SOCIETY IN TRANSITION

Robert W. Winslow

SOCIETY

A social approach

Fp

THE FREE PRESS, NEW YORK
COLLIER-MACMILLAN LIMITED, LONDON

in transition

to deviancy

The Free Press. A Division of The Macmillan Company. 866 Third Avenue, New York, N.Y. 10022. Collier–Macmillan Canada Ltd., Toronto, Ontario. Library of Congress Catalog Card Number: 74–116604.

printing number
1 2 3 4 5 6 7 8 9 10

To Ginny and Cindy

Contents

Preface

This text is designed for courses in deviancy, social disorganization, social pathology, social maladjustment, and social problems. It provides a somewhat different approach from most current texts in these fields, being designed for the student who wants to study deviancy using the framework of general sociological theory rather than by simply focusing on isolated social problems. Specifically, I have attempted to show the relevance of the classical social theories of Marx, Weber, Durkheim, Tönnies, Parsons, and others to the current sociological study of deviancy.

The relevance of these theories is discussed in Chapters 1 and 2, where it is shown that there are, in historical social thought, alternatives to the "sick society" approach of current deviancy theory. Durkheim, for example, saw contemporary society as cohesive rather than disorganized. The question is raised as to whether contemporary society is in fact disorganized. The tentative answer given is that contemporary society is quite cohesive when compared with underdeveloped countries (which are often held up as ideal "folk societies"). Yet, despite this relative stability, certain forms of deviant behavior seem to be more prevalent in contemporary society, perhaps accounting for the assumption of a "sick society" taken by many deviancy texts.

In Chapter 3, social disorganization theory is examined with this in mind, and it is shown that the trend has been away from theories of social disorganization and toward the more recent anomie and mass society perspectives. The focus has shifted from the post-Depression emphasis upon social disequilibrium to the Cold War emphasis upon the alienation and loneliness of modern man. Society is quite stable but, in social organization, is definitely "mass" in nature.

In Chapter 4, it is argued that, although there is widespread deviancy in modern society, deviancy is not necessarily disorganizing or disruptive, but rather it may lead to necessary social changes, which eventually may enhance stability. Instead of social disorganization, it is suggested that society-in-transition would be a more appropriate term, incorporating the possibility of "moving equilibrium." Certain forms of deviancy are disruptive, however, and a typology is suggested for distinguishing the more seriously disruptive deviant acts from those that may in fact prove "functional" for social change.

In Chapter 5, current theories of deviancy are examined and a new theory of deviancy, based on general social theory and broader in scope than current deviancy approaches, is suggested. This theory holds that problems of deviancy cannot be traced directly to the social structure of society-at-large, because that structure is an essentially cohesive and stable one. Deviancy, instead, is traced to the kinds of institutions and organizations that exist in modern society. This view is examined in the light of current prevalence, trend, and cross-cultural data on deviancy.

In Chapter 6, in keeping with the conclusion of Chapter 5, it is argued that the proper focus of deviancy theory is the study of the organizational bases of deviancy—that is, what forms of social organization are conducive to what forms of deviancy. Various formal organizational contexts are discussed in relation to specific forms of deviancy.

In Chapter 7, the same organizational analysis is applied to informal settings of deviancy, including such major forms of deviancy as professional crime, organized crime, vice, delinquency, and mental disorder.

In Chapter 8, forms of deviancy that can apparently be traced to the absence of organizational ties are discussed, such as mental disorder, suicide, alcoholism, and prejudice—increasingly important problems in contemporary society.

In Chapter 9, a fairly unique ending for a deviancy text is presented: not a portrait of gloom or immanent societal distruction, but a preview of programs and tendencies toward positive social change, some of which are now under way.

The major purpose of this text, then, is to cast doubt upon the belief that the study of deviancy is a narrow, specialized discipline and, in fact, to show the significant ties between the study of deviancy and the general domain of social thought and the study of organizations. The outcome of this work, it is hoped, is an integrated approach to deviancy.

SOCIETY IN TRANSITION

Social equilibrium, social change, and deviancy

Current approaches to deviancy

The study of deviant behavior has traditionally focused on one of two major textbook perspectives. The first, the social problems approach, views deviancy eclectically as a product of various social and psychological causes. This approach may involve bringing to bear various "theories of deviancy," or it may entail a study of problems from an atheoretical point of view—that is, without a theoretical framework—and study social problems primarily from a statistical orientation.[1] The second, the global-theory emphasis, takes some particular theory of deviancy, such as social disorganization, cultural lag, differential association, anomie, or containment theory, and applies this approach to various forms of deviant behavior.[2] In these global-theory approaches, however, no attempt is made to link the approach taken in the text with "major" sociological theories, those usually dealt with in sociological courses on "theory."[3] There is an ever-present implication that deviancy should be treated as though it were entirely separate from sociological theory. For example, social disorganization theory,

Notes for this chapter are on page 369.

I

one of the major ways of looking at deviancy, may indeed have roots in classic social theories, such as Tönnies' theory of gemein-schaft—gesellschaft, Weber's theory of the rise of capitalism, or Durkheim's theory of anomie; however, nowhere in the disorgani-zation literature is this link with classical social theory made explicit. Perhaps in the past, authors of various theories of deviancy consid-ered it unimportant or irrelevant to survey the theoretical under-pinnings of their approaches. However, it is becoming increasingly important in sociology that assumptions and value implications be made evident to the reader, so that he may be able to assess intel-ligently an author's work in the light of alternative approaches.

This text will attempt to show the theoretical roots of some current perspectives on deviance. It will be seen that consideration of classical social theories not only provides rich sources of hypoth-eses, but also presents to the reader several alternative ways of view-ing the phenomenon. For example, if it can be shown that social disorganization theory is historically related to anomie theory and that anomie is only one among many perspectives for the analysis of contemporary society (for example, "pluralism" or "totalitari-anism" might also be used as alternative analytical concepts), then the reader might elect to analyze society from still another perspec-tive. Certain social problems might be prevalent if society is disor-ganized or anomic, others if it is pluralistically organized, and others if it is totalitarian in organization. When the problem is so stated, the reader is free to consult his own value framework for the analysis of society and social problems.

In this text we will view current deviancy theory as being based on major classical sociological theory, as having its roots in the writings of Durkheim, Tönnies, Pareto, and other "sociological pioneers." It will be shown that the current emphasis on anomie theory in the study of deviancy or disorganization can be traced to one particular perspective in sociological thought: a "gesellschaft" view of society. There are a number of assumptions implicit in this approach—for instance, that society is less organized than in the past, that deviancy can be curbed through increasing corrective sanctions, and even that deviancy is increasing in modern society—and thus it is important that it be distinguished from other ap-proaches. It is possible that our society may, on the contrary, exhibit characteristics of stable organization, or may even take the form of oligarchy. The important thing to consider is that there are various and alternative approaches to deviancy, depending upon the theoretical framework one accepts and applies.

It might be argued that deviancy theory is by its very nature normative theory and that it is really misleading to try to present an "objective" view.[4] However, there should be some attempt to acquaint the reader with alternatives. This book does in fact take a stand, but only after delineating the wide range of alternatives. When these alternatives are presented, the reader may either agree or disagree with the approach taken in this text. In light of the wide spectrum of views in sociology, this would seem to be an appropriate reaction to any text on deviancy.

Study of social organization and social change

As has been suggested above, previous texts on deviancy contain, either implicitly or explicitly, some "image of society." Texts on social disorganization, for example, present a rather clear and concise diagnosis of society: it suffers from insufficient social integration, breakdown in its norm and value structure, dissensus or lack of consensus, and the like. In other deviancy approaches, the social diagnosis is less explicit, but nevertheless involved in the analysis. Clinard, for example, traces deviancy to the growth of world urbanism, pointing out that crime and most other forms of deviancy are more prevalent in the city than in the country.[5] He says, further: "Urbanism, with its mobility, impersonality, individualism, materialism, norm and role conflicts, and rapid social change, appears to be associated with higher incidence of deviant behavior."[6]

The focus on urbanism as the source of problems is closely interrelated with the disorganization perspective. Also closely related to the concept of disorganization are concepts such as "sick society," the "missing community," social malaise, mass society, anomie, and "insane society." These ideas are referred to in explaining contemporary deviancy.

The disintegration of our traditional culture, with the decay of the ideas, conceptions, and beliefs upon which our social and individual lives were organized, brings us face to face with the problem of treating society, since individual therapy or punishment no longer has any value beyond mere alleviation of our symptoms.

The conception of a sick society in need of treatment has many advantages for diagnosis of our individual and social difficulties and for constructive therapy.[7]

The accumulation of the missed and compromised revolutions of modern times, with their consequent ambiguities and social imbalances, has fallen, and must fall, most heavily on the young, making it hard to grow up. [Italics in original text.] . . . A successful revolution establishes a new community. A missed revolution makes irrelevant the community that persists. And a compromised revolution tends to shatter the community that was, without an adequate substitute.[8]

We live in an age of malaise. It is difficult to deliniate the general pattern of disorder. Strains are seen in such diverse areas as the fabric of the American family, the incidence of criminal activity, psychoneurotic disorders, and alcoholism.[9]

The mass society, whether one likes it or not, has had a number of consequences. . . . The mass society appears to require a fragmentized life for the participant in it. . . . Within the mass society there is a great deal of personal movement. . . . Another aspect of the mass society which has attracted the attention of many observers is a seemingly growing casualness about traditional moral precepts where the collective enterprise is concerned.[10]

Culture may be such as to lead individuals to center their emotional convictions upon the complex of culturally acclaimed ends, with far less emotional support for prescribed methods of reaching out for the ends. . . . As this process of attenuation continues, the society becomes unstable and there develops what Durkheim called "anomie". . . . Contemporary American culture appears to approximate the polar type in which great emphasis upon certain success-goals occurs without equivalent emphasis upon institutional means.[11]

Mental health cannot be defined in terms of 'the "adjustment" of the individual to society, but, on the contrary, it must be defined in terms of the adjustment of society to the needs of man.[12]

Terms such as "mass society," "social disorganization," and "sick society" are used by social pathologists somewhat unsystematically and in a way only remotely related to more general theory. As such, the reader of books on deviancy cannot assess the adequacy of these concepts as a frame of reference as compared with alternative views (for example, compare the relative utility of mass society *versus* pluralist society as a perspective for analysis of modern society). Thus, generalities about society that use these concepts are more often platitudes than scientific or axiomatic theories. Although it cannot be denied that the way society is organized is relevant to deviancy, it is not valid to assume that if certain forms of deviancy appear widespread in modern society, then modern society is necessarily disorganized rather than organized, mass rather than plural, "sick" rather than healthy, insane rather than sane, and the like. Indeed, it is worth considering that the very problems typical of modern society might stem from the excessive stability of larger social organization, *vis-à-vis* individual personality organization, in that it, in Cooley's words, "drains away the energies of human nature."[13] The Freudians, for instance, have asserted that there is an inherent opposition between man and society. Social organization implies the repression of instinctual forces in man and thus of man's basic nature. It may be that the very state of health or sanity of society presupposes the illness or insanity of man within society.

We are assuming neither that society is sick nor that man is sick. Rather, in the following chapters we will explore the relatively wide range of models that can be drawn upon for the analysis of man and society. Through a brief review of representative "classic" theories of society, it will be shown that the organization of contemporary Western society is not a singular or monolithic phenomenon. It is largely meaningless to speak of "modern society" or even "human nature" without specifying what type of society or culture we are dealing with. Once such a framework is laid down, we can be free to select a theory which, based upon current empirical data, appears to be appropriate for the analysis of contemporary society.

The remainder of the present chapter will present an overview of the various concepts of social organization and society that form the basis of theories to be discussed in detail throughout subsequent chapters in the book. Fortunately, such a grand typology has been attempted by Talcott Parsons, upon whom the next few pages will rely heavily.

Theories of transition

Societies and perhaps civilizations may develop through stages of evolutionary growth. Parsons has suggested that stable phases can be described by the "AGIL" sequence of adaptation, goal attainment, integration, and pattern maintenance. Parsons has used these terms implicitly as a frame of reference for the study of sociological theories.[14] Thus, they are intended in part as heuristic devices, aids for study that may serve us well in typing and categorizing various theories of transition. If one studies social theory at length he is at once confused by the staggering number of terms that are used by various social theorists to describe society in its various stages. It may be useful to preview the terms that will be discussed at length in Chapter 2. We will use Parsons' general categories—adaptation, goal attainment, integration, and pattern maintenance—as general categories for conceptualization. Parsons suggests numerous applications of the AGIL paradigm, one of which is its use to describe an evolutionary sequence of society (any society). *Patterns maintenance* refers to the earliest and simplest form of stable social organization. When society develops a market exchange and division of labor in order to cope with expanding populations or other environmental demands, it passes into the *adaptation phase.* Subsequently, having adapted to its environment, society enters the *goal attainment phase.* Finally, it reaches a new stage of *integration,* achieves *pattern maintenance,* and eventually begins the cycle again.

Though the theories and concepts to be discussed in Chapter 2 are diverse, they can be viewed as part of a general framework. The Parsonian scheme previously discussed is useful for grouping these concepts; however, we will not rely upon it exclusively. Instead, we shall attempt to develop a "constructive typology" based more directly upon the various theories that will be discussed in Chapter 2. This constructive typology, in turn, will provide the basis for subsequent analysis. Parsons' scheme will serve by way of introduction.

PATTERN MAINTENANCE

A number of nearly synonomous terms are used to refer to societies whose organization has been described as "simple equilibrium." These are small scale societies variously called "folk society," "communal society," "primary group relationships," "gemeinschaft," "mechanical solidarity," "sacred society," and the like. It will be shown that such societies are necessarily isolated and have managed to subsist adequately, given available resources. They are societies in which all functions are merged and performed by one or two dominant institutions—namely, the family and/or religion. Such societies have, in Parsons' terms, for the most part solved the problems of adaptation, goal attainment, and integration; thus, they are concerned primarily with pattern maintenance—logically their only functional problem.

ADAPTATION

There are probably few examples of simple equilibrium in the world today. This is because most societies are ultimately faced with problems of an "external" nature: population expansion, competition for land and other resources with other societies, famine, disease, and the like. This results in a shift in emphasis from pattern maintenance to adaptation. In order to adjust to population pressures, for example, societies must develop a social organization capable of incorporating larger populations. Social differention or division of labor and the development of a market economy may result, maximizing the available resources in developing individual efficiency and in exploiting what is available. However, when society devotes priority to economic matters, other functions may necessarily receive secondary emphasis. Thus, traditional patterns may breakdown, deviancy may increase, and individual gratification may decline. Various concepts have arisen in social thought to describe such situations, including "gesellschaft," "anomie," "normless society," "secondary group relations," "social disorganization," "social pathology," "rule of the foxes," "capitalism," and "civilization."

GOAL ATTAINMENT

The period of disorganization that is likely to characterize the adaptation phase of society would typically be followed by a period of goal attainment. For the members of society, there may be relative affluence. For the whole society, it may be a period of territorial aggrandizement. Examples include the Elizabethan era in England, the Napoleonic period in France, the Middle Ages generally in Europe. In social theory there are a number of related concepts for these phases of society, including "militant society," "forced division of labor," and "totalitarianism." The last of these, totalitarianism, may carry the connotation of unpopular government. Only if such societal orientations were inappropriate to its stage of development, however, would such government ordinarily be unpopular.[15]

INTEGRATION

The final phase of development typically would be a society in which economic problems had been solved and resources had been distributed on a continuing basis. In addition, institutions would have been developed—especially the legal institutions—which would serve to maintain the functional relations in society, preventing the domination of any special functional interests. Such are the ideal, or utopian, societies of many social theories: "positivistic society," "socialism," "associative society," "organic solidarity," "pluralism," "principled secular society," and "reorganized society."

Summary and conclusion

There are two major textbook approaches to deviancy. At one extreme is the eclectic, highly factual "social problems" approach, an approach which is characterized by descriptions of various social problems, with little attempt at theoretical integration. The global theory approaches are at the other extreme. These include texts on "disorganization," "social pathology," "social maladjustment," and the like. The global theory approaches utilize a single theory to explain all deviant behavior, a theory usually arrived at by the author and seemingly unrelated to the framework of classical social theory. The implication appears to be that the study of sociological theory is unrelated to the study of deviancy or that deviancy theory should develop separately.

It is the position of this text, however, that current deviancy approaches may carry ties to larger theories that have previously been overlooked. This text will attempt to make those ties manifest. This, it is hoped, will yield new perspectives on current deviancy theories; alternative theories and hypotheses; and a basis for criticizing current deviancy approaches. It is hoped that a more explicit tie between deviancy theory and empirical data can result from this synthesis and codification of theories.

A major advantage of this approach is that the reader of this text will not be exposed to merely one theoretical approach or perspective on deviancy but will instead be shown a gamut of theoretical possibilities. Thus, the question may arise, Is American society disorganized, or perhaps well integrated or maybe even excessively rigid in organization?

By way of introduction to the range of "images of society" from which we may select for our theoretical analysis, four basic types of social organization are delineated using Parsons' four types "adaptation," "goal attainment," "integration," and "pattern maintenance" (AGIL). With this many types to select from, many theoretical possibilities exist. We shall see that classic social theories generally portray society as passing from one of these four types to another. We shall see that though there are twelve possible combinations, only about four have been selected in classic social theory, and only one of these four is used in current American deviancy theory. It is the position of this text that deviancy theory should take into account at least four and possibly other combinations.

Social theories of transition

2

We have seen that there is a variety of types of social order or social organization, and that these have been represented in various ways in the classical social theories. Most of these theories, it will be seen, are "ideal," or polar, typologies—those that focus upon and contrast logical though extreme types that do not necessarily exist in reality.[1] As such, a given theorist may select certain types as a framework for contrast. While it is conceivable that there could be as many as twelve directional polar typologies from the four societal types (AGIL), there are only three or four actually used.

The first, which might be called *evolutionary theories,* view society as progressing either from pattern maintenance or goal attainment phases to the integration phase described above. These include the theories of Comte, Spencer, Marx, Weber, and MacIver.

It is significant that both the pattern maintenance and goal attainment types have been generally described in the literature as "folk society," when in fact there are important differences between them. Although they are often lumped together, there is an important distinction between "folk society" and "feudal society."[2] The concept of "folk society" refers to small-scale, isolated, nonliterate,

unstratified, sacred primitive societies; while the term "feudal society" refers to large-scale, heterogeneous, complex, highly stratified, caste-like societies. Perhaps the two have been confused, due to
the presence of traditional resistance to social change in both; however, feudal society, due to its complex organization, its elite system
of monarchs, landlords, and priests, and its literacy, is far more capable of defending itself against encroachment from foreign powers,
than is folk society.

The second class of theories, which might be called *cycle or
equilibrium theories,* view society neither as progressing nor retrogressing, but vacillating back and forth from one to another type of
organization. Still a third class, the *devolutionary theories,* view
society as declining from the stable pattern maintenance phase to
the more disorganized adaptation phase of history.

Evolutionary theories of transition

Many of the major social theories of transition were
developed in Europe, for it was in Europe during the nineteenth
century that sociology took the form of theorizing on a grand scale
about society at large. Most of these theories were progressivistic
and developmental and, in the broadest sense of the term, evolutionary. The term "evolutionary theories" is used here to refer to
theories that treat society as developing or growing by a process of
stages. As such, the term "evolutionary" is not confined to the strict
biological usage, say, of the social Darwinists, implying adaptation,
survival of the fittest, and natural selection. The term "evolution"
will be used here to refer to developmental, progressive processes
of all kinds. In this sense, a number of classic European sociologists,
including Comte, Marx, Durkheim, and Weber, as well as historical
and current American social thinkers, such as Sumner, Giddings,
Ward, MacIver, Lerner, and Service, can be designated evolutionary
theorists.

There are no doubt sizable differences between the perspectives
of the various social theorists mentioned above.[3] But perhaps the
major point of difference between these approaches concerns not
the final stage of development predicted, the utopia, but rather the

starting point or point of origin. In many respects, the ultimate utopias or ideal societies of these various theorists, such as Comte's positivism, Marx's socialism, MacIver's associationism, are quite similar.

EVOLUTION FROM FOLK SOCIETY

Generally, contrasts made between contemporary "mass society" and earlier "folk society" tend to favor, perhaps somewhat sentimentally, earlier folk society. However, it is feasible to view both contemporary and primitive society as stable forms of equilibrium, and even to realize certain advantages of contemporary society, such as greater freedom, more interdependence, more widespread participation. This approach was taken by Émile Durkheim, Robert MacIver, and, to some extent, Max Weber.

Émile Durkheim   Although the sociology of Émile Durkheim (1855–1917) goes far beyond his evolutionary model, the development of society from mechanical to organic solidarity is both the starting point and underlying theme of the majority of his writings.[4]

To Durkheim, *mechanical solidarity* and *organic solidarity* were polar opposites. Mechanical solidarity is characterized by little division of labor, by repressive or punitive law, and by strong collective conscience as a basis for organization. *Organic solidarity,* by contrast, entails complex division, restitutive law, and the relative importance of individual personality rather than collective conscience. Mechanical solidarity implies the attraction of like to like element, while organic solidarity involves the interdependence of opposites. Under mechanical solidarity there is little or no government apart from the rules of kinship, while under organic solidarity government emerges as a specialized agency and comes to symbolize the collective conscience. While both types of organization are cohesive and solidary, as Durkheim sees them, Durkheim's sentiments favor organic solidarity based upon its wider universality and greater stability. Mechanical solidarity is easily breached by the introduction of foreign elements into the division of labor, but organic solidarity is more impermeable, due to the prior incorporation of a variety of elements into its division of labor.

Durkheim's theory will be discussed at greater length in Chapter 3, where it will be shown that organic solidarity does not always result from this transition, but that certain abnormal phases of the division of labor—anomic division of labor and the forced division of labor—may occur.

Max Weber   Though Weber (1864–1920) is probably more well-known for other aspects of his sociology, his distinction between *communal social relationships* and *associative social relationships,* which is an application of his more general theory, is relevant to the present discussion. Basic to Weber's distinction between communal and associative social relations were the four basic types of social action of Weber's general theory: the *wertrational,* the *affectual,* the *traditional,* and the *zweckrational.*

> Action is *zweckrational* ("rationally purposeful") when it is addressed to a situation with a plurality of means and ends, a situation in which the actor is free to choose his means purely in terms of efficiency: Action is *wertrational* ("rational in terms of values") when the means are chosen for their efficiency but the ends are fixed in advance. Action is *affective* when emotional factors determine the means and ends of action: and action is *traditional* when both means and ends are fixed by custom.[5]

Various types of action might range all the way from attendance of religious services (traditional), to enjoyment of friendship relations (affective), to negotiation of a business deal (wertrational), to going to a department store "bargain basement" sale (zweckrational). Church attendance is generally a customary activity and once a given religion and denomination is selected the means and ends of worship are ritualized. Friendship relations generally bring emotional gratification, and generally such gratification is not a function of the rational intellect of the friend but how "attractive" the person is physically and emotionally, and whether or not the person expresses a degree of liking for others. In Linton's terms, friendship is largely controlled by ascribed rather than achieved characteristics. By contrast, business activities may follow no traditional pattern and may seem quite "cold" emotionally, and the paramount objective of economic profit may be achieved through various sales schemes. The "bargain basement sale" may represent an extreme situation where an individual may seize upon any article or product with a minimum of concern for the rights or feelings of competitors.

The first two situations, church attendance and friendship relations, are organized into *communal social relations,* while the second two, business and bargain basement shopping, exemplify *associative social relations. Communal social relationships* are based upon affectual or traditional rationality. Such relationships, either based upon emotional bonds or traditional ties, are cooperative rather than conflicting, and are founded upon subjective feeling of belongingness. Weber mentioned erotic relationships, national community, and family as examples of communal social relationships. *Associative social relationships* are either wertrational or zweckrational in orientation. The former is termed absolute value rationality, while the latter is termed expedient rationality. Associative social relationships are based upon rationally motivated adjustment of interests through mutual consent, as in contract and market exchange, and are characterized by a compromise of rival, potentially conflicting interests, rather than cooperation *per se.* Conflicts exist outside of areas of compromise.[6]

Weber's polarity of communal and associative social relations cannot unequivocally be termed evolutionary. While Weber recognized the greater stability of modern associative relations and the consequent emergence of rational handling of various aspects of life, he did regret certain negative consequences of bureaucracy in its effect on personality and personal freedom.

> Weber thus identifies bureaucracy with rationality, and the process of rationalization with mechanism, depersonalization, and oppressive routine. Rationality, in this context, is seen as adverse to personal freedom. Accordingly, Weber is a nostalgic liberal, feeling himself on the defensive. He deplores the type of man that the mechanization and the routine of bureaucracy selects and forms. . . . Indeed, he feels this type of man to be a petty routine creature, lacking in heroism, human spontaneity, and inventiveness.[7]

This dual awareness is not so clearly evident in other evolutionary theorists as it is in Weber. Because of Weber's belief that history was indeterminant, he never really took a progressivistic perspective. However, his analysis has been presented here because of its similarity to that of Robert M. MacIver, who views "associational society" more favorably than would Weber.

Robert MacIver: communal and associational society   MacIver's formulation of *communal* versus *associational society* follows quite closely upon Weber's typology of communal and associative relationships.[8] However, it is more clear in MacIver's analysis than in Weber's communal–associative polarity that associational society represents a continuous progression away from communal society.[9]

Communal society is characteristically segmental or compartmental rather than composed of functionally interdependent groups.[10] It is elaborate in kin distinctions and ceremonial offices, lacking in social differentiation apart from age and sex divisions, totally without great specialized associations, communal in sharing of goods, and repressive of differences.

Associational society, by contrast, is characterized by functional interdependence of groups, especially of the complex, great associations;[11] few kin distinctions and autonomous family; conflict rather than cooperation with regard to special interests; and encouragement of differences.

It is on this last point of individual differences that MacIver seems to clearly favor associational society. The core of MacIver's thinking is a focus upon "attitudes" and "interests." Attitudes are states of consciousness within a person with respect to objects, while interests are the objects toward which people are oriented.[12] The advantage of associational society, claims MacIver, is that every attitude finds social corroboration, every interest its own association to represent it.

EVOLUTION FROM FEUDAL SOCIETY

It will be shown that historical and current theories that portray contemporary mass society negatively tend to contrast it with folk rather than feudal society as an earlier form of society. The opposite is true of evolutionary approaches, which tend to compare contemporary or future society with former feudal society. Thus, the differences between various theories may lie largely in the different "strawman" picked for criticism. Among the feudal-evolution theories are those of Comte, Marx, and Lerner.

Auguste Comte   Auguste Comte (1798–1857), a forerunner of Émile Durkheim and a pioneer of sociology, developed a theory of successive and progressive developmental stages of society based upon his theory of evolution of intellectual thought. He felt that each era of history had its own mode of explanation of phenomena. The earliest stage, the *theological period,* involved a view that all phenomena, including supernatural behavior, could be explained by analogies drawn from human behavior. In the theological period of thought, all phenomena were viewed as caused by sovereign arbitrary will of a supernatural servant of man, God. By contrast, in the most advanced phase of history, the *positive stage,* explanation is restricted to investigation of phenomena themselves, by the scientific method, eschewing all theories of cause or ultimate origin. A third stage of history, the *metaphysical* period was transitional between theological and positivistic stage, with few unique characteristics.[13]

Comte, who followed a Hegelian tradition of idealism, viewed all aspects of social organization as dependent upon prevailing systems of thought. The earliest philosophy, theological philosophy, provided the basis of social organization itself by promulgating common beliefs, providing the basis for a speculative class, and by fostering a dominant military established to defend theology and uniting isolated families through conquest. The ultimate result was the emergence of the nation state and the substitution of law and a defensive military during the metaphysical stage. Ultimately, however, positivism comes to provide the basis for large-scale industrial society, serving no higher causes than man, oriented toward changing nature for the benefit of man.

Comte felt that the positivist state is an advanced phase of history. Theology is absolutistic and unchanging, and mankind was divided into limited domestic groups during the theological era. Positivism would bring with it the preponderance of reason, exploratory relativism, benevolence as a dominant sentiment, and the universal organization of mankind.

Karl Marx   Like Comte, Marx (1818–1883) traced the development of social organization from feudalism onward. The similarity ends there, however. Marx's theory of society amounted to an outright repudiation of Hegel's idealism. Hegel had earlier used the concept of the dialectic drawn from Greek drama to describe the intellectual course of history. Hegel had posited that thought followed the process of the dialectic. As a process, any idea cast up by thought (thesis) necessarily is followed by its opposite (antithesis) after which thought must reconcile the conflict (synthesis).[14] Marx differed markedly from Hegel, however, in his emphasis upon materialism as opposed to Hegel's idealism. While in Hegel's evolutionism, changes in the social structure of society were caused by changes in intellectual thought or ideas, for Marx the social class structure of society was a fundamental substructure upon which ideas and other aspects of society depended. As the social structure changes, the superstructure of ideas changes, the former preceding the latter.[15]

Marx is said to have "turned Hegel's dialectic scheme upside-down" by applying the scheme not to fundamental spirit, as Hegel did, but to matter. That is, Marx applied the process of thesis, antithesis, synthesis, not to the development of human spirit, but to the evolution of the social class system of society. Every system of economic production starts as an affirmation or thesis, since it is the best system for that particular time. Once entrenched, however, the system becomes an obstacle to the application of new technological inventions and the use of newly discovered markets and supplies of raw material. The entrenched order must be overcome by revolution, creating a new order of production, a synthesis of the old and the new.

Using the process just described, Marx traced the development of human society from the earliest times to the present. "The history of all human society past and present has been a history of class struggle."[16] The earliest society, the ancient or Asiatic society, is a military society, the dominant social class being the warlords who controlled the means of warfare and rule over the slaves. This ultimately was followed by feudalism, in which the dominant class of lords rule over serfs, power being based upon ownership of land. With the advent of industrialization, feudalism is not longer appropriate. Ultimately, the bourgeoisie, those who own means of production, overthrow the feudal lords. The revolution of the bourgeoisie was not a violent revolution, but rather a gradual one, almost subtle. For example, Marx argued that the peasant based *coup d'etat* of Louis Bonaparte in actuality benefited not so much the peasants as it did the bourgeoisie, who managed to appropriate feudal lands from the peasants.[17]

The emergence of capitalism was a technological rather than violent revolution, because the means of production could be invented and thus acquired peacefully. Marx emphasized the importance of capitalism in history as a necessary antecedent to socialism. The bourgeoisie destroyed the sacred ties that historically justified class society, establishing only secular relations in their place. They secularized social relations by converting all positions into wage labor. The bourgeoisie centralized power by the development of cities, the state, bureaucracy, and industrial production and by creating dependency of rural and uncivilized countries upon urban, civilized ones. They eliminated all previous ruling classes. Thus, the bourgeoisie increased alienation to its maximum in history, laying the basis for the final *coup* against class society in general. The bourgeoisie then had sown the "seeds of its own destruction," for in order to exploit labor, it had to arm it with education and other weapons, which in turn will be turned back against the bourgeoisie. When the bourgeoisie is in turn overcome, there will be no further basis for domination. Thus, socialism and classless society will be established and all property will be communized, the state owning all.

In sum: Like the other theories examined above, Marxian theory postulated that society undergoes progressive development through a series of stages. The earliest, the *ancient* or *asiatic,* is followed by *feudalism,* then *capitalism,* and ultimately *socialism.* Each stage except the last is characterized by a dominant and subordinate class: the ancient by master and slave classes, the feudal by lord and serf, the capitalist period by the bourgeoisie and proletariat. Only socialism lacks a ruling class and constitutes a classless society.[18]

Daniel Lerner   Lerner has posited that society evolves from *traditional society* to *participant society,* a typology similar to MacIver's. *Participant society* is characterized by its complex division of labor, literacy, extensive development of mass media, high level of participation by members of society, representative government, and by the existence of a transpersonal doctrine of stratification which places strangers. In *traditional society,* by contrast, all relations and concepts are personal and kin-based, literacy is rare, mass communication absent, and participation in the government largely absent.[19]

Cycle or equilibrium theories

While evolutionary typologies stress the transition from small to large scale societies, another set of theories, the *cycle* or *equilibrium theories,* look at the great civilizations and societies that have developed throughout the world and attempt to assess the periodic trends and phases that they have gone through. We have already seen two theories that have been viewed as cycle theories: those of Talcott Parsons and Max Weber. Parsons suggests that all societies undergo the AGIL sequence, and upon reaching L, the pattern maintenance phase, cycle back to A and begin the sequence again. Weber viewed history as undergoing cycles of charismatic authority, followed by traditional authority, which ultimately is broken once again by charismatic authority. However, despite the recurrent cycles expressed in these theories, there nevertheless is a general on-going trend in history. Weber saw the trend of history as one of gradually declining charisma and emerging bureaucracy. Parsons describes a general trend from small-scale, simple equilibrium to large-scale, complex equilibrium. Thus, neither of these theories constitute "pure" or thoroughgoing cycle theories, because as defined here a cycle theory states either that society does not reach higher, better states of organization but remains the same (Pareto), or proposes that society may develop but inevitably will retrogress to its point of origin (Sorokin).

Vilfredo Pareto Perhaps the epitome of cycle theory is found in Pareto's elite theory. Vilfredo Pareto (1848–1923), an Italian sociologist, was influenced by the Machiavellian school of Italian sociology, a school which emphasized the importance of rule by elites and saw society as a kind of equilibrium of forces. Machiavelli believed that men originally banded together, electing "the strongest and most courageous from amongst themselves and placing him at their head, promising to obey him. Thence they began to know the good and the honest, and to distinguish them from the bad and vicious."[20] Eventually, however, sovereignty becomes nonelective, and there is no guarantee against inferior stock. Excessive luxury in a prince would lead to envy of others, which in turn would lead to conspiracy. Fear of a conspiracy turned the prince into a tyrant who is eventually overthrown and aristocracy is formed. Aristocracy is corrupted and replaced by democracy, which moves step by step toward anarchy, leading eventually to a new dictatorship.

Like Machiavelli, Pareto conceived of society as a system in equilibrium and a balance of forces. As does Machiavelli, he focuses upon elites and assumes the necessity of oligarchy for large-scale social organization. Pareto also saw society as cycling from democracy or plutocracy on the one hand to aristocracy on the other. Whether a society was democratic or aristocratic depended upon its state of equilibrium, as well as the distribution of instinctual forces in the society.

Elites consist of those of highest performance in their respective fields. There are two principle classes of elites: (1) a governing elite, comprising individuals who directly or indirectly play an important role in the manipulation of political power, and (2) a nongoverning elite, consisting of capable men not in power positions. The *foxes* were those elites whose instinctual inclinations were in the direction of *combinations,* or the ability to associate diverse aspects of reality and to manipulate the environment in terms of these insights. The *lions* are those elites whose inclination is toward what Pareto termed the *persistance of aggregates* — that is, the inclination to preserve what is, rather than to alter or change the situation creatively. In the economic sphere, the counterpart of the foxes are the *speculators;* while parallel to the lions are the *rentiers.* [21] The *rentiers* are those who live by fixed incomes, such as bonds, bank securities, and unspeculative real estate found most often in stable, crystalized societies. The *speculators* live on variable income, such as stocks and speculative real estate and are most predominant in unstable societies. The *foxes* and *speculators* constitute the ruling elite in democratic states, while the *lions* and *rentiers* constitute the ruling elite in *aristocratic* states.

Circulation of elites occurs because each of the two types contains the "seeds of its own destruction." The lions rule by force, maintaining a strong central government through their use of military power. Eventually, however, they find they cannot maintain social organization through force alone. Thus, the foxes, being gifted at persuasive manipulation of people, are permitted to infiltrate the ranks of the lions, rising socially into the upper classes. However, the democracy that the foxes establish is unstable, eventually descending into anarchy, which calls forth the man of force to bring order out of chaos. Consequently, both elites rotate in positions of political power. When an elite of one type has ruled for some time, superior elements accumulate in the governed classes and conversely, inferior elements develop in the ruling classes. One elite makes mistakes which eventually opens the way for the other. [22]

Pitirim Sorokin   Pitirim Sorokin (1889–1968) was a historical sociologist whose theories may be viewed in part as a reaction to current pessimistic historical theories, notably those of Spengler and Toynbee. While Sorokin agreed that history may be described as a straight-line progress up to a point and the reversal of this linear trend after that point, he believed that history once again reverses and continues in this fluctuation pattern indefinitely. [23]

Specifically, Sorokin asserted that history swings from *ideational* to *sensate* cultural poles. Transitional, or "in between" types are the *idealistic* culture and the *mixed* type in the sensate direction. The basic characteristic underlying each type is the kind of reality perceived as "true" by the members of the given sociocultural system. Among the *sensate* systems truth is sensory: there is no reality except that perceived by our sense organs. In the *ideational* systems there is primary emphasis upon a super-sensory, super-rational God and a belief that the sensory is an illusion, or at least unimportant. In the *idealistic* systems there is an integration of the two types, while combinations that are not integrated are called *mixed*.[24]

Sorokin illustrated his theory by tracing the whole history of Western culture, which he believed could be traced to ancient Greece. Greek culture is described as ideational until the end of the sixth century B.C.; then followed the century known as the Golden Age of Athens, which was idealistic. For the next eight centuries the sensate Roman Empire thrived and flourished. This was followed by mixed culture and then a period of ideational culture up to the twelfth century. This was followed by the Gothic period of idealism from the late twelfth to the early fourteenth century. This gradually gave way to sensate culture, which characterizes the present era; however, symptoms indicate change in the direction of the ideational pole.

It would seem that the death of culture could occur if it reached either extreme of the pure ideation or pure sensate form. However, Sorokin, in contrast to Spengler and Toynbee, conceived that every cultural supersystem is incompletely integrated, so that the trend is reversed before the limit is reached.

Devolutionary theories

In the previous sections of this chapter, a number of theories of society have been examined that take either an optimistic, evolutionary view of society in transition, or a cyclical, equilibrium view. While these theories are important to historical sociology, the prevailing emphasis, especially in American sociology, is to use the idea of "mass society" to describe modern large-scale society.[25] Alienation and the widespread nature of deviant behavior are a prevailing theme in American sociology. This prevailing orientation is reflected in the following statement, drawn from a major social-problems text:

> Probably the most fundamental features that have transformed the historical Western society, which is now called a "mass society" by many professionals, are growing homogeneity and conformity. . . . *The mass society is a growing and engulfing system of human relationships for which few, aside from the present generation of youth, have much compatible precedent.* [26]

Theories with this focus may be termed "devolutionary" or "retrogression" theories. Indeed, the most relevant typologies to the contemporary study of deviancy are those that view society as being in transition from more integrated, more cohesive forms of social organization to less cohesive, disorganized forms of social organization. In this section, only the general theories of social organization in historical sociology will be discussed, leaving for a later chapter the more specific social disorganization theories of contemporary sociology. Specifically, devolutionary or retrogression theories include those of Freud, Tönnies, and Redfield.

Sigmund Freud Like Vilfredo Pareto, Sigmund Freud (1856–1939) saw instinctual forces as basic to social organization. Unlike Pareto, however, he saw an incompatibility between their expression and the existence of large-scale social organization. [27] Although Freud focused upon individual psychopathology in most of his writing, in his later years he began to develop the implications of his theories for the study of history. He believed that the history of the human species was analogous to events in the life of the individual.

At various stages in the development of the human individual, conflicts of a sexual-aggressive nature occur, leaving permanent traces. These conflicts occur due to incompatible demands from the individual's *id* (inherited instinctive forces, such as life, sex, and death instincts) as opposed to his *superego* (parental attitudes determined by cultural standards). The *ego* plays the function of "umpire" in the inner conflict, adapting inherited drives to each other and to environmental standards. Often reconciliation cannot be made, however, and the ego must resort to irrational defense mechanisms—a move leading to neurosis, or even to psychosis.

Normally the individual encounters various psychosexual stages. If the ego is unsuccessful in reconciliation at any given stage the result is a neurotic personality type. At the earliest stage, the *oral stage,* the sucking impulse, if frustrated by early weaning, may lead to the *nutrient* or the *oral personality,* an overly dependent type. Later on, at the *anal stage,* early toilet training may interfere with the desire for feces manipulation (personal "scheduling" of bowel movements) and may lead to the "anal," stingy personality: parsimonious, petty, and punctual. The anal stage is followed by a period of relative calm—the *latency stage*—during which conflicts are held in abeyance. However, this is followed by the most tumultuous stage of all, the final stage of psychosexual development, which is the *genital stage,* in which a most devastating conflict may occur between father and son for the affections of the mother, resulting in the *Oedipus complex.* Another variant of this is the mother-daughter rivalry, resulting in the *Electra complex.*[28]

Thus, for Freud, each stage of psychosexual development represented a unique conflict resulting in fixation, and each stage represented enhanced repression of the individual. So it is with civilization in general.

For Freud, social organization implies repression of instinctual gratification and therefore is responsible for the neurotic personality types. As civilization advances, conflict between the superego and id increases, and increasing anxiety and the use of defenses result in increased psychosis and neurosis, making societal disintegration imminent.[29]

Freud viewed history as a transition from the earliest phase of the primeval horde to the highest stages of civilization. This transition corresponds to increasing social organization and also to increasing repression. The primal horde was dominated by a strong male. According to Freud, the "original sin" that formed the basis for later civilization was the killing of this strong male, the primal father, by his sons, who then ate the body, thus identifying with the father by incorporating some of him. The guilt generated by this act inevitably lead to the first forms of social organization, whose cardinal purpose was to assuage guilt through renunciation of instinctual gratification and through totemism. Morality (especially the incest taboo), the law, and recognition of mutual obligations all served in renouncing instinctual gratification, and the ceremonial eating of the totem as father substitute was a means of atonement for killing the primal father.[30]

Despite its inhibitions, this early stage of civilization was not as severe as later phases of civilization, due to the permissive, matriarchal form of authority. In fact, it is with the return of the father as a deity, through the vehicle of monotheism, that guilt and repression are increased in later forms of civilization. In this later civilization a personal God comes to replace the totem as the father, although in Communion the ceremonial eating of the flesh is still practiced. This return of the repressed was further aggravated by the advent of Moses, and later Christ. Both were killed, just as the primal father was killed, due to the anxiety and guilt they provoked. Their death however, brought with it consciousness of guilt, anxiety, and the memory of the primal act or original sin, which led to increasing repression through morality, the law, and mutual obligations.[31]

Thus civilization, for Freud, involves greater repression than primitive life, due to the repressive influence of religion, especially Christianity. "Civilized people," then, have high rates of neurosis and psychosis. The perspective that civilization envolves greater repression is generally accepted in the behavioral sciences.

Ferdinand Tönnies   Unlike the historical theories of Freud and Toynbee, Ferdinand Tönnies' (1855—1936) now classic ideal type of *gemeinschaft–gesellschaft* (roughly translated; "community-society") is historically general, not applying to particular civilizations, and it is a typology of societal development rather than of civilizations. Tönnies' approach is a more specifically sociological one, in that it presents a typology of general social organization.

Although for the historical theorists, historical development might lead to degeneracy, for Tönnies the development of society is clearly from one type of organization to another. While it is clear that Tönnies favored gemeinschaft, it does not follow from this analysis of gesellschaft that the destruction of society is imminent. Gesellschaft is, perhaps, an inevitable, although perhaps unfortunate condition of large-scale society.

The distinction between gemeinschaft and gesellschaft is given, as with most polar typologies, by a series of opposing characteristics.

In contrast to Durkheim's terminological usage, gemeinschaft, the small-scale phase, is "organismic," while gesellschaft is "mechanical" in structure. Gemeinschaft relationships are organismic in the sense that they are interrelated as a whole or totality whose epitomy is found in blood or kin relations, especially mother–child, husband–wife, and brother–sister relationships (in order of decreasing "instinct" but increasing psychic bond). By contrast, gesellschaft relationships are machine-like, interdependent parts with no *a priori* unity or common value orientation (except exchange values), each part exchanging what is easiest to produce for something better.[32]

Gemeinschaft relations are typically altruistic, while gesellschaft relationships are egoistic in nature. Gemeinschaft relations are mutually beneficial relations, though not necessarily reciprocal relations, and in such relations, authority (for example, authority of age, of force, or of wisdom) is defined as aid used for the benefit of a subordinate based on sacred agreement. By contrast, gesellschaft relations are loose, necessarily reciprocal union of independent wills, whose common orientation is only apparent and not real.

Related to the above is a distinction between equalitarian and inequalitarian relations. Gemeinschaft relations are characteristically equalitarian, authority having definite limits such that despite the physical distance separating such relations there is always social nearness. By contrast, gesellschaft relations are an arena of opposing wills and abilities.

Gemeinschaft relations tend to be particularistic and ethnocentric while gesellschaft relations are cosmopolitan. Gemeinschaft relations are private, exclusive, intimate, life-long, spontaneous, and "oriented to the center of locality," while gesellschaft relations are public, limitless, transitory, superficial, polite, without boundary, and oriented to the world at large.

Last, and perhaps most important, is the underlying distinction based upon the volitional bases of the relationship. Gemeinschaft relations are based upon "natural will," while gesellschaft relations are based upon "rational will." Gemeinschaft relations are based upon understanding and consensus, the reciprocal binding sentiment expressed in language, which forms the basis of intimacy, fondness, affection, holistic orientation, equalitarianism, and mutual furtherance. Gesellschaft relations are, by contrast, aritificial and calculative, as epitomized by convention, a working agreement or coalition of potential enemies, which encourages or at least corresponds with individualistic, exploitative, cosmopolitan, market relationships.[33]

Tönnies, throughout his work, emphasizes that gemeinschaft—gesellschaft orientations are "ideal types" of relationships, and thus, the typology has unlimited application to a variety of social structures. This type of analysis is a forerunner of the notion of "constructive typology" which will be discussed below.

Robert Redfield   Robert Redfield (1897–1958) was inspired by Tönnies' distinction, as well as by a caricature of urban life drawn up by sociologists of the "Chicago School" of sociology.[34] The Chicago School of the 1920's and 1930's portrayed urbanism as a way of life characterized by extensive conflicts of norms and values, by rapid social change, by increased mobility of the population, by emphasis on material goods and individualism, and by a marked decline in intimate communication. Redfield focused upon the transition from "folk society" to "urban society." Both types have their positive and negative aspects. The negative aspects of urban society were perhaps given the greatest degree of emphasis, however.

In folk societies, the core of society is kinship relations. All statuses are kinship statuses. All categories for thought are kinship categories. All behavior is customary and ritualized, and all social relationships are personal. Such societies are necessarily "small, isolated, nonliterate, and culturally homogenous."

Urban societies, by contrast, are contractual, market economies, with a highly developed division of labor. Such societies are large, cosmopolitan, literate, and heterogenous. The core institutions of folk society—family and religion—become specialized, and thus there is a decline of the sacred and increase of the secular, an increase of impersonality and decline in sense of solidarity, a decline in partriarchal or matriarchal authority within the family, and increasing scepticism and scientific reflection.[35]

Despite the continuum nature of Redfield's folk-urban polarity, he applied his analysis empirically to actually existing societies. Thus he studied the Tepoztlan of South Central Mexico, as an intermediate type, transitional between "folk" and "demos." Later he studied four communities in Yucatan, each representing a phase of development from folk to urban: a tribal village (Tusik), a peasant village (Chan Rom), a town (Dzitas), and a city (Merida).[36] Thus Redfield, like Tönnies, is a forerunner of constructive typology.

Constructive typology

The polar or ideal typologies we have discussed have been criticized from a variety of points of view: (1) they don't refer to empirical reality and thus cannot be verified or rejected; (2) there is a tendency to emphasize one pole or another of the typology; (3) a continuum is implied which may not be an accurate portrayal; (4) the typologies present a stereotyping of types into one pole or another when it may be more accurate to describe several subtypes; and (5) the concepts used imply a value judgment or a subjective point of view.[37]

A number of theorists have sought to overcome the disadvantages of ideal typologies through the development of what might be termed "eclectic typologies" or "constructive typologies."[38] We have already seen an attempt at such a typology in Parsons' theory of social action. Parsons' categories of the AGIL paradigm are derived from and inclusive of the wide range of theoretical concepts and orientations that he had earlier studied.[39]

Durkheim, whose mechanical *versus* organic solidarity typology has been discussed above, qualified his analysis by including three "abnormal phases" of the division of labor: anomic division of labor, forced division of labor, and another form which he simply designated "mixed." Howard Becker, known for his "sacred–secular" typology, introduced several subtypes of sacred and secular poles based upon a study of all polar typologies in extant. Another scheme, based upon several transitional stages of evolution, is suggested by the anthropologist Elman Service.

These schemes will be presented in detail in the pages to follow. In addition, an original constructive typology will be proposed, based upon existing ideal *and* constructive typologies.

Émile Durkheim's "Abnormal Types" Durkheim was essentially an evolutionist. He believed that societies normally progress from mechanical to organic solidarity, accompanied by increasing complexity of division of labor, the decline of collective conscience and rise of individual conscience, increase of restitutive law over and above repressive law, and increasing cohesive bonds. However, Durkheim also recognized that societies do not always fall neatly into this pattern. He described "deviant or abnormal" forms of social organization: the *anomic division of labor,* the *forced division of labor,* and a third, *mixed* form.[40]

An *anomic* division of labor may result from excessively rapid change in the population or in the number of competing groups. "Anomic division of labor" refers to a state of society in which there is a "lack of adjustment of functions" or a conflict between functions.[41] This state of anomie involves either the loss or breakdown of rules regulating relations between functions or the failure of government to play its proper role as moderator between these conflicting groups, or both.

Forced division of labor refers to an essentially opposite condition of overregulation of relations between these groups—in a sense, too many rules. Society lacks "equality in the external conditions of conflict."

The *mixed* form that Durkheim simply terms "another abnormal form" is characterized by a lack of coordination of functions—that is, "functions are disturbed in such a way that they do not offer sufficient material for individual activity."[42] This cannot be corrected merely through general regulative activity (as in the anomic division of labor) but rather through economical management.

Durkheim viewed the above types as temporary and brief, however. Anomic division of labor is usually alleviated by the spontaneous agreement or consensus of the conflicting functions through developing a division of labor. This brings a state of comfort or well-being which prevents violation. Forced division of labor may be broken up through violence directed at the ruler to reestablish equality of opportunity. The mixed form of division of labor can be corrected through more economical allocation of functions.

Durkheim's theory will be examined in greater detail in Chapter 3 on anomie theory. Durkheim is often cited as the "father" of current anomie theory.

Howard Becker   Like Durkheim, Becker has isolated four types of social organization. These are based upon his primary distinction between *sacred society* and *secular society*.[43] *Sacred societies* are characterized by their social isolation and related characteristics such as fixation of habit and neophobia, relations of avoidance, and traditional in-group–out-group attitudes. As in Durkheim's typology of mechanical solidarity, Becker's sacred society is characterized by an emphasis upon extended family, simple division of labor, and informal social control. It is called sacred society because of the dominance of nonrational behavior in favor of supernaturalism and an impermeable value system.

Secular society, by contrast, is highly changeable, characterized by frequent innovation, a permeable value system, and scientific rationality with regard to the pursuit of happiness. The division of labor is complex. The family system declines in influence in favor of the nuclear family. Formal control emerges to replace declining informal control.

These two ideal types cannot be found in empirical reality. However, their major subtypes are constructive types and can be approximated. The *folk-sacred society* is best exemplified by old-fashioned and primitive groups of the world, sometimes referred to as "folk societies." The *prescribed-sacred society* is approximated by the Geneva theocracy of Calvin, the Jesuit state of Paraguay, Fascist Italy, Nazi Germany, and Soviet Russia. The *principled-secular society* is an advanced form of equilibrium in which the extreme aspects of the sacred are lost, and yet a principle derived from the sacred value system puts a check on rampant change and reduces the potential of mental accessibility. The *normless-secular society* is the anomic form of secular society characterized by confusion regarding norms and by social disorganization.

Elman Service   In still another attempt to classify several types of societies, an evolutionary scheme has been developed by the anthropologist Elman Service.[44] Service distinguishes five different levels or stages of societal development. *Band societies* are small, rudimentary, lacking in government, and regulated exclusively by the rules of kinship. Examples of band societies include the Eskimo, Arunta, Yahgan, and Andaman Islanders. *Tribes* are actually several combined bands regulated by subband sodalities, regulatory organizations (including clans, kindreds, and secret societies) with no residential basis, which unify residential groups. Though there is more division of labor and greater size, there is no permanent government, and society is still divided into segmental groups. Examples include the Nuer, the Navaho, the Jivaro of South America, and the Cheyenne. At the next level, the *chieftain level,* organic solidarity first emerges. The chief performs the governmental function, and a division of labor emerges with the development of economic and labor specialization and a market exchange. Examples include the Nootka of British Columbia, Trobriand Islanders, natives of Tahiti, and the Kalinga (Philap). The next level, the *state* level, is characterized primarily by the emergence of socioeconomic classes and the monopoly of force by the government. The highest level, the *imperial level,* incorporates a significant urban rural difference as well.

A new typology (synthesis)

Thus far in this chapter we have examined the wide range of ideal typologies and constructive typologies that come to us from historical and contemporary social theory. The sheer volume of these typologies may create confusion in the mind of the reader. This is part of the reason for the development of the constructive typologies that have been discussed in the last few pages. However, we are still left with a choice of which constructive typology to use. The purpose of presenting the multitude of theoretical typologies in this chapter is to provide a basis for assessment of current-day theories of deviancy. However, for other purposes, these typologies will have to be simplified. Hopefully, it will be possible to develop a typology that incorporates the concepts and characteristics of the typologies discussed so far.

This "grand typology" will have multifold uses in comparative analysis of deviancy throughout the text. First, it will enable us to discuss cross-cultural social systems, to predict patterns of deviancy cross-culturally (and over time), and to assess the existing evidence in terms of these predictions. Second, similar analysis can be done comparing subcultures within a society. Third, comparative analysis of behavior in complex organizations can be done using an adaptation of our "grand typology." Fourth, the typology can be applied to smaller institutional settings: communities, classrooms, primary work groups, gangs, and even families. Thus, we can study deviant behavior from the point of view of its group context, rather than basing our generalizations about group behavior upon the kinds of deviancy found in groups, or ignoring groups context altogether, as is so often done in textbooks on social problems. The basis of this constructive typology might be found in a now-classic article by DeGré.[45]

Although DeGré's analysis focuses upon freedom and conditions for freedom, the result of his analysis is a five-fold typology which will be shown useful in organizing concepts, in grouping organizational types, and in analyzing societies historically and in terms of size. It can be used accurately to categorize contemporary societies, as well as historical ones, and it can be used for comparative purposes. Thus it meets the criteria of our constructive typology.

DeGré pointed out that the term "freedom" is itself ambiguous. It is defined particularistically by both conservatives and revolutionaries to apply only to their own narrow class interests. Freedom refers to the number of things a person can do without interference from others. Freedom flourishes when groups relationships are in a state of equilibrium involving reciprocity and equality with regard to each other.

> Freedom may be defined in terms of the probability that specific groups or individuals can formulate their ends of conduct and initiate a course of action with a minimum degree of constraint from other persons, and with a high degree of predictability of the consequences of their acts within the institutional and associational structure of the community.[46]

In a hyper-individualized or atomized society, groups cannot organize to attain their ends due to the debilitating conflict that goes on with other rival groups, while when one or two groups obtain control of the social structure, the resulting oligarchy can dominate the majority for its own purposes. It is thus possible that freedom cannot be optimized either under conditions of underorganization or overorganization, but is optimized somewhere in between. DeGré showed this in Figure 2–1.

DeGré isolated five different forms of social organization, based upon "degrees of freedom" and degree of concentration of power. The minimal degree of group integration is correlated with a low degree of freedom, illustrative of Hobbes' "war of all against all," termed *atomistic society*. Historical examples include frontier democracy and the cut-throat, competitive economy of Dobu. The *minoral* degree of social integration involves a multitude of small competing groups, characterized by low stability, paving the way to dictatorship and the monolithic state. This is characteristically a disorganized society, with many autonomous economic organizations, a large number of competing sects, a multi-party system in which no one group can achieve a parlimentary majority or significant minority, and a society lacking a basic consensus concerning its ends, institutions, or organization. This is termed *multipartite society*, exemplified by the Holy Roman Empire and the Italian city-states, and the French political scene during the thirties. By contrast, in *pluralistic society*, indicated by the presence of large, well-integrated groups representing significant divisions of interests

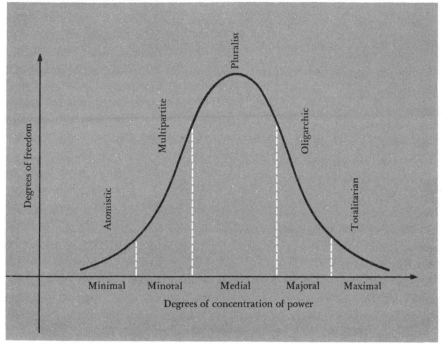

Figure 2–1. DeGré's curve: Freedom as related to concentration of power. SOURCE: Gerard DeGré, "Freedom and Social Structure," *American Sociological Review*, 11 (October, 1946), 534–536.

and values, there is maximum freedom, though medial concentration of power. All power or interest groups in the society have equal countervailing groups to take into account; the government must take organized public opinion into account; business must placate labor; management and labor look out for consumer interest; each religious group balances the other; religion is countervailed by independent, secular thought in free media; and there are a variety of types of productive organization. Examples include the United States, Great Britain, and Sweden. By contrast, the term *oligarchy* characterizes the next step on the declining curve. Power is concentrated in the hands of specific vested interests, irrespective of whether these interests are aristocratic, bourgeois, military, proletarian, ecclesiastic, or bureaucratic. Last, at the bottom of the declining slope is *totalitarian society,* total in the sense that it has systematically destroyed all independent groups and autonomous opinion. The individual, though appearing "atomized," is actually "massified" by the omnipotent Leviathan state, not present in atomistic society.

Though DeGré does not claim his curve has any empirical validity, with some modifications it would appear to serve as an adequate constructive typology under which all of the foregoing concepts can be subsumed.

A problem with DeGré's analysis, however, is that it fails to take into account scale or size of society. That is, in a small, relatively isolated, preindustrial society, the absence of groups and "atomization" of individuals may not necessarily lead to war of all against all. As has been shown, there may be a highly developed collective conscience and/or family organization uniting the society as a whole into a community. Such groups have been variously referred to as folk society, tribe or band, communal society, gemeinschaft, and mechanical solidarity. Though they correspond to the condition of low individual freedom, they can hardly be said to be highly individualized or characterized by a "war of all against all." Thus, we must adjust for this in making our analysis. Instead of DeGré's term atomistic we shall use the term communal society to refer to the small-scale phase of societal equilibrium. When this adjustment is made, DeGré's typology appears highly adequate for classifying societies of the world, and for grouping various theoretical types that have been studied. This classification serves as the basis for our constructive typology.

CRITERIA FOR CONSTRUCTIVE TYPOLOGY

In reviewing the organizational types developed above, essentially five criteria appear to be significant: (1) the extent of division of labor or the extent to which various institutions, occupations, and interest groups have been separated; (2) the degree of cohesion or attractiveness of group members or large groups to each other; (3) the typical sanction or form of punishment for wrongdoing; (4) the adaptability of society or capacity of society to handle change; and (5) the modal personality type or dominant personality type. We will now proceed to apply these criteria to selected constructed types.

Communal society   Several classical sociological concepts seem to refer to the small-scale, isolated, preindustrial version of communal society, including Redfield's "folk society," Cooley's "primary group," Tönnies' "gemeinschaft," Becker's "folk-sacred society," Durkheim's "mechanical solidarity," MacIver's "communal society," and Service's discussion of "band" and "tribe." In DeGré's formulation these would all involve few if any subgroups and little or no concentration of power.

Communal societies have a simple *division of labor.* They are homogeneous, and if subgroups exist at all, they are segmental rather than associational or specialized groups. Family and religion are undifferentiated and central to all experience. The only division of labor is sexual division between males and females.

Cohesion in this society type is relatively strong. There is a strong "we" feeling, or attraction of like elements. Relations are personal, familial, and face-to-face. Self and group are merged, and collective conscience exerts a significant influence over individual behavior. The individual is directly related to society. There are no classes, few status distinctions apart from family position, and no government.

The typical *sanction* for deviancy is repressive. Such sanctions tend to be informal rather than formal, and sacred rather than secular. Examples include such spontaneous sanctions as gossip, sorcery, ostracism. Such societies, however, cannot easily *adapt* to changes in the external environment. They are isolated and non-literate. All behavior is handled by customary ritualized rules, which do not cover new unanticipated environmental circumstances.

Based upon a strong collective conscience and the extremity of sanction for deviancy, conformity would be more pervasive than in modern society, but any deviant personality would polarize toward philistinism. Two variants of this are ritualism and retreatism. The ritualist conforms reluctantly, while the retreatist withdraws into a schizophrenic fantasy world such as that of the shaman, an accepted form of deviancy in primitive society.

Multipartite or anomic society   The term "anomic" seems more descriptive of the next level of social organization than the term multipartite, because multipartite refers to a rather specific aspect of government. A number of classic social concepts can be subsumed under this type, including Thomas and Znaniecki's "disorganization," Pareto's "combinations," Marx's "capitalism," Spengler's and Toynbee's "civilization," Kornhauser's "mass society," Tönnies' "Gesellschaft," Becker's "normless-secular," and Durkheim's "anomic division of labor."

Implied is at least some level of industrialization and relatively complex *division of labor,* in that there exist rival, conflicting, independent, schemes, associations, functions, institutions, occupational groups, and interest groups insufficiently regulated due in part to relatively weak government, which can be traced to the lack of dominance of any one traditional scheme.

Because of the absence of common values and of conflicting values, beliefs, wills, and interests, cohesion is relatively weak. This is due to the decline of tradition and custom and the absence of a transpersonal stratification doctrine and adequate regulatory government. Government may be entrenched with unscrupulous men, oriented toward their own self-interest and not at all interested in the people. The only basis holding society together is trade or market relations, because of the existence of labor specialization and the need for exchange. Common ground is thus found in interdependence of interest. Due to the weakness of the government and the absence of tradition, effective *sanctions* for deviancy may be absent. *Sanctions* are inconsistent, misdirected, and often excessively restitutive rather than repressive, and supportive of the society's principles or values.

Due to the lack of commitment to tradition or domination by some specific group, the "rules of the game" are constantly changing, as shown in frequent fashions and fads. Patterns of behavior are in flux and there is no group identity. Relations are characteristically cosmopolitan, superficial, and transitory. Individual behavior is nonconforming, migratory, or *bohemian.*

Pluralistic society Such societies are characterized by the highest industrialization and most complex division of labor among great specialized associations, representing all attitudes and interests. Though individualism is thus fostered to a high degree, individuals are deeply involved in associational groups which interdepend in a cooperative manner oriented toward a mutually recognized, common value system or set of principles. Individuals are related to larger groups by way of a transpersonal stratification doctrine, which nevertheless incorporates achieved rather than ascribed criteria for placement. On the individual level, there develops an attitude of mutual tolerance and understanding, or even benevolence, toward members of specialized groups or status levels other than one's own, due to the absence of conflict in larger groups relations and to a sense of fairness in the distribution of reward values. Though restitutive sanctions are more highly used than in primitive society, repressive sanctions are necessary occasionally to support the basic principles of society.

In such societies, individual and group freedom is highest, due to the division of labor, conditions of mutual tolerance, and an agreed-upon stratification doctrine. Also, facilitative of freedom is the recognition of the place of scientific, innovative thought and the existence of a mechanism — the mass media — for communicating knowledge to a literate public. The typical personality is a creative man, capable of achieving his personal and group ends to the highest degree. A number of conceptual counterparts fit this type, including Lerner's "participant society," Comte's "positivistic society," Spencer's "industrial society," MacIver's "associational society," Kornhauser's "pluralistic society," Becker's "principled-secular society," and Durkheim's "organic solidarity".

Oligarchic or coercive organization While in pluralistic society there is an effective integration of diverse groups, in oligarchic society one or another special interest group has come to dominate society, restricting through force the free play and interchange between existing groups. Such groups are best described as coercive rather than oligarchic, because organizational studies show that oligarchy is a condition of nearly all large-scale organization. Corresponding concepts include Sjoberg's "feudal society," Comte's "theological society," Pareto's "aggregates," Freud's "civilization," Spencer's "military society," Becker's "prescribed-sacred" society, and Durkheim's "forced division of labor." These concepts refer to a variety of dominating interest groups: feudal land-owning aristocracy, clerical elites, military groups, and the like. Marx's capitalism was excluded because of his description of the covert nature of bourgeoisie domination and the high degree of conflict with labor. Anomic organization does not necessarily mean that all interests are served equally. Oligarchy, however, differs in the quelling of all opposition through the force of custom or arms.

Because of the domination of one group, the division of labor is not allowed to develop beyond a point or along lines other than those favored by the entrenched elite group. There is an emphasis upon citizen emulation of the elite group rather than the development of individual personality. Cooperation is compulsory. All operations or functions are directed from central control points. Jobs are assigned rather than freely chosen. Status is predominantly ascribed, based upon some sacred, quasi-sacred, or even pseudo-

TABLE 2-1 Constructive typology of social organization

Type of social organization	*Communal*	*Multipartite*
Concepts and authors	Folk Society (Redfield) Primary Group (Cooley) Tribe–Band (Service) Communal Society (MacIver–Kornhauser) Gemeinschaft (Tönnies) Folk-Sacred Society (Becker) Mechanical Solidarity (Durkheim)	Social Disorganization (Thomas and Znaniecki) Combinations–Foxes (Pareto) Mass Society (Kornhauser) Gesellschaft (Tönnies) Normless–Secular Society (Becker) Anomic Division of Labor (Durkheim)
Degree of concentration of power	Minimal: No groups	Minoral: Poorly integrated groups
Extent of division of labor	Simple and sexual No specialties No associations Homogeneity Segmentalization	Complex Independent rival associations Domination of none
Basis of cohesion	Elaborate and all-inclusive kinship "We" unity No government	Interdependence of self-interest No common values Weak and corrupt government
Dominant sanction	Repressive, informal or sacred sanction	Restitutive "normlessness"
Adaptability of society	Rigid, isolated, non-literate, bound by custom and ritual	Constant change and turmoil
Dominant personality type	Philistine	Bohemian

sacred transpersonal stratification doctrine, generally established and altered only by the ruling interest group. Thus freedom is relatively low, and there is little equality of opportunity to individuals outside the elite group.

Sanctions for deviancy are generally violent and repressive,

TABLE 2–1   Continued

Pluralistic	Oligarchic	Totalitarian
Participant Society (Lerner)	Feudal Society (Sjoberg)	Totalitarianism (Kornhauser)
Positivistic Society (Comte)	Theological Society (Comte)	
Associational Society (MacIver)	Aggregates–Lions (Pareto)	
Pluralistic Society (Kornhauser)	Civilization (Freud)	
Principled–Secular Society (Becker)	Prescribed–Sacred Society (Becker)	
Organic Solidarity (Durkheim)	Forced Division of Labor (Durkheim)	
Medial: Well-integrated groups	Majoral: Power concentrated in special interest groups	Maximal: All groups destroyed
Complex, interdependent functions and associations, none dominating	Complex but rigid due to domination of one association	Atomistic: No associations
Specialized government Common values Interdependence	Government direction	Absolute dictator run government
Balance of restitutive and repressive	Repressive, violent sanction	Repressive, violent
Innovative Relativistic Literate	Rigid, absolute	Resistant to change Free speech suppressed
Creative Man	Philistine	Philistine

either formal or informal, based upon the recognition of widespread discontent and the necessity of quelling possible revolution.

The elite group resists social change, rigidly expressing absolute belief systems, because social change can only be in the direction of some other interest group or elite system. Thus, it rigorously suppresses all inquiry and use of media that might bring about that social change.

The individual faced by the threat of violence and the sacredness of tradition has only one choice: philistinism—to conform rigidly even though disagreeing.

Totalitarianism This type is relatively rare, but as described by Kornhauser, appears to be primarily a more extreme extension of the characteristics of oligarchy. Totalitarianism differs from oligarchy primarily by the greater concentration of power and destruction of all opposing interest groups that might serve as a potential basis of opposition.

Summary and conclusion

It has been demonstrated that there is a wide variety of concepts and perspectives for the analysis of contemporary society. In fact, the same society may be criticized or idealized by portraying it in terms of one concept or another. For example, current-day elite theories, such as those of C. Wright Mills and Floyd Hunter, stress the presence of coercive and oligarchical elements in modern society. By contrast, disorganization theory utilizes an anomic or multipartite model as a basis for criticism. On the other hand, the current theory of political pluralism stresses the integrating and balancing aspects of the various organizations that proliferate in contemporary society.

It will be shown that current deviancy approaches explicitly or implictly adopt a particular theoretical perspective. However, it is necessary to examine critically the prevailing perspective in comparison with alternative perspectives, and in addition to look at the empirical evidence for each. This approach will at least sharpen previously "fuzzy" perspectives as to the social context of deviancy. It could potentially totally revise images of society utilized in current popular deviancy theories.

Table 2-1 is a paradigm that shows in summary form the constructive typology developed in this chapter, and the various concepts and meanings that it subsumes. This will prove useful for quick reference to the basic constructive types that will be constantly referred to in the chapters that follow.

Social disorganization and related contemporary approaches

There are a multitude of theoretical approaches to the study of deviance in American society. A number of these theories are somewhat parochial—that is, confined to a particular substantive area, such as criminology—and have no explicit link with the larger theories of society, such as those discussed in Chapter 2. These include culture conflict theory, status deprivation theory, theory of cultural discontinuity, differential association theory, social control theory, theory of social isolation, cultural transmission theory, and containment theory. These are essentially middle-range or microtheoretical approaches[1] which make no explicit statements about the type of society that generates one or the other form of deviancy.

These more narrow middle-range theories have been developed in reaction to "sick society–disorganization theories" because critics attacked such theories as value laden, fallacious, narrowly conservative, and methodologically unsound. This reaction against large-scale disorganization theory is part of the reaction in all areas of social theory to the lofty "grand theories" that dominated early

Notes for this chapter are on pages 372–380.

sociology. However, recently there has been a revival of interest in large-scale theorizing in general sociology. In part this is because of the awareness that middle-range approaches imply an often undefined larger theory of society. Similarly, in the study of deviancy, there has been a revival of interest in earlier anomie and disorganization theories, but yet under the guise of middle-range theory, notably in the works of Robert K. Merton and his followers.

The end result of the reluctance of deviancy theorists to discuss large-scale theory is that one prevailing image of society—a vague disorganization or mass society image—though unacceptable to many, has remained unchallenged by alternative images of society, and has been uncritically employed by social pathologists (implicitly or explicitly). Nobody has dared to suggest that indeed society may not be disorganized but highly organized, perhaps supraorganized. Instead, it is always assumed that there must be something disordered or unhealthy about the social organization of a society in which large amounts of deviancy are found to take place. This lack of attention by deviancy writers to larger theoretical issues is not a minor flaw but a major one. Without adequate theory it is not possible to predict, control, or even to understand. A different theoretical orientation could totally reorient expectations. These reformed orientations may not be in accord with current empirical research on deviancy, especially that based on official reports. However, future field study might reveal the methodological errors of present studies. One impetus for such criticisms might be the development and crystalization of alternative theories of society in relation to deviancy.

The narrow "microtheories" discussed above are not of direct concern to this book. In fact, our objective is to redirect attention toward large-scale theory in relation to deviancy. For this reason, this text will focus upon three related approaches to deviancy—social disorganization, anomie, and mass society—which contain definite statements that may be linked to larger theory. In a sense, therefore, these are true sociological theories of deviancy, inasmuch as they contain such statements. These approaches will be critically examined in this chapter, and will be placed within the constructive typology discussed in Chapter 2. Alternative approaches will be empirically examined using cross-national data and trend data for the United States.

Social disorganization

It has been shown from a brief examination of early sociological theories that many of the European approaches were progressivistic in their view of society. Society was developing toward higher, more complex, and superior stages. Comte emphasized the superiority of the positivistic stage. Durkheim favored organic solidarity. Weber saw the tendency toward rationality and bureaucratization as in some respects a favorable one. Marx saw future socialism as a utopian prospect.

THE EARLY AMERICAN SCENE

Early American theorists did not break with this tradition. The early American sociologists were "grand theorists," looking at society-at-large as developing through phases toward higher, better forms. William Graham Sumner, perhaps the earliest of these grand theorists, saw as the basic law of man the law of evolution: a spontaneous, irreversible process, which cannot be changed by social effort. He insisted that the folkways, the ways of doing things that are commonly accepted in a society, evolved toward better forms. By trial and error, from various ways of acting, the best and the fittest folkways are elected.

Sumner was an economic determinist, in the sense that he believed that political and social institutions find their basis in economic fact, and that what determines the state of both is the stage of the industrial organization existing at a given time. He believed that the existence of society is conditioned by natural and social forces and that its phenomena are subject to laws. Man must learn these laws, obey them, and conform to them, and not try to intervene or change the laws. The basic law is evolution, which is an automatic process.[2]

Other early theorists on the American scene carried, with certain variations and qualifications, this theme of progressivism and evolutionism. A. W. Small, another early theorist, saw society as evolving from an isolated agrarian form to a modern metropolitan one, and stressed that this evolution brought more complete persons and more complete institutions, and that it had no fixed limit.[3]

Another prominent pioneer in American sociology was Lester

F. Ward. In his theories, Ward recognized *genesis* or emergent evolution of human society, but differed with Sumner and Small in his reference to *social telesis,* the conscious control and direction of social development by the human mind.[4]

DEVELOPMENT OF THE CONCEPT OF SOCIAL DISORGANIZATION

The concept of social disorganization in American thought can be seen, in part, as a reaction to this tradition of progressivism and evolutionism.

Thomas and Znaniecki The earliest approach to social disorganization, that of Thomas and Znaniecki,[5] amounted to a denial of both economic determinism and progressivism as scientific law. They insisted that objective or social causes were only a partial explanation for the development of society. Subjective factors, they insist, not explained by objective, social causes, always enter into definition of the situation and subsequently into development of society. Thomas's theorem "if men define situations as real they are real in their consequences" is reminiscent of Weber's *verstehen* — the subjective "free-will"–based factor of history. The result of taking a particular stand is crucial. Through arbitrary decision, history and evolution can be manifestly altered. The fate of a society or of the whole world is sometimes dependent on the whim of one man.

It is based upon this voluntaristic context that Thomas and Znaniecki became concerned with the possibility of social disorganization. It is possible that valid social rules may be violated by significant individuals, precipitating a disruption of group life and a breakdown in social control.

For Thomas and Znaniecki, social disorganization occurs when there is a deviation from traditional rules of behavior. Traditional society consists of one large complex of schemes or definitions of situations, evolving slowly, but easily disorganized by contact with rival schemes of rival cultures. After the breakdown of traditional society, society undergoes a phase of disorganization in which a variety of traditional schemes or complexes exist independently and in conflict or competition with one another. One or another of these schemes may dominate from time to time; however, none are able to regulate all group activities.

The existence of these diverse schemes produces conflicting demands upon the individual. Each scheme vies with the other for individual allegiance. However, this does not mean that the existence of social disorganization necessarily implies personal disorganization. Personal disorganization, they say, consists of "a decrease of the individual's ability to organize his whole life for the efficient, progressive, and continuous realization of his fundamental interests." It is possible, however, that *through deviating from the societal norms and values* an individual may achieve those fundamental interests.

> An individual who breaks some or even most of the social rules prevailing in his group may indeed do this because he is losing the minimum capacity of life-organization required by social conformism; but he may also reject the schemes of behavior imposed by his milieu because they hinder him in reaching a more efficient and more comprehensive life organization. On the other hand also, the social organization of a group may be very permanent and strong in the sense that no opposition is manifested to the existing rules and institutions; and yet, this lack of opposition may be simply the result of the narrowness of the interests of the group-members and may be accompanied by a very rudimentary, mechanical and inefficient life-organization of each member individually. . . . It is therefore impossible to conclude from social as to individual organization or disorganization or vice versa.[6]

The thesis of non-correspondence between personal and social disorganization has many ramifications which led to wide controversy among those who followed Thomas and Znaniecki. For that reason, they should be examined in detail.

1. *It is possible to have social disorganization without personal disorganization.* The individual may realize his interests through violating the traditional rules. Thomas and Znaniecki termed this adaptation that of the *creative man.* He is capable of selecting from several traditional schemes, deriving the best elements from each, due to his dynamic internal organization.

2. *It is possible to have personal disorganization without social disorganization.* A person may fail to obtain his life goals precisely because he conforms to a stable traditional organization. This mode of adjustment is termed *philistine adaptation.* The individual becomes a specialist within one traditional scheme and is inefficient in obtaining life goals due to his blindness to alternative prospective schemes.

3. *Personal disorganization may result from social disorganization.* If the individual rejects all of the traditional complexes,

passing from one to the other, he will fail in the attainment of his life goals. This is termed *bohemian adaptation.*

4. *Personal and social organization may be counterparts.* "A strong group organization may be also the product of a conscious moral effort of its members and thus corresponding to a very high degree of life-organization of each of them individually."[7]

Though social disorganization is viewed as a present reality by Thomas and Znaniecki, it is not necessarily a perpetual state of society. As a matter of fact, in contrast to many of the subsequent approaches to disorganization, they viewed it as normally transitory. Ultimately, the rival complexes would develop interdependence, mutual tolerance, and cooperative relations, as well as an integrated, common value orientation.

Charles Horton Cooley   Charles Horton Cooley is perhaps the second of the pioneers in the study of social disorganization. His analysis differed in a number of ways from that of his predecessors, Thomas and Znaniecki, especially his analysis of the relation between individual and social disorganization.

Cooley's analysis begins with his analysis of the primary group:

> By *primary groups* I mean *those characterized by intimate face-to-face associations and cooperation.* They are primary in several senses, but chiefly in that they are fundamental in forming the social nature and ideals of the individual.[8]

Key examples of the primary group include the family, the play group, and intimate neighborhood associations. They are primary in the sense of development of self, giving the individual his earliest and most complete experience of social unity. Even more important, however, the primary group experience gives rise to universally found social ideals such as sympathy, love, resentment, ambition, vanity, hero-worship, and feelings of social right and wrong.

Cooley's analysis of the primary group in fact roughly parallels Freud's analysis of the family as a basis for larger social organization.[9] Cooley, like Freud, believed there were certain inherited instincts: anger, fear, love, and self-assertion. In socialized beings these are expressed as the passions of lust, greed, revenge, and pride. Through one's experience in the primary group these are channeled in the direction of the ideals of love, freedom, justice, and morality, becoming internalized forces in the mature personality, forming the basis for large-scale social organization. If the primary group fails in its function, the individual will not be socialized and society will be disorganized by rampant passions.

To Cooley, society develops out of the primary group as a construction of primary ideals. Large-scale institutions, such as democracy and Christianity, are merely an expression of primary group sentiments. However, with the development of large-scale institutions inevitably comes dissipation of the energies of human nature and social disorganization, due to mechanization and formalization of behavior.[10]

> The organization of society may not only fail to give human nature the moral support it needs, but may be of such a kind as actively to promote degeneration. On its worst side the whole system of commercialism, characteristic of our time, is of this sort. That is, its spirit is largely mechanical, unhuman, seeking to use mankind as an agent of material production with very little regard, in the case of the weak classes, for breadth of life, self-expression, outlook, hope, or any kind of higher life. Men, women, children, find themselves required to work at tasks, usually uninteresting and often exhausting, amidst dreary surroundings, and under such relations to the work as a whole that their imagination and loyalty are little, if at all, aroused. Such a life either atrophies the larger impulses of human nature or represses them to such a degree that they break out, from time to time, in gross and degrading forms of expression.[11]

Perhaps the most significant feature of Cooley's analysis is the one-to-one relation he drew between individual organization and social disorganization. If the spirit of the primary group is dissipated in large-scale formal institutions, so is the spirit of human nature. For Cooley, human nature is primary group nature as found universally, so that as society becomes disorganized, personality becomes disorganized, and, as a matter of fact, one follows the other in a kind of cyclical process. The existence of personality disorganization fosters a consciousness of common needs which results in institutional organization to fulfill these needs. However, institutionalization brings formalization, controlling the individual externally but leaving him without internal guidance or control— namely, personality disorganization. This results in rebellion from institutional forms and social disorganization, followed by reorganization starting over again.[12]

Cooley's assumption of a one-to-one correlation between personal and social disorganization paved the way for the wider usage of social disorganization as an explanatory framework. Thomas and Znaniecki's earlier usage had been confined to the Polish community, while envisioning the possibility of disorganization of the larger society during periods of transition. If we can assume with Cooley that personal and social disorganization are one and the same thing, and if we can acknowledge the widespread nature of deviancy in modern society, then we are ready to perceive that disorganization is a pervasive and chronic condition of modern society. In essence this is the stand taken by the early textbook approaches to disorganization.

TEXTBOOK APPROACHES TO DISORGANIZATION

Despite a widespread usage of the term "social disorganization" in sociology, relatively few texts have been written with that title or even with the word "disorganization" in the title.[13] Almost all of these were written in the 1930's and 1940's,[14] and only two of these are currently in print.[15] Generally, a course on social disorganization is taught using a text on a related topic such as "deviant behavior," "social pathology," or "social problems," as a variety of current texts are available on those topics.[16]

In terms of the definition of social disorganization, there is general agreement among the various early texts on the subject. Drawing from these texts generally, social disorganization is defined as a weakening of group relationships, a breakdown in institutions, a decline in consensus, and a failure of group task attainment. There is similar agreement in the use of the term "personal disorganization" as disruption of pattern of behavior toward life goals, statuses, roles, values, and purposes. Another commonality is the approach to causation. Most of the textbook approaches trace disorganization, directly or indirectly, to social change, especially to rapid social change utilizing such theoretical approaches as cultural lag and culture conflict. Mowrer, for example, viewed social disorganization as a normal result of social change:

> As variations from the approved pattern become more clearly defined, they meet with social disapproval varying all the way from tolerant skepticism to moral indignation. If this disapproval is met positively by attempting to find approval among those whose own divergencies . . . are in harmony with one's own, the result is to attempt

consciously to introduce a new element into the social order. Social disorganization is the inevitable result until such time as the new behavior pattern loses group support or becomes incorporated into the social order. . . . All social change thus involves some social disorganization.[17]

The texts, in addition, generally agree as to the relationship between social and personal disorganization. Personal disorganization is generally viewed as a normal outcome of social disorganization and/or a factor leading to further disorganization. Thus, a variety of instances of personal disorganization, such as crime, suicide, mental disorder, drug addiction, and alcoholism, may be viewed within a larger theoretical scheme of social disorganization.

Finally, there was general agreement as to measurement. Generally, social disorganization was to be measured by the variety and prevalence of social problems existing in a given society—for instance suicide rates, insanity rates, divorce rates, delinquency rates, and the like.[18]

> Community disorganization may be indicated by the literacy rate of the population, figures for irregular school attendance, rates of social mobility and transiency, political corruption, suicide, vice, and crime. Indices for personal and social disorganization may thus overlap.[19]

It will be shown below that this somewhat oversimplified approach to the study of deviant behavior has met with much criticism. Before examining the various opposing points of view, however, it is necessary to review briefly the basic empirical literature upon which this early social disorganization approach was based. The criticisms directed at social disorganization theory often are based on the kind of empirical data adduced to support disorganization theory.

EMPIRICAL APPROACHES TO DISORGANIZATION

Social disorganization was at one time a theory and a perspective for grouping or codifying various empirical studies. A variety of studies have been cited by disorganization theorists to show the relevancy or applicability of social disorganization theory. First, a variety of *ecological studies,* studies dealing with the spatial distribution of various social problems, showed that social disorganization could be used to explain the distribution of various phenomena such as delinquency and mental disorder throughout the city. Second, *case studies,* as suggested by the earlier approach of Thomas and Znaniecki, showed that disorganization could be seen through the eyes of the deviant. Third, *community studies* were used to portray the development of disorganization in various settings. Last, a few *national studies* were used to illustrate disorganization.

Ecological studies   Perhaps the very basis of disorganization theory are the various studies of the distribution of various disorders throughout the city—the ecological studies. While several ecological approaches have been suggested, the most generally accepted and most thoroughly corroborated are those based on the *concentric zone theory* of Burgess and Park.[20]

Burgess and Park conceived of the city as divided into circular areas or concentric zones spanning out from the central city. Although many zones were conceived in the original analysis, these were reduced to five basic zones going from the inner city to the suburbs: Zone I, the central business district; Zone II, an area known by such names as slums, zone in transition, or interstitial area; Zone III, an area of two- and three-family flats or dwellings; Zone IV, an area of single-family dwellings; and Zone V, the suburban or commutation area. The circle is seen as constantly expanding outward, since the central business district is constantly expanding into the slum much as many persons living in each zone move outward.

Two of these areas in the inner city, the zone in transition and the central business district, were of interest to social disorganization theorists. It is here that there was most evidence of social disorganization. It is here that there are the widest variations in age, sex, nationality and racial origins, occupation, social class, home ownership, condition of housing, literacy, and education, and such variations were considered indices of social disorganization. Concurrently, much to the satisfaction of the social disorganization thinkers, a variety of types of deviation were concentrated in these two areas.

> Conventional crime, delinquency, mental illness in general and schizophrenia in particular, suicide, prostitution, vagrancy, dependency, illegitimacy, infant mortality, as well as associated problems such as high death and disease rates, have been found to vary with the areas of the city. The highest rates are in Zones I and II, and become successively lower out from this area. The evidence on alcoholism and

the manic-depressive psychoses does not show quite this pronounced pattern for, although there are probably higher rates in Zones I and II, the differences are not as marked from one part of the city to another. White-collar crime, on the other hand, is greater in Zones IV and V of the city. Gambling and prostitution are prevalent not only in Zone II but sometimes beyond the suburban fringe of the city.[21]

These patterns have stood up under tests in many cities, particularly in the case of juvenile delinquency. The early analysis of the delinquency areas of Chicago by Clifford Shaw and his associates set off a wave of studies in other cities.[22] A 1931 study of the National Commission on Law Observance found that the characteristic patterns for delinquency rates in Chicago could also be found in Philadelphia, Richmond, Cleveland, Birmingham, Denver, and Seattle.[23] These patterns have also been found in Mexico City and Honolulu.[24]

Case studies Another empirical approach to the study of disorganization, that of the case study, derives from the premise that social disorganization is best described by those most subject to it—that is, by deviants themselves.

> The concept of social disorganization refers to a social process and is most meaningful if comprehended in terms of the group–individual relationship. . . . In the last analysis, social disorganization refers to a state of interpersonal relations. . . . This restatement would seem to imply that the sociologist, in order to study and understand social disorganization, must study the influence of group relations by studying the individual. . . . We can see whether the group breakdown is a "real" occurrence by observing disruptions in the life organization of an individual.[25]

Thus, even if social disorganization could be shown to exist only in the eyes of the deviant, it would be an important phenomenon in terms of the consequences of this belief for his behavior. Thomas and Znaniecki used this case study approach extensively in *The Polish Peasant,* and Thomas expressed the importance of the subjective factor in his well-known theorem, "If men define situations as real, they are real in their consequences."[26]

It is hardly coincidental that Clifford Shaw and R. E. L. Faris did both ecological studies and case studies.[27] Both produced case studies of "typical" deviants from the ecologically most disorganized slum areas.

Shaw's two case studies, *The Jack-Roller* and *The Natural History of a Delinquent Career,* reveal the existence of disorganization in slum areas and the ways in which social disorganization lead to delinquent and criminal patterns of behavior. The *Jack-Roller* tells the story of a slum youth who, rejected by parents and school, spent much of his adolescence in reform school, and later in adult prison. Shaw cites one of the poems of Stanley, the young delinquent, which reveals that Stanley places responsibility for his misconduct upon external circumstances indicative of disorganization:

LIFE'S CIRCUMSTANCES

Life's a gale of wind
On a storm-swept sea
Gathering its victims
Into its paw
Swiftly the undercurrent
Takes its hold
And surrounds its victim
Down more and more.

Some men are rich
Others are poor
But fate takes a hand
In guiding out lives
It weaves its web
In a noiseless way;
Be it night or day
It holds full sway.

It follows us through the years and years
And never stops its ceaseless work
We are nothing but straws
In this strife-swept world
And the man with the gold
Is the man with the hold.[28]

In another case study, *The Natural History of a Delinquent Career,* a case study of Sidney, Shaw reveals the role of the temptations of the central business district in drawing Sidney into delinquency:

Sidney's earliest delinquencies assumed the character of a fascinating game. It was the element of thrill and adventure, rather than the desire for monetary gain which comprised one of the dominant incentives in his earliest delinquencies. . . . initial excursions into the Loop opened up an entirely new world to Sidney and contributed to the development of attitudes and interests which were to play an important part in the natural history of his delinquent career. . . . Initial delinquencies tend to defined attitudes and interests which conventional behavior find it difficult to compete. There was nothing in Sidney's home and school which could rival his fascinating excursions into the Loop.[29]

Faris did a similar analysis, but in this case, on a schizophrenic patient.[30] The case study of "Albert Ritter" (pseudonymn) revealed a whole history of interpersonal problems among family, friends, and work relationships which led to a paranoid schizophrenic personality. Faris commented that Albert's problem was not one of "mental disorder," because he had actually developed an elaborate and orderly system of thought, privately worked out as a solution to a number of severe life problems. This case study, Faris concluded, showed that disorganization relates to schizophrenia in essentially three ways: (1) by intensifying personal problems; (2) by providing a social environment in which no conventional solutions are available; and (3) by providing an environment in which the patient's private solutions are considered unintelligible and unacceptable to other persons.

Community studies   Community studies are a useful means of illustrating the *process* of social disorganization. One example of such a community study was done in Harlan County, Kentucky.[31] What happened in this relatively small town illustrates the process of disorganization as it occurs in society-at-large. That is, the history of "Bloody Harlan" illustrates many of the problems of social disorganization that accompany the sudden impact of industrial civilization upon a self-sufficient, isolated agricultural society.

Originally a small, rural, kinship-oriented community with few if any class distinctions, Harlan underwent a transformation to a coal town in which 70 per cent of the population were miners. Several events contributing to disorganization occurred. The population tripled over a short period of time. With the Depression came destitution. The class system polarized into a rigid caste system of mine bosses *versus* laborers. When unions were suppressed, Communist-influenced violence erupted. Competition and exploitation in pursuit of the dominant value of money replaced friendly mutual aid social relations. Human relations became casual and impersonal. Concurrent with these changes was a rapid increase in many areas of deviancy. There was an 80 per cent increase in divorce rates. Vice and crime increased. Typically drunken brawls in bars would often lead to murder and other crimes of violence. The rate of venereal disease was highest in the nation. Politics became corrupt, as seen in stuffing of ballot boxes, and political assassination became frequent.

This trend of social disorganization was not irreversible. With the end of coal expansion and the development of the union shop and compulsory arbitration came peace. The population growth leveled off. As a result, various indices of deviancy—homicide, divorce, venereal disease, and the like—showed a marked decline.

Another example of community disorganization is given in the case of Shanghai in 1948 following World War II. The disorganization of Shanghai was a prelude to impending Communist control of China.[32]

> In the days following the long war with Japan and before the impending Communist control of China, disintegration took place with increasing rapidity. . . . Long-term contracts could not be made with confidence that the political system would endure as long as the contracts. Corruption was encouraged by this condition. . . . The short-run point of view was reflected in the tendency to take profits from properties without maintaining them in good condition. The result, by 1948, was a severe physical deterioration of buildings and utilities in the cities. . . . With loss of confidence in government went lack of faith in the currency, and China suffered from severe inflation after the war. . . . Merchants and customers made free use of black markets. . . . In the face of failure to control the people by ordinary means, the government undertook increasingly drastic methods, but these failed in the face of great difficulties. . . . The ineffectiveness of the power of the government to maintain order is illustrated by an incident in 1947, in which a crowd of students seized a railway train and started toward the capital to stage a demonstration over certain grievances. . . . Groups of soldiers wandered about the streets, entering restaurants and offices to ask for money. If refused, they sometimes returned with a larger crowd to wreck the place. . . . Many western businessmen were forced to withdraw from China, causing a further loss to the economy, and those who survived were most likely to have done so by bribing officials, sometimes amassing fortunes in the process while adding to the breakdown of morality and the attitudes of cynicism and defeatism which along with other factors brought about the fall of China.[33]

Both of the above examples illustrate the process of social disorganization. The Harlan County example showed the importance of rapid change, especially rapid industrialization, in leading to the breakdown of a community. The Shanghai example showed, in some detail, what happens when a city becomes disorganized. The most important features of Shanghai during this phase were the decline through corruption of the effectiveness of the elites in government and business.

Studies of national disorganization   Whereas there have been no national studies specifically oriented toward testing social disorganization theory, there are countless national studies that could be used drawn from contemporary ethnology, comparative sociology, and political science.[34] Although these will be discussed in a subsequent chapter, a study done in Indonesia is illustrative of the type of information such studies yield.[35] This study shows the disruption that accompanies the transition of that country. In Indonesia there is a continuing conflict between a part of the population that is Westernized and the old indigenous population. The Westernized segment is attempting to change the nation and integrate it, thus disorganizing the folk society.

> Western economic theories of price, demand, thrift, or investment do not operate in the village economy, indeed are regarded frequently as antithetical to the community's way of life and inimical to its traditional existence. As a result, Western concepts of production are only with difficulty brought into existence; where they penetrate, the traditional self-reliance and independence of the village economy is broken. . . .
>
> In attempting to Christianize a given section of the Indonesian people, the missionary . . . attacked the social and political traditions of the group . . . under the impact of missionary activity there has arisen a class of people who no longer are part of the traditional socio-religious environment of their ancestors but who are not Christians either; at best they seem to have become rootless individuals who do not find a home either with their own communal environment or with a Christian atmosphere. . . . Taken together, these aspects of Western influence in Indonesian society today show above all the incompletion of the assimilation process now under way. The overt, technical aspects of Westernization appear to make the greatest impression on the population. . . . There is much evidence of a glib, superficial emulation of Western ways, particularly in the towns, but most everywhere traditional patterns of behavior continue to flourish. The danger in this process is that no stable social framework exists which permits Indonesia to become relatively uniformly "Westernized." Society is in a state of flux. . . . For a long time to come, Indonesia will have to cope

with a marginal culture, with rootless individuals who search for some cohesion in their existence and who are prone to seek the solution of their problems in the espousal of extremist, highly authoritarian patterns of government and social behavior.

CRITICISMS OF SOCIAL DISORGANIZATION THEORY

Though some of the literature on social disorganization that followed these early theoretical and empirical attempts was an extension of social disorganization theory,[36] much of it was directed toward criticising these early approaches, especially the textbook approaches, in terms of assumptions, bases of measurement, predictions, and the like.

Perhaps the earliest of these criticisms was made by Herbert Blumer,[37] who stressed, contrary to the textbook approaches, that "social disorganization may arise and persist without being an expression of personality disorganization"—and, contrarywise, that the opposite need not occur either:

> Passing beyond the age of early childhood, it would seem that the subsequent role of social disorganization is merely that of occasioning distressing experiences which test the already established dispositions of the child.[38]

Thus, there may be social disorganization without individual disorganization and individual disorganization without social disorganization.

In a later article, Louis Wirth attacked the concept of social disorganization as a normative or "value-laden" concept:

> To refer to a society as disorganized implies some criteria of disorganization and conversely some marks by which an organized society can be identified. . . . The concept of social disorganization thus has a normative basis.[39]

Wirth goes on to point out that, contrary to approaches prevailing at that time, the existence of deviant behavior did not necessarily imply disorganization.

> Not all deviations from norms are to be regarded as prima facie evidence of social disorganization. It is possible to have a wide range of individual differentiation and deviation from norms in a society without approaching a state of social disorganization.[40]

If society succeeds in isolating the deviant, it may proceed on a highly organized basis.

In a subsequent article, Mowrer (who later wrote a text on disorganization) also emphasizes the normative and subjective nature of the concept of social disorganization.

> As a condition, social disorganization has been analyzed in terms of social problems, social pathology, and social disease. The distinctive characteristic of this approach is that certain conditions are looked upon as inimical to social welfare and call for concerted action on the part of the group in order to eliminate these conditions. What constitues a social problem is, therefore, a matter of judgment as to what constitutes social welfare. In turn, social welfare tends to be a subjective concept unless some device can be evolved for eliminating its evaluative character.[41]

Mowrer further points out that the most significant approaches to social disorganization were those of Cooley, on the one hand, and Thomas and Znaniecki, on the other hand. However, neither of these approaches, he says, has consistently stated the relationship between social and personal disorganization.

In a later article, Kramer points to two flaws in the major disorganization approaches. First, these approaches tend to view disorganization as a condition rather than a process. Second, a false dichotomy is drawn between the disorganized society, on the one hand, and the individual on the other. Actually they are part and parcel of the same process and can be understood only together.

> The sociologist, in order to study and understand social disorganization, must study the influence of group relations by studying the individual. . . . We can see whether group breakdown is a "real" occurrence by observing disruptions in the life-organization of an individual. . . . The reality of a sociological process is manifested in the effects it has on an individual.[42]

Probably the most penetrating analysis of all was given by Whyte,[43] who looks at the social disorganization approach from both the theoretical and empirical point of view. Whyte acknowledges that the primary empirical study of disorganization has been done in slums, on the assumption that the slum is the most disorganized part of the city. He cited Zorbaugh on this assumption:

> Throughout the Near North Side [a slum in Chicago], then, community life, where it has not already disintegrated, is in the pro-

cess of disintegration. Community institutions are ceasing to function. The church, the school, the family, the occupational group, government, and the news have ceased to bear any direct relationship to local life. Behavior is individualized in the extreme. . . . Life is highly disorganized—lived without the law, and without the mores of the larger society. The Near North Side is a section of the old frontier transplanted to the heart of a modern city.[44]

Whyte goes on to cite Zorbaugh's analysis of politics in the slum:

Politics on the Near North Side is nothing more than a game, a game played without well-defined rules, a game played only incidentally in the local community and bearing little or no relationship to the problems—they can scarcely be called issues—of local life.[45]

Zorbaugh, Whyte adds, is simply saying that politics in the slum district is not like politics in the middle-class district. Because it does not meet middle-class standards, it is "nothing more than a game."

Whyte thus criticized Zorbaugh's somewhat typical analysis of a slum district as disorganized, mainly because Whyte believed that some slum areas were disorganized, especially rooming house areas, but other districts, though socio-economically similar, are highly organized immigrant family settlements. From his observations of three and a half years of research in an Italian slum district of "Cornerville," Whyte concluded that immigrant slums were not disorganized. There existed subdivisions of associations and interrelations of associations within a slum. The problem was not lack of organization but failure of the slums own social organization to mesh with the structure—the middle-class structure—of society around it.[46] Furthermore, the existence of family disorganization did not necessarily imply social disorganization of the larger community.

While the family does not play the role in directing slum life that it assumes in peasant European communities, other groupings have arisen to provide organization. The corner gangs, well described by Thrasher, mobilize the young men of the district and . . . they form the building blocks of the community-wide organizations of the rackets and politics. The informal ties of the corner gang provide a network of personal relations and mutual obligations upon which these larger organizations are based.[47]

Lastly, Whyte commented on the Thomas–Znaniecki definition of social disorganization:

If social disorganization involves a "decrease of the influence of existing social rules," and the rules referred to are those of the peasant society from which the immigrants came, then the slum is certainly disorganized. However, that is only a part of the picture. It is fruitless to study the area simply in terms of the breakdown of old groupings and old standards; new groupings and new standards have arisen. . . . The major conflict is that between the organized life of the slums and organized "respectable" middle class society. . . . The character of slum social organization cannot be understood until more sociologists shift their emphasis from social disorganization in order to investigate the process of social reorganization.[48]

SOCIAL DISORGANIZATION AS COMPARED WITH EARLIER APPROACHES

As has been shown in the first and second chapters of this book, there are a number of views with regard to society in transition. Some approaches are optimistic. For example, Durkheim sees the trend from mechanical to organic solidarity as a favorable one. Other approaches are neither committed to a thesis of progress nor retrogression. Pareto, for example, saw society as rotating from "combinations" phases to "aggregates" phases, depending upon the composition of elites in the society. Still other approaches, and these are the ones of most interest here, look with disfavor upon the transition of society from earlier forms to later ones. Let us review these approaches briefly here.

Freud, the first of these, saw the development of mankind toward civilization which he viewed negatively as a continuously increasing manifestation of repressed instinctual impulses. Large-scale society thus implies the repression of basic self.[49]

Spengler also looked upon civilization negatively as the last phase of life for a society. He linked it with such undesirable features as megalopolis, scientific irreligion, mass society, and pecuniary materialism.

Toynbee similarly viewed civilization as the near point of breakdown, disintegration, and the nemesis of the creative minority needed to rule society.

Tönnies saw the trend from *gemeinschaft* to *gesellschaft* forms as an unfortunate one. *Gesellschaft* is dissipated life or even dead forms, mechanical in nature, of social relationships. It is characterized by interdependence without common bond. Such relations are egoistic, calculating, even hostile, transitory, superficial, and cosmopolitan.

Redfield, similarly, viewed the trend to urbanism as a negative one. Relations decline in intimateness, become secularized, skeptical, and contractual. The family declines as a criterion of place.

It is the position of this text that *the theory of social disorganization, as well as the anomie approaches and mass society approaches to be described in the next two chapters, are forms of devolutionary theory* like those of Freud, Spengler, Toynbee, Tönnies, and Redfield. Briefly, their common points may be outlined as follows:

1. *In both classic devolutionary theory and contemporary disorganization theory society is declining, retrogressing, breaking down, disintegrating, or at least is developing toward less integrated forms.*

2. *In both, large-scale society is seen as precipitating a decline of consensus with regard to meanings, norms, values, and beliefs. Individualism comes to take precedence and the group secondary importance.*

3. *In both, relationships are seen as increasingly impersonal, calculative, and superficial as society develops.*

4. *In both, the individual is viewed as isolated, cut off from kinship or intimate ties in modern society.*

5. *Both, by inference, are conservative approaches ideologically, implying that the ideal society is to be found in the past, and perhaps, that it is necessary to reverse certain tendencies in our society to make that ideal possible.* Thus, current fashions, trends, standards, and ideals are viewed negatively as symptomatic of decadence, requiring control to prevent the dissolutionment of society.

We have seen that devolution is only one among several alternative theoretical approaches to contemporary society. It follows that disorganization represents one among many approaches to deviancy. It is not, as one is often led to believe, the only accepted view of society, nor is it the consensus of opinion in current or historical sociology. This is why alternative theories have been dealt with at such length in this text. These alternatives will be considered just as seriously as disorganization and empirically examined both within institutional settings and in larger society. Hopefully in this way we will not fall heir to the major error of most texts on disorganization, that of assuming *beforehand* the presence of disorganization in modern society without considering the evidence for alternative views. At the same time, we will be able to provide the reader with a perspective for viewing society or social organization in relation to deviancy, as current microtheories do not do.

MEASUREMENT OF SOCIAL DISORGANIZATION

Traditionally, social disorganization has been measured by indices of various social problems. For example, Elliott and Merrill state:

> Community disorganization may be indicated by the literacy rate of the population, figures for irregular school attendance, rates of social mobility and transiency, political corruption, suicide, vice, and crime.[50]

This procedure is methodologically invalid. The fallacy involved is one of "contamination" of independent and dependent variables.[51] The independent variable (social disorganization) is being measured by a predicted outcome (social problems). Statistics on "political corruption, suicide, vice, and crime" are used to measure social disorganization. When this is done, *the theory of social disorganization becomes nothing more than a theory of social problems.* The social disorganization approach has been bitterly criticized for such a methodological fault.

Perhaps the main reason for this weakness is the feeling that it is difficult or impossible to measure social disorganization *directly.* Consequently, an "index" is selected. However, such an assumption is not true. A number of indices have been suggested to independently measure disorganization and allied concepts such as social integration and political stability. Durkheim, in fact, suggested a way to measure social integration. He suggested that organic solidarity, the advanced form of social integration, could be indicated by the ratio of restitutive to repressive sanctions in a society.[52] Empirically, this would mean counting the total number of sanctions that could be termed restitutive and those termed repressive, using the ratio of one to the other as an index. One problem with this approach would be that many laws are passed but never applied, and thus in actuality are not the effective law. However, indices of the application of penal or repressive law could be a rough index of laws applied. Thus, the ratio of prisoners to population might provide an even better index than that suggested by Durkheim. Disorganized society would in Durkheim's framework refer to insufficient application of repressive law, while forced division of labor could be measured by excessive application of repressive law.

Another measure related to disorganization is social differentiation. It has been argued that the greater the differentiation, the greater the disorganization.[53] Marsh suggests two measures of social differentiation: the percentages of males in non-agricultural occupations, and gross energy consumption per capita.[54] These two measure a kind of industrialization, which has been equated with disorganization. Another corollary of disorganization is the variable political stability that has been empirically measured by political scientists.[55]

At this point, it would not be appropriate to designate one or another of these indices as our measure of disorganization. In some ways, it will be shown, these measures do not work out the way we would expect them to, and our view of measurement will have to be changed, along with our view of theory. Our purpose here was to show that disorganization can be measured apart from its predicted consequences. It remains for future chapters to show exactly how this is done.

A NEW APPROACH

It can be seen from the above analyses that the social disorganization approach has been criticized from a variety of points of view. These criticisms are summarized effectively by Clinard.

> There are a number of objections to this [social disorganization] frame of reference. (1) Disorganization is too subjective and vague a concept for analyzing a general society. . . . (2) Social disorganization implies the disruption of a previously existing condition of organization, a situation which generally cannot be established. . . . (3) Social disorganization is usually thought of as something "bad," and what is bad is often the value judgment of the observer and the members of his social class or other social groups. . . . (4) The existence of forms of deviant behavior does not necessarily constitute a major threat to the central values of society. . . . (5) What seems like disorganization may actually often be highly organized systems of competing norms. . . . (6) It is possible that a variety of subcultures may contribute, through

their diversity, to the unity or integration of a society rather than weaken it by constituting a situation of social disorganization.[56]

Perhaps the early social disorganization approach contains still another flaw: *that of equating social disorganization with its causes or consequences—namely, a decline in consensus.* Although it is fair to say that Cooley was definitely committed to the consensual folk society of the small town—friendly feelings, intimate neighborliness, and the like—it is not fair to accuse Thomas and Znaniecki of such a value orientation. Thomas and Znaniecki saw the possibility of societal "reorganization" based upon modified social rules, possibly with the intervention of their idealized "creative man." However, it is fair to assert that they failed to perceive the essential aspect to be incorporated into the definition of social disorganization—that is, the *nature of relations of actually existing parts of society, apart from the body of rules shared by the members of society.* Putting this another way, it is possible for a society to share rules, meanings, and values and yet to be in an utter state of anarchy and chaos. For example, a highly stable folk society can be intensively disorganized by a natural catastrophe, such as an earthquake, or a man-made catastrophe, such as a nuclear explosion, in spite of the existence of consensus on rules, meanings, and values.

The core of the concept of social disorganization, therefore, lies not in the rules, but in the *actually existing relations between people and functions* in a society. A social system, from this point of view, is a system of interacting parts. Thus, the so-called social insects, bees and ants, exhibit social organization even though sharing no consensually agreed-upon rules. Among insects, function is biological and the division of labor is hereditary. Similarly, among human caste societies, there may be disagreement on rules but rigid organization due to division of labor between hereditary castes. If one of the functions fails to operate, relations between all parts will be disrupted, and social disorganization will ensue. Dissensus on rules, values, and meanings may precede or follow this event. In fact, in some cases social change in norms, values, meanings, and standards is necessary in order to prevent the social disorganization that might occur from changed relations between parts of society, changes which may be both endogenic (originating from within the society) and exogenic (originating from outside of the society).

Based on the above considerations, we shall define social disorganization as *the disruption of relations between the functioning parts (functions) of a social system so as to jeopardize the attainment of common values.*[57] It can immediately be seen that this definition is quite congruent with Durkheim's conceptualization of the "anomic division of labor" (anomie).

The term *anomie,* as Durkheim originally defined it, referred to a state of society characterized by a lack of regulation over the relations between functions. The term "function" is used to refer to vital parts of the larger organismic whole: society.[58] These vital parts might be corporate groups in society at large or outstanding personal leaders in a smaller group context.

Durkheim, it will be shown, of all the European sociologists discussed above, presents a clearcut theory of social disorganization which is both relevant in today's modern world and, complying with our definition of social disorganization, overcomes fallacies of the early pessimistic approaches. The orientation of this text, therefore, will be to redirect social disorganization theory back to the long-standing European tradition of progressive, evolutionary organicism.

The revised concept overcomes many of the criticisms that have been directed at the early concept. First, it will be shown that the concept is empirical, operational, and fairly objective, rather than subjective and vague. Second, it is possible to measure social disorganization as a variable apart from establishing disruption of previous organization. Third, the revised concept does not stigmatize social disorganization as something bad, but leaves room for the possibility that periodic anomie may precede the emergence of newer, higher, more cohesive forms of organization. Fourth, it is possible that social problems and deviant behavior may be functional for social change of existing rules so as to be congruent with changed functional relations in society. The revised concept distinguishes between social differentiation and social disorganization. It incorporates a recognition that solidarity may be based upon differences or complementarity of dissimilar interest. Last, it pinpoints the single universal characteristic of disorganization—functional disintegration—so as to apply logically to all cases known. It focuses upon the phenomena of social disorganization apart from its causes of effects.

Anomie approaches to deviancy

RISE OF ANOMIE THEORY

A quick glance at a list of articles and books on social disorganization indicates that the term "social disorganization" was most used during the 1930's and 1940's, then gradually fell from use, probably due to the heavy criticism that was directed at the social-disorganization approach during the late 1940's and 1950's. As the term "disorganization" fell from use, the concepts of "anomie" and "alienation" became frequent in the journals and in monograph publications. This trend can be seen in the Table 3–1.

TABLE 3–1   Articles published on social disorganization, anomie, and mass society (alienation) 1907–1968

	Disorga- nization	Anomie	Alien- ation
1907–1915	NL	NL	NL
1916–1919	NL	NL	NL
1920–1923	NL	NL	NL
1924–1927	NL	NL	NL
January 1928–June 1931	NL	NL	NL
July 1931–June 1934	NL	NL	NL
July 1934–June 1937	NL	NL	NL
July 1937–March 1940	NL	NL	NL
April 1940–March 1943	6	NL	0
April 1943–March 1946	1	NL	0
April 1946–March 1949	2	1	1
April 1949–March 1952	5	0	0
April 1952–March 1955	1	NL	0
April 1955–March 1958	0	2	1
April 1958–March 1960	2	7	6
April 1960–March 1962	NL	5	1
April 1962–March 1964	NL	5	12
April 1964–March 1965	NL	1	4
April 1965–March 1966	SD–A	6	12
April 1966–March 1967	SD–A	4	10
April 1967–March 1968	SD–A	8	15

NL = not listed
SD–A = social disorganization cross reference to anomie
SOURCE: *Social Sciences and Humanities Index (International Index).*

Although the growth of anomie theory no doubt parallels the growth of sociology itself during the post-World War II period, the concept of disorganization declined in usage during the same period. Two possibilities present themselves, both of which may be true. First, the concept of social disorganization fell from use due to certain undesirable implications of the concept, discussed in the previous chapter. Second, the concept of anomie came to replace disorganization as an explanatory framework for primarily the same empirical phenomena—that is, "social problems," "social pathology," and "deviant behavior." The link between the two concepts has long been recognized by students of deviancy. However, the trends in usage of the concepts have never been made explicit. Similar assumptions, explanations, kinds of data, and theories are used by both anomie theorists today and social disorganization theorists of the past. But if it is true that social disorganization approaches have been largely repudiated, it would seem that many mistaken notions are turning up under the guise of a new concept. To some extent that it may be said of anomie theory, in the words of Santyana, that "Those who do not understand history are doomed to repeat it."

The anomie view of society is, like the disorganization approach a devolutionary view. We shall see that this term "anomie" is defined in a variety of ways (as is disorganization); however, all of them when applied to larger society imply an unfortunate state of society, perhaps an undesirable state. Current theories of anomie are purported to be based upon the works of the French sociologist, Émile Durkheim, the founder of anomie theory. This is ironic, because we have classified Durkheim as an "evolutionary" theorist. Perhaps this paradox is resolved when it is seen that Durkheim, though he discussed anomie and studied its relation to the problem of suicide, was not an "anomie theorist." He did not believe that anomie was problematic for modern society, but rather that it was an "abnormal" phenomenon, occurring only in exceptional circumstances. Contemporary anomie theory may not be in congruence with Durkheim's thinking as much as it agrees with the assumptions of another classic theorist, Max Weber.[59] For various reasons, however, it will be fruitful to examine Durkheim's approach to anomie theory in detail here. First, Durkheim defined the concept in ways still relevant today. Second, Durkheim's approach in some ways presents an *alternative* to contemporary anomie theory. Last, it is necessary to examine Durkheim's theory in detail in order to see its exact relatedness (or lack of relationship) to contemporary anomie theory.

DURKHEIM'S ANOMIE THEORY

In the previous section, the concept of social disorganization was defined as "a disruption of functional relations . . . between the functional parts of a group." When social disorganization is defined in this way, the concept of social disorganization is close in meaning to the way Durkheim defined "anomie." The link with anomie theory is found in the phrase "disruption of functional relations." Anomie, according to Durkheim, refers to "a state of society in which various functions are not adjusted to one another." The term "function" plays a central part in this theoretical congruence. A "function," according to Merton, may refer to: (1) a public gathering, (2) an occupation or interest group, (3) activities of a status— namely, roles, (4) a mathematical relation between variables, or (5) a part played with respect to a whole.[60] (It is no mere coincidence that Merton is both a functionalist and an anomie theorist). Durkheim's "functions" probably refer to occupations or interest groups, but the phrase "lack of adjustment of functions" certainly implies a disruption of functional relations in the sense of part–whole.

Like the early disorganization theory and like recent texts on social disorganization, Durkheim's analysis begins with social organization and conditions for social organization as a point of departure. But, unlike the disorganization theorists, he recognizes that there is more than one "type of organization." One form corresponds to large-scale society. Thus, Durkheim differs from Thomas, Cooley, Mead, and more recent writers like Elliott and Merrill, Faris, and McGee, in recognizing that large-scale urban societies are not necessarily "disorganized." Durkheim's theory contains an image of solidarity in large-scale society not found in American social disorganization theory. Durkheim also differs in proposing the possibility of "over-organization" as a possible "abnormal form of society."

Types of solidarity   In his most well-known work, *La division du travail social (The Division of Labor in Society)*, Durkheim develops "ideal types" of what he termed "mechanical solidarity" or folk society, as opposed to "organic solidarity" or urban solidarity. The two types are ideal in the sense that they can never be achieved by existing societies, and probably they never existed anywhere in history, but stand as a direction from which or to which societies tend. Several basic parameters distinguish these two types: (1) the extent of the divison of labor, (2) the relative influence of individual *versus* collective conscience, (3) the typical reaction toward deviation, and (4) adaptability of society to crisis.

Extent of division of labor. Mechanical solidarity is characterized by a low level of the division of labor, while organic solidarity typically has a highly complex, well-developed division of labor. This refers essentially to the amount of differentiation of roles and tasks within smaller social groups, occupations, and interest groups within larger social groups. The example that Durkheim cites for mechanical solidarity on the small group level was the matriarchal family. The matriarchal family is characterized by a sparcity of mutual obligations and a looseness of ties between spouses, but close relations between mother and children.

Collective versus individual conscience. Collective conscience refers to a sense of sharedness of common beliefs, sentiments, rules, and values. Because the governmental power of a particular society is responsible for setting rules, defining values, and fostering shared sentiments and beliefs, the government is said to be the symbol of collective conscience. Consequently, all political offenses are viewed as if they were an offense to the collective conscience (thus, explaining the severity with which many political crimes—treason, espionage, assassination, and the like—are punished). The term "collective conscience" refers essentially to what is today referred to as "cultural integration."[61] According to Durkheim, collective conscience has a greater, more direct relative importance and influence under the condition of mechanical solidarity, while under organic solidarity collective conscience declines, as shown by the development of specialized rather than diffuse government (that is, government is not equated with society, but is a specialized agency) and by the relegation of government to the role of moderator of divergent groups, interests, and so on.

While collective conscience declines with the emergence of organic solidarity, individual conscience or personality develops. Under mechanical solidarity, there is little or no conflict between individual and society. All behavior is defined by the all encompassing "collective representations"—ways of thinking shared by members of society. Such representations or symbols do not change from generation to generation under mechanical solidarity. These representations shape, or even determine for the individual what his needs ought to be. In Ralph Linton's terms, there are no alternatives in culture, only universals. There are no problems of choice, because all choices are already made by the group's definition of the situation. Because an individual is not inclined to elect alternatives, he is incapable of differing with society in terms of his own beliefs, needs, values, attitudes, and the like.

Under organic solidarity, the individual may be quite unique. Organic solidarity is based upon a certain degree of tolerance of difference. This is essentially based upon the principle of interdependence of self-interests.[62] Consequently, under organic solidarity, deviant behavior of previous times may become defined as acceptable. While women were not permitted to smoke during the last century, smoking has become an aspect of sociability in some circles.

Under organic solidarity, the "autonomous man" becomes possible. Such phrases as self-actualization, personality development, freedom of choice, independent thought, and the like become a goal in the popular culture because of the recognition that one will become wanted for some specialized talent or role. Thus, while collective conscience—society's directing power—declines in influence, the individual's self-directing power—individual conscience—increases. Simultaneously, the individual becomes indirectly related to government or central regulatory power through intermediary organizations, no longer being directly controlled and influenced by society.

Reaction to Deviation. Two basic forms of law exist, according to Durkheim. The first, repressive law or penal law, is oriented toward inflicting suffering on the offender, while the second, restitutive law, is oriented toward restoring things as they were or affecting a "return in state." While repressive law characterizes mechanical solidarity, restitutive law characterizes organic solidarity. Repressive law, represented in modern society by criminal law, is designed to repress the deviant, especially if the act is serious or a felony. However, Durkheim would envision an increasing tendency to adjudicate offenses under restitutive law. Civil, commercial, and constitutional law are forms of restitutive law which are increasingly covering more offenses.

Adaptability of society to crisis. Although Durkheim did not discuss social change specifically, a theory of change can be inferred from his theory. Mechanical solidarity, by its very nature, is relatively inflexible, incapable of social change to meet extraordinary demands—such as population explosion, war, volcano eruption, or invasion. The rules, norms, mores, and folkways are incapable of meeting with unpredicted events, by virtue of the lack of development of a specialized regulatory agency—the government. When changes occur calling for cultural innovation, the rules cannot be modified to cope with the cultural change. The roles played by the individuals and the functions played by different occupations are not adapted to the new situation.

Organically solidary societies, on the other hand, are stable in times of crisis. The government is capable of defining new goals for the society, of developing new rules, and of allocating new roles and functions. It is for this reason that organically solidary societies are superior in terms of survival capability. A small, organically solidary country could provide a great threat to larger but less differentiated countries.[63]

The age-old axiom *divide et impera,* "divide and conquer," seems to have relevance here. A more differentiated group can overcome a less differentiated group merely by its contact with that group. The introduction of foreign elements into the mechanically solidary group leads to social disorganization, while the organically solidary group most likely incorporates such solidary elements.[64]

One peculiarity noted by Durkheim was that truly foreign elements would be more disrupting to organic solidarity. Truly foreign elements are incapable of being incorporated, due to intense interdependence.

Abnormal forms of society   Durkheim's anomie has been reinterpreted by American sociologists to refer to practically a universal condition of modern urban society. One is mislead into thinking that Durkheim saw modern societies as typically disorganized, when in fact it is clear from his writings that anomie as well as the forced division of labor were *abnormal forms* of the division of labor. By "normal," Durkheim is referring to that most frequently distributed—the modal type—for a given stage of development of society.[65] Durkheim viewed as normal the two types of solidarity: mechanical, and organic. In a sense then, Durkheim, at least in his early work, was not an anomie theorist.

Anomie. Durkheim did not see anomie as endemic to large-scale society. However, he perceived that periodically anomie occurs in modern society. This periodic anomie is traced to many factors that contribute to social differentiation. Specifically, anomie and conflict between functions occur as results of the development of new functions. Periodic anomie is probably inevitable in the transition from mechanical to organic solidarity, as "functions must emerge before they can be either regulated or before they can adjust mutually." Thus, social change and division of labor result in functional disintegration or disorganization which lead to a higher form of social organization. Periodic anomie probably occurs in any ongoing developing social group and, for that matter, there is a personality counterpart to social anomie. Durkheim stressed the conflict between labor and management that developed during the nineteenth century in society at large; but he also showed that the concept of anomie could be applied to smaller settings, such as the social sciences, which he characterized as anomic. Within the social sciences, there is a latent conflict between different disciplines— psychology, sociology, anthropology, and political science—all endeavoring to explain the same or similar phenomena.

We shall apply anomie theory to more specific institutional settings. Within particular institutional settings, the conflict between functions may be most intense because of the possibility of interaction and close contact. For example, within a university there often occurs cleavage between administration and academic personnel. Within industrial organization, there is a conflict between staff and line. All of these represent anomie or a state of social group in which there is a conflict between functions whose basis, according to Durkheim, is the competition for the same or similar goals. The result of this conflict or moderation of higher power is a division of labor which becomes stated in the form of formal and informal rules. The conflict is due to the absence of rules regulating functions, but may in fact be due to the application of old, inappropriate rules. A division of labor becomes customary based upon a sense of comfort or well-being which it brings, as in the case of a useful innovation within a formal organization.

Anomie exists, therefore, where there is a conflict between interest groups, occupations, roles, or other "actors" in a larger social system. Lacking are rules regulating relations between these functional parts. However, the conflict between the functions may actually be instrumental in leading to an agreement upon rules. A consensus is in part "worked out" through competition and conflict, assuming the proper functioning of government as a moderator.

Forced division of labor. Critics of Durkheim have pointed out that he was committed to social order and consensus as a basic value, that his ideal society was a static society, and therefore that he was a conservative.[66] However, it is clear that Durkheim recognized the danger of excessive regulation over functional relations. He perceived that another abnormal type of society, the forced division of labor, existed when different parts of society are forced to cooperate and were prevented from conflicting by a system of rules drawn from past, archaic society. He thus recognized the possibility of totalitarianism, as we know it today. In societies based upon a forced division of labor, individuals are assigned tasks or roles and groups are assigned functions that are not appropriate to their abilities. He noted that such societies were lacking in "equality in the external conditions of conflict." This phrase shows clearly that Durkheim recognized the importance of conflict as a positive influence in formulating rules appropriate to differential abilities, aptitudes, interests, value orientations, and the like. In fact, he acknowledges that violence may be necessary in order to re-establish this equality of opportunity. In a sense, then, Durkheim felt that small-scale periodic anomie was in fact necessary to the emergence of the division of labor and therefore to organic solidarity.

Causes of anomie If Durkheim saw societies as basically solidary and cohesive rather than disorganized, it would seem that the social disorganization approach would be incompatible with his basic assumptions. However, Durkheim did specify the conditions for the development of organic solidarity. If one can assume that anomie occurs as a result of *excessively rapid change* in these conditions, Durkheim's anomie theory becomes more applicable in the world of the twentieth century in which such changes have taken place. Assuming this, we may draw from Durkheim's analysis in listing the conditions under which social disorganization and anomie occur.

Population changes. One basic condition for anomie would be an excessively rapid increase in the volume and density of population. The result is conflict between people, occupations, and interest groups. The conflict occurs because all seek the same goals and values. For example, conflict occurred in frontier towns in the old west of the United States due basically to the rapid westward migration. Farmers competed for the same land and "feuds" were fought over land rights. Cattlemen competed with sheep-farmers for grazing land and water rights. "Forty-niner" gold miners often conflicted over grubstakes. The result of these clashes were typical frontier crimes—such as assault, arson, cattle stealing, and robbery. The "lawlessness" of the west never really ended until commercial and trade interests gained a foothold—interests oriented toward non-land values.

Conflict is mitigated when different parts of society pursue different goals or values: ". . . units develop different needs and pursue different objects." "The soldier pursues military glory, the priest moral authority, the statesman power, the businessman riches, and the scholar scientific renown."[67]

Gouldner has suggested that another avenue to cohesion is *specialization of function.* A larger system-unit may threaten to destroy another smaller one pursuing the same function. The smaller unit survives by becoming a specialized part within the larger one.[68] For example, large discount houses often threaten to bankrupt smaller businesses. Owners of those businesses often may be offered a managerial job within the discount firm, which serves both the interest of the small businessman and the large discount house.

Thus, rapid population development may lead to social disorganization until specialization and division of labor mitigate the changes. However, this is almost bound to happen sooner or later, according to Durkheim, if there is adequate communication: "Since a body of rules is the definite form which spontaneously established relations between social functions take in the course of time, we can say, *a priori,* that the state of anomie is impossible wherever solidary organs are sufficiently in contact or sufficiently prolonged."[69]

Durkheim did not view increasing population as generally disorganizing. Usually there is a dynamic density of population and a "progressive preponderance of organic solidarity." Thus, Durkheim was anti-evolutionist in the sense that he viewed the division of labor as mitigating natural selection.

Just as a "population explosion" may be disorganizing, a dangerous situation may also be created by a "population implosion"—a sudden *decline* of population.[70] Thus, the basis of anomie is not to be found in any particular set of rules, but rather in the inappropriateness of a given set to a particular form of social organization.

Rapid urbanization. Critics of Durkheim have seized upon his emphasis on population expansion as an explanatory variable, saying that population is an ecological or demographic factor and ultimately a biological phenomenon, therefore, Durkheim is violating his own methodological rules in explaining a social fact by a biological one—that is, that he is a reductionist.[71]

This allegation, however, is not entirely true. In Durkheim's analysis, it is not population density, *per se*, which is causative, but "moral density" or "dynamic density." The presence of such density indicates the presence of organic solidarity, while the absence of moral density, we may infer, would bring an abnormal form of division of labor, perhaps "anomie." If Durkheim had been writing in the twentieth century, he probably would have focused on urbanism and the nature of urban organization as explanatory. Much of the work done in urban sociology might very well be an elaboration of Durkheim. In fact the term "anomie" has been used to describe the disorganized nature of the inner city. Therefore, a brief discussion of urbanism will be helpful in elaborating the causes of anomie.

Certain aspects of urban organization in large cities have been traditionally linked to social disorganization. These factors are both social and ecological in nature—social in the sense that they are influenced greatly by the amount of planning or anticipatory regulation, ecological in the sense that natural boundaries are also influential.

One of the earliest concerns with urbanism is found in the work of Park and Burgess.[72] Their now-classic "concentric zone theory" is very much an expression of anomie theory. The city has essentially five concentric zones. Zone 1, the central business district; Zone 2, the zone of transition; Zone 3, two- and three-family flats or dwellings; Zone 4, an area of single family dwellings; and Zone 5, the suburban or commutation area. Zones 1 and 2 are heaviest in most social problems—crime, delinquency, mental illness, suicide, prostitution, vagrancy, and the like—all decreasing toward the periphery of the concentric circles. Two exceptions, however, are *white-collar crime* and *manic–depressive* disorder, disproportionately prevalent in Zones 4 and 5.

All features of *anomie* and social disorganization are to be found in the zone in transition. The population is highly and rapidly concentrated, due to a high influx of immigration. Population elements are highly heterogeneous in terms of racial, ethnic, and national background—socio-economic heterogeneity precipitating conflict over economic values. The zone in transition, possibly traced to larger urban organization, is thus a disorganized area

Urbanization is not by itself a cause of disorganization. Only cities that develop planlessly without central organization are susceptible to disorganization. Many cities in the United States have developed "master plans" which determine the nature of urban growth. When land is allocated beforehand, the phenomenon "zone in transition" or urban slum, is prevented before it happens. These slums are created by predatory speculation—investors holding land that will bring a high price from industrial concerns, while not permitting adequate housing and neighborhood development.

Rapid transit. Durkheim could not have anticipated the development of rapid means of transportation that took place in the present century. However, such development is relevant to his theory and thus may be listed as another cause of anomie. The development of rapid means of transportation and communication leads to problems of a social nature sometimes worse than the traffic problems mitigated. This has been pointed out by Ogburn in his "theory of cultural lag"—rapid change in material culture causes needed readjustments in non-material culture which lags far behind material culture.[73]

In Durkheimian terms, when transportation and communication improve, diverse peoples and groups are brought into contact with one another. The result is a conflict of norms and values. If divergent elements are introduced, mechanical solidarity breaks down. For example, knowledge of other cultures derived from anthropologists has led to a breakdown of many traditional mores with regard to family organization, sex, and religion in American society. Only over a period of many years are these divergent norms and values incorporated into the American social organization. During the interim, a period of social disorganization has occurred with respect to the traditional family structure.

International relations can be viewed in similar terms. Contact between organically solidary societies and mechanically solidary societies may be disorganizing for the latter. Many of the "underdeveloped countries" have fallen easy prey to the more organized European countries, based upon the disorganizing influence of Western mores. The result in these countries is a relatively long period of disorganization, internal subversion, many social movements, high crime rates, and the like. The increasing development of transportation and communication can only aggravate this problem.

The major solution is the intervention of a central governmental apparatus to promote more gradual introduction and moderation of divergent elements. Educational programs promoting international understanding are of special importance. It is necessary that Westerners learn about underdeveloped countries to understand the importance of traditional mores to their social organization. Innovations must be introduced in such a way as to mesh with social organization to corresponding with the growing functional needs of underdeveloped countries. A similar generalization applies to backward segments of large industrialized countries.

Demographic imbalance. Another factor relevant to Durkheimian theory is demographic imbalance, which is disproportional with respect to sex and age. In any developing society different age and sex groups play different functions. These functions may clash under certain conditions.

In general, the older segment of the population is the "carrier of culture." It is its function to transmit culture—norms and values—from one generation to the next. Young people, by contrast, as well as being future adults, serve a crucial function ot modifying old rules to meet changed conditions. A sudden loss of young people, through war or disease might be highly disorganizing in the sense that necessary reforms would be thwarted.

A trend in the demographic transition has been toward a pyramid-like population curve, with more young people and fewer old people. The result is a relative lack of influence of older people in exercising their traditional regulatory function. One manifestation is the development of "youth culture" and the alienation of modern youth from society. Young people have developed a very strong sub-culture in American society of nearly revolutionary proportions. Social changes are promoted which are in conflict with old norms and values supported by the older generation.[74]

Another possible basis for social disorganization is the development of a sex imbalance. This occurs very often in frontier areas and nations that attract large numbers of immigrants, where population tends to overrepresent males. Such areas will tend to be disorganized in the sense of unstable government and lawlessness.

This occurs as a result of two basic factors. First, females play an essential role in the family in their function as homemaker and socializing agent. Without these functions, there is no basis for the development of local culture and transmission of norms and values. Second, in the words of Durkheim, marriage serves to regulate the biological and psychological needs of males more so than females, based upon differences in phylogenetic makeup and in function of the two sexes. Marriage regulates the passions of men, preventing a rampage of gratification and providing a more stable everyday basis of need satisfaction. Without this regulation over the needs of men, personality disorganization—a disruption of the relation between personal goals and means of attaining them—may occur. Thus, men may seek goals beyond their abilities, suffering severe setbacks upon failure, or may become doomed to an endless myriad of gratification of always increasing psychological needs. Both alternatives are equally frustrating. (Both will be discussed more fully below).

Crisis or disaster. While population explosion, urbanization, rapid transit, and demographic imbalance occur over a period of many years, (and may be termed predisposing factors), certain conditions may cause a sudden disruption of a society (and may be termed precipitating factors). These conditions are extremely rare during the life of most societies but occur in times of crisis or disaster. A crisis may be defined as any event suddenly interrupting the customary activities of a group. This is more or less a "waste-basket category" including floods, earthquakes, bombings, tidal waves, volcanoes, invasions, war, and the like.

Perhaps the most interesting aspect of crises is that they very often lead to a form of communal or mechanical solidarity. People may band together to help one another as a means of coping with the treat of social disorganization. Society returns to an earlier form of solidarity, a kind of social regression. If society is large, forced division of labor may result.

Perhaps the best example of this is the situation of war. War creates needs that must be met rapidly upon the threat of devastation by an enemy. Society must be reorganized on a much tighter basis so as to meet the threat. Internal conflict jeopardizing group goal is not permitted, and a more monolithic division of labor is called for. Wartime industry is devoted to fewer functions due to the dominant function of manufacture of war machinery. Companies previously manufacturing many products must specialize on one or two wartime items, devoting all resources to that cause.

The nation unites toward one common goal. In this unity, people come to identify with their government as if it were a close-knit primary group. People come to believe that the fate of their family is inseparably tied in with the fate of their government. During wartime, the government may even assume the role of one of the family members—such as an uncle: Uncle Sam. Wartime propaganda—movies, songs, radio broadcasts, movies, newspaper articles—stresses likenesses, basic values that unite. For example, one central theme has been that Americans are fighting for the "American way of life," for the flag and "democracy." The French fought for "liberty, equality, fraternity." There is, in Cooley's terms, a basic stress upon primary group values—love of country, patriotism, faith, and so on. War brings about Cooley's image of institutions.

It has often been pointed out that wartime brings an increase of *crime and delinquency*, although a decrease in suicide. In terms of the above discussion, this trend results not from social disorganization but from "over-organization" of society. Youngsters, demoralized by the loss of parents and frustrated by the regimentation of wartime curfew, draft regulations, school demands, and food shortages strike back against society in the form of delinquency. Black market violations increase as a retaliation against government regulation—price ceilings, rationing, rent ceilings, and record keeping.

Suicide rates decrease, however, based upon the lower rates of anomic suicide—a form resulting from personality disorganization—although there is no way of determining how many "altruistic suicides" occur in battle.

War therefore presents the threat of disorganization and very often disorganization and chaos itself. However, very often disorganization does not occur until after a war is over. When there is no longer any basis for wartime regulations, people rebel against such regulation, such rebellion leading to both inner conflict and conflict between the government and subgroups.

Another outcome of the war is the disorganization of the family. Many families have been upset by the loss of the father. Others may be disrupted by the return of the father from war. War experiences may change one's personality, leading to marital incompatibility. Wartime marriages are very often unstable, based upon short courtships and short acquaintance periods. The father may return to a family in which the wife has adjusted to playing the father and mother role.

In short, the aftermath of a war may very often be a period of social disorganization, which only time will reconcile. Perhaps, it is at this time that a country is most vulnerable to invasion.

This discussion of societal regression raises an essential point about the development of organic solidarity. Though Durkheim portrays societies developing organic solidarity, it would be false to view mechanical solidarity as absent from large-scale societies. In our large-scale societies, we take the common conscience or common values for granted. There is a basic confidence in shared sentiments upon which our division of labor is based. Mechanical solidarity, in a sense, is a fundamental substratum upon which organic solidarity is based. Social disorganization may in fact occur due to a lack of confidence in shared sentiments—such that resulting from a scandal in government—preventing needed social changes from occuring.

Anomic suicide   In his earliest work, *The Division of Labor,* Durkheim viewed anomie as an abnormal phase of the division of labor. However, in his classic volume, *Suicide,* Durkheim devoted considerably more attention to and emphasis upon anomie as a concept.[75] In so doing, he reformulated the concept of anomie.

The reformulation took place based upon extensive, painstaking analysis of a mass of data on suicide. To Durkheim, the presence of suicide indicated the existence of anomie as he had conceptualized it. He found suicide was most frequent in times of economic depression or in times of economic prosperity. Both shared a common denominator, the lack of adjustment that people faced with the sudden changes in society's economic organization. People faced a sense of confusion, panic disorientation, insecurity, and discomfort. They suffered because their previous "means–ends framework" was no longer meaningful. In such situations, society's normative structure ceased to regulate the pursuit of life goals. Individuals facing sudden prosperity no longer believe the impossibility of anything, and come to strive for unattainable or even nonexisting goals. Under such conditions, people are prone to suicide, in particular, anomic suicide.

Using this explanatory framework, Durkheim was able to explain high rates of suicide among certain groups. It was highest among the wealthy due to the loss of object or purpose that accompanies having achieved wealth. It is high among divorced people and childless families as compared to families with children, due to the loss of the regulatory effect of family life. It was highest among males rather than females, but marriage was found to protect males from suicide more than females due to the more overt nature of the male biological and psychological needs or passions.

Other types of suicide were suggested by Durkheim: egoistic, altruistic, and fatalistic. These, however, will be discussed in detail in a later chapter. The important point here is that in *Suicide* Durkheim redefined suicide to refer to a situation in which the relationship between means and ends is not regulated by societal norms: ". . . human activity naturally aspires beyond assignable limits and sets itself unattainable goals."[76]

This sense of the term "anomie" has subsequently been termed "normlessness," the absence of norms or existence of insufficient norms regulating the pursuit of goals. This sense of the term "anomie" is by no means inconsistent with Durkheim's earlier "anomic division of labor." Rather, it is an application of it to the interpersonal sphere. It is quite conceivable that a society in which the "functions are not adjusted to one another" is one in which individual behavior is insufficiently regulated as well. The common denominator is the absense of or insufficiency of regulatory norms and the failure of government as a regulatory apparatus.

> For a whole century, economic progress has mainly consisted of freeing industrial relations from all regulation. Until very recently, it was the function of a whole system of moral forces to exert this discipline. . . . The influence of religion was felt alike by workers and masters, the poor and the rich. . . . Temporal power, in turn, restrained the scope of economic functions by its supremacy over them and by the relatively subordinate role it assigned them. . . . We do not mean to propose this organization as a model. Clearly it would be inadequate to existing societies without great changes. What we stress is its existence, the fact of its useful influence, and that nothing today has come to take its place.

> Actually, religion has lost most of its power. And government, instead of regulating economic life, has become its tool and servant. . . . Industry, instead of being still regarded as a means to an end transcending itself, has become the supreme end of individuals and societies alike. Thereupon the appetites thus excited have become freed of any limiting authority. . . .

Such is the source of the excitement predominating in this part of society, and which has thence extended to the other parts. There, the state of crisis and anomy is constant and, so to speak, normal. From top to bottom of the ladder, greed is aroused without knowing where to find the ultimate foothold. Nothing can calm it, since its goal is far beyond all it can attain. Reality seems valueless by comparison with the dreams of fevered imaginations; reality is therefore abandoned, but so too is possibility abandoned when it in turn becomes reality. A thirst arises for novelties, unfamiliar pleasures, nameless sensations, all of which lose their savor once known. . . . All these new sensations in their infinite quantity cannot form a solid foundation of happiness to support one during days of trial. . . .

Anomy [*sic*], therefore, is a regular and specific factor in suicide in our modern societies; one of the springs from which the annual contingent feeds. So we have here a new type to distinguish from the others. It differs from them in its dependence, not on the way in which individuals are attached to society, but on how it regulates them. Egoistic suicide results from man's no longer finding a basis for existence in life; altruistic suicide, because this basis for existence appears to man situated beyond life itself. The third sort of suicide, the existence of which has just been shown, results from man's activities lacking regulation and his consequent sufferings. By virtue of its origin we shall assign this last variety the name of *anomic suicide*.[77]

Thus, Durkheim's extension of anomie theory to inter-personal behavior lead to the concept of "normlessness" or a state of deregulation with regard to pursuit of life goals.

It should be noted at this point that Durkheim's usage of the term anomie refers primarily to situations of disruption of life goals (sudden prosperity, depression, divorce, etc.) such that the individual is confused about life goals, perhaps striving for nonexisting goals. A somewhat different sense of the term anomie is discussed by Merton in which the goals may be relatively well-known, but the individual may be prevented by economic conditions from obtaining them.

MERTON'S APPROACH TO ANOMIE

The foundation of American anomie theory is an article written by Merton in 1937, "Social Structure and Anomie,"[78] revised in 1949, and printed in its final expanded version in 1957.[79] Of it, Cohen has said:

Without any doubt, this body of ideas, which has come to be known as "anomie theory," has been the most influential single formulation in the sociology of deviance in the last 25 years, and Merton's paper, in its original and revised versions, is possibly the most frequently quoted single paper in modern sociology.[80]

While Merton's anomie is by implication an extension of Durkheim's anomie theory, the language and kinds of statements made about anomie are somewhat unfamiliar to followers of Durkheim:

Our primary aim lies in discovering how some social structures exert a definite pressure upon certain persons in the society to engage in nonconformist rather than conformist conduct. . . . Among the elements of social and cultural structure, two are important for our purposes. . . . The first consists of culturally defined goals, purposes, and interests. . . . The second phase of the social structure defines, regulates, and controls the acceptable modes of achieving these goals. . . . There may develop a disproportionate, at times, a virtually exclusive, stress upon the value of specific goals, involving relatively slight concern with the institutionally appropriate modes of attaining these goals. . . . Aberrant conduct, therefore, may be viewed as a symptom of dissociation between culturally defined aspirations and socially structured means. . . . Of the types of groups which result from the independent variation of the two phases of social structure, we shall be primarily concerned with the first, namely, that involving a disproportionate accent on goals. . . . The technically most feasible procedure, whether legitimate or not, is preferred to the institutionally prescribed conduct. As this process continues, the integration of the society becomes tenuous and anomie ensues.[81]

Merton's definition of anomie is couched in pretty much the same terms:

Cultural structure may be defined as that organized set of normative values governing behavior which is common to members of a designated society or group. And by social structure is meant that organized set of social relationships in which members of the society or group are variously implicated. Anomie is then conceived as a breakdown in the cultural structure, occurring particularly when there is an acute disjunction between the cultural norms and goals and the socially structured capacities of members of the group to act in accord with them.[82]

Thus, on the surface, Merton appears to be carrying forth Durkheim's analysis of "normlessness" and its consequences in society.

Society fails to provide regulatory norms with regard to certain aspirations (or the "passions," in Durkheim's analysis).

In another respect, Merton's analysis is an extension of Durkheim's. There is an implicit polar typology of social organization in Merton similar to Durkheim's three variants of anomic division of labor, organic solidarity, and forced division of labor.

> There may develop a disproportionate, at times, a virtually exclusive, stress upon the value of specific goals, involving relatively slight concern with the institutionally appropriate modes of attaining these goals. The limiting case in this direction is reached when the range of alternative procedures is limited only by technical rather than institutional considerations. . . . A second polar type is found in groups where activities originally conceived as instrumental are transmuted into ends in themselves. . . . Finally, there are the intermediate types of groups where a balance between culture goals and institutional means is maintained. These are significantly integrated and relatively stable, though changing groups.[83]

The first of these is clearly reminiscent of Durkheim's "anomic division of labor" in which "rules regulating the relations between the functions" are absent. The second of the polar types call to mind Durkheim's "forced division of labor" in which the division of labor is not in accord with differential abilities, and equality of opportunity is lacking. The third would then be the counterpart of Durkheim's "organic solidarity."

Despite these obvious continuities between Durkheim and Merton, in many ways Merton's analysis goes beyond Durkheim's by being more explicit on certain important points:

1. Durkheim talked in terms of certain drives or needs as being part of man's biological nature:

> Unlimited desires are insatiable by definition and insatiability is rightly considered a sign of morbidity. Being unlimited, they constantly and infinitely surpass the means at their command; they cannot be quenched. Inextinguishable thirst is constantly renewed torture. It has been claimed, indeed, that human activity naturally aspires beyond assignable limits and sets itself unattainable goals.[84]

Merton, by contrast, views these drives and aspirations as induced by society. The goals themselves are emphasized in culture.

> It no longer appears so obvious that man is set against society in an unceasing war between biological impulse and social restraint. The

image of man as an untamed bundle of impulses begins to look more like a caricature than a portrait. . . . Whatever the role of biological impulses, there still remains the further question of why it is that the frequency of deviant behavior varies within different social structures and how it happens that the deviants have different shapes and patterns in different social structures.[85]

2. Merton accounts for a spectrum of types of deviant behavior, including crime, delinquency, mental disorder, drug addiction, suicide, and many other phenomena, while Durkheim discusses only one form of deviancy, suicide, as an illustration of his broader anomie theory. Merton's typology of deviant behavior is based upon his dichotomous separation of institutional means and cultural goals. By varying "acceptance" or "rejection" of each of these, Merton derived a fairly exhaustive typology of deviancy, including five alternative adaptations to anomie: conformity, innovation, ritualism, and rebellion.

3. To Durkheim, anomie was a temporary, transitory, and perhaps abnormal phenomenon, while to Merton, anomie is a constant in modern American society:

> Durkheim's concept of anomie . . . might be defined as a *situation characterized by the sudden disharmony of normative expectations and everyday experiences.* . . . Merton conceived of anomie as a chronic condition; Durkheim as an acute fracturing of the social world.[86]

Thus, Merton suggests that anomie is a widespread problem and that it can be used as a framework for the analysis of contemporary social problems.

4. While Durkheim largely ignores social class, racial, ethnic, and other differences in anomie, Merton stresses that anomie can be found to differ significantly according to position in the social class system, ethnic status, and the like. Deviancy, especially innovation, will be disproportionately concentrated in the lower class stratum of society:

> Whatever the differential rates of deviant behavior in the several social strata, and we know from many sources that the official crime statistics uniformly showing higher rates in the lower strata are far from complete or reliable, it appears from our analysis that the greatest pressures toward deviation are exerted upon the lower strata. . . . The occupational opportunities of people in these areas are largely con-

fined to manual labor and the lesser white-collar jobs. Given the American stigmatization of manual labor *which has been found to hold rather uniformly in all social classes,* and the absence of realistic opportunities for advancement beyond this level, the result is a marked tendency toward deviant behavior.[87]

Putting it in Durkheim's terms, "functional conflict," absence of norms, or normative breakdown, would be greatest in the lower class. There is, however, no counterpart in Durkheim's thinking on anomie or on the anomic division of labor in emphasis upon the relevance of stratification considerations for anomie theory. Ironically, however, there is some discussion of social stratification in Durkheim's discussion of the "forced division of labor."

> In effect, if the institution of classes or castes sometimes gives rise to anxiety and pain instead of producing solidarity, this is because the distribution of social functions on which it rests does not respond, or rather no longer responds, to the distribution of natural talents. . . . For needs to flow from one class to another, differences which originally separated these classes much have disappeared or grown less. Through changes produced in society, some must have become apt at functions which were at first beyond them, while the others lost their original superiority. . . . In accordance with these transformations, the agreement between the aptitudes of individuals and the kind of activity assigned to them is found to be broken in every region of society; constraint alone, more or less violent and more or less direct, links them to their functions. Consequently, only an imperfect and troubled solidarity is possible.
>
> Thus, this result is not a necessary consequence of the division of labor. It comes about only under particular circumstances, that is, when it is an effect of external force. . . .
>
> The forced division of labor is, then, the second abnormal type we meet. But the sense of the word "forced" must not be misunderstood. Constraint is not every kind of regulation, since, as we have just seen, the division of labor cannot do without regulation. . . . Constraint only begins when regulation, no longer corresponding to the true nature of things, and, accordingly, no longer having any basis in customs, can only be validated through force.[88]

The above description portrays the individual of lower-class background as desiring a higher place in life and yet being held in check and not allowed access to opportunities to better himself. This essentially corresponds to Merton's description of anomie, except for Merton, constraint does not play such a strong role, because the individual does not perceive the socially structured bases of his inopportunity.[89]

The parallel of Durkheim's forced division of labor with Merton's anomie is significant, since, as the empirical data in a forthcoming chapter will show, what Durkheim described as the forced division of labor may be a "form of anomie." This is a form of anomie to be found in countries possessing oligarchic or even dictatoral forms of government, coercive in nature, and yet characterized by constant civil war, violence, assassination, and instability of other types of aggression. It is interesting to note, however, that this "form of anomie" is characteristic of many "transitional" Latin American countries, but not characteristic of American society or countries in Europe of Scandinavia.

Thus, the final effect of Merton's anomie analysis is to extend anomie theory to include two forms of anomie: (1) a form in which there are differentials in availability of means to commonly wanted goals, which discrepancy is induced by the social structure, and which differentials produce a basis of *conflict* between functions and individuals in society, and (2) a second form, more central to Durkheim's analysis, in which a person's means–ends schema has been upset by some sudden change, especially sudden improvement in conditions, resulting in endless striving for something new, something nonexisting.

Recently, other typologies of anomie have been proposed. Mizruchi terms the first situation "bondlessness" and the latter situation "boundlessness."[90] De Grazia's distinction between "simple" and "acute" anomie is also related.[91]

In a later chapter in this book, the two will be described as "anomie of conflict" versus "anomie of isolation." In both cases, society may be said to be anomic insofar as certain forms of deviancy appear problematic in each. In this situation of anomie of conflict, functional differentiation is held in check resulting in internal instability manifested in crime, delinquency, and vice. By contrast, in anomie of isolation, differentiation is at its highest peak, resulting in the isolation of the individual from society, which in turn results in more inward deviancy, such as suicide, mental disorder, and drug addiction. Although in anomie of conflict the central problem is relative deprivation, in anomie of isolation the central problem is loneliness, confusion of goals, or even vacancy of goals due to social division and the ethic of affluence. While anomie of conflict is characteristic of lower-class people, anomie of isolation characterizes upper-class people. The former characterizes emergent nations, the latter characterizes highly industrialized ones.

Social psychological outcomes of anomie   The current view in the field of social disorganization is that personality disorganization is the primary outcome of social disorganization. However, this approach arises from the fault of equating small-scale society with *organized society*. In small-scale societies there is, no doubt, a fairly direct relation between the condition of society at large and personality organization; however, in large societies, the fate of the individual is not nearly so determined by the condition of the society. Thomas and Znaniecki recognized that personality disorganization was only one outcome of social disorganization, and this knowledge led them to postulate three reactions to social disorganization: the bohemian or "disorganized personality," the creative man or "adjusted personality," and the philistine or "over-organized personality."

The major explicit discussion of social phychological reactions to anomie is found, as discussed above, in the work of R. K. Merton.[92] In formulating a typology of adaptations, Merton states a few assumptions about stratification which are not stressed in Durkheim's work. As we have seen, Merton sees anomie as problematic within societies midway between caste societies (forced division of labor) and open class societies (organic solidarity). In the former, stratification has no particular relation to abilities, while in the latter there is a perfect relation. In societies such as American society, which are quasi-caste in nature, the problem of anomie occurs. It is created by the orientation of all people toward the same culture goals or values, when in fact only a few have either the opportunity or ability to achieve them. This cultural egalitarianism is essentially based upon our frontier background, in which goal attainment was possible for all. However, in Durkheim's terms, the conditions for anomie—population explosion, rapid urbanization, rapid transity, demographic inbalance, and crisis—all have occurred. Only those who are specialized in some needed skill can succeed. This specialization is necessarily associated with differentiation of function or division of labor and orientation toward different cultural goals according to positional stratification. Division of labor mitigates the conflict between individuals, groups, and functions.

Merton thus sees the problem of anomie arising essentially from the problem of stratification. Anomie, according to Merton, is a strain on the cultural structure due to the social structure. The continuity with Durkheim is in the emphasis upon common value orientations as causative and in the recognition that reduction of anomie requires differentiation of value orientation and of function. Merton's typology of reactions to deviation is, due to his emphasis upon stratification, correlated with position in the social stratification system. Certain people whose position and opportunity make easier the pursuit of cultural goals are in a better position to conform with the "rules of the game" specified in the cultural structure. Other people in positions of less advantage tend to disregard the rules in favor of the more highly emphasized cultural values. Normlessness results in these sections. Individuals and groups under the greatest pressure to achieve, but who have least opportunity, may follow a pattern of rebellion (the rejection of cultural norms and values, and the substitution of new ones) or retreatism (the rejection without the substitution). Those under great pressure to succeed but little pressure to conform to cultural norms may follow innovation as a pattern: the rejection of cultural norms while oriented toward cultural values. Others may choose ritualism, a scaling-down or abandoning of success goals, permitting conformity to cultural norms. This analysis is summarized in Merton's deviancy paradigm below (Table 3–2).

TABLE 3-2 Merton's paradigm of deviancy

A TYPOLOGY OF MODES OF INDIVIDUAL ADAPTATION

Modes of Adaptation	Cultural Goals	Institutionalized Means
I. Conformity	+	+
II. Innovation	+	—
III. Ritualism	—	+
IV. Retreatism	—	—
V. Rebellion	±	±

(+) = acceptance
(—) = rejection
(±) = rejection and substitution

SOURCE: Robert K. Merton, "Social Structure and Anomie," Chapter IV in Robert K. Merton, *Social Theory and Social Structure* (New York: The Free Press, 1957), p. 140.

Merton's typology is not a typology of personality types but of adaptations. Such adaptations can be followed by a person, a group, an institution, or any other social entity. However, Merton's typology clearly implies that "personality disorganization" is only one adaptation to the societal situation of anomie. Merton's ritualism, like Thomas' philistine adaptation, is a rigid form of adaptation. Roles are too well integrated in terms of lowered aspirations. Retreatism and rebellion are analogous to bohemian adaptation, while innovation is a quasi-category, in some ways analogous to "creative personality."

DEVELOPMENT OF ANOMIE APPROACH

Though some of the literature following the classic work of Durkheim and Merton involved extensions of the theoretical framework, most of the literature has been of an empirical nature. The empirical studies are divided into two types: studies of "anomie" and studies of "anomia." The former refers to a property of a social system, while the latter is a psychological entity:

> The first thing to note about the sociological concept of anomie is that it is — sociological. Anomie refers to a property of a social system, not to the state of mind of this or that individual within the system. It refers to a breakdown of social standards governing behavior and so also signifies little social cohesion. . . . Anomie, then, is a condition of the social surrounding, not a condition of particular people. People are *confronted* by substantial anomie when, as a matter of objective fact, they cannot rely upon a high probability that the behavior of others will be in rough accord with standards *jointly* regarded as legitimate. To prevent conceptual confusion, therefore, different terms are required to distinguish between the anomic state of individuals and the anomic state of the social system, for though the two are variously connected, they are nevertheless distinct. . . . Some fifteen years ago, Leo Srole proposed the term *anomia* to designate an anomic state of the individual,[93] and this term has since passed into common sociological usage.[94]

There has been a confusion of these two aspects of anomie in the empirical literature, somewhat reminiscent of the earlier confusion between social disorganization and personal disorganization. Since anomia is, as will be shown, readily operational and much easier to employ in empirical studies than anomie, it has been widely used as a measure, sometimes mistakenly, of anomie. In addition to the multitude of empirical studies of anomie and anomia, as with the social disorganization literature, there is an increasing tendency toward criticism of the anomie approach.

Extensions of anomie theory   Although much of the empirical literature has indirectly contributed to the body of anomie theory, an important area of strictly theoretical essays and books has contributed significantly to the anomie approach. Merton has formally acknowledged some of these:[95]

> The psychological conception of anomie has been simultaneously formulated by R. M. MacIver and David Riesman. Since their formulations are substantially alike, what is said of one may be said of both. . . . As has been noted, MacIver's approach is thus psychological (*i.e.,* anomie is for him a state of *mind,* not a state of society—though the state of mind may reflect social tensions) and his psychological types correspond to the elements (anxiety–isolation–purposelessness) which form the subject aspect of Durkheim's concept.[96]

As Merton points out, this psychological conception of anomia has been operationalized by Srole, who defines anomia as "a rejective orientation toward out-groups in general and minority groups in particular.[97] Srole's anomia has five components: (1) a sense that community leaders are detached from or indifferent to one's needs, (2) a sense that the social order is fickle and unpredictable, (3) a feeling of retrogression from goals already reached, (4) a sense of loss of internalized norms, and (5) a sense that immediate personal relations are no longer predictive or supportive. As will be shown in the next section, Srole's anomia scale has been the basis of much empirical research. Meier and Bell, who have used this scale extensively, comment that it seems to measure *despair* or a sense of hopelessness and discouragement and perhaps "personal disorganization." This statement is significant for pointing to the continuity between anomie theory and social disorganization theory.

Merton also commented on DeGrazia's contributions:

> An effort has been made to catch up the psychological and sociological concepts in a distinction between "simple" and "acute" anomie.[98]

> Simple anomie refers to the state of confusion in a group or society which is subject to conflict between value systems, resulting in some de-

gree of uneasiness and a sense of separation from the group; acute anomie, to the deterioration and, at the extreme, the disintegration of
value systems, which results in marked anxieties. This has the merit of
terminologically ear-marking the often stated but sometimes neglected
fact that, like other conditions of society, anomie varies in degree and
perhaps in kind.[99]

DeGrazia's contributions are not, however, limited to his distinction
between simple and acute anomia. He also extends Durkheimian
theory by showing how subjective anomia may be traced to the help-
less position of being a child in the family, and later in adult life
to failure of political rulers:

> The clues to anomie left by Durkheim sufficed to call attention
> to four important situations of anxiety in the early history of the human
> organism: absence of attendants, withdrawal of affection by attendants,
> discovery of the limitations of attendants, and, lastly, partial abandon-
> ment by attendants.[100]
>
> The deterioration of beliefs follows fast on any revelation that the
> reigning *ruler* is either unable or unwilling to perform his commit-
> ments. The unexpected crumbling of old idols should have an effect
> on adults similar to the shock of the child upon discovering the limita-
> tions of his attendants.[101]

Merton goes on to acknowledge the contribution of Parsons
and Bales[102] to the study of typologies of deviancy. Parsons has built
upon Merton's paradigm of deviancy whose major components are
acceptance *versus* rejection of institutional means *vis-a-vis* cultural
goals:

> Talcott Parsons has taken up this typology and has derived it,
> in motivational terms, from his conceptual scheme of social interac-
> tion. . . .
>
> In the words of Parsons and Bales, "Deviance was shown to involve
> four basic directions, according to whether the need to express aliena-
> tion from the normative pattern—including the repudiation of attach-
> ment to alter as an object—or to maintain compulsive conformity with
> the normative pattern and attachment to alter, and according to wheth-
> er the mode of action was actively or passively inclined. This yielded
> four directional types, those of aggressiveness and withdrawal on the
> alienative side, and of compulsive performance and compulsive accep-
> tance, on the side of compulsive conformity."[103]

Parsons' typology is presented in paradigm form in Table 3–3.
It can be seen as parallel to Merton's typology. The alienative *versus*

TABLE 3-3   Parsons' paradigm of deviancy

	ACTIVITY		PASSIVITY	
	Compulsive performance orientation		*Compulsive acquiescence*	
	Focus on social objects	Focus on norms	Focus on social objects	Focus on norms
Conformative dominance	Dominance	Compulsive enforcement	Submission (*e.g.*, sick role)	Perfectionist observance (Merton's ritualism)
	Rebelliousness		*Withdrawal*	
Alienative dominance	Aggressiveness toward social objects (Hell's Angels)	Incorrigibility (dropouts)	Compulsive independence (*e.g.*, Black Muslims)	Evasion (*e.g.*, hobo)

SOURCE: Talcott Parsons, *The Social System* (New York: The Free Press, 1951), p. 259.
NOTE: Examples in parentheses are added by author for clarification.

conformative dimension is parallel to Merton's acceptance *versus* rejection. The parameter of social object orientation *versus* social norm orientation is roughly congruent with Merton's cultural goal *versus* institutionalized means polarity. The unique contribution of Parsons' typology is, however, the inclusion of active *versus* passive response. This, no doubt, is an important refinement; however, what Parson's paradigm gains in refinement, it loses in simplicity and intuitiveness of application, primarily because Parsons has not illustrated in detail each possible variant as painstakingly as has Merton. As a result, Merton's typology still remains more useful and more widely used in empirical research.

Another significant contribution to Merton's anomie approach is that of Albert Cohen. Although self-consciously a non-anomie approach and oriented in the "Chicago cultural transmission" tradition of Shaw–McKay, Thrasher, and others, there are implicit points of congruence between Cohen and Merton. Again, in Merton's words:

In his theoretically sensitive book, Albert K. Cohen suggests that this theory is "highly plausible as an explanation for adult professional crime and for the property delinquency of some older and semi-professional juvenile thieves. Unfortunately," he goes on to say, "it fails to account for the non-utilitarian quality of the subculture. . . ." Were the participant in the delinquent subculture merely employing illicit means to the end of acquiring economic goods, he would show more respect for the goods he has thus acquired. Furthermore, the destructiveness, the versatility, the zest and the wholesale negativism which characterizes the delinquent subculture are beyond the purview of this theory."[104]

Merton goes on to explain the ways in which Cohen's approach is not entirely inconsistent with his own:

> But in exploring this matter further, it should be remembered for purposes of theoretical clarity, that this theory does not maintain that the resulting deviant behavior is rationally calculated and utilitarian. Instead, it centers on the *acute* pressures created by the discrepancy between culturally induced goals and socially structured opportunities. . . . Cohen does, in fact, examine the social and cultural sources of these pressures in much the same terms as those we have been considering. His thoroughly sociological analysis considerably advances our understanding of certain forms of deviant behavior commonly found in delinquency groups and does so by extending the type of structural and functional theory now under review.[105]

More recently, Cohen has taken a stance even more antagonistic to Merton's anomie approach, and this will be discussed in a subsequent section.[106]

Cloward and Ohlin have suggested reformulations of Merton's approach even more congruent than Cohen's.[107] Although this approach will be discussed in a later chapter focusing on delinquency, three general points are important enough to cite here:

1. Merton does not give enough importance to the differential availability of *illegitimate means,* only treating legitimate means as analytically important.

2. When this extension is made, a basic compatibility between the "cultural transmission view" (that deviancy is learned and passed on from generation to generation) and the anomie view is evident, whose key link is the notion of "differential opportunity structures."

3. An individual may have access to neither legitimate nor illegitimate opportunity structures, which makes for a "retreatist" pattern of behavior.

Empirical studies of anomie and anomia   Although the term "anomie" integrates a wide variety of literature, three separate traditions in the empirical study of anomie and anomia have emerged:

1. Studies of anomie as a *condition* of a social system in the sense of anomic division of labor in the tradition of Durkheim.

2. Studies of anomie as a variable within a social system in the tradition of Durkheim's study of suicide and Merton's social structure and anomie.

3. Studies of the personal counterpart of the situation of anomie following Srole's "anomia." The third of these areas has had the greatest concentration of studies, perhaps due to the ease of measurement of major variables involved.

Anomie in the tradition of Durkheim. Relatively few studies have been done in the Durkheim tradition of anomic division of labor, the state of societal deregulations, and probably none explicitly so. However, there is an interesting thesis that seems to emerge from those that have been done, that anomie is associated with coercive subjugation. This may be best expressed by William J. Goode.[108] Goode, for example, traces illegitimacy rates to the existence of anomie or non-integration. Anomie, used in a relative rather than an absolute sense, refers to several possible variables: cultural disintegration, social disintegration, and lack of local–national, social, or cultural integration. Goode examines several historical examples of high illegitimacy rates: Northwestern Europe during recent times; industrialized sub-Saharan Africa; immigrant populations in the United States during 1910–1935; ante-bellum United States South; the Caribbean; and mainland Iberian countries in the New World. In all of these cases, illegitimacy is found high among the subjected peoples (for instance, slaves in the United States, Indians in Latin America) and is traced to the breakdown of the village normative structure, resulting from conquest. This breakdown is eventually reconciled, however, when the native population is assimilated into the norms of the conqueror. Thus anomie and illegitimacy are viewed as a phase of development in the assimilation to a new culture as characteristic of a subordinated, dominated population.

In a similar fashion, Powell[109] has characterized anomie as a phase in the development of Buffalo, New York. Powell found that violent crimes in Buffalo, as measured by official reports, were most prevalent during the 1970's, declined steadily until the turn of the century, rose again until 1918, and then receded to the precivil war level by 1940. Since 1946, arrests of all forms have decreased in Buffalo. Powell's explanation for trends in violent crimes is similar to Goode's explanation for trends in illegitimacy. The post-Civil War chaos was produced by the rise of a new dominant class of industrial capitalists, whose dominance led to corruption and dislocation of the institutional order of the total society. However, with the readjustment of society to capitalism, means and ends were brought into closer harmony, and the crime rate subsided. While corruption characterized the dominant class, violence characterized the subjected classes during the emergence of capitalism. The leveling of class systems, however, brought a reduction of anomie among the subjected class and a decrease in crime.

Following a similar line of analysis, though in smaller settings, several studies have portrayed the anomie of inmates in concentration camps of Nazi Germany, of Soviet Russia during the Stalin period, of the North Koreans during the Korean War, and of the confederacy during the United States Civil War.[110] Cressey and Krassowski have argued that anomie is, in fact, cultivated by prison staffs to allow them to control inmates effectively.[111]

The Mertonian Tradition. Merton's theory postulates a relationship between socio-economic status, on the one hand, and success opportunities, success pressures, and deviancy, on the other hand. Thus, empirical studies relevant to Merton's approach are those showing the presence or absence of social class differentials in the three variables. Despite the volume of studies on these variables, a clear-cut picture has not yet emerged.

Several studies have indicated the existence of differentials in success aspirations and success pressures according to parental social class. Of these most have shown lower-class youngsters lower in aspirations and success pressure than middle- and upper-class youngsters.[112] Though these findings contradict Merton's assumption that success values are held equally by all social classes, the findings are not so strong that they by themselves dismiss Merton's theory. Merton in defending his theory against these findings has asserted that, "It is . . . sufficient that a *sizable minority* of the lower strata assimilate this [success] goal for them to be differentially subject to this pressure as to achieve monetary success."[113]

No studies of differentials in actual opportunities have been undertaken, probably because it is taken for granted that lower-class people are faced with more limited opportunities. Studies have been done of differentials in perceived opportunities, however, and on this point the findings are inconsistent. Nearly half of the studies indicate that lower-class youngsters perceive equal opportunities or anticipate future opportunities on par with middle- and upper-class youngsters, while the other half portray perceived opportunity as lower in the lower class.[114] Thus, based on available data on perceived opportunity, Merton's theory can neither be challenged nor confirmed.

To the neglect of all else, the major controversy with regard to the Merton theory has centered about social class differentials in various forms of deviant behavior. Proponents have looked to official records (including police reports, court records, welfare reports, hospital statistics) with some satisfaction showing mental disorder, delinquency and crime, alcoholism, illegitimacy, and the spectrum of deviancy problems as inverse corollaries of SES.[115] However, recent field studies using participant observation, self-report, and survey techniques have yielded a not-so-unanimous picture. The majority of self-report studies of delinquency show no relation between delinquency and SES.[116] Thus, though Merton's theory of anomie has received much more attention in empirical research than Durkheim's, it has neither received a clear-cut mandate nor repudiation from the empirical research. Conflicting findings have led to conflicting explanations, pointing to the need for larger-scale research intended to clarify the contradictions.

The Srole Continuity. Following Srole's development of his scale in 1957,[117] a host of articles have been published using anomia as a dependent variable.

Meier and Bell have followed Merton's thinking, suggesting that anomia results when individuals lack access to the means for achievement of life goals. Their data indicate anomia to be highest among the poor, uneducated, the old, the unmarried, the urban dweller, and the socially isolated, in accord with the Merton model.[118]

The empirical literature utilizing Srole's anomia scale or similar index is vast, although in a broad way it can be codified in terms of various applications of the Meier and Bell differential access hypothesis. In agreement with Meier and Bell, other investigators have found anomia inversely related to socio-economic status,[119] urbanism,[120] and amount of social contact.[121] Also supportive is the finding that anomia is higher among Negroes than Caucasians[122] and that anomia is inversely related to level of aspiration.[123]

Indirectly, the success–access hypothesis has been corroborated by evidence that anomia is correlated with variables usually linked with success or access to success goals, or more generally to the amount of frustration. Thus, anomia has been found directly related to authoritarianism and prejudice,[124] directly to religious orthodoxy,[125] to years spent in a V.A. domiciliary,[126] and inversely related to readiness for desegregation,[127] and to voting and being politically informed.[128] Only in regard to religion as a dependent variable has there been any disagreement with the deductions made by Meier and Bell. In contrast to the Meier and Bell finding that Catholics rate higher in anomia than Protestants or Jews, two studies have found anomia highest among Protestants.[129] Too little research has been done to determine the basis of this inconsistency.

In spite of this one negative find, the mass of literature on anomia bears a striking consistency as compared with empirical findings in other fields of social research. This seems to lend support to the Meier and Bell interpretation that Srole's anomia is a measure of despair and that it is a corollary of failure or lack of access to life goals. Because Meier and Bell are linking Srole's anomie with Merton's anomie through their analysis, the corollaries found linked with anomia offer support and elaboration of Merton's theory. As Merton's theory states, lower status and minority group people suffer from despair (anomia) and isolation. This, in turn, may be manifested in prejudice, authoritarianism, political apathy, and religious orthodoxy. Further investigation using the anomia scale might clarify the relation between low status and deviant behavior whose relationship is confusingly portrayed in current literature.

Key characteristics of multipartite or anomic organization are excessive competition or conflict between groups, values, beliefs, interests, and wills; by ineffective, corrupt government and unscrupulous, self-interested leadership; by the absence of common values, with the exception of market exchange as a value; by the breakdown in social control; by excessive tolerance of deviancy; and the like. The personal counterpart is the nonconforming, migratory bohemian or cosmopolitan personality.

The concepts of disorganization and anomie (in addition to the mass society theory discussed below) are historically related to each other and to such classic concepts as Marx' "capitalism," Pareto's "combinations," Becker's "normless-secular society," and Tonnies' "gesellschaft." Social disorganization is usually defined in terms of breakdown in consensus on norms, values, beliefs, (that is, normlessness) or in terms of intergroup conflict, as is anomie. Images of personality in these related theoretical areas are very similar. Classic theory emphasizes the blasé, cosmopolitan type of personality—what Thomas and Znaniecki termed bohemian. Disorganization approaches stress personality disorganization. Anomie approaches are using anomia as a personal counterpart of anomie.

The bohemian cannot adjust or gain satisfaction in one institutional sphere. The disorganized personality and the anomic type have characteristically been portrayed as failing to achieve life goals.

One main difference between the disorganization and anomie perspectives is that the latter perspective has been more thoroughly researched. In fact, most of the classical theoretical approaches were largely impressionistic "armchair philosophy." As such, the classical approaches offered little hope of viewing society objectively, but became merely the basis of ideological dispute rather than consensual acceptance. However, the extensive empirical investigation of disorganization and anomie has given rise to sensitive criticism of those concepts as applicable to modern society. The criticism of disorganization, we have seen, led to its decreasing usage. However, the need for an explanatory framework for large scale deviancy has led to the emergence of anomie as a fashionable concept.

However, currently the concept of anomie and anomie theory are receiving criticism from all sides. This dissatisfaction with anomie as a concept has coincided with an emergence (and perhaps transference) of interest in alienation and mass society as explanations. In fact, very recently the term alienation has been substituted for anomia in research using the Srole anomia scale.

It will be suggested in chapters to come that much of the difficulty with the anomie and disorganization perspectives is the lack of cognizance of alternative images for the description of modern society, mainly pluralistic and oligarchic society. The recognition of these alternatives may correct current deviancy perspectives and adjust sociological explanations of deviancy so as to answer diverse criticisms. The nature of current deviancy may derive from pluralistic or oligarchic rather than anomic social organization. If these possibilities are considered, new predictions about types of deviancy, trends in deviant behavior, and the extent of various types of deviancy might be made, which predictions "better fit" the current data available on deviancy.

Although deviancy researchers have not yet attempted such theoretical clarification, such attempts have been made by students of mass society and alienation. Although mass society literature has been largely confined to the areas of political sociology and collective behavior, there is no reason to suppose that the mass society outlook will not spread into the field of deviancy. In the next section, we shall look at mass society theory and attempt to show how some of the insights gained in the study of mass society theory might be useful in explaining deviancy.

Mass society theory

Of recent interest and influence, yet of great scope of relationship to classic theories, is the theory of mass society. The theory of mass society may be defined narrowly by the writings of a few relatively recent pessimistic writers, including Ortega y Gasset, Karl Mannheim, Emil Lederer, Hannah Arendt, and Erich Fromm; however, the term also has a broader meaning. If we agree with Bramson that "the parable of alienation is the theory of mass society,"[130] the scope of mass society is open to all theories that have touched upon the phenomenon of alienation in modern society and, as Glazer has pointed out, alienation is perhaps the implicit perspective of most classic social theories, including Marx, Durkheim, Veblen, Weber, Tonnies, Simmel, Cooley, and Mead.[131] All focus upon the decline of intimacy and estrangement of modern man that accompanies rational large-scale society.

Because of its broad scope, it has been asserted that there is no *theory* of mass society—just a *perspective* which may be termed mass society, or that the theory of mass society is as broad as sociology itself.[132] Admittedly, mass society theory is broad and general, but that by itself does not discount its adequacy as a theory. The primary criteria of excellence of a theory in sociology are whether the theory refers to something sociologically important and whether the theory is subject to empirical test. It is my belief that the theory of mass society meets these criteria. But before evaluating the theory, it is necessary to review the body of theories that are usually termed mass society theories.

Is there a logically interdependent set of empirical propositions—that is, a theory of the middle range—that can be derived from these theories? Kornhauser has asserted that there is, and it is upon his analysis that the following pages shall rely extensively.[133] Kornhauser stresses that there are actually two types of mass society theories, *aristocratic* and *democratic. Aristocratic theories* are motivated by a defense of elite values against the rise of mass participation. By contrast, *democratic theories* defend democratic values against the rise of elites bent on total domination. Included among the aristocratic theorists are Le Bon, Ortega y Gasset, and Mannheim, while democratic theorists include Lederer, Arendt, and Fromm.

ARISTOCRATIC THEORISTS

Aristocratic theorists see mass society as a set of conditions under which elites are exposed to non-elite pressures. The earliest of these, Le Bon, looked upon his times as an "era of crowds," speaking of crowds as vehicles in the downfall of civilization.[134] Ortega stressed the "revolt of the masses" in which modern culture was vulgarized by its expression of mass values, and in which qualified elites were replaced by unqualified elites.[135] Mannheim similarly emphasizes that in mass society the many come to intervene in areas previously reserved for the few and determine social policies and cultural standards which they are not competent to determine.[136] Kornhauser sums up the aristocratic analyses as follows:

> The conception of mass society contained in such writings as these includes three major terms: (*a*) growing equalitarianism (loss of traditional authority); (*b*) widespread readiness to support anti-aristocratic forms of rule (quest for popular authority); (*c*) rule by the masses (domination by pseudo-authority).[137]

DEMOCRATIC THEORIES

Democratic theories focus more upon the protection of non-elites from elites than upon the danger of mass rule. While for aristocratic critics, mass society is a condition under which there is too much control by the many over the few, for democratic theorists, mass society is a condition of too much control by the few over the many (unlimited democracy *versus* unlimited tyranny). Democratic theorists obscure the difference between mass society and totalitarianism. They are one and the same. For Emil Lederer[138] and Hannah Arendt,[139] mass society refers to atomized society, a society in which there are no group identifications except the larger group. Individuals are related to each other only in terms of their relatedness to a common authority. As a result they are alienated, anxious, and inclined to extreme behavior to escape from their tensions and feelings of isolation.

Kornhauser summarizes democratic theory as follows:

> There are three major terms implied in the democratic criticism of mass society: (*a*) growing atomization (loss of community); (*b*) widespread readiness to embrace new ideologies (quest for community); (*c*) totalitarianism (total domination by pseudo-community).[140]

SYSTEMATIC THEORY OF MASS SOCIETY

The larger theory of mass society contains an abundance of statements about society and modern man in contemporary society, so much so that the theory, when expressed in a general form, appears confusing, vague, and all-inclusive. Daniel Bell has attempted to summarize the theory of mass society:

> The conception of "mass society" can be summarized as follows: The revolutions in transport and communications have brought men into closer contact with each other and bound them in new ways; the division of labor has made them more interdependent; tremors in one part of society affect all others. Despite this greater interdependence, however, individuals have grown more estranged from one another. The old primary group ties of family and local community have been shattered; ancient parochial faiths are questioned; few unifying values have taken their place. Most important, the critical standards of an educated elite no longer shape opinion or taste. As a result, mores and morals are in constant flux, relations between individuals are tangential or compartmentalized rather than organic. At the same time greater mobility, spatial and social, intensifies concern over status. Instead of a fixed or known status symbolized by dress or title, each person assumes a multiplicity of roles and constantly has to prove himself in a succession of new situations. Because of all this, the individual loses a coherent sense of self. His anxieties increase. There ensues a search

for new faiths. The stage is thus set for the charismatic leader, the secular messiah, who, by bestowing upon each person the semblance of necessary grace, and of fullness of personality, supplies a substitute for the older unifying belief that the mass society has destroyed.[141]

Indeed, the characteristics of mass society as expressed in this form are so global that they would seem to apply to all contemporary societies, and thus the mass society scheme would explain nothing except perhaps differences between folk and urban society, gemeinschaft and gesellschaft, and the like. However, Kornhauser has insisted that there is a *theory* implicit in the mass society writings, which emerges from the global maze of societal attributes. One of the problems to be overcome, however, is that mass society theorists may confuse mass societies and, logically distinct, totalitarian societies:

> Democratic critics tend to construe totalitarianism as mass society, because elite domination based on a mobilized population is the central meaning of their conception of totalitarianism. However, they also tend to designate societies that are vulnerable to totalitarianism as mass society. For example, both Weimar Germany and Nazi Germany have been called mass societies. This obscures the problem of developmental patterns, since factors which encourage totalitarian movements in political democracies are not necessarily the same as those which *sustain* totalitarian regimes once they are in power. It is necessary, therefore, to distinguish between a mass society and a totalitarian society.[142]

Thus, Kornhauser's solution to the apparent ambiguity in mass society theory is to draw a precise distinction between mass society and other forms of social organization:

> *Mass society is a social system in which elites are readily accessible to influence by non-elites and non-elites are readily available for mobilization by elites.*
> This conception of mass society may be better understood by comparing it with other types of societies. For this purpose, we shall consider communal society, pluralist society, and totalitarian society, insofar as they can be characterized by other combinations of the two variables of (*a*) accessibility of elites and (*b*) availability of non-elites.[143]

The terms *access* and *availability* are key terms and their meanings are quite important. Though their meanings vary with different contexts, Kornhauser suggests a general definition:

As a rough indicator of the degree of access to elites we shall use the extent to which members of the society participate in the selection of elites, and as a comparable measure of the degree of availability of non-elites we may use the extent to which members of the society lack attachments to independent groups.[144]

Kornhauser proceeds to characterize the four types of society:

Communal society requires inaccessible elites and unavailable non-elites if it is to sustain its traditional structure—as in certain medieval communities. Elites are inaccessible in that elite elements and standards of selection are fixed by traditional ascription. Non-elites are unavailable in that people are firmly bound by kinship and community.

Pluralist society requires accessible elites and unavailable non-elites if it is to sustain its freedom and diversity—as in certain liberal democracies. Elites are accessible in that competition among independent groups opens many channels of communication and power. The population is unavailable in that people possess multiple commitments to diverse and autonomous groups. . . .

Mass society requires both accessible elites and available non-elites if it is to exhibit a high rate of mass behavior. Elites are accessible and non-elites are available in that there is a paucity of independent groups between the state and the family to protect either elites or non-elites from manipulation and mobilization by the other. In the absence of social autonomy at all levels of society, large numbers of people are pushed and pulled toward activist modes of intervention in vital centers of society; and mass-oriented leaders have the opportunity to mobilize this activism for the capture of power. As a result, freedom is precarious in mass society.

Totalitarian society requires an inaccessible elite and an available population if it is to sustain a system of total control from above—as in certain modern dictatorships. The elite is inaccessible in that elite elements are selected and fixed through co-operation, by virtue of a monopoly over the means of coercion and persuasion in the hands of those at the apex of the structure. The population is available in that its members lack all those independent social formations that could serve as a basis of resistance to the elite.[145]

Kornhauser's four-fold typology is reminiscent of many reviewed above, including Durkheim's mechanical solidarity, organic solidarity, anomic division of labor, and forced division of labor; Becker's folk-sacred, prescribed sacred, normless-secular, and principled secular society. The virtue of Kornhauser's approach is that it lends itself to empirical verification. Using the terms of his definition of mass society, he formulates the following central proposition:

> *A high rate of mass behavior may be expected when both elites and non-elites lack social insulation; that is, when elites are accessible to direct intervention by non-elites, and when non-elites are available for direct mobilization by elites.*[146]

Having laid out an empirically testable proposition Kornhauser proceeds to define his terms:

> *Mass behavior* is a form of collective behavior exhibiting the following characteristics: (*a*) The focus of attention is remote from personal experience and daily life. . . . (*b*) The mode of response to remote objects is direct. (*c*) Mass behavior also tends to be highly unstable, readily shifting its focus of attention and intensity of response. Activist responses are likely to alternate with apathetic responses. . . . (*d*) When mass behavior becomes organized around a program and acquires a certain continuity in purpose and effort, it takes on the character of a *mass movement.*[147]

Mass society is characterized by an abundance of mass movements. As such it is important to distinguish *mass movements* from *totalitarian movements.*

> Mass movements generally have the following characteristics: their objectives are remote and extreme; they favor activist modes of intervention in the social order; they mobilize uprooted and atomized sections of the population; they lack in internal structure of independent groups. . . . The distinctive character of totalitarian movements lies in their effort to gain total control over their followers and over the whole society. Totalitarian movements are highly organized by an elite bent on total power, whereas mass movements tend to be amorphous collectivities, often without any stable leadership.[148]

Each type of society seems to foster its own kind of social movement. Mass society favors mass movements. Communal society contains generally traditional movements. Pluralist society incorporates only reform movements. Totalitarian society, however, favors only the one dominant totalitarian movement.

ALIENATION AND MASS SOCIETY AS A PERSPECTIVE

Despite Kornhauser's explicit formulation of mass society theory discussed above, a number of writers continue to use mass society and alienation as perspectives for viewing modern society generally.[149] The mass society perspective consists for many of "a set of historically grounded descriptive statements about contemporary social structure"[150] (much like social disorganization theory described above).

Shils has summarized this global concept of mass society adequately:

> [Mass society consists of] a territorially extensive society with a large population, highly urbanized and industrialized. Power is concentrated in this society, and much of the power takes the form of manipulation of the mass through the media of mass communication. Civic spirit is poor, local localities are few, primordial solidarity is virtually non-existent. There is no individuality, only a restless and frustrated egoism. It is like the state of nature described by Thomas Hobbes, except that public disorder is restrained through the manipulation of the elite and the apathetic idiocy of the mass. The latter is broken only when, in a state of crises, the masses rally around some demagogue.[151]

It was suggested above that *mass society theory* might one day replace anomie theory as a deviance approach. Clearly, mass society *as a perspective* is already being used by deviance textbooks.[152] Most of the recent literature on mass society theory pertains to alienation in mass society. Thus, the foregoing discussion will focus specifically on the relation between alienation and mass society. This would seem an appropriate emphasis in a text on deviancy, because alienation though not mass society has been constantly been referred to in deviancy literature under the rubric of "antisocial sentiment."[153] It should be forewarned, however, that throughout this discussion mass society is used as a perspective and not a theory. Some suggestions as to how mass society theory relates to deviancy will be made later in this chapter.

MASS SOCIETY, ALIENATION, AND DEVIATION

The literature on mass society and alienation contains essentially five different kinds of statements: (1) statements about the nature of mass society and alienation, (2) theoretical discussions of the causes of mass society and alienation, (3) empirical studies of the concept of alienation, (4) empirical studies of the causes of alienation, and (5) studies of the correlates of alienation.

The nature and causes of mass society and alienation The most outstanding voice on the topic of alienation is that of Melvin Seeman, whose commentary on alienation and mass society serves as an excellent introduction to the literature, especially of much of the empirical literature on alienation follows upon his work.[154] Seeman has pointed out five essential structural elements of mass society noted in mass society perspectives: (1) the development of impersonality and the decline of kinship as a criterion of place; (2) the development of bureaucracy, resulting in secularization and the decline of sacred elements and rationality of beliefs and values; (3) social differentiation and specialization of tasks; (4) increasing social mobility; and (5) the enlargment of scale or bigness. These underlying factors contribute to three alienation-relevant structural factors: (1) loss of control over work and product; (2) lack of integration into the larger organizational structure; and (3) low access to reward values.[155]

Seeman lists five possible social psychological outcomes of objective alienation in mass society; powerlessness, normlessness, isolation, self-estrangement, and meaninglessness.[156] *Powerlessness* refers to the expectancy held by the individual that his own behavior cannot determine the reinforcements he seeks. *Normlessness* is a high expectancy that socially unapproved behaviors are required to achieve given goals. *Meaninglessness* refers to a low expectancy that meaningful predictions can be made about future outcomes of behavior. *Isolation* is a tendency to assign low regard values to goals or beliefs that are typically highly valued. *Self-estrangement* indicates a degree of dependence of the given behavior upon anticipated future outcomes of behavior.

These psychological types of alienation have been attributed to all three of the objective alienation factors in the literature. For instance, Browning, *et al.* see these five types as developing in stages based upon (3) low access to reward values. As they see it, alienation develops in three logical stages (*a*) a *predisposing stage,* arising from frustration and inability to cope with life situation, and consisting of powerlessness, meaninglessness, and normlessness; (*b*) a *stage of culture disaffection,* in which the person becomes isolated from cultural values; (*c*) an *adaptation phase,* in which the person becomes *self-estranged* as an outcome.[157]

Other usages of the term "alienation" Though Seeman is perhaps the most outstanding spokesman for the concept of alienation and the most often quoted, the term is not restricted to his usages. In fact, Seeman's operational types have been criticized for failing to incorporate the "classic" meaning of alienation as found in the writings of Marx.[158] Seeman's concept of alienation, it is said, departs from classic alienation by excluding the objective conditions of alienation in society and by subsuming all alienation under the concept of powerlessness. It is then concluded that "It would have been better for Seeman not to refer to Marx or any of the historical literature than to do so superficially and then narrow and distort the meaning to his own purposes."[159] However, it can be shown that Seeman's concept of alienation is not so inconsistent with classic alienation as is proposed. First, subjective or psychological components of alienation (as opposed to objective conditions or behavioral manifestations) are of great importance in Marx's concept of alienation (that is, the class concept). Second, Seeman's concept of self-estrangement takes in a major part of the original Marxian meaning, while clarifying it so as to make it operational.

Rediscovery of alienation Daniel Bell substantiates the above view by pinpointing essential components of classic alienation which are reflected in Seeman's types (as shown in the discussion below). Marx's usage of the term "alienation" includes "marketability" and "estrangement from self," while neo-Marxists adhere to a different idea of alienation involving "estrangement from society or community" and "reification."[160]

Content analysis of the essays on classic alienation by Erich Fromm[161] and Karl Marx[162] was performed by the author in the light of Seeman's and Bell's categories. The following components were abstracted:

A-1. *Powerlessness:* Lack of perception of self as an acting agent as reflected in inactivity; receptivity in manner of experiencing world; negation of productivity; feelings of loss of object of production; and desire to possess, use, or have.

A-2. *Normlessness:* Market orientation as reflected in lack of consciousness of species life; desire to establish an alien power over others; and orientation toward possession of money for this purpose.

A-3. *Self-estrangement:* Sense of involuntary obligation to work in pursuit of non-work needs as shown by physical exhaustion and mental debasement resulting from work; sense of resentment over working for others rather than self; sense that creativity is not rewarded in the work situation; and sense of loss of life to object of production.

A-4. *Reification:* Sense of separation from and deference for man-made objects given personal significance; dependency upon objects for sense of self-respect; feeling that objects have independent power; and substitution of symbols for experience.

An analysis of the above components reveals they are, for the most part, subjective feelings rather than objective conditions, and that a major portion of these subjective elements can be subsumed under Seeman's concepts of powerlessness, normlessness, and self-estrangement. It can also be seen that Marx's concept of alienation omits two components of alienation found in Seeman's article: meaninglessness and isolation. If one agrees with Daniel Bell that the concept of alienation must stand on its own feet apart from the crutch of Marx, and if it can be said that isolation and meaninglessness are significant components of alienation, Seeman's omission of the concept of reification may be compensated for. In addition, it has been pointed out by Russell Middleton that other components of alienation, including reification, may be dependent upon and be centered upon the concept of self-estrangement.[163]

While Bell (above) restricts contemporary usage of the term alienation to the dual meaning of "estrangement from society or community" and "reification," other usages have been exploring the dimension of "market orientation" (Seeman's normlessness). Alienation for Fromm involves idolatry of money and objectification of self as a thing to be employed successfully on the market rather than as an active agent.[164] Keniston focuses upon estrangement from society and self:

> In societies in which the transition from childhood to adulthood is unusually painful, young people often form their own "youth culture" with a special set of anti-adult values and institutions, in which they can at least temporarily negate the feared life of the adult. . . . [Self-alienation refers to] alienation of man from his own creative potentialities, imbedded in his fantasy life.[165]

Stroup has opened up still other dimensions of alienation, including in his typology indifference, isolation, self-estrangement, powerlessness, loneliness, meaninglessness, disenchantment, and anonymity.[166] By contrast, Greene has narrowed the concept to incapacity of role taking, "the wrenching or failure of role action by limitation of the abstractive."[167]

Empirical studies of the concept of alienation   While Seeman's and Marx's versions of alienation seem to be reconcilable as
psychological variables, a controversy goes on between those who
view alienation as a single unidimensional "global" condition of
man in the tradition of Marx, on the one hand, and those who agree
with Seeman, who insists that alienation consists of several independent variables or dimensions.[168] On this point, the empirical data
seems to be overwhelmingly in favor of the multidimension school.

The development of the recent empirical studies of alienation—
the concept—may best be viewed chronologically. In 1961, Dean,
in a study conducted in Columbus, Ohio, found that the three
dimensions, powerlessness, normlessness, and social isolation were
high intercorrelated, but there was enough independence between
them to warrent treatment as independent variables.[169] In 1963,
Middleton, in a study of residents of a small Southern city, found
a high intercorrelation between all of the Seeman variants except
isolation—evidence that alienation was not totally unidimensional.[170] That same year, Neal and Rettig published their finding
that powerlessness and normlessness, when controlled for socio-
economic status, were separate and unrelated dimensions.[171]

In 1964, Blauner showed that the generality of alienation varies
with the work setting. In unskilled assembly line work, workers are
alienated in multiple senses, while in the semi-skilled textile industry, workers suffer powerlessness and meaninglessness but not normlessness or isolation, due to close ties with fellow workers.[172] Recently, Neal and Rettig have shown that the different operational
measures of alienation do, in some degree, relate to a general theme
of alienation while contributing, at the time, to different portions
of its variance.[173] Thus, all empirical studies of alienation have
yielded the conclusion of at least some independence between alienation dimensions, in contrast to the Marxian assumption of generalized alienation.

In all fairness to the Marxian school, however, it should be
stated that all of the above studies have been limited to paper-and-
pencil questionnaire methodology. Thus, what is measured is conscious or verbal attitudes, and no attempt has been made to check
the validity of such measurements or the spuriousness of responses
through polygraph of even "lie scale" measurement. Future studies,
using projective devices such as the Rorschach or TAT, may yield
radically different conclusions. Since such studies have not been

done, the Marxian approach cannot be dismissed, in spite of the unanimity of the above findings.

Correlates of alienation   Though the empirical study of alienation began only a decade ago, there has been a multitude of studies correlating alienation with various social and psychological variables. Despite the plentitude of studies, alienation has been investigated in breadth but not depth. That is, alienation has been related to a long list of variables, but little replication of findings has been done. With these reservations, we can state in a preliminary way the direction of the findings.

Several studies have probed the causes of alienation (especially the variant "powerlessness"). Psychological studies have indicated that alienation is related to parental authority and is highest among those whose parents were either domineering or excessively lax,[174] especially and most frequently in the case of the mother's authority.[175] Generally, alienation (especially powerlessness) seems related to rejection in or exclusion from various group settings. It is directly related to isolation from peers[176] and being an outsider in high school.[177] Perhaps the most widely substantiated relationship is the inverse relationship between alienation and organizational participation (especially though not necessarily informal or voluntary organizations).[178]

In addition to these interpersonal contexts, alienation seems to be tied in with authority structure and social class position, or more generally "social structural variables." Alienation has been shown inversely related to social class standing,[179] inversely to level of position in a bureaucracy,[180] directly related to centralization and formalization of organizational structure,[181] and directly to the disparity between one's own position in a bureaucracy and one's supervisor's.[182]

The general conclusion emerging from these findings is that there is fertile soil in the study of alienation for both psychologists and sociologists to employ explanatory variables germane to their separate disciplines. Moreover, alienation might better be explored as a social psychological variable through interdisciplinary collaboration between psychologists and sociologists.

The most important question for our purposes is whether or not alienation has been shown relevant to the study of deviancy. One difficulty with such studies is that alienation has generally been measured with attitude questionnaires while deviance is generally studied through the analysis of official records (police arrest reports, court records, hospital admission records, coroners' reports, and the like). Nevertheless, there have been a few attempts to overcome these difficulties and to probe the relationship between alienation and deviance. In fact, one study indicated a general relationship between alienation and general deviance or non-conformity to the expectations of others.[183]

Two variants of alienation have been stressed in the deviance studies: isolation and powerlessness. Isolation has been found directly related to mental illness,[184] to extremist political behavior,[185] and to political deviancy.[186] One study of isolation deserves special note. Nettler correlated a scale of isolation with self-reported criminality, and discovered that the most alienated were not the most crime-prone, but rather that the moderately alienated were most criminal-istic.[187] The most alienated tended toward escapist offenses such as excessive use of alcohol or narcotics abuse, while the moderately alienated tended to perform hard core crime. While this study properly permits very little generalization, one cannot help speculating that extreme isolation may be conducive to either mental illness or extremist behavior or political deviancy, while criminal behavior appears to entail, as Merton has suggested, some degree of commitment to the values of the social system in which it occurs.

Powerlessness has received less attention empirically. It has been found positively related to religious liberalism,[188] and to failure to vote in local elections.[189] However, powerlessness has been shown to have little bearing on national political behavior.[190]

Actually, the number of studies cited above is relatively few in light of the importance of the topic of the relation between alienation and deviance. This may indicate that a number of investigators have had difficulty finding meaningful relationships between alienation or its components and various forms of deviancy. My own research has indicated such a difficulty in the case of juvenile delinquency.[191] I am not suggesting, however, that alienation is irrelevant to deviancy. If it is true that alienation has not "panned out" in studies of deviancy, there are two possible reasons for this failure.

First, the object of alienation is not specified so as to make it relevant to the form of deviancy at hand. For example, powerlessness in national political affairs might show no correlation with indices of crime, but powerlessness in local business affairs might indeed bear a relation to crime, for instance, white collar crime. Deviants and conformists alike may share alienation toward objects not germane to the deviancy at hand. This is not to say that larger alienation contexts are irrelevant to deviancy; they might be relevant cross-nationally. Thus, political powerlessness might lead to high rates of crimes in one nation as compared to another. Both powerlessness and crime might be part of a general cultural adaptation but not covariants of each other within a given society. Both might be learned through exposure to culture and not be related in a cause–effect sense.

Second, and related to the first point, most studies do not specify the group context of alienation. Blauner's study has shown the importance of specifying that group context.[192]

Both alienation and deviation can be viewed sociologically as outcomes of group experience. Inmates in a prison may feel powerless and may be inclined toward certain patterns of deviancy. Both are patterns of behavior learned through interaction with other inmates, and it may be only the more socially acute leaders within the inmate social system who make the intellectual connections between positional powerlessness and the necessity of deviancy. Other inmates may follow patterns set by leaders, without really sensing the relationship between attitude and behavior. Thus, what I am saying is that differences in alienation patterns and correlated patterns of deviancy may occur between different types of groups, but not necessarily between individuals. Individual correlations between alienation and deviancy may thus be relatively low without jeopardizing the parallel study of both variables.

THE NEED FOR COMPARATIVE STUDIES OF ALIENATION AND
DEVIANT BEHAVIOR

Throughout the last few pages, Kornhauser's systematic theory of mass society has largely been ignored in favor of the global studies of mass society and alienation perspective. However, this digression has not been without purpose. It seems that current usage of the term "mass society" is very close in meaning to what Kornhauser terms "pluralistic society." Mass society is seen as a highly industrialized, large-scale, bureaucratized, stable, and in other ways highly organized society whose participants are characterized by mass apathy and "alienation." Furthermore, data to be presented in a later chapter indicates that countries dominated by coercive governments are generally rampant with violence and intergroup conflict, and thus are by Kornhauser's definition, "mass societies." Thus, it will be suggested that two basic pathological group structures exist: one characterized by largeness and perhaps excessive stability (in the sense of making group intimacy unnecessary), and the other characterized by excessive group conflict and violence. The former might be characterized by individual attitudes of powerlessness, normlessness, meaningless (the essential components of Srole's anomia), while the latter might be conducive to violent, generalized, alienative attitudes (in the Marxian sense, unidimensional).

CRITICISM OF MASS SOCIETY THEORY

Criticisms of mass society theory have been quite similar to those addressed to the earlier social disorganization approach, underlining the similarity of the two approaches. For the most part, criticism has entailed denying that the underlying conditions for mass society are present in contemporary United States. As noted above, there are five basic conditions noted in mass society perspectives: (1) impersonality and the decline of kinship; (2) bureaucracy, secularization, and rationality; (3) social differentiation and specialization of tasks; (4) increasing social mobility; and (5) enlargement of scale or bigness.

Impersonality; kinship decline Opponents of mass society theory have stressed that urban, contemporary life may not be so void of kin and personal ties as has been assumed by mass society theorists and that the romantic view of the past found in mass society theory masks a number of undesirable features of previous social organization, such as the coercive, autocratic government of feudal society.[193] Several recent empirical studies have supported this view, showing that the majority of urban dwellers have regular and intimate contacts with friends, relatives, co-workers and neighbors.[194]

Bureaucracy, secularization, and rationality These are not necessarily negative features of modern society. They may be viewed, rather, as emancipating features of contemporary society, ensuring privacy, freedom of choice, equality of opportunity, consensus, mass education, mass affluence, and objectivity.[195]

Social differentiation and specialization It may be argued that social differentiation brings a new form of cohesion which results from functional interdependence and attraction of opposites.[196]

It has also been argued that the diverse aspects of functional differentiation are being counteracted by unifying, centralizing elements of modern society, mainly the state, mass education, mass media, and mass entertainment.[197]

Increased social mobility While social mobility may make for some degree of rootlessness, one could stress the liberating aspects of social movement and the expanding opportunity for freedom from material deprivation.

Bigness Larger scale enables greater output and less work for all. The current development of society cannot be set back. Smallness by itself may not be the problem.

Summary and conclusion

In the foregoing chapter it was shown that social disorganization is one among many deviance perspectives. Social disorganization theory developed in the United States largely as a reaction to progressivistic grand theory. The term disorganization came to refer basically to decline in consensus on meanings, norms, values, beliefs, and the like. The disorganization approach began to lose its foothold when it was subjected to severe criticism for its vagueness, conservative and middle-class value slant, lack of operational meaning, and dubious relevance to contemporary organization, even the organization of slums. The difficulty with disorganization theory may be seen retrospectively in that its advocates failed to consider alternative models of contemporary society described in historical social theory, such as the evolutionary model that views society as evolving toward more cohesive, more stable, and in other ways superior forms. Disorganization is a devolutionary theory, although its proponents did not label it as such or indicate their awareness of alternative types of societal development. Because of its difficulties, interest and usage have shifted in favor of anomie theory and mass society theory. The terms social disorganization, anomie, and mass society are, in fact, often used synonomously. These newer approaches are an improvement over disorganization theory in the sense that they are defined and made operational more precisely, more thoroughly researched, and viewed in a context of alternative images of society; however, these new approaches are to some extent "old wine in new bottles"! Much may and has been lost by ignoring earlier disorganization approaches, in the sense that mistakes made by these early approaches may be repeated by the newer approaches. It is my position that disorganization is still a useful concept, in fact one commonly used in sociology today, and yet since the movement to anomie and mass society theory, very little has been done to refine the concept of disorganization. Thus, it would be fruitful to redefine the concept of disorganization in terms of what these newer approaches can teach us. What I have suggested is that disorganization may be defined clearly and operationally in much the same terms as Durkheim used to describe anomie in his early work. As Durkheim stresses conflict between functions and resulting deregulation or normlessness in his concept of anomie, our new concept of disorganization entails a disruption of relations between the functioning parts of a social system jeopardizing the attainment of common values. In short, I am suggesting that there would be no harm done by treating disorganization, anomie, and mass society as virtually the same area or theory.

Looking at anomie theory and mass society theory, it can be seen that there is much to be gained from these approaches. Durkheim clarifies the nature of anomie by contrasting it with other forms of organization: mechanical solidarity, organic solidarity, and forced division of labor. Kornhauser performs the same service with the theory of mass society, contrasting mass society with communal society, pluralistic society, and totalitarian society.

A second major contribution of the new approaches has been the comparatively rigorous operationalization of concepts. Durkheim suggested that the four types of solidarity could be measured in terms of the extent of division of labor, of individualization, and of the types of law. Durkheim's discussion of personal reactions to social anomie is later elaborated and made more clear by Merton's delineation of types of adaptation to the situation of anomie. There are, however, important differences between Durkheim's and Merton's anomie. Merton stresses barred access to existing goals, which might be termed the "anomie of failure." By contrast, Durkheim stresses in his concept the striving for unattainable goals, nonexisting goals, or for a definition of goals, which might be termed the "anomie of success." Despite these differences, the discussions on personal counterparts of anomie have gone beyond in clarity and delineation the global, all-inclusive concept of personal disorganization, although capturing the essence of its meaning.

While mass society theory has not been extensively applied to the study of deviancy, it shows promise of perhaps being the next great emphasis in deviancy theory. One advantage is that while disorganization and anomie perspectives tend to localize deviancy in one sector or area of the country, mass society perspectives shift the emphasis to deviancy as a societal problem (as opposed to a problem of disorganized slums or inner-city areas). This shift in emphasis may lead sociologists to investigate deviancy in all sectors of the population. Thus, for example, the incidence of "hidden" crime and delinquency in middle- and upper-class areas may become of more concern to social investigators. Thus, with the mass society perspective comes a needed shift to concern with the "anomie of success." Related to mass society theory is the study of alienation, and this study provides a direct link with the multitude of deviancy theories which postulate alienation as a causal variable. The study of various types of alienation suggested by Melvin Seeman has import for understanding the attitudinal component of deviant behavior. The study of alienation bears directly on the topic of "anomie of failure" versus "anomie of success." A still more important byproduct of the study of alienation and deviancy is the linking current theories of deviancy with classic theories of alienation.

In the foregoing chapters of this text, the focus will shift to the study of deviancy proper. However, deviancy will be viewed at all times in terms of the social contexts discussed in this chapter and the two previous chapters.

The concept of deviancy

We have examined three alternative images of society that are relevant to the study of deviancy, all of which are possible frameworks to be utilized in the analysis of contemporary society. While contemporary deviancy writers focus on the anomie image of society, they ignore two other alternative perspectives:pluralistic and oligarchic organization. In this chapter it will be suggested not only that these alternatives are relevant to the study of deviancy, but that deviancy cannot be understood cross-culturally or cross-organizationally without considering these types as possibilities. In fact, in a later chapter it will be argued that the two alternative images better fit the cross-cultural data on deviancy that are available, and that the anomie image of society seems to have the greater utility not in describing modern or industrialized society, but rather in describing pre-industrial and transitional societies undergoing rapid industrialization and social change.

The nature of deviance: deviancy as an index and instrument of social change

There is a variety of perspectives on deviancy today, each representing a different perspective on social change and the nature of social organization.

Notes for this chapter are on pages 380–383.

DEVIANCY AS DISORGANIZING

The first and earliest of these views is that deviancy is strictly a negative phenomenon: undesirable, pathological maladjustment to be studied so that it can be predicted and controlled. Deviancy is viewed as strictly dysfunctional for society, in the sense that it disorganizes both society and the individual deviant, and because disorganization represents an abnormal disruptive breakdown of society, deviancy, which causes disorganization, must be eliminated. This view is seen in the following quote from a popular text on disorganization:

> In deviating from the expected group behavior, the deviant may weaken the group ties and thus contribute to social disorganization. The person who consistently deviates from many group norms becomes disorganized himself, so close is the relationship between the individual and society. Effective functioning of the group depends upon the relationships which bind the members together as a functioning whole. The deviant usually (although not always) weakens these group ties and himself at the same time.[1]

Horton has suggested that this definition of deviancy contains an implied value judgment as to whether society or man is more important.[2] The "transcendental" view holds society as more important than man, while the "immanent" conception views man as primary, with society developing to serve man. According to this analysis, the view above would hold society as superior and man as needing to "adjust" to the demands of society for the "good of all," rather than society organizing and reorganizing to meet the needs of man.

DEVIANCY AS RELATIVE TO STATISTICAL NORMS

Probably the most prevalent definition of deviancy is that of behavior relative to a statistical norm. This view recognizes that some deviations are viewed as normal and are tolerated in a given society and that what is deviancy in one society may not be so in another society. "Only those situations in which behavior is in a disapproved direction, and of sufficient degree to exceed the tolerance limit of the community, constitute *deviant behavior* as it will be used here."[3] Figure 4–1 illustrates this view of deviancy.

This view has merit in that it defines deviancy as culturally relative and a functioning of labeling of the deviant act within society.

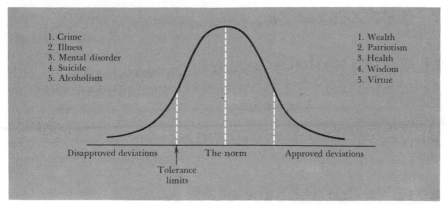

Figure 4–1.   The normal curve of conformity and deviance

Thus, this approach to deviancy allows objectivity, and permits the author to agree or disagree with society's definition of deviancy as such, in the light of the study of various forms of deviancy. The end result of this definition is not at variance with societal prescriptions. There is the implicit assumption that deviation beyond the tolerance limits of society is dangerous for society and for the individual.

> Deviant behavior that exceeds the tolerance limit of the community usually results in public action designed (*a*) to *protect* society, (*b*) to *reform* the offender, and (*c*) to *warn* everyone that deviations beyond a certain point will not be tolerated.[4]

This assumption of danger is shown even more by the way deviancy is approached in texts using this definition in such a way that various instances of deviancy are enumerated and explored separately, and it is suggested that these problems can be overcome through one or another treatment, therapy, or rehabilitation technique. Thus, usually in texts on deviancy it is assumed that it is better not to have deviant behavior than to have it, and that social problems would be best eliminated. Seldom is it acknowledged that because deviancy is relative to cultural and statistical norms, that certain forms of deviancy may actually prove functional if accepted as normal behavior in our society, as they have proven functional elsewhere.

DEVIANCY AS RELATIVE TO ABSOLUTE, UTOPIAN VALUES

Still another view is that deviancy cannot be defined in terms of the narrow, parochial norms of a given society, but can only be validly conceived as relative to the norms of utopian or ideal society.

This definition is congruent with the immanent conception of man discussed above. In terms of this definition a number of authors have attempted to redefine deviancy and conformity. Thus Fromm has redefined "mental health":

> Mental health is characterized by the ability to love and to create, by the emergence from incestuous ties to clan and soil, by a sense of identity based one's experience of self as the subject and agent of one's powers, by the grasp of reality inside and outside of ourselves, that is, by the development of objectivity and reason. . . . Mental health cannot be defined in terms of the "adjustment" of the individual to the society, but, on the contrary, that it must be defined in terms of the adjustment of society to the needs of man.[5]

Similarly, Goodman redefines "delinquency" in a positive vein as adaptive behavior oriented toward objects the society deprives of, while he views conformity to dominant society as leading only to apathy, disappointment, cynicism, and waste. Goodman asserts that what is usually seen by society as delinquent behavior could be better conceptualized on other ways.

> Let us expand the subject matter as a series of possible punishable relations obtaining between the boy struggling for life and trying to grow up, and the society that he cannot accept and that lacks objective opportunities for him. Roughly, we can name six importantly distinct stages in this series: (1) acts not antisocial if society had more sense, (2) acts that are innocent but destructive in their consequences and therefore need control, (3) acts antisocial in purpose, (4) behavior aimed at getting caught and punished, (5) gang fighting that is not delinquency yet must be controlled, and (6) delinquency secondarily created by society itself by treating as delinquents those who were not delinquent and by social attempts at prevention and reform.[6]

Likewise, Barron has seen delinquency as normal, purposive, adjustive behavior to frustrations and deprivations, and a means of self-expression where socially acceptable behavior has been thwarted.[7] In a similar way, Keniston has suggested that contemporary alienation and deviancy may be seen as a quest for new positive values to replace those that are held in question today.[8] Thus, in terms of the absolute value perspectives, what is currently regarded as deviancy may actually be conformity to absolute utopian norms and values, and what is regarded as conforming behavior may actually be a form of sickness, inhumanity, and alienation.

DEVIANCY AS AN INDEX AND INSTRUMENT OF SOCIAL CHANGE

Both the "transcendental" and the "immanent" approaches discussed above have their advantages and limitations. The "transcendental" view of deviancy has the advantage of commonness of usage and consensual agreement within society, but the disadvantage of carrying a commitment to the prevailing "order" in society, when order may actually be detrimental to the future welfare of society and its participants. The "immanent" view of deviancy has pejorative value as advocating change, and deviancy as fomenting that change, while lacking customary usage and consensual agreement, as well as having no other validity than that in the mind of the theorist who specifies the norms and values of the ideal utopian society. Although the "transcendental" view is almost universal in deviancy texts, the "immanent" view has received little or no recognition. Our perspective will be somewhere between the extremes of immanent and transcendental viewpoints. Some deviancy is functional for positive social change. Some is dysfunctional for positive social change. The decision about functionality may be independent of the current opinion regarding the seriousness of an act of deviancy. To say that deviancy is functional in terms of social change is not to say that deviancy is not painful, harmful, disruptive, and the like. Thus, patriots of the American Revolution may have been jailed in large numbers for having disobeyed colonial law, and yet their deviancy can in large part be held as accounting for American independence and freedom from colonial rule.

Because the prevailing emphasis in the study of deviancy is upon the dysfunctional aspects of deviant behavior, it would be well at this point to list some ways in which various forms of deviant behavior may be functional for society. The decision as to which forms of deviancy are functional or dysfunctional in our society cannot be dictated by this text, as it would involve several predictions and perspectives that cannot be indicated with any high degree of certainty: (*a*) the type of society in which we live, (*b*) the future changes and organization of society, and (*c*) appropriate innovations (deviations) that would facilitate that change. Nevertheless, several possibilities may be enumerated:

1. The first and most obvious way that deviancy may be functional is in the sense of cultural and physical innovation. Certain forms of deviant behavior, viewed negatively at first, are later

accepted as needed and positive innovations. There are many examples in the history of science. Sir Isaac Newton was nearly burned at the stake for contradicting the Copernican system of physics which was widely held at his time. Put even more broadly, following Durkheim, even negative deviancy—deviancy that never proves functional for society—may serve a purpose, in that its existence makes the norms more flexible, permitting creative deviancy to occur. Society cannot always distinguish creative from destructive deviancy. "Where crime exists, collective sentiments are sufficiently flexible to take on a new form, and crime sometimes helps to determine the form they will take."[9] Deviancy may bring to public attention ways of behaving that otherwise would have been considered impossible or not even imagined, and that later prove worthwhile. For example, Synanon, a communal, inter-racial, heterosexual colony of ex-drug addicts, organized for self-help, has met resistance in all communities in which it has attempted to organize, but it has received considerable recognition, and its methods are being used in prison settings today.

2. Deviancy may be functional, in the sense that without it collective sentiments would be ill-defined and less capable of forming the basis for mass action. "Crime is, then, necessary; it is bound up with the fundamental conditions of all social life, and by that very fact it is useful, because these conditions of which it is a part are themselves indispensable to the normal evolution of morality and law."[10]

3. The deviant may symbolize and expound upon an alternative norm and value system which otherwise might not be considered by society, but which is later accepted and proves functional for society. "Socrates was a criminal, and his condemnation was no more than just. However, his crime, namely, the independence of his thought, rendered a service not only to humanity but to his country. It served to prepare a new morality and faith which the Athenians needed, since the traditions by which they had lived until then were no longer in harmony with the current conditions of life."[11]

4. Deviancy in the form of violent conflict may prove functional in a number of ways described by various "conflict theories." Conflict leads to communication and association, it may integrate a group and resolve tension between contrasting ideas, it may define boundaries and provide a basis for balance of divergencies, it serves to preserve individuality against the threat of enslavement, it may

provide a form of play or recreation—perhaps reducing hostility, it may lead to greater intimateness within a group, it may lead to revolution and reformulation of group objectives, and it may lead to the individual's sense of devotion to larger group ties.[12]

Because our theme is that deviancy can be either functional or dysfunctional, the purpose of this book will not be to suggest panaceas for solving the contemporary problems of deviancy or for controlling them. We will examine contemporary problems in their social context with an eye to their functionality (or dysfunctionality) and to the direction of social and institutional change necessary to ameliorate these problems. The emphasis will be not upon eliminating or "curing" deviancy, but the socio-cultural conditions that foster it. The final outcome of our quest will be a vision of the necessary social changes for improvement of contemporary social life, and the correction of deviant behavior is only one criterion of that improvement. Our goal should be to specify the conditions under which our society could be more pleasant for both deviants and conformists, such that it is possible to have a new kind of commitment from those who may have previously conformed fearfully or reluctantly.

Typologies of deviancy

A brief look at the table of contents of any text on deviancy or social disorganization will show that most of what is generally termed deviancy is covered under the topic of "crime." Thus, the study of deviancy includes for the most part such problems as theft, murder, white collar crime, professional crime, organized crime, drug addiction, alcoholism, forgery, prostitution, vandalism, sex crime, homosexuality, and the like. This link between deviancy and the study of crime is so great that in various cross-reference indexes—for example, *Sociological Abstracts*—the concepts of deviancy and disorganization are cross-referenced to the concept of crime. The study of criminology is often considered synonymous with the study of social disorganization. However, the study of deviancy does include other problems, notably mental disorder, divorce, intergroup relations, and suicide (although suicide is sometimes considered a crime).

Nevertheless, because the scope of the study of crime is so broad, it is proper that in developing a general typology of deviancy we begin with crime. This will prove valuable for a number of reasons: First, more typologies have been developed for criminal behavior than for any other area of deviancy. Second, an examination of types of crime and criminals will yield insights germane to the study of other forms of deviancy. Third, and related to the second point, our approach will view crime on a continuum with other social problems. Because crime refers to the largest group of specific problems, our continuum typology will probably be more inclusive if we approach the problem of taxonomy from the point of view of crime.

The object of our quest will be to produce a continuum that can be used for viewing a large variety of current forms of deviant behavior. This continuum will also provide a theoretical basis for an empirical rank-ordering of deviancy acts, this rank-ordering to be tested out through opinion and attitude survey.

CRIME TYPOLOGY

There are various ways of classifying crime and the criminal. Although much confusion arises from the fact that type of crime and type of criminal are separate phenomena, in actual usage these are often mixed or considered concurrently. It will be shown below that evaluation of a criminal act generally involves some evaluation of its perpetrator and his possible motives and background. These evaluations may or may not be valid; nevertheless, it is a fact that they do exist in public opinion. Ultimately, it will be argued that the most reasonable way of viewing crime will be to take into account both the characteristics of the criminal and of the criminal act itself. This is useful to theory, in the sense that it corresponds to public attitude and reaction to crime, and it is this reaction to crime that may explain the prevalence or absence of various forms of crime in different group or societal settings. Thus, in certain countries, violence is expected and considered normal in certain circumstances and is prevalent in those countries, while in other countries theft may be expected and normal. This reaction to and tolerance of various forms of crime may be shown even more generally to tie in with characteristics of a society's social organization, as discussed in previous chapters. In countries in which there is great emphasis upon conformity to tradition (namely, Durkheim's "mechanical solidarity"), violence is seen as a normal means of ensuring that conformity. By contrast, in countries characterized by constant change and diversity of functions, there is less tolerance of violence, which is seen as jeopardizing solidarity, but greater toleration of innovation of both the legitimate and quasi-legitimate type, on the assumption that certain quasi-legitimate operations may one day be conceived as legitimate.

As a means of approaching a general typology, let us first look at some common typologies, for they contain various aspects that will contribute to a final all-inclusive typology.

A number of typologies of crime are available for consideration, and each should be critically evaluated for strengths and weaknesses. Probably the most influential typologies to which we are exposed are the legal typologies and the sociological typologies. Legal typologies are those that are actually applied by the public at large and by legal authorities within our society. In addition, a number of typologies have been suggested by sociologists as either alternatives to legal typologies or as bases for understanding legal typologies.

Legal typologies   The most elementary legal typology is the legal classification of different offenses—murder, burglary, arson— terms referring to specific actions or behaviors involved.

Most of these crimes are defined by the statutes of each state, which definitions are derived historically from English Common Law. Take, for example, the offense called "murder." Most states define murder as:

> The crime of killing a person under circumstances precisely de- fined by statute: as A: first-degree murder that deserves either capital or severe punishment because of being willful and premeditated, being committed with atrocity or cruelty, being committed in the course of the commission of a serious felony (as arson, burglary, or kidnapping), or being committed after lying in wait for the purpose of killing the victim B: second-degree murder that in most states is all other murder not classified as first-degree murder.[13]

In the same way a multitude of definitions of various offenses are specified in the law. The major difficulty with the offense typol- ogy is it may contain overlapping categories that are not mutually exclusive. Thus, quite often police have difficulty determining which offense category to use in a given instance. Another difficulty is that without some auxiliary typology, offenses cannot be viewed in groups whose characteristics are similar. One may also question whether or not these typologies contain all elements of the specific situations, including the particular circumstances of a crime and the nature of the offender–victim relationships. Thus, in extreme cases some inequities may occur before the law. A 41-year-old man who sexually assaults a 6-year-old girl may be charged with the same offense (forcible rape) as a 21-year-old man who seduces a bar maid.[14] In our quest for an improved typology of crime, however, we may not be able to improve much upon those acts specified in the statutes, but may be able to provide a basis for subclassifying offenses in terms of seriousness categories. Our quest will focus instead upon finding the most suitable general typologies for grouping these particular offenses.

Legal authorities have long been aware of this limitation of the offense typology, and two more general legal typologies are designated in criminal law, the first based upon the penalty attached to a given offense and the second based upon the nature of the object of the act. The former include *felonies,* defined basically as offenses punished by state or federal detention for at least one year, and *misdemeanors,* those punished by county detention of less than one year. The classification of offenses as either felonies or misdemeanors derived from judicial precedent, and consequently there are no clear-cut, objective criteria for classifying an act as a felony or a misdemeanor. Thus the felonies–misdemeanors typology is not specified operationally, this lack leading to difficulties. A felony in one jurisdiction may be a misdemeanor in another.

The lack of objective criteria for distinguishing felonies and misdemeanors leads to a certain amount of arbitrariness in the application of justice. For example, two men engage in a street fight and one is seriously injured. If the case is brought to court, both may be charged with "disorderly conduct," a misdemeanor, or one may be charged with assault, possibly a felony depending upon the judge's perception of the nature of the situation. He may be called upon in instances like this to exercise his judgment without the counsel of objective criteria for making a choice of legal labels specified in the law. This may explain why much effort in the social sciences has been directed at determining such criteria.

Before we dismiss the topic of legal typologies, it should be pointed out that some attempts have been made to classify crimes by some objective standard. The first of these has to do with the object of criminal offense. In terms of object or goal orientation, crimes are typed as: crimes against person, crimes against property, and crimes against public order. While such a typology incorporates goal orientation as a consideration, and is thus operational, it leaves out considerations of punishment attached or seriousness of offenses, and has not been systematically linked with the typology of felonies–misdemeanors.

Perhaps the most rigorous of all legal typologies is that developed by the Federal Bureau of Investigation. The classification

TABLE 4-1 Uniform Classification of Offenses

Part 1
1. Criminal homicide
   (*a*) Murder and nonnegligent manslaughter
   (*b*) Manslaughter by negligence
2. Forcible rape
3. Robbery
4. Aggravated assault
5. Burglary—breaking and entering
6. Larceny—theft (except auto theft)
   (*a*) Fifty dollars and over in value
   (*b*) Under fifty dollars in value
7. Auto theft

Part 2
8. Other assaults
9. Arson
10. Forgery and counterfeiting
11. Fraud
12. Embezzlement
13. Stolen property: buying, receiving, possessing
14. Vandalism
15. Weapons: carrying, possessing, etc.
16. Prostitution and commercialized vice (except forcible rape)
17. Sex offenses: prostitution and commercialized vice
18. Narcotics drug laws
19. Gambling
20. Offenses against the family and children
21. Driving under the influence
22. Liquor laws
23. Drunkenness
24. Disorderly conduct
25. Vagrancy
26. All other offenses
27. Suspicion
28. Curfew and loitering laws (juvenile)
29. Runaway (juvenile)

SOURCE: John Edgar Hoover, *Crime in the United States: Uniform Crime Reports,* 1966.

contains 29 categories, as seen in Table 4–1. These are used in standardizing the reporting of crimes by local agencies. The offenses are reported not according to the specific designations of criminal law but by the code numbers and title used in the uniform classification.

Though the FBI classification is more rigorous and systematic than the other legal classifications, it really does not carry analysis much further, as it is a more or less arbitrary classification. There is an implied typology of seriousness in the selection of seven crimes—criminal homicide, forcible rape, robbery, aggravated assault, burglary, larceny, and auto theft—as "index crimes," those used in a regional or state "total crime index." The implication is that these crimes represent "real crime." These seven crimes were selected in 1927 and modified in 1958 by a special advisory committee of the International Association of Chiefs of Police on the basis of three criteria: seriousness, frequency, and reliability of reporting from citizens to police.[15]

The major limitation of the UCR typology is that it excludes from consideration as serious offenses a number of crimes that would ordinarily be considered serious (e.g. arson, drug abuse, and homosexual behavior). Furthermore, the UCR typology makes only gross distinctions (Part 1 *vs.* Part 2 offenses) and does not provide a basis for rank, ordering crimes in terms of their seriousness or forming a continuum, which we have stated as the objective of our quest.

Psychological typologies   A number of psychological typologies of crime and delinquency have been developed primarily by psychiatrists using a Freudian framework of ego–id–superego (see the discussion of Freud in Chapter 2). These have been summarized and reviewed by Ferdinand.[16]

Alexander and Staub propose a two-way typology of *chronic* and *accidental* criminal types. Accidental crime results from "unkind fate" and has two subtypes: *mistaken* crime, due to the weakening of the ego by circumstances; and *situational* crime, due to the weakening effects of crisis. While *accidental* crime is due to environmental circumstances, *chronic* criminality arises from the psychological make-up of the criminal. There are five variations of ego, id, and superego among chronic types: *organic or toxic types,* including mental defectives, alcoholics, drug addicts; *compulsive* types, in which unconscious needs keep breaking through to otherwise sublimated, normal personality; *neurotic* types, distinguished from the compulsive only by a more willing ego; the *normal criminal,* whose superego actually contains criminal standards; and the *genuine criminal,* whose behavior is motivated purely by the id.[17]

Abrahamsen, like Alexander and Staub, distinguishes *chronic offenders* from *momentary offenders.* For momentary offenders, illegal behavior is traced to unusual circumstances, while for chronic offenders, delinquency is immediately related to psychodynamics. Momentary offenders are of three types: *situational,* those confronted with an irresistible though illegal opportunity; *accidental,* who suffer from a lapse in judgment; and *associational,* drawn into crime by friends. *Chronic offenders* include *neurotic offenders,* driven by an irresistible compulsion but haunted by guilt; those with *character disorders,* driven by compulsion without guilt; *psychotics* and *mental defectives,* compelled to crime by mental illness or defect; and *cultural delinquents,* directed to crime by a faulty superego that leads to identification with a criminal way of life.[18]

Sanford describes a similar typology, but because his typology focuses upon prison inmates, it neglects the accidental or momentary offender described in the above typologies. Sanford sees essentially three types of chronic offenders, based upon variations of ego and superego: *Presocial criminals* are characterized by weak superego and ego. *Antisocial criminals* have both strong superego and strong ego, which the criminal has rebelled against, and he must neutralize his guilt by constant reassurance from compatriots. The *asocial criminal* has a strong ego but weak superego.[19]

Weinberg has suggested still another psychological typology of criminals, based primarily upon the presence or absence of affectionate ties in childhood. The *true psychopath*—egocentric, irresponsible, and impulsive—has had few if any childhood attachments. The *acting-out neurotic* is capable of forming attachments, but due to inner hostility becomes alienated and inevitably isolated from his relations. The *self-centered, overindulged person,* typically exploitative, and unscrupulous, has had some emotional ties with parents or one parent, usually the mother. Finally, the *cultural delinquent* has had affectional relations which, however, have enculturated him with a deviant value system.[20]

Ferdinand has suggested that these typologies can be synthesized into an all-inclusive three-fold scheme.[21] The *impulsive delinquent* is characterized either by undeveloped superego or excessive id development. The *neurotic delinquent* suffers from conflicts between a more-or-less normal id and superego which the ego cannot reconcile. The *symptomatic delinquent* suffers from excessive id pressure, but differs from *impulsive delinquency* by indirect rather than direct acting out.

The impulsive delinquent type contains four variations: the *unsocialized child* pattern, characterized by inoperative superego; the *self-centered, indulged delinquent,* with an intense and volatile emotional structure; the *psychopath,* characterized by uninhibited exploitative desires; and the *sexual pervert,* primarily characterized by abnormal sex desires.

The neurotic delinquent type contains two subtypes: the *inadequate delinquent,* whose socialized ego cannot handle responsibilities, the conflict being resolved through aggression: and the *crystalized delinquent* who uses delinquency as a way to banish guilt, for example, through combative gang delinquency.

The symptomatic delinquent type contains three sub-types, each characterized by a particular indirect expression of unconscious desire: the *kleptomaniac,* whose pilfering symbolizes attempted recovery of something lost, such as the castrated penis; the *pyromaniac,* whose interest in fire-setting may represent an indirect way of gaining urethal pleasure; and the *sexual delinquent,* whose primary fear is that of being castrated.

While the above typologies may appear at first to be relatively confusing, as Ferdinand has pointed out, there seems to be a common core of analysis which, in fact, may be used to tie the various concepts into one typology. Most of the conceptual types mentioned above refer to some variation of ego–id–superego combinations. A meaningful polar typology can be constructed, as seen in Figure 4–2, if concepts referring to *dominant id* or *faulty superego* (which implies weak ego and superego) are polarized at one end, concepts referring to dominant *superego* (implying repressed id forces) at the other, and concepts referring to id–superego conflict mediated through ego are in the middle. Such a typology has the advantage of rank-ordering psychological criminal types in a sense from most serious or threatening to society (id dominant) to least serious to society (superego dominant). The merit of this approach furthermore is to make the psychological typologies complementary to social types that will be discussed below. Specifically, it will be shown that the deviant act or the offender can be classified socio-

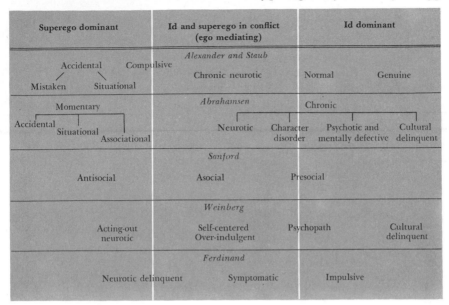

Figure 4–2.   Psychological typologies on the Id–Superego continuum

logically as to value orientation such that a value orientation can be said to correspond with a drive state. If an offender has a faulty superego, it can be said that his value orientation is likely to be "subterranean" rather than conventional, while offenders who are conscience-stricken by their deviancy may hold the dominant values of society as their primary orientation.

Social typologies   Social typologies are as numerous and diverse as psychological typologies. Each has its own limitations. Although the psychological typologies can be viewed roughly in terms of the amount of libidinous *need* gratification, social typologies focus upon the environmental counterparts of needs: *values* and the means to obtaining these values. Although there are a multitude of social typologies, four deserve special note here. Two of these stress the extent of orientation of the criminal toward social or antisocial values. Another focuses upon the acquisition by illegitimate means of obtaining these values. A fourth typology is eclectic, drawing from a variety of minor typologies, and seems to incorporate both the idea of illegitimate means and value orientations.

Clinard's Typology: Focus on Illegitimate Means. [22]   One way to view crime and crimes is the extent to which the individual has been socialized to the techniques and ideologies of criminals. This refers to the extent to which crime has become a career or profession. Clinard argues that individual criminals can be classified in terms of their degree of professionalization. He classifies some typical crimes on a continuum from career to non-career crimes, based upon role crystallization, identification, and progression in crime. Such a scale indicates a measure of "criminality" better than the above legal typologies. It could provide a feasible basis for revision of criminal statutes and related penalties. Sex offenders, for example, are considered a "good risk" in terms of rehabilitation as they are in general non-career types, and should receive a lenient sentence for their offenses. Bank robbers, on the other hand, are professional offenders and should be more severely dealt with. Thus, one could use Clinard's classification to distinguish felonies from misdemeanors.

While Clinard does not suggest any particular usage of his typology, if one were to apply his typology in this way it might prove awkward in certain cases. For example, murderers are non-career types and would thus be treated leniently, while pickpockets are career types and would be treated severely. In the most extreme case, this application would involve setting murderers free and executing pickpockets.

This application would no doubt be functional in terms of maximizing rehabilitation of offenders. Offenders least inclined to continue a career are leniently treated, while career criminals are severely treated. However, in other ways and in terms of other applications, such an application might prove dysfunctional.

Clinard's typology would have its least application in small towns or communities in which a crime has come to public attention. In Durkheim's words, in such communities there is a mechanical form of solidarity, a common agreement upon norms and values, which is threatened by crimes against basic common values. In sanctioning a deviant act repressively, society is not concerned with the welfare of the deviant. In fact, society is at war with the deviant because he has threatened society's basis of solidarity. In small societies, if severe normative deviations are allowed to exist, social disorganization will occur.

This occurs, although to a lesser degree, in large-scale societies, especially where a criminal offense has become publically known, such as an offense against a well-liked government official. An assassination of a President leads to a public reaction against the offender which makes the death sentence a mild penalty for his crime.

In sum, Clinard's typology can be criticized as containing no reference to the value-orientation of an offense—whether or not a basic societal value has been breached, thus threatening the solidarity of society.

On the other hand, in certain cases, lenient punishment of a crime may be functional for society if society's organization is inappropriate to its scale or size. Large-scale societies whose organization is absolutistic (pseudo-mechanical) may well benefit by a permissive judiciary. The Nuremberg trials showed that the judiciary plays an essential role as a check against totalitarianism through its application of the law.

Ferdinand's Eclectic Social Typology. While Clinard's typology emphasizes socialization to illegitimate means and ignores acceptance or rejection of conventional or antisocial values, a typology constructed by Ferdinand seems to take all of these factors into account.[23] Ferdinand identifies six separate patterns of delinquent behavior: (1) the mischievous–indulgent pattern, (2) the aggressive–exploitative pattern, (3) the criminal pattern, (4) the fighting pattern, (5) a theft pattern, and (6) the disorganized acting-out pattern.

The *mischievous–indulgent* pattern includes such acts as vandalism, sexual indulgence, consumption of liquor, and unsystematic property crimes. Such a pattern characterizes the weakly integrated, marginal cliques of alienated, unsuccessful youngsters in upper upper-class private schools.

The *aggressive–exploitative* pattern refers to the interclique fracases, drinking bouts, and sexual licentiousness, which characterizes lower upper-class and upper middle-class youngsters. Such activity is pursued by well-organized clubs and groups, only moderately alienated from the adult community, and more or less without the knowledge of the adult community. The remaining typologies are characteristically lower class.

The *criminal* pattern characterizes upper lower-class youngsters oriented toward a career in lower-class crime. Despite this and a relative rejection of middle-class norms, the youngsters neither reject nor are rejected by the adults in the community and are loosely organized in cliques subordinate to adult criminals in the community.

By contrast, the vicious, marauding *fighting pattern,* also characteristic of the upper lower class, involves a tight gang organization, a disorganized community setting, and an alienated relationship between the delinquent and the adult community.

The *theft pattern,* like the *criminal pattern,* characterizes the upper lower class and is tolerated by the community, but involves nonutilitarian adventurous theft, vandalism, and some combat and sexual activity.

Lastly, the *disorganized acting-out pattern* is a largely structureless pattern of theft, narcotics use, appetite indulgence, and assault characterizing the lower lower-class, inner-city slum.

Ferdinand's typology is derived eclectically through combining features of several typologies, and as was pointed out above, it seems to incorporate reference to both illegitimate means and value orientations. Thus, in both the *mischievous–indulgent pattern* and the *aggressive–exploitative pattern,* typical and somewhat conventional values (sex, liquor, material goods, thrills) are achieved through illicit means (fake I.D's, secret clandestine parties, hidden pilfering, and the like). The same is true of the *theft pattern* and *criminal pattern,* except that in these two patterns, especially the criminal pattern, there is greater commitment to and involvement in illegitimate means. By contrast, the *fighting* and *disorganized acting-out pattern* involve both an endorsement of antisocial values (such as the narcotic stupor) and illicit means to those values (theft, violence).

One difficulty with Ferdinand's typology, however, is that it was derived intuitively, and the "means–ends" distinctions are not explicit. In the next two typologies, the focus will shift to antisocial ends made explicit in the typology.

A Typology of Convicted Offenders. Another typology is given in the President's Crime Commission Report, based on a 1956 NIMH project which cross-tabulated a number of delinquency typology systems.[24] The typology is a four-fold scheme based upon acceptance or rejection of conventional norms and values. The *prosocial offender* is one who actually holds conventional norms and values but may have committed an impulsive act due to extraordinary environmental pressures—for instance, a crime of violence or a naively executed property offense. The offender suffers great remorse and is unlikely to repeat his offense and thus requires little or no punishment or treatment. By contrast the *antisocial offender,* usually from a disorganized family, rejects societies norms and values, blaming society for his condition. Group therapy is recommended in redirecting normative value orientations, self-concept, and attitudes toward associations. Also rejecting conventional standards is the *pseudosocial manipulator,* who because of a hostile, competitive family and environmental background is resistant to any kind of treatment. The *asocial offender* lacks any background of intimate relations, cannot identify with others, and spontaneously acts out primitive impulses. The last requires elementary training in human relations.

While this typology is similar to psychological typologies above, it qualifies as a social typology in that its major comparative parameter is the value orientation of the offender.

Cavan's Typology. Cavan has proposed still another typology, also based primarily upon the value orientation of the offender.[25] Hers is a typology of both criminal and delinquent offenses. However, since the typologies are essentially similar, her typology of criminal offenses will be discussed here. Cavan utilizes a normal curve to portray seven separate adaptations representing degrees of criminality. Not all of her categories, however, are criminal adaptations. They include: (1) criminal contraculture (underworld), (2) "average" conformity, (3) minor underconformity, (4) extreme underconformity, (5) minor overconformity, (6) extreme overconformity, and (7) ideological contraculture (reform groups). Of these types, only 1–4 and perhaps 7 are conceivably criminal types.

The most extreme adaptation, *contracultural criminality,* is that of the professional criminal, the drug addict, and the participant in organized crime. These reject society and identify with crime as a way of life, and are rejected by society, as shown by their imprisonment when caught.

The *extreme underconformer* commits systematic and irresponsible offenses, but is ambivalent about criminal values and crime as a way of life.

The *minor underconformer* accepts conventional values and views himself as a conventional person, but commits occasional offenses. While the minor underconformer is tolerated, the extreme underconformer is disapproved of by the community. Cavan recognizes that there are also some offenses committed by "average" conformers, including white collar crime, pilfering, casual offenses, and cooperation with organized crime. Such behavior is actually approved by the conventional community and the offender considers himself a law-abiding citizen.

The *minor overconformer* and the *extreme overconformer* are somewhat disapproved because of his exact, rigid obedience to law and social norms, while the *contracultural overconformer* may actually be rejected because of his fanatical and insistent adherence to ultimate standards of culture, such as Puritanism, asceticism, or conscientious objection. Thus, the contracultural overconformer may become involved in criminal behavior due to the extremity of his departure from "normal deviancy."

Constructive typology In the above analysis a number of typologies have been examined, each representing a particular point of view. Most of these in a way may be seen as attempts to rank-order offenses or offenders in terms of the seriousness of the deviant act committed. One decisive advantage of this approach is that typologies seen in this way are not merely nominal classification schemes but also ordinal or rank-order schemes, which are more meaningful in that relationships between types are quite clear. Thus, the common denomination in these typologies is the criterion of seriousness—each typology however viewing seriousness from a somewhat different point of view. Clinard seems to view seriousness from the point of view of the capacity of the offender for rehabilitation. Ferdinand presents essentially a nominal scheme. However, implicit in this scheme is the view that crimes can be distinguished in terms of the goal-orientation of the offender or perhaps typical patterns of behavior. This value criterion is made even more explicit in the President's Crime Commission typology, and forms the basis for Cavan's typology.

Like the psychological typologies presented above, the social typologies may be viewed (see Table 4–2) on a continuum of conventional *versus* antisocial value orientation. It is interesting to note the parallel between the psychoanalytic id–superego dichotomy and the social dichotomy of conventional *versus* antisocial values orientation noted in parentheses in Table 4–2. This further substantiates the view that the various typologies can be grouped into rank-order seriousness categories. Only Clinard's typology is excluded, in that his typology refers primarily to the background of the criminal rather than the motive or intent of the criminal act. However, though the value dimension is the primary one in evaluating the seriousness of different types of crime, it would be unrealistic and out of touch with both court practice or public opinion to evaluate the seriousness of a deviant act (and what type of act it is) without considering the past history of the deviant. A hardened gangster found guilty of, say, sale of narcotics, would justifiably be treated less leniently than an adolescent first-offender. Thus, our final typology will contain reference to both value and career aspects of seriousness. Each of these typologies has its advantages and disadvantages. We have found the disadvantages of one typology overcome by another typology. None of the typologies we have considered have overcome all criticisms. It would be well to develop a typology incorporating all advantages, in order to be able to make decisions concerning certain acts of delinquency and crime.

Such a typology could provide a basis for distinguishing felonies and misdemeanors which as yet is not clear in the law. Our typology must include a general measure of *seriousness*. It must incorporate the factor of social rejection accompanying an act. The more serious acts imply a rejection of the offender by society, but also imply a rejection of society by the offender. In part, seriousness can be measured by value orientation of the act. Our typology must also incorporate some reference to the career-nature of an act. If an act is probably that of a chronic offender, it should be given a more severe sanction.

What results is essentially a typology of two dimensions: (1) Value orientation—whether the offender's orientation might be

TABLE 4-2   Social typologies viewed on a polar continuum of conventional versus antisocial value orientation

Conventional value orientation ("Ego mediating")			Antisocial value orientation ("Id motivated")	
		Ferdinand		
Mischievous–indulgent	Aggressive–exploitative	Theft–criminal	Fighting	Disorganized–acting-out
		PCC		
Prosocial	Pseudosocial manipulator		Asocial	Antisocial
		Cavan		
"Average" conformity	Minor underconformity	Extreme underconformity		Contracultural criminality

"normal" or "contracultural", and (2) career orientation—whether the offender might be a chronic or first time offender.

Cavan incorporates only crime and delinquency into her typology; however, there is ample basis for incorporating most other major forms of deviance into the typology. There is reason to believe that mental disorder, suicide, and minority-group prejudice may be conceptualized in terms of "overconformity". In agreement with the analysis, these disorders are found to be in contrast to crime and delinquency in a number of ways. While crime may be a product of gang or nongang association, mental disorder, suicide, and prejudice have been widely traced to an absence of or estrangement from association. All can be conceptualized in terms of response to stress, anxiety, and frustration resulting in an attempt at compulsive conformity with traditional parental standards as opposed to changing standards of society, while most crime may be viewed as a rebellion against parental standards in favor of new standards.

It can be seen that perhaps what Cavan means by "overconformity" is strict conformity to parental standards (that is, philistine adaptation) rather than to contemporary peer group norms and values. Furthermore, what Cavan means by "overconformity" is what Merton means by "ritualism," and thus much of the problem that the overconformer faces is that his ultraconformity to parental conceptions of legitimate means may hamper pursuit of various success goals. However, remembering Merton's analysis, it can be seen that if this conformity is carried too far, it becomes retreatism, thus entailing rejection of both legitimate means and conventional values (and thus leading to public rejection and condemnation as contracultural behavior).

Our three types of deviancy—mental disorder, suicide, and prejudice—may be viewed in this framework. Prejudice may be seen as a way of coping with stress and frustration, as are other neurotic defense mechanisms. Psychotic "breakdown," however, may occur if prejudice and neurotic defense mechanisms fail to cope with stress. What about suicide? Is suicide a form of mental disorder? Clearly it is not, and in fact studies show a low correlation between suicide and mental disorder.[26] However, the difference may only be one of time and development. Most forms of psychosis develop over long periods of time and in fact are usually traced to childhood experiences. By contrast, suicide may be largely the adaptation of an individual to an extremely and suddenly disruptive and stressful experience. Thus it is possible to view both psychosis and suicide as retreatist phenomena.

The argument that I have been developing as to the three forms of deviancy—mental disorder, suicide, and prejudice—depends upon three types of evidence: (1) that these disorders are a response to or concomitant of "overconformity" or conformity to traditional standards (and a rejection of current ones), (2) that such deviancy results from or is concomitant with isolation from peer-group association, and (3) that the public rejects these disorders in rank-ordered degrees in accord with the amount of "overconformity" and "loss of touch with reality" that can now be seen as referring to the reality of contemporary standards (rather than material reality *per se*). Let us examine the evidence on these three propositions.

SUICIDE, MENTAL DISORDER, AND PREJUDICE AS OVERCONFOMITY

These three problems have much in common, but let us first look at mental disorder, then prejudice and neurotic defense, and then suicide.

The most frequent form of psychosis is schizophrenia, and it is the most researched disorder. Studies have shown, in accord with our framework, that the schizophrenic is an overconformist to adult standards, an over-achiever, a "shut in" or "seclusive" personality smothered by maternal guidance, a highly anxious individual, one whose aspirations are beyond abilities, one with strict disciplinarian family background, one with over-protective parents, and one whose schizophrenic breakdown was precipitated by environmental circumstances which make it impossible to conform to these expectations.[27] There is even some evidence that the schizophrenic thinks of himself as conforming to an ordered, traditional system, though one which is not understood by the average person.[28] In a sense, then, the neurotic is one who is somewhat capable of conforming to parental traditional standards, while the psychotic cannot, due to the circumstances, and therefore suffers a break with reality.[29]

The relation of prejudice to overconformity is a little less obvious than psychosis. Studies have shown that prejudice is a widespread phenomenon in American society and perhaps characteristic of the "average man."[30] Myrdal and Williams have argued that racism and group superiority themes are part of American culture. While it may be that most Americans harbor racist and prejudiced beliefs or adhere to them unwittingly, the "all-out racist" or "authoritarian personality" is nevertheless viewed as a deviant by most people. Thus, studies have found that authoritarian personality and extreme forms of prejudice are associated with "status concern," "enhanced status striving," downward social mobility, frustration, and the like.[31] Quite congruent with our view, then, is the general theme that the prejudiced person is one who fears rejection and failure and thus overconforms to what he considers to be a tradition of racism and group superiority in American society.

In a similar way, suicide has been found correlated with overconformity. Durkheim's anomic suicide is one traced to a sudden disruption of life goals of an individual who is overinvolved in the social order—for instance, the world of work.[32] Henry and Short have argued that suicide is aggression expressed inward toward self, where the individual cannot direct aggression toward others due to constraints about the expression of aggression—that is, "overconformity."[33]

Isolation and overconformity The major arena of goal frustration for the overconformist is interpersonal ties. The isolate is one rejected from a group, physically or psychologically or both. A typical response to this isolation process is overconformity to what the individual conceives are group standards. There is growing evidence of a high relation between schizophrenia and isolation from peer group ties.[34] There is some evidence that the authoritarian personality or highly prejudiced person is "isolated in association."[35] Lastly, since the beginnings of the study of suicide, suicide has been found correlated with various indices of isolation.[36]

Rejection and overconformity Finally, our whole argument rests upon the premise that suicide, mental disorder, and racism are subject to public rejection. There is mounting evidence that the mentally ill and even the topic of mental illness are both rejected to the extent of severity.[37] One study bears directly on this question. Phillips found that the public rejects the mentally ill in terms of the severity of mental illness in the following order: (1) normal, (2) phobic–compulsive, (3) simple schizophrenic, (4) depressed neurotic, and (5) paranoid schizophrenic.[38] Phillips also found a rejection to the degree that specialized professional help is sought for mental disorder.[39] National studies indicate that the mentally ill are viewed prejudicially and categorically in terms of stereotypes of violent and unpredictable behavior to be dealt with by confinement in a mental hospital.[40]

There have been few if any studies to document the extent of public acceptance or rejection of extreme racism and authoritarianism, probably because the focus in most studies has been upon the widespread nature of prejudice. However, some evidence of rejection is given by the fact that the Ku Klux Klan has been listed as a subversive organization by the U.S. Attorney General. Similarly, there is little or no evidence on public attitudes toward suicide, but suicide is against the law in most states.

CONSTRUCTIVE TYPOLOGY

Several social typologies have been suggested in this and previous chapters. It has been shown that the social typologies are essentially congruent with the psychological typologies. However, because each psychological type can refer to various specific types of criminal acts (for instance, the term "antisocial" can include everything from rape to vandalism), we will not attempt to incorporate the psychological types into our final typology (except by inference). In accord with the emphasis of this text, ours will be a social typology of deviancy. Several typologies will bear specific reference in our manifold scheme: (1) Merton's typology of deviancy, including conformity, innovation, ritualism, retreatism, and rebellion, (2) Thomas and Znaniecki's typology of philistine, bohemian, and creative man adaptation, (3) Clinard's career *versus* noncareer crime, and (4) Cavan's typology collapsed into five basic types, including contracultural overconformity, overconformity, normal conformity, underconformity, and contracultural underconformity.

These four typologies are combined in a constructive social typology of deviance as seen in Table 4–3. While the combining of these typologies may depart slightly from the original intent of their authors, they do seem to "hang together" coherently and

TABLE 4–3   Constructive Typology of Deviance

Typologies	*Major characteristics*	*Examples*
Retreatism (1) Contracultural overconformity (4)	(1) Rejection of legitimate means and cultural goals (4) Rejection of contemporary standards and rejection by community	Suicide Psychosis Reactionary social movements
Ritualism (1) Philistine (2) overconformity (4)	(1) Rejection or scaling down of cultural goals; acceptance of legitimate means (2) Rigid conformity to tradition (4) Rejection of goal orientation of average person; toleration or disapproval by community	Neurosis Altruistic suicide Authoritarian personality
Conformity (1) Creative man (2) Normal conformity (4)	(1) Acceptance of both institutional means and cultural goals (2) Reconciliation of traditional values with diversity of schemes and specialties (4) Acceptance of conventional values and acceptance by community	Heterosexual relations Pilfering Minor vandalism Social drinking Ethnic prejudice Gambling
Innovation (1) Bohemian (2) Noncareer (3) underconformity (4)	(1) Rejection of institutionalized means; acceptance of cultural goals (2) Lack of stable conformity with tradition, and drift from specialty to specialty (3) Once only offense (4) Ambivalence about conventional values, and guilt concerning deviancy	Petty theft Vandalism Drunkenness Disorderly conduct Exhibitionism Some homosexual relations Marihuana use
Career (3) underconformity (4)	(3) Chronic deviancy (4) Tolerated or disapproved by community	Organized crime Prostitution Pickpocketing
Rebellion (1) Noncareer (2) contraculture (4)	(1) Rejection of old and substitution of new means and ends (4) Rejection of conventional values; substituting criminal values without feeling of guilt; rejected by conventional community (3) Once only offense	Murder of rival or relative Violent sex acts Assault Assassination Arson Rioting Guerrilla warfare
Career (3) contraculture (4)	(3) Chronic deviancy	Professional murder Drug addiction Gang violence Overt homosexuality

meaningfully. Merton's types are used as the main headings in Table 4–3 because they take into account both acceptance or rejection of illegitimate means (and thus the extent of career orientation) and extent of acceptance or rejection of conventional values.

Retreatism   The retreatist is tradition-oriented, so much so that he is rejected by the community-at-large and/or rejects the standards of the average person (both the institutionalized means and cultural goals). However, because of his inability to live up to his own standards, and/or because of his isolation and rejection, he may suffer breakdown in the form of psychosis (especially schizophrenia), he may commit suicide, or he may join an extremely reactionary political movement through which he may accomplish his ends. The latter adaptation is that of the "true believer," a person who is so dependent upon participation in social movements that he might suffer extreme neurosis or psychosis if such movements were not available. This "retreatist" behavior can easily be converted into "rebellious" behavior, that is, the individual may swing to the extreme opposite end of the continuum. As Hoffer points out, mass movements are often interchangeable, in the sense that they draw from the same population of frustrated individuals.[41] Thus, it would be easy to view the latter adaptation (reactionary mass behavior) as "rebellion" in Merton's terms. There difference is that contrary to the rebellious adaptation, the individual seeks to revive traditional norms rather than institute new ones.

Ritualism   The ritualist also conforms to tradition. He may be either tolerated or disapproved by the community, but he is not rejected, probably because the ritualist is capable of accepting the institutionalized means of the community and thus may be able to work within a bureaucratic setting. However, he rejects the cultural goals or revises them, perhaps on grounds that they involve crass materialism, or because they are unreachable, or on moral grounds such as "greed is sin." Because the ritualist can at least live in formally organized or bureaucratic settings, rigidly conforming to the rules of bureaucracy, he is not totally isolated, at least from formal organizational ties. Because of his overachievement and overconformity to pristine tradition, however, he is often rejected from intimate association with peers. He may overcompensate for the loss of personal ties through even further overachievement in the vain hope that this will lead to peer group recognition or at least that it will allow the individual to maintain a sense of pride despite rebuff from fellows.

The result of interpersonal rebuff may be an excessive use of neurotic defense mechanisms such as escapism, compensation, rationalization, reaction formation, displacement, intellectualization, dissociation, identification, introjection, projection, repression, undoing, and the like.

The authoritarian personality syndrome is typical of this adaptation, and may be seen in this framework as an overstatement of values which the person conceives to be higher morality and may be an unconscious attempt to gain community approval. It is remarkable how much the authoritarian personality syndrome fits the pattern described above as seen in the following description:

a. *Conventionalism.* Rigid adherence to conventional, middle-class values.

b. *Authoritarian submission.* Submissive, uncritical attitude toward idealized moral authorities of the ingroup.

c. *Authoritarian aggression.* Tendency to be on the lookout for, and to condemn, reject, and punish people who violate conventional values. . . .

h. *Projectivity.* The disposition to believe that wild and dangerous things go on in the world; the projection outwards of unconscious emotional impulses.

i. *Sex.* Exaggerated concern with sexual "goings-on."[42]

The ultimate in this pitiful quest for community approval may be the voluntary taking of one's own life in the form of altruistic suicide. The individual may expect to receive social acclaim in the hereafter.

Conformity   The "conformist" in a changing society is not necessarily obedient to tradition, but selects those aspects of tradition that agree with current standards. The conformist is acceptable to the larger community because he is able to work within institutional means and cultural goals. The conformist views every work setting critically, conforming to rules generally but without emotional devotion and never to the extent of interfering with his goal attainment. While he may on occasion deviate from the rules, he strives to change them rather than chronically evade them when he disagrees with them. Because of his problem-oriented stance and and because of the general acceptability of his behavior to the community, he is acceptable for both formal and informal association. As he can generally arrive at his objectives legitimately, his deviancies are minor and rare, generally ritualized as "reversal rites" or celebrations. He may engage in occupational pilfering or minor vandalism, both of which are written off by his employer as normal losses. Other of his "deviancy" acts can hardly be called such by current informal standards, including such acts as heterosexual relations, social drinking, traffic offenses, and minority group discrimination.

Innovation   Innovation is subdivided into two subtypes, both of which imply the use of illegitimate means but varying in the degree of involvement and socialization to these means (Clinard). In both cases, the individual rejects traditional means but accepts or even overaccentuates the culturally induced goals of society, wealth, power, status, and the like. While emphasizing material success, innovators may be somewhat ambivalent about other conventional values (family, home, education, frugality, and so on). Because of this marginal acceptance of institutionalized means and selective acceptance of cultural goals, innovators are merely tolerated or perhaps disapproved by the community.

Because the innovator is capable of some degree of conformity, he can function within work and other institutional settings, but when confronted with undesirable rules he evades them or obeys them only when necessary, calculating his behavior as such to maximize material goal-attainment. For the innovator, the end justifies the means. Innovation may vary, however, in degree of commitment to illegitimate means. Those marginally committed will commit occasional or hidden offenses, such as white-collar crime, petty theft, vandalism, secret use of marihuana, private excessive drinking, and the like. However, with greater commitment and association with others who agree and corroborate one's definitions, full scale forms of revenue gaining crime may ensue, including professional crime, organized crime, ordinary crime, prostitution, and pickpocketing.

Rebellion   The rebel thoroughly repudiates all aspects of tradition and formal organizational rule. As such he cannot live in conventional neighborhoods or pursue a conventional career or job for extended periods of time, or if he does hold such a career and family status, it is a status split with a secret "other life" which may even be unknown to the deviant himself. Generally, this involves subcultural deviancy, if the individual's offenses have been chronic. He comes to associate with others who agree with his definitions. However, an act of rebellion may be a single act, generally of high visibility, and as such the probability of continued commitment to the community is low. Noncareer types include such violent acts as family murders, violent sex assault, assassination, rioting, arson, and guerilla warfare. If rebellion has become a way of life, it may take the form of subcultural drug addiction, gang violence, or murder as a profession.

Measuring seriousness of deviancy

The above analysis has indicated that the variety of "nominal" typologies that exist in the study of deviancy can be consolidated into rank-order categories. When rank-ordered in this way the categories represent and correspond to varying degrees of seriousness. Two basic dimensions stand out: (1) the extent of socialization to illegitimate means, and (2) the extent of rejection of conventional or institutionalized values implied by a given deviant act. We have attempted above to combine and subcategorize both dimensions, and to suggest examples of each subcategory. However, as it stands, the typology is not complete, nor very useful, nor is it scientifically or empirically validated. More deviancy acts need to be added. Unless specific instances of deviancy are indicated the typology cannot be directly used in everyday research. Furthermore, examples have been assigned on purely speculative grounds. Ultimately and ideally what is needed is a list of deviant acts rank-ordered in degrees of seriousness. This list could be used in various ways:

1. It would tell us how various deviant acts are viewed in our society.

2. It may be conceptualized as a curve of deviant acts which can be compared with like curves found in other societies or, comparing social organizational contexts, in one or another social organizations within society.

3. It would help to separate for research purposes sets of deviant acts, for instance, "real crime" as opposed to minor delinquency for special study.

4. It ultimately could be used officially (by police, courts, probation authorities, and so on) as a basis for making penal decisions.

5. It could help us locate acts potentially functional in the sense that they may be tolerated or publically rejected based on believed incompatability with current value orientations (this decision cannot be made by a sociologist, but must be ascertained through a knowledge of public belief).

Thus what we will attempt to do is to construct, with empirical detail and validity, applications of the above constructive typology. Of the two dimensions discussed above (socialization to illegitimate means and rejection of conventional values) we shall focus on value rejection. The "illegitimate means" aspect of a deviant act can be (and has been) determined by an examination of recidivism records for individual crimes. Clinard has done this. What needs to be explored here, however, is the public attitudes regarding the rejection of conventional values implied by various acts. This can only be derived through public opinion survey and cannot be arbitrarily designated by a given researcher (because his designation would reflect only his values or perceptions and not the consensus of public opinion). The final typology, combined with a typology like Clinard's "career-noncareer" typology, would provide an "objective" basis for evaluating a wide variety of deviant acts.

STUDIES OF SERIOUSNESS

The bulk of the studies existing on the topic of public attitudes toward seriousness of deviancy are those pertaining to juvenile delinquency. This is probably owed to the fact that delinquency is the most empirically researched area of deviant behavior. Our empirical study of deviancy will focus on delinquency and crime for this reason and for the reason that this is the broadest general area of deviancy.[43] The insights gained through this study can be applied to other areas of deviancy.

Sellin and Wolfgang's Study   Sellin and Wolfgang's study represents the most advanced attempt to date to measure the qualitative differences of delinquent events, and accordingly—though our research objectives are somewhat different—various procedures of the present project are based on the attempts of these authors to measure the differential seriousness of delinquent acts.[44] Initially, in attempting to establish a range of variation of offenses, Sellin and Wolfgang drew a ten per cent sample of the juvenile offenses committed in Philadephia for the year of 1960, compared this subsample with the total offenses known to the police, and on the basis of the elements contained within the offenses, constructed 141 offense descriptions.[45]

The major focus of Sellin and Wolfgang, as reiterated throughout their monograph, was:

> . . . to examine the possibility of arriving at an index of delinquency that would be usable in testing the effectiveness of social action aiming at the reduction or prevention of delinquency, in other words *an index that would, as accurately as possible, measure the real or actual incidence of delinquency during a given period or in a given area.*[46]

As is apparent in the above quote, the researchers' major concern revolved around an attempt to develop a sensitive index of delinquent events that would have utility in assessing the effectiveness of a prevention program in a given area over a given period of time. Thus, the authors' explicit interest is trend analysis ". . . of real juvenile misconduct which violates the criminal law and inflicts personal injuries and/or property loss."[47]

In attempting an accurate assessment of differential seriousness, the authors based the derivation of their scale of seriousness on what they label as Category I offenses. Offenses within this classification involve variations of the three objective components of bodily harm, property damage, and theft. Further, the authors maintain that only offenses known to the police, as well as only these offenses containing some variation of the objective components, form an acceptable base for the construction of the index. Accordingly, Sellin and Wolfgang, in utilizing the offenses, concentrated on the elements involved in the commission of an act. Thus, the major focus is centered upon the act itself and not on the attributes of the offender.

Subsequent to the selection of the offenses, the acts were rated in terms of seriousness by the use of both an eleven-point category scale and a magnitude ratio scale. The raters consisted of four groups: (1) university students, (2) police line officers, (3) police assigned to the Juvenile Aid Division, and (4) juvenile court judges.[48] In considering the results of the scale analysis, Sellin and Wolfgang selected, as a basis for index construction, the magnitude ratio scale over the category scale. In applying the derived scale, each individual delinquent receives a score value based upon the number of elements the particular act contains.[49]

In brief, Sellin and Wolfgang have exhibited major advances over the previous attempts to assess the qualitative differences of delinquent acts. First, the authors have rank-ordered an expanded range of acts. Second, concern is expressed over the elements contained in an act, and accordingly, variations of bodily harm, property damage, and theft are included within the offense categories. Third, the researchers have included an expanded sample of raters in their utilization of four different sources.

Although Sellin and Wolfgang's study represents the most elaborate attempt to measure the seriousness of delinquency, certain questionable methodological procedures and assumptions will be delineated in the next section.

Evaluation of Sellin and Wolfgang's study　　In assessing Sellin and Wolfgang's contribution, it is evident that the major focus of the researchers revolves around the construction of an index with which to assess qualitative changes in delinquencies in a given area over a given period of time. As a basis for index construction, primary consideration is given to the presence or absence of the three objective components of bodily harm, of property damage, and of theft.

Sellin and Wolfgang state that by focusing on the objective components of an event, they are necessarily limiting the range of offenses with which to construct their index. Accordingly, many offenses do not contain any of the components. Consider, for example, moral acts such as gambling, prostitution, and homosexuality. Are such acts to be assumed before the fact to be of a less serious nature for lack of at least one of Sellin and Wolfgang's three objective criteria? It is apparent that their major concern is with the degree of harm received by a personal victim and a respect for property as major values. However, criteria other than Sellin and Wolfgang's three objective components should be considered.

In continuing the discussion of the methodological procedures underlying Sellin and Wolfgang's research, additional points can be raised. Discrepancies can be noted among judges, particularly between the policemen and the university students with respect to the assessed seriousness of moral offenses. The policemen tended to rate the moral acts as being substantially more serious than did the college students. Sellin and Wolfgang maintain that there is no significant difference in the ratings. Such notable divergencies would suggest an avenue for future empirical research.

In considering the choice of potential raters, the divergencies between the university students and the policemen would suggest an additional concern. Are the rankings of the various raters in Sellin and Wolfgang's study an accurate assessment or reflection of the "collective sentiments"? Stated differently, do the police, or for that matter, does the sanctioning, as provided for by the statutes, accurately reflect the evaluation of seriousness by the general public? Granted—and Sellin and Wolfgang forcefully state—that this is a society based on the middle-class value system. However, it is feasible that groups of raters from the various strata of society would differentially assess the relative gravity of particular acts. In fact, numerous delinquency theorists[50] suggest that members of the lower class possess value systems divergent from the middle-class and upper-class strata of American society. Therefore, Sellin and Wolfgang, by utilizing raters of the middle-class value stance, may have been unable to detect any appreciable difference in the assessment of the seriousness of acts relative to socio-economic status. Accordingly, the authors are struck by the marked invariance in the rankings over the range of their raters.[51]

Still, although Sellin and Wolfgang present justification for their particular selection of raters, there is present a sufficient degree of variance among the respondents to suggest a refinement in procedures. It is posited that the rank-ordering of acts relative to seriousness will vary by socio-economic status. A similar view has been expressed by Rose, who, in addition, questions the basic proposition underlying Sellin and Wolfgang's study.[52] As empirical support for differential assessment, Rose presents ratings of differential seriousness by middle-class as opposed to working-class respondents. In a subsequent rejoinder, Akman and his co-authors attempt to dismiss Rose's criticism by maintaining that: ". . . faults can be found with the choice of sample in many studies if one were to evaluate it from the lofty plateau of empirical research where funds are unlimited. . . ."[53] Such a reply appears to miss Rose's basic point, in which he questions whether, in fact, Sellin and Wolfgang's choice of subjects and their ratings ". . . accurately reflect the social values of the community as regards the seriousness of crime. . . ."[54]

In the end analysis, the possibility of differential ratings by socio-economic status remains an empirical question that warrants further research. In the absence of an area probability sample, a crude indication could possibly be obtained by comparing the rank-ordering of seriousness by the father's occupation. Such a procedure may be of limited utility, in that the majority of university students are usually a product of the middle-class value system. Still, it is conceivable that by controlling for father's occupation, significant differences may or may not be noted.

SERIOUSNESS IN RELATION TO SOCIAL TYPOLOGY

The typology of deviation developed in the first part of this chapter suggests that serious crime involves a rejection by the deviant of the values of society (as well as a career commitment to crime as a way of life). The studies of seriousness cited above take into account the value-rejection dimension and attempt to derive a rank-ordered list of crimes as rated by representatives of public morality: police officers, judges, probation officers, students, and so on. Sellin and Wolfgang go even farther to suggest that two values—freedom from bodily harm and protection of private property from theft and damage—are central to the evaluation of crime in our society. However, by their own admission, Sellin and Wolfgang have ignored other major values in forming their index system, and thus have no basis for scoring such serious crimes (in American society) as drug sale and use, homosexuality, abnormal sex, incest, prostitution, and the like. Sellin and Wolfgang's survey findings could suffice as a rank-ordered list of deviant acts if one ignores their separate discussion of index construction. However, for purposes of checking out some of the methodological difficulties discussed above, and for purposes of corroboration of the Sellin and Wolfgang findings, a small-scale replication of the Sellin and Wolfgang study was attempted on a San Diego sample.

THE MEASUREMENT OF SERIOUSNESS

A shortened version of the instrument developed by Sellin and Wolfgang was constructed for the foregoing survey. Offense selection was based on the Federal Bureau of Investigation's Uniform Crime Report classificatory Labels.[55] These 29 categories appeared to present an adequate cross-section of delinquent events. The legal categories were refined through use of Sellin and Wolfgang's offense descriptions.[56] As an example, in considering the index crime of "forcible rape," three variations were used: (1) "A person forcibly rapes a woman. Her neck is broken and she dies." (2) "A person forces a female to submit to sexual intercourse. No physical injury is inflicted." (3) "A person drags a woman into an alley, tears her clothes, but flees before she is physically harmed or attacked."

Sixty acts were chosen for analysis. Because of the time and budget limitations of this study, all 60 items were administered collectively in questionnaire form, randomly ordered for position in the questionnaire (rather than being administered in smaller groups as in Sellin and Wolfgang's study). It was felt that the smaller sample of 60 items would not cause undue fatigue.

The 60 acts were ranked by 190 respondents included in two nonprobability samples. The first sample consisted of 150 upper-division male and female undergraduate students enrolled in four sociology classes at San Diego State College. The second sample was composed of 40 police science students attending courses at Grossmont Junior College in San Diego. The majority (80 per cent) were full-time police patrolmen. These samples differed in a number of ways, such that the reliability of the ratings could be tested on contrasting groups. The police sample was exclusively male, while the student sample was 64 per cent female. Forty-seven per cent of the police were age 30 or over, while only 11 per cent of the students were. The police sample was junior college level of education, while the student sample was exclusively upper division level education. Two-thirds of the students were single, while the same proportion of police were married. Both samples were alike in racial composition. Ninety-one per cent of the students were Caucasian, as compared with 97 per cent of the police. In terms of socio-economic standing, the students came from diverse SES levels while, by definition, the police sample was of one occupational level.

As indicated above, the procedures employed in this survey were somewhat different from those used by Sellin and Wolfgang. As we have pointed out, the items were administered in questionnaire form. A seven point magnitude scale was used. Instead of merely telling the respondents to rate the acts in terms of seriousness, we specified what we meant by seriousness. The questionnaire instructions read "Please record a number from 1 (least offensive) to 7 (most offensive) to indicate how offensive each particular act is to *your own moral beliefs*." The purpose of this qualification was to direct the respondent to the value dimension in rating deviant acts and to rule out other possible criteria of seriousness, as value acceptance or rejection is the basis of our typology.

EMPIRICAL TYPOLOGY OF SERIOUSNESS

Average scores on all 60 deviant acts were calculated and are shown in Table 4–4 (San Diego State students only). The items are arranged in four groups divided according to first, second, third, and fourth quartiles of the average score distribution. There is a surprising correspondence between Table 4–4, the empirical typology, and Table 4–3, our theoretically derived typology. In the former table the fourth column on the right, labeled "rebellion," includes primarily acts of violence, implying bodily harm. There is, however, no clear-cut distinction between career and noncareer contraculture within the rebellion column, probably because violence is relatively rare among career criminals and thus does not become a consideration in the typology.

The next two columns are labeled "innovation," in that they both involve normative violations. These two columns differ, as in Table 4–3, primarily in the extent of career involvement.

The acts labeled "career underconformity" are of two types: those that emphasize crime as a professional career (receiving stolen property, breaking and entering, major embezzlement, pickpocketing, and forgery) and those that emphasize the rejection of conventional values ("underconformity") (failure to pay child support, drunk driving, auto theft, arson, and heroin addiction).

The next column seems to fit well the "noncareer underconformity" column in Table 4–3. A number of these are utilitarian or impulsive acts of a "once only" variety: draft card burning, book stealing, throwing rocks through a window, peeping-Tomism, placing an obscene phone call, embezzlement of $5, a marihuana sale, adultery, a bicycle theft, passing a bad check. Other acts listed in this column may be of a chronic variety, but imply agreement or conformity to conventional values: unlawful sale of liquor, running house of prostitution, illegal abortion.

The acts listed in the "conformity" column are quite likely normal acts of average people: playing dice, violating curfew, premarital intercourse, runaway, intoxication, disturbing the peace. While not all acts perfectly fit the category assigned, there are enough acts in correspondence to lend at least face validity to the constructive typology discussed above.

Reliability of the typology   The first question a critic of the

TABLE 4-4 Criminal offenses classified according to seriousness

LEAST
SERIOUS

←

Conformity	$\overline{\times}$	*Innovation*	$\overline{\times}$
(Normal conformity)		*(Noncareer underconformity)*	
Dice game	1.53	Burns draft card	3.23
Curfew violation	1.55	Unlawful sale of liquor	3.25
Premarital sexual		Runs house of prosti-	
intercourse	2.12	tution	3.31
Racial protest march	2.12	Steals library book	
Firing rifle without		worth five dollars	3.32
permit.	2.18	Throws rocks through window	3.44
Runaway juvenile	2.31	Homosexual—willing	3.54
Intoxicated in public	2.34	Peeping Tom	3.55
Illegal possession		Obscene phone call	3.67
of a knife	2.46	Embezzles five dollars	3.72
Vagrancy	2.50	Gets customers for	
Customer in illegal		prostitute	3.87
gambling establishment	2.58	Sells marihuana	3.89
Disturbing peace	2.68	Adultery—married male	3.96
Smoking marihuana	2.82	Steals bicycle	3.98
Sex intercourse between		Performs illegal abortion	3.98
person over sixteen and		Passes bad check	4.00
under sixteen	3.14		
Prostitute in house			
of prostitution	3.16		
Runs gambling house	3.17		

above findings might ask is: To what extent are these ratings reliable? Our sample is a student sample and therefore may not be representative of the opinion of the community at large. One way to test this assertion is to correlate our ratings against those taken on samples that differ from our own in background characteristics;

TABLE 4-4 **Continued**

			MOST SERIOUS $\longrightarrow$
Innovation *(Career underconformity)*	$\overline{X}$	*Rebellion* *(Contracultural nonconformity)*	$\overline{X}$
Fails to pay child support	4.00	Breaks into residence, forces	
Receiving stolen property	4.02	open cash box, steals one	
Shows pornographic movie		thousand dollars	4.05
to a minor	4.04	Uses physical force to rob	
Driving under the influence		a victim of one thousand	
of alcohol	4.36	dollars—no physical harm	5.12
Breaking into a private		Beats victim with fist—victim	
residence, stealing five		requires hospitalization	5.18
dollars from cash box—		Forces female to submit to	
forced	4.46	sexual intercourse—no injury	5.46
Embezzles one thousand		Sexual intercourse with	
dollars	4.62	stepdaughter	5.49
Steals, damages unlocked		Stabs victim with knife—no	
car	4.70	medical treatment required	5.57
Deserts family	4.76	Sells heroin	5.57
Sets fire to a garage	4.77	Armed with blunt instrument,	
Picks pocket of one		robs victim of one thousand	
thousand dollars	4.80	dollars—victim requires	
Breaks into a locked car—steals,		hospitalization	5.66
damages, abandons	4.94	Father beats wife and	
Defaces public statue—one		children	5.76
thousand dollars damage	4.51	Drags woman into alley,	
Signs someone else's name		tears clothes, flees—woman	
to a check—cashes	4.52	not harmed	5.76
Administers heroin to self	4.55	Fires gun—major wound	
Breaks into department		extensive hospitalization	6.08
store, forces open cash		Robs victim using gun—	
box, steals five dollars	4.60	victim struggles resulting	
		in death of victim	6.41
		Robs victim of one thousand	
		dollars—victim shot to death	6.62
		Forcibly rapes woman—her	
		neck is broken, she dies	6.70
		Stabs person to death	6.80

this is why a sample of police science students was included. Table 4–5 indicates that the San Diego State student ratings (both male and female) are highly intercorrelated with the police science student ratings. This is confirmatory in that the police science students were shown to differ significantly from the San Diego State student sample in age, sex, marital background, education, and socio-economic standing. Even more confirmatory, a correlation was run between the San Diego State male ratings and the Sellin and Wolfgang male student ratings. The relatively high correlation of .77 between these two sample ratings is surprising in light of the differences in geographical location and in wording and questionnaire administration procedures between our study and Sellin and Wolfgang's.

Since the start of this project it has been learned that the Sellin and Wolfgang findings have recently been replicated in various settings with this same high level of correlation. One study was done in all the Canadian provinces on a sample of male and female university students.[57] Several other studies have been done which have not yet been published — one on tribal groups and university students in the Belgian Congo (1967), another in England on a sample of union workers (1966–67), still another done on inmates in a New Jersey prison, and a national study done by Peter Rossi of the National Opinion Research Center, for the President's Crime Commission. All of these studies have correlated highly (r's $= 0.900$ to 0.999) with the original Sellin and Wolfgang ratings.

TABLE 4-5   Intercorrelation matrix for ratings taken on different samples

Variable	x_1	x_2	x_3
SDS male ratings (x_1)	1.00	0.85	0.91
SDS female ratings (x_2)		1.00	0.82
Grossmont police science ratings (x_3)			1.00

Results of tests bearing on criticisms of Sellin and Wolfgang Two possible areas of criticism of Sellin and Wolfgang's findings were stated above: (1) Separate examination of "morals offenses" might yield significant variability between police and student samples, as these areas are areas of disagreement between police and students. (2) Similarly, socio-economic class differences might exist on the same grounds. We tested these assertions through intercorrelating students and police ratings and blue collar and white collar ratings on eleven sex offenses drawn from our larger sample of 60 offenses. The results are shown in Tables 4–6 and 4–7. In both, intercorrelations between subsample ratings are extremely high, further demonstrating the reliability of the Sellin and Wolfgang scale.

TABLE 4-6   Correlation matrix: ratings of sex offenses by police and student samples

| | STUDENTS | | |
	Male	*Female*	*Police*
Male	x	0.84	0.96
Female	x	0.87	x

NOTE: All computations are based on Spearman rank correlations.

TABLE 4-7   Correlation matrix: ratings of sex offenses by respondents whose fathers' occupations were "white-collar" as related to ratings by respondents whose fathers' occupations were "blue-collar"

| BLUE-COLLAR OCCUPATIONS | WHITE-COLLAR OCCUPATIONS | | | |
	1	2	3	8
5	0.93	0.89	0.80	0.95
6	0.89	0.79	0.77	0.95
7	0.74	0.79	0.71	0.94

Occupation:
1 Salesman or salesclerk
2 Owner or manager of a business
3 Clerical, secretarial or similar work
4 Service worker*
5 Semi-skilled worker
6 Skilled worker or foreman
7 Work for government
8 Professional work

NOTE: All computations are based on Spearman rank correlations.
*Limited number of respondents on which to base comparisons.

Summary and conclusion on typology of deviancy

The foregoing chapter has been concerned extensively with the development of typologies of deviancy, both theoretical and empirical. In the first part of this chapter theoretical typology was developed based on the study of various theoretical typologies developed primarily in the study of crime. This theoretical typology was extended to include not only crime, but additional forms of deviancy, including suicide, mental disorder, and intergroup prejudice and discrimination. Similarly, the empirical typology developed in the second part of this chapter was based upon previous typological attempts, primarily in the area of crime and delinquency. This focus on crime is justified in part by the fact that crime covers the broadest area of deviancy, and empirical studies of seriousness of crime have been done which lend themselves to our research. Suicide, mental disorder, and intergroup relations have not been explored empirically with regard to the development of a taxonomy of seriousness. However, it is hoped that the corroboration that our findings on seriousness of crime have lent to the "conformity" and "underconformity" sides of our theoretical typology also lend at least some credibility to the "overconformity" side of the taxonomy. It nevertheless remains for future research to explore this side empirically.

Now that concrete reference and meaning has been supplied for a large gamut of types of deviancy, we can go on to explore the relation between deviant behavior and the social organization–disorganization theory discussed in previous chapters—the stated purpose of this text. We shall look at deviant behavior in various settings: "macro" settings such as large nations, and "micro" settings such as formal or complex organizations and informal organizations, such as communities, gangs, families, and the like. Now that the various individual types of deviancy have been discussed, it is hoped that we can develop a truly sociological approach to deviancy, viewing deviancy within the context of various group or organizational settings (rather than viewing each form of deviancy as a different social problem to be explained by a potpouri of unrelated theories). In all of these settings, our basic typology of deviant behavior will remain the same. It will, however, be applied differently at different levels of social organization.

Deviancy and social transition

The typology of deviancy developed in the last chapter will provide a basis for the theory of deviancy we will now develop. Before presenting this theory, we shall look at some major theories of deviancy, both historical and current, with an eye to assessing their limitations and synthesizing, whenever possible, their contributions. Later in this chapter a theory will be presented which attempts to overcome these limitations and draws together these approaches. This theory is not merely a synthetic approach. It not only draws from older theories and attempts to combine them, but also takes into account new empirical evidence that is contrary to earlier theories. In the second section of this chapter, we shall examine some empirical data in the light of this theory—both cross-cultural and trend data for the United States. Other data relevant to this theory will be presented throughout the remainder of the book.

Theories of deviancy

First we shall examine several theories which, for the most part, are now considered defunct. Among these will be he-

Notes for this chapter are on pages 383–385.

donistic psychology, the thermal theory of deviancy, the theory of the born criminal, the psychogenic theory, and two early social theories: the theory of imitation and the theory of economic determinism. Next, we will consider various social theories of deviancy — theories which may be viewed as reactive and antithetical to the above-mentioned earlier theories. We may note a number of limitations of these theories. For example, they have no particular relationship to larger general theories of society, having been developed rather narrowly within the disciplines of crime and delinquency. They are cross-sectional and ahistorical theories based on the authors' own perceptions of particular instances of deviancy at a particular time. In addition, these theories have not been cross-culturally validated nor has there been any attempt to test their assumptions through looking at broad trends in the United States.[1]

EARLY THEORIES OF DEVIANCY

Before examining current deviancy theories, it will be informative to review briefly some historical theories of deviancy. These theories help us to understand current approaches, which are reactive to some of the historical theories and an outgrowth of others. It will also be useful to study the reasons for which these earlier theories were rejected. We will consider essentially six theories developed in Europe, some of which are still prominant today: (1) the "classical" school of crime; (2) the "thermal theory"; (3) the theory of the "born criminal"; (4) two early social theories — (a) the theory of imitation, and (b) economic determinism; and (5) the psychogenic school.

The "classical" school   Near the end of the eighteenth century, the "classical" school, whose main exponents were Cesare Beccaria in Italy and Jeremy Bentham in England, proposed that crime was simply an act wherein the pleasure derived from illegal behavior exceeded the possible pain that might be imposed in punishment. This school was based on an underlying philosophical belief in rationalism. Rationalism or the "contract theory of society" held that man contracts intellectually to enter into certain relationships with his fellows. Man thus has the power to choose right from wrong. Thus, crime could be understood by the principles of hedonistic psychology, which proposed that all behavior was motivated by a pleasure–pain calculus. In a famous essay,

Beccaria expressed the view that uniform penalties for given crimes should vary according to the severity of the crime, so many years for robbery, so many for burglary, and so on.[2]

Despite the fact that this approach has many limitations, criminal law in nearly all countries today is based upon the classical theory of crime. However, it should be acknowledged that for its time, the classical theory was revolutionary and progressive. Previously, crimes were punished differently by different judges, with differential justice applied to different social classes. The utilitarian or pain–pleasure principle at least provided an external criterion that would at least allow some equity before the law.

The thermal theory of crime　Early in the nineteenth century, geographers became impressed with the variation in crime according to climatic conditions. This "thermal theory of crime" proposed that crimes against persons were induced by hotter climates, and crimes against property were induced by colder climates. The thermal approach was first suggested by the French philosopher Montesquieu, who proposed that criminality increases as one approaches the equator, but drunkenness increases in proportion as one approaches the poles. A century later, Quételet formed his famous "thermal law" of delinquency, which states that crimes against persons predominate in the south during the warm seasons, while crimes against property predominate in the north and during the wintertime. The next significant work on climate and crime was done by Dexter in 1904 and titled *Weather Influences*. Dexter analyzed certain criminal cases in New York City and Denver and found that crimes of violence were most numerous during the warm months of the year, during periods of low barometric pressure, and during periods of low humidity.[3]

Despite the interesting correlations revealed by these early studies, criminologists have devoted little or no attention either to verifying or refuting geographical theories.

The theory of the "born criminal"　The classical school of criminology was developed before the advent of biological sciences; therefore, it neither reflected the method nor the knowledge developed in biology. When biological science was applied to criminology in the late nineteenth century by Lombroso, the classical school of criminology was considered repudiated. Lombroso reflected the Darwinian belief in evolution in his theorizing. Different persons might represent different stages of human evolution.

It is probable that criminality is an inborn tendency. The "born criminal," as indicated by his physical and mental characteristics (stigmata or anomalies), is a throwback to primitive man (atavism). Lombroso's theory has been summarized as follows:

1. Criminals constitute a distinct born type.

2. This type can be identified by certain stigmata or anomalies, such as protruding jaws, asymmetrical skull, retreating forehead, large outstanding ears, low sensitivity to pain, etc.

3. The stigmata are not the causes of crime but rather the symptoms of atavism (reversion to a more primitive type) or degeneracy, especially that characterized by epileptic tendencies. Thus, according to Lombroso, atavism and degeneracy are the causes of crime.

4. The person who is the criminal type *cannot refrain* from committing crime unless he lives under exceptionally favorable circumstances.[4]

Although his early work was general in scope, Lombroso later allowed for the effects of epilepsy and brain pathology on born criminals, and even later allowed for others who were not born criminals but criminaloids. His final work considered the effects of a bad environment along with hereditary criminality. Lombroso's theories were modified and extended by the Italians Garofalo and Ferri. However, the whole Italian School was soon to come under attack. Lombroso had based his conclusions only upon the study of prison populations, without comparing them to non-criminals. Goring, an Englishman, made a comparative study of several thousand criminals and noncriminals and concluded that there is no anthropological criminal type, no physical stigmata of crime, and that criminals are not differentiated significantly among themselves as to these traits. Goring, however, did report two differences between criminals and the general population. They were less developed physically (except violent criminals who were better developed), and their intelligence was lower than that of the general population.[5] Goring, while refuting the idea of a physical type, asserted the existence of a "criminal diathesis," or constitutional factors causing criminal behavior, which was inherited. Thus Goring did not completely break with the explanation of inherited criminality prevalent in his time.

Another theory, originally proposed by Franz Joseph Gall, parallels Lombroso's theory of the born criminal. Gall's theory, which he termed "craniology" (later to be call phrenology), asserted that various qualities of character, acquisitiveness, combativeness, and the like were related to the conformation of the brain and the development of its various parts or "faculties. " The development of these faculties was indicated by the bumps on a person's head. Gall believed that the shape of a criminal's head would be different from that of the noncriminal, and therefore, criminality could be diagnosed through examination of head bumps.

Gall's phrenology, as well as other theories of the born criminal—theories of arrested development, degeneracy, and the pathological nature of crime—have been largely repudiated. Phrenology lost repute when it was discovered that the mind was not composed of "faculties," as was originally proposed.

More recent attempts to portray the born criminal have not met with much greater success. In 1939, Hooton published a more moderate postition based on a comparative study of 13,873 male convicts in ten states and 3,203 noncriminals, including patrons of a Massachusetts bathing beach, firemen in Nashville, members of a military company, and a few out-patients in a hospital. While Hooton claimed no stigmata attached to criminality, he did assert that biological inferiority, both mental and physical, was primary in a complex of social, psychological, and biological causes of criminality. He concluded that an increase in criminality could be checked through sterilization of defective types.[6]

Hooton's findings have not been accepted in criminology for a variety of reasons: his sample was neither representative of criminals nor noncriminals, he presented no objective evidence of inferiority of the criminal population, there was no proof that inferiority was inherited rather than acquired, and his findings have been reversed by more recent studies.[7]

More recently, Sheldon has published a thesis that criminal behavior is a function of body structure (in particular, mesomorphic as opposed to endomorphic or ectomorphic). While Sheldon's study seems the most well-designed of any in the positivist school, it is difficult to determine the extent to which social-environmental interpretations are the bases of interpretation of a given type, and therefore not causal.

The psychogenic school of thought   We shall discuss both traditional psychiatric and psychological approaches as belonging to this school, for they both share the common assumption that family dynamics—the interaction between father, mother, and offspring—serve as the basis of explanation of crime. This school differs from the positivist school by treating criminality not as determined by heredity and physical constitution, but due to childhood experiences within the family. As indicated in the discussion of psychiatric typologies of deviance, criminality is usually traced to faulty development of the ego and superego. Basically, the psychiatric school sees delinquency and subsequent criminality as a result of the inability of the ego to control impulses in terms of superego standards.

Exemplary of the psychoanalytic school are the works of William Healy.[8] During the first part of the twentieth century Healy led a movement away from the search for single traits to a multiple-factor approach. As director of the Juvenile Psychopathic Institute, organized in Chicago in 1909, he studied 1,000 juvenile delinquents who had been treated at his institute. His observations are based on these case studies. In Healy's framework, delinquency is a form of substitution for an object lost through frustration. Nondelinquents are better able to find substitutes through acceptable channels than were delinquents. Delinquents suffered from severe emotional disturbances.

Healy's approach, as well as psychiatric approaches to crime generally, have come under attack primarily on the basis of methodological flaws. Though Healy compared his delinquent subjects with nondelinquent subjects, the use of case-study method is highly subjective. It is relatively easy for a case analyst to find emotional and other disturbances more prevalent in delinquents, insofar as what one perceives is often determined by what one expects and wants to perceive. The case analyst may select only those aspects of a case study that are corroborative, ignoring aspects that contradict his theoretical point of view.[9]

Another approach focusing upon the family as a basic agency is the psychological theory that feeble-mindedness is related to criminality. Henry Goddard, in 1920 the director of the research laboratory of the New Jersey Training School for Feebleminded at Vineland, argued that the greatest single cause of delinquency and crime was "low-grade mentality." This view came to be quite popular in the United States—part of the folklore of crime. However, it has been thoroughly repudiated by American psychologists. Using multivariate control techniques, prisoners were not found to differ from law-abiding persons in intelligence. In fact, it may be argued that if white-collar criminals are considered, the criminal population may well be more intelligent than the conventional population.[10]

ROOTS OF THE SOCIOLOGICAL APPROACH

Two early theories, the theory of imitation and the theory that crime is economically determined, may be seen as predecessors of many modern sociological theories of crime. Although these theories have passed from acceptance, we can see elements of them in current ways of viewing criminality.

Gabriel Tarde, though a contemporary of Lombroso, was an outspoken opponent of biological theory. Crime, he said, was not inherited, but learned through "imitation," and transmitted through suggestion. If a man steals or murders, he is merely imitating someone else. Crime spreads from the city into rural areas, and from those of higher prestige to those of lower social status. Thus, crime originates in the cities and spreads to rural areas. Aristocratic antisocial acts spread to the masses.[11]

Although imitation has not been considered a valid explanation of human behavior, the emphasis on the diffusion or spread of criminal patterns of behavior through social interaction in groups has influenced many contemporary crime theories, notably Sutherland's theory of differential association.

Another foundation social theory was expounded by William A. Bonger, a Dutch criminologist. Bonger, a Marxist, believed that crime was due to the capitalist system. Theft was due to a desire of the poor to acquire the necessities of life in a system in which such were lacking to them. Vagrancy was due to unemployment, which was a chronic condition of capitalism. Alcoholism, prostitution, and other vices are traced to the market orientation of persons under capitalism and exploitation of others. Ostensibly, many crimes are property crimes; however, crimes of violence and against public order can be traced to the capitalist system. The solution, according to Bonger, is to reorganize the system along socialist utopian lines.[12]

Although many of the conditions that Bonger traced to capitalism (mass poverty, exploitation) have been removed in today's society, and although Marxist predictions did not come true in Western capitalist countries, Bonger's emphasis upon the relation between socio-economic class and crime has endured, and is seen today in many theories of crime.

DIFFICULTIES WITH EARLIER APPROACHES

Most of the above theories have lost favor with contemporary criminologists and do not receive much serious consideration in current texts on deviance. These approaches have not received corroboration of scientific research. The initiation of a science of human behavior led to the downfall of rationalistic hedonistic psychology as it became known that not all human behavior is rational, but rather that biological and psychological forces not controlled by the individual's conscious mind influence behavior. Scientific studies have denied the existence of inherited criminality or even criminal tendencies, and have found no difference between criminal and noncriminal populations in presumed biological traits (stigmata of degeneracy, skull bumps, brain faculties). Even the psychological approaches are held in doubt, because of the limited case study method used in these studies.

In general, then, the above approaches are attacked for being "arm chair theory," on the one hand, and "common sense theory" on the other. These approaches were basically those of philosophers, physicians, and psychiatrists who in the course of their practice developed "hunch hypotheses" about the biological or psychological bases of deviancy. These early theories were largely subjective, and did not receive the objective validation either of derivation from more general theories of social organization or of generalization from wide varieties of extant sources of data on deviancy. In short, these theories are seen as somewhat limited or parochial—that is, particularistic rather than universalistic.

Current social theories of deviancy developed in reaction to these early approaches. These are in part an extension of Tarde's insistence that deviancy is learned, not inherited, and Bonger's view that deviancy is largely a product of capitalism, which forces the proletariat or working class to steal and perform other acts of deviancy. Bonger's view would contradict not only inheritance theories, but theories that reductionistically trace deviancy to individual psychology rather than to the true cause which is the structure of society. We shall see, however, that despite advances made by these frameworks, they are still limited in some of the ways of earlier theories, by their lack of foundation in general social theory, and by an inadequate and limited data base.

SOCIAL THEORIES OF CRIME

A number of social theories of deviancy have developed in America in reaction to these early approaches. Though there may be a common framework implied by all of these theories, they may be treated separately, based upon different foci. Sutherland's pioneering work, the *differential association theory* of criminality, emphasized the learned nature of criminal behavior. Later theories, notably those of Cohen and Merton, attempt to explain the development of *deviant adaptations* and *delinquent subcultures* of norms and values in opposition to middle-class society. Other theories have emphasized the importance of *cultural transmission* of delinquent attitudes as causative factors in deviancy. Still other theories show how deviancy arises from conflict, notably *class conflict*. These various schemes have been integrated into a theory that associations, legitimate or illegitimate, may differ in their availability to an individual in the sense of differential opportunity structures. Last, we may list a separate theoretical area of *cultural discontinuity* theory.

The theory of differential association   Like Tarde's imitation-suggestion theory, Sutherland's theory of differential association emphasizes the learned nature of delinquent and criminal behavior. Sutherland's theory is perhaps more systematic than Tarde's, stating that (1) criminal behavior is learned rather than inherited; (2) criminal behavior is learned in interaction with other persons in a process of communication; (3) the principle part of the learning of criminal behavior occurs within intimate personal groups rather than impersonal agencies such as movies and newspapers; (4) the learning includes (*a*) techniques of committing the crime, and (*b*) the specific direction of motives, drives, rationalizations, and attitudes; (5) the specific direction of motives and drives is learned from definitions of the legal codes as favorable or unfavorable; (6) a person becomes delinquent because of an excess of definitions favorable to violation of law over definitions unfavorable to violation of law (principle of differential association); (7) differential associations may vary in frequency, duration, priority, and intensity; (8) this process involves all the mechanisms involved in any other learning; and (9) criminal behavior is not explained by needs and values, as non-criminal behavior is an expression of the same needs and values.[13] Although this theory represents a fairly bold step away from inheritance theory, its major limitation is that it fails to account for the selection of criminal *versus* non-criminal behavior patterns.[14]

Glasier[15] has suggested that the theory of differential association should be expanded to include identification with the behavior of persons or groups of persons that are not directly part of one's membership group (*i.e.*, reference groups behavior). However, Glasier admits that his "theory of differential identification" does not account for forces driving a person to one model or another.

The theory of cultural transmission   A number of theories have developed along similar lines as the differential association theory, in the sense that they emphasize the learned nature of criminality, but differing from differential association theory primarily by emphasizing the transmission of delinquent patterns through lower-class culture. The major impetus for these theories was the earlier work of Shaw and McKay, Thrasher, and others of the "Chicago School," which showed the existence of a deviant code in lower-class, disorganized neighborhoods. This criminal subculture existed side-by-side with the legitimate value system and may be transmitted intergenerationally in certain areas.

Representative of this school include Walter Miller, William Kvaraceus, and Solomon Kobrin.[16] Kobrin has observed that there are certain areas in which most boys acquire delinquent records before their adulthood, though they may not necessarily become chronic delinquents. In these areas, youngsters are exposed to both conventional and criminal value systems. As adulthood is approached, a choice is made and the boy enters one or the other spheres, criminal or conventional, on a predominant basis. If the criminal sector is integrated with the legitimate sector of a neighborhood, delinquency will be controlled and restricted by the adult community. However, if the two spheres are separate, independent systems, where adult crime is sporadic and unorganized, delinquency is unrestricted by any element of the adult social structure and becomes violent, wild, and irrational.

Walter Miller has proposed an explanation of delinquency which is more purely a cultural transmission theory than Kobrin's.[17] Miller sees delinquency as a product not of subcultural forces, but of the entire lower-class community, which conflicts in its focal concerns or values with the middle-class value system. Lower-class values of autonomy, fate, excitement, smartness, toughness, and trouble are passed on through the agency of peer group. The lower-class peer group serves the emotional function of the middle-class family, a function that is lost to lower-class youngsters due to the disorganization of the lower-class matriarchal family. Thus, gang activities, such as assault and theft, are self-consciously law-violating and motivated by a strict alternative code of moral standards.

Kvaraceus and Miller[18] have further focused upon the basis of delinquency in lower-class culture. They stress that delinquency is not a product of emotional disturbance among lower-class youth but is primarily a product of lower or alternative aspirations. While lower-class youngsters focus upon trouble, toughness, smartness, and so on, middle-class youngsters orient toward achievement, deferred gratification, responsibility, accumulation of material goods, cleanliness, and ambition. Lower-class culture contributes to delinquency by containing patterns that are a violation of legal norms, portraying illegal patterns as an easier route to valued objects than legal patterns, and demanding responses to situations entailing illegal acts. The NEA project found most lower-class youngsters are nondelinquent due to the relative prevalence of high aspiration levels, which lead to conformity in hopes of future reward value rather than short-run status and object orientation. Middle-class youngsters differ in part because of concealment of norm-violating behavior, but middle-class delinquency may increase in the future, due to the borrowing of lower-class patterns.

The theory of delinquent subculture   While differential association theory and culture transmission theory explain how criminal patterns are learned and transmitted from generation to generation, the theory of delinquent subculture, primarily the work of Albert K. Cohen, attempts to explain how these patterns come about in the first place, why they are more prevalent among lower than middle- or upper-class people and why they take the forms they do among adolescent gang members.[19] Cohen's theory, unlike the former two schools, stems from Merton's anomie theory. Cohen's primary focus is upon socio-economic status frustration as a major component in the causation of delinquent behavior. The lower-class boy in a middle-class world competes for success goals which he has limited ability to achieve. He must adopt middle-class attitudes toward ambition, individual responsibility, skill, the necessity of postponing immediate gratification, and so on, in order to succeed. However, failing in these respects he comes to reject middle-class and conventional values. The gang offers an alternative status system with alternative values antithetical to middle-class values. The gang legitimizes anti-middle-class hostility and aggression and emphasizes actions that are malicious, negativistic, and nonutilitarian, and thus are incomprehensible to middle-class society.

In a later article, Cohen and Short attempted to identify several types of delinquent subcultures, including the *parent-male subculture,* described in *Delinquent Boys;* the *conflict-oriented subculture* characterized by its "turf" or territory, subgang structure, and conflict involvement; *the drug-addict subculture,* oriented toward income-producing delinquency and drugs rather than violence; and the *semi-professional theft subculture,* primarily found among older adolescents who are beginning a life of professional crime; and, last, the *middle-class delinquent subculture* (all other forms being lower class) emphasizing such attitudes as deliberate courting of danger and a sophisticated, irresponsible "playboy" approach to sex, liquor, and automobiles.[20]

The conflict theory   A relatively recent conflict theory approach to crime has been suggested by George B. Vold.[21] Differential association and cultural transmission emphasize socialization into deviant norms and values, while conflict theory emphasizes actual direction of aggression toward antagonistic out-groups. By contrast with Cohen's delinquent subculture theory, conflict theory emphasizes group determination of individual behavior rather than psychological bases of gangs.

Gangs and criminal groups are interest groups conflicting with other groups, defending an in-group code. The juvenile gang conflicts with the adult community. Conscientious objectors conflict with the government. Labor groups may conflict with management and in the process commit crimes: crimes against property, and crimes of violence and disorder. Race riots may result in the commission of crimes—looting, murder, arson, and the like. Organized criminal groups can be seen as conflicting with legitimate business and with each other. However, Vold's conflict theory has broader implications than indicated by these statements about group conflict. Dominant groups in the society incorporate their vested interests in the law, and the police as well as other agencies of social control, who enforce these interests to the disadvantage of the less powerful and politically less sophisticated, who in turn are driven to conflict to obtain what they are deprived of.

The theory of delinquency and opportunity   Another theory, based directly upon Merton's anomie approach, is that of Cloward and Ohlin: delinquency and opportunity.[22] According to Merton, crime results from anomie or the disjunction between means and ends—a high emphasis upon success motivation in the cultural system but limited opportunity to achieve these goals, in the case of lower-class groups due to the social system. Anomie, it may be recalled, results in four possible deviant adaptations in American society: *innovation,* the rejection of legitimate means but acceptance of cultural success goals; *ritualism,* the adherence to legitimate means but scaling down of aspirations toward success goals; *retreatism,* the rejection of both means and ends; and *rebellion,* the rejection of both, but the substitution of an alternative means-ends system.

Starting with Merton's anomie theory, Cloward and Ohlin have developed an eclectic approach, claiming to integrate almost all the various social theories of deviancy we have discussed so far in this chapter. The logic of the synthesis is as follows: Anomie theory views deviancy as an individual response to available, consciously recognized, illegal alternatives. However, anomie theory ignores the relative availability of illegal alternatives—for instance, lower-class people have greater access to illegitimate alternatives. The "Chicago School" (the cultural transmission and differential association approaches) focuses upon differentials in availability of illegal means—that is, on the processes by which a person gains admission to criminal gangs and subcultures. The synthesis of these two approaches can be found in the concept of differential opportunity structures—that is, both legitimate and illegitimate opportunity structures. Thus, ordinary criminal careers ordinarily require lower-class backgrounds, because such illegitimate opportunity structures are not available to middle-class people. White-collar criminal opportunities, however, are not open to lower-class people. Furthermore, illegitimate opportunities may not be equally prevalent in all lower-class neighborhoods.

Three types of delinquent subcultures develop, based upon the presence or absence of these illegitimate opportunities. In "integrated neighborhoods," those in which the adult criminal sector has infiltrated the legitimate business and political sector as described by Kobrin above, the *criminal pattern* emerges, characterized by rational, disciplined crime-oriented delinquency. By contrast, the *conflict subculture,* characterized by violence and non-utlitarian delinquency, arises where social disorganization and disintegration prevails. The legitimate and illegitimate sectors are not integrated with each other; thus the young are deprived of both conventional and criminal opportunities. Violence arises as a means of achieving frustrated status goals. If an adolescent cannot find a place in either the criminal or conflict subculture—that is, if he fails to obtain access to either legitimate or illegitimate means toward status or success—he becomes a "double failure" and a candidate for the *retreatist subculture.*

However, Cloward and Ohlin recognize that not all lower-class youngsters become delinquents. They point out a relatively long process of thinking that precedes attempting to join a gang. The individual may feel a sense of status deprivation. In order to seek gang membership, he must be aggressive and rebellious, and that presupposes that he blame the social order rather than himself for his deprivation. Otherwise his status deprivation might lead to neurosis or conformity rather than delinquency, or some other form of inner problem solving. Feeling alienated, the individual must attach sentiments to illegitimate norms, and neutralize the guilt feelings that accompany such attachment. Last, he must be admitted to gang membership, which is not assured strictly by lower-class background.

The cultural discontinuity theory Last among our list of theories of crime is the theory primarily developed by Bloch and Niederhoffer.[23] They believe that gang delinquency may be explained by what Benedict refers to as "discontinuities in cultural conditioning." Adolescents are deprived of symbols of adulthood, including money, personal autonomy, and sexual relations. There are no "rites de passage," such as the puberty ceremonies found in primitive societies, which bridge the transition to adulthood. These puberty rites not only prepared youth for adult status but also satisfied concealed needs of youth (such as the need to overcome anxiety and doubt). The gang serves this function in modern society, as seen in the informal rituals of modern American gangs, reminiscent of the puberty rites of tribes. In the gang, a youngster may also gain adult status in the eyes of his peers through demonstrating that he is independent, tough, and capable of flaunting adult authority.

Unlike the above theories, however, delinquency is seen as both middle- and lower-class based, since it is primarily a product of the underprivileged state of adolescence rather than of social class.

The implication of this theory is that gang delinquency can be lessened by incorporating rites de passage into our social structure. Bloch and Niederhoffer are focusing upon a new aspect of the problem of delinquency and crime: youth culture, the adolescent system, and the like. To some extent, this line of analysis is antithetical to the delinquency approaches discussed above. Delinquency is viewed as more prevalent among the middle class than in traditional theories. There is some evidence for this assumption, which will be discussed in the chapter on "white-collar crime."

PERSPECTIVE ON SOCIAL THEORIES

The above analysis indicates that extensive controversy is going on currently between deviancy theorists. This diversity of opinion may be largely traced to differences in focus. That is, perhaps all are talking about different aspects of the same phenomenon. Sutherland's analysis and Miller's theory may be appropriate in describing the stable "corner boy" gang subculture. Merton's analysis may best fit the "semi-professional gang." Cohen's framework seems to refer specifically to the conflict gang. Bloch and Niederhoffer's gang approach may apply best to the middle-class gang. All of this indicates that the different theories are limited, parochial, or particularistic, the same basic criticism directed at the early approaches to deviancy — Cloward and Ohlin have attempted to "universalize" these approaches, drawing them together in one framework. Despite some shortcomings, the Cloward-Ohlin synthesis does this quite well. However, in some ways it falls short of the objective of universalism.

The most serious of its limitations is that it holds most delinquency to be exclusively confined to lower-class neighborhoods. In the pages to follow it will be shown that crime is found throughout our society and the extent of crime is increasing. Because the number of lower-class people is decreasing, the Cloward-Ohlin framework (and its antecedents) cannot account for this trend. Furthermore, there is mounting evidence that juvenile delinquency is far more extensive in the middle class than previously believed, and there has been considerable attention to the extensiveness of white-collar and other occupational crime. Since the Cloward-Ohlin theory focuses on lower-class deviancy, it is useless in explaining these phenomena. Moreover, none of the deviancy theorists discussed above have attempted to come to grips with cross-cultural data (thereby necessitating universality) or to derive their theories systematically from larger (universalistic) theories of society.

In the following pages we shall examine some of the data that deviancy theory must explain. Then, in the conclusion of the present chapter, we shall attempt a tentative formulation of a theory which is compatible with the data and which is axiomatically derived from general theory. It may be noted that the deviancy theories discussed above are pertinent primarily to the more-or-less limited areas of crime and delinquency. When our theory is universalistically formulated, it will be seen that other forms of deviancy — suicide, mental disorder, and alcoholism — may be viewed under the auspices of the same general theory of deviancy.

Empirical assessment of deviancy theories

Various forms of data can be brought to bear to assess the amount of deviancy, including data on amount, trends, and cross-cultural differences in deviancy. The foregoing analysis of amount and trends will be confined primarily to crime, although our cross-cultural analysis will include other forms of deviancy. For purposes of assessing the extent of and trends in deviancy in the United States, crime statistics are more accurate, reliable, and available than statistics on other disorders. Moreover, crime statistics are most relevant in assessing the above theories. Statistics on other disorders may prove important in corroborating our final general theory of deviancy, and will be cited after that theory is formulated.

For the time being, let us look at the crime data for the United

States with an eye to revising the above particularistic theories of deviancy.

THE EXTENT OF CRIME

Extent may be assessed either from the point of view of the victim or the offender. In terms of available statistics, current studies, and present theories on crime, there are thus several ways of looking at the extent of crime:

1. Extent of crime victimization in the United States as noted in official statistics.

2. Extent of victimization, whether or not recorded in official statistics—unreported crime.

3. The number of offenders, as recorded in official records.

4. The number of offenders, whether or not recorded in official records.

Thus, 1, 2, 3, and 4 represent all combinations of victim-offender and official-unreported crime variables. Each of these can be further subdivided according to "categories of risk"—age, sex, social class, race, and so on. These delineations in turn provide the basis for many of the major theories of crime and delinquency.

Officially recorded victimization The number of crimes involving the American public is large—over 2,800 Federal crimes and a much larger number of state and local crimes. Generally, they include crimes against persons, against property, against public order or morals, against the government, and against the economy. The FBI has constructed an index of crimes felt most serious to most Americans, including criminal homicide, forcible rape, aggravated assault, robbery, burglary, larceny of $50 and over, and auto theft. These crimes make up different proportions of the index.

The crimes of violence—murder, forcible rape, aggravated assault, and robbery—make up only 13 per cent of the index. Of these, only robbery is an offense usually committed by a stranger. UCR and other studies indicate that about 70 per cent of all willful killings,[24] nearly two thirds of all aggravated assaults,[25] and a higher percentage of forcible rapes[26] are committed by family members, friends, or other persons previously known to the victim. In Wolfgang's study, 85.6 per cent of murder victims were at least casually acquainted with their attackers.[27] A special survey made by the UCR in 1960 of 564 cities showed that more than 65 per cent of all aggravated assaults occurred either within the family (22 per cent) or among neighbors or acquaintances (43.3 per cent). Of the 131 aggravated assaults studied by the D.C. Crime Commission, 81 per cent involved offenders previously known to their victims; 20.7 per cent of the offenders were relatives. Only 19 per cent of the offenders were strangers.[28] The D.C. Crime Commission Report indicated that only 36 per cent of all rapes surveyed were committed by complete strangers.[29] A study in Philadelphia showed that only 42.3 per cent were strangers, 9.6 per cent were strangers whose identity was known, 14.4 per cent were acquaintances, 19.3 per cent neighbors, 6.0 per cent close friends, 5.3 per cent family friends, and 2.5 per cent relatives. Nationally, about one half of all robberies (taking of property by use of force) are street robberies, 20.2 per cent commercial house, 5.9 per cent gas or service station, 2.7 chain store, 9.1 residence, 0.9 bank, and 9.9 miscellaneous.[30] The situations in which robberies occur indicate that the offender is most often a stranger. Available evidence indicates that injury occurs in 25 per cent of robberies, 84 per cent of aggravated assault, and less than 25 per cent of forcible rapes.[31]

An overall assessment of offenses involving injury indicates that, on the average, the likelihood of a serious personal attack on any American in a given year is about 1 in 550. The rate of serious body harm from crimes of violence for 1965 was 184.7 per 100,000 population for all crimes of violence; 5.1 for murder; 11.6 forcible rape; 61.4, robbery; and 106.6 aggravated assault.[32] Interestingly, more than half of these serious injuries were inflicted by spouses, family members, friends, or acquaintances.[33] Furthermore, studies indicate that the injury inflicted by family members or acquaintances is likely to be more severe than from strangers.

The relatively large rate of homicide in the United States is perhaps accounted for by the large part played by motor vehicle offenses. In 1965, negligent manslaughter—primarily a motor vehicle offense—accounted for more than 7,000 of the 49,000 motor vehicle deaths.[34] The risk of injury from crime, however, is somewhat higher than UCR figures indicate, since the UCR index does not include all crimes involving injury. Excluded are such crimes as arson, kidnapping, child molestation, and simple assault. In a Philadelphia study, offenses other than the seven index crimes constituted 62 per cent of all cases in which there was physical injury.[35]

Victimization, of course, does not include only crimes of violence. In fact, of the index crimes, property crimes—burglary, automobile theft, and larceny of $50 and over—make up 87 per cent.[36] Thus, the total risk of victimization for all index crimes would be about one in 70. Furthermore, studies indicate that more dollar value is lost through crimes such as fraud and embezzlement not figured in the FBI index than by index offenses.[37] Statistics on certain economically costly crimes, such as crimes connected with corporate activity (white-collar crime) and organized crime, are not even compiled by the FBI. Furthermore, the extent of victimization from professional crime is difficult to assess, because professional criminals develop highly proficient techniques in evading legal sanctions.

Existing studies indicate that more serious and more violent crimes are reported more reliably than less serious crimes.[38] In the more serious crimes, arrests are more often made for crimes reported. For example, there is a high percentage of reported cases in which arrests are made for murder (91 per cent) and a relatively low percentage for larceny (20 per cent). Furthermore, crimes reported to the FBI are for less than 70 per cent of the population.[39] Thus, crimes of a less serious nature in FBI statistics would tend to be underestimates of the true crime picture. Even so, non-index crimes are by far more prevalent than index crimes, as measured by arrest statistics. In fact, nearly 45 per cent of all arrests are for relatively minor offenses without victims, or against public order, such as drunkenness, gambling, liquor law violations, vagrancy, and prostitution. Drunkenness alone accounted for 31 per cent of all arrests. Thus, even the official crime picture in the United States is relatively extensive, with five million arrests for the year 1965 in FBI statistics alone.

The extent of unreported victimization　　Although police and FBI statistics indicate much crime in the United States today, they fall short of indicating the total amount. For a variety of reasons, some crimes are not reported to law enforcement agencies, and thus some guilty parties are not apprehended. Citizens may fear reprisals from the offenders, or may even wish to protect them. Too, public apathy often leads to the non-reporting of crimes. And in some cases public complicity, such as involvement with gambling or vice, may negatively influence the reporting of crimes to police.

Very often, crimes may be reported but an arrest is not made—

also for a variety of reasons. The offender may have concealed all evidence that could lead to his capture. Probably more usually, the police may not have the resources to track down the offender. The offender may be known to the police but an arrest cannot be made due to lack of evidence and/or the socially acceptable position of the offender in the community. Thus, in some cases, the "true incidence" of crime in the community may be much larger than the reported incidence.

The first national survey of crime victimization was taken in 1966–1967 by the National Opinion Research Center of the University of Chicago.[40] The survey of 10,000 households involved asking whether the person questioned or any member of his or her household, had been a victim of crime during the past year, whether the crime had been reported, and if not, the reasons for not reporting. The NORC survey showed that the actual amount of crime in the United States today is several times that reported in the UCR. The amount of personal injury crime reported to NORC was almost twice the UCR rate. The amount of property crime was more than twice as much as the UCR rate for individuals. Forcible rapes were more than 3½ times the reported rate, burglaries three times, aggravated assaults and larcenies of $50 and over more than double, and robbery 50 per cent greater than the reported rate. Even these rates were probably an understatement because respondents reported more offenses committed against self than against other members of his household.

There were several reasons mentioned by respondents as to why they had not reported crimes. The reason most frequently mentioned for all offenses was that the police could not do anything. The next most frequent reason was that the offense was a private matter or that the victim did not want to harm the offender. Fear of reprisal was least often cited, but was highest in cases of assaults and family crimes.

Table 5–1 shows the distribution that occurs when crimes are ranked according to the percentage of cases in which police are not notified. As it turns out, the crimes most often reported (auto theft, robbery, aggravated assault, larceny of $50 and over, and burglary) are among the seven major crimes reported in the UCR index. Because fear of reprisal is relatively negligible as a reason for non-reporting, this order appears to suffice as a rough measure of public tolerance of crime—that is, a measure of seriousness. This order

TABLE 5–1   Percentage of cases in which police are not notified

1. Auto theft	11%
2. Robbery	35%
3. Aggravated assault	35%
4. Larceny ($50 and over)	40%
5. Burglary	42%
6. Sex offenses (other than rape)	49%
7. Family crimes (desertion, nonsupport, etc.)	50%
8. Simple assault	54%
9. Larceny (under $50)	63%
10. Other fraud (bad checks, swindling, etc.)	74%
11. Consumer fraud	90%

SOURCE: NORC Survey

corresponds quite well with Cavan's order of crime seriousness as reported in Chapter 4. Of the most serious offenses, those most often reported are professional crime, according to Cavan. Thus, robbery, larceny, and burglary rank high. Occasional crimes are disapproved by the public. Thus, occasional offenses, such as family crimes, simple assault, larceny, and sex offenses, are ranked middle in seriousness. The least serious offenses are white-collar crimes, as in this case various forms of fraud. Seriousness is here defined in terms of the values of our own society. While violence is not condoned by our society, the illicit appropriation of money, as in fraud, which does not involve coercion or threat, may be tolerated, or even in some cases approved. Even more interesting, this rank-order of seriousness corresponds quite well to the rank order of frequency of crime, the more serious crimes are less often committed.

Implications of victimization studies   A number of relevant conclusions can be drawn from the above statistics. First, crimes of a relative serious nature are quite widespread in American society. Roughly 1.5 per cent of Americans are victimized by serious crime each year, as indicated by official records; unofficially, ten times that figure. It is doubtful that all or even a sizable majority of these crimes are committed by lower-class offenders, as the deviancy theories assume. Second, a minority of crimes of violence (excepting robbery) are committed by strangers to the victim. Since crimes of violence occur in every social class, it is doubtful that the offender (who is quite likely a friend or relative) is invariably a lower-class person, as assumed by deviancy theories above. Last, studies of public toleration of crime indicate that crimes are often not reported because the victim does not want to harm the offender, indicating the strong possibility that offenders are of the same or higher social class as their victims, and as such a number of crimes are committed by upper- and middle-class offenders but never reported.

Offenders—official versus unofficial   When the emphasis is shifted from victimization, which refers to the total number of offenses committed during any period of time, to incidence or prevalence of crime, a somewhat different picture is drawn. Data on offenders is badly needed, as generalizations based solely on arrest figures may produce a biased picture. That is, an exaggerated estimate of crime may result if the same person is arrested more than once during a year, as often occurs in drunkenness offenses and other crimes against public order.

Oddly enough, although statistics are available on incidence—that is the number of persons convicted of crime and under correctional supervision—there are no official records on prevalence. Incidence figures indicate 0.65 per cent of the United States population were under correctional supervision in 1965.[41] The closest approximation to prevalence figures are estimates of the prevalence of juvenile delinquency. Rough estimates by the Children's Bureau, supported by independent studies, indicate that one in every nine youths—one in every six male youths—will be referred to juvenile court in connection with a delinquent act (excluding traffic offenses) before his eighteenth birthday.[42]

Studies of unreported crime and delinquency have, as in the case of unreported victimization, yielded higher estimates. These studies have indicated that as many as 90 per cent of juveniles and 99 per cent of adults have committed offenses meriting jail terms.

Implications of offender studies   The estimates of the number of offenders in the United States vary widely from roughly 11 per cent to 90 per cent of the population depending upon statistical source used. In either case, it can be doubted that all of these offenders are lower-class.

Extent of crime among certain social categories   As in the case of the overall amount of crime, the distribution of crime among various social categories—SES, sex, race, age, religion, and so on—can be studied either from the point of view of the victim or the offender. In this case, however, there seems to be more information available on offender variations than victim. While the FBI Uniform Crime Reports classify crime by region and state, there are no national crimes statistics showing the variation of official crimes by such categories as SES, race, sex, age, and so on. However, the NORC survey described above did classify self-reported victimization by these categories, and these findings will be summarized briefly here.[43]

Region. The Crime Commission report compared NORC survey findings with FBI data. Comparing four regions, Northeast, North Central, South, and West, the following findings were noted. In general, the FBI and NORC findings were comparable for both Part I and Part II offenses, with the exception of the North Central region, in which the survey showed a higher rate than the UCR. The relative rankings by regions for both types of offenses were the same: the West highest, North Central next, Northeast, and South lowest. However, some discrepancies were noted between NORC and UCR findings. Aggravated assaults are highest in the South, according to the UCR, but the survey shows a much higher rate in the West. Robbery is high in the North Central and Western regions in UCR statistics; the survey, however, shows robbery rates equal in the North Central and the South, but indicates a rate three times that of the UCR in the Northeast.

Community type. The Commission also studied victimization by degree of urbanization, using three areas: (1) central cities of metropolitan areas; (2) suburban communities of the metropolis; and (3) non-metropolitan communities. Traditional beliefs about the association between urbanization and crime were confirmed by Commission findings. The central cities produce more crimes of violence than the non-metropolitan communities. Petty theft and malicious destruction of property are reported most often in the suburbs. However, crimes of false pretenses—forgery, counterfeiting, frauds, and consumer frauds—proved anomalous by being equally concentrated at each level.

Socio-economic status. Traditional theories stress that crime is most often committed by persons from lower socio-economic background. However, if it can be assumed that criminals victimize their own social class, there appears to be little evidence for traditional theory. Both Part I and Part II offenses are equally divided among four different income levels and among both whites and non-whites. In only three crime areas—robbery, burglary, and family crimes—

is the lowest income category (less than $3,000) victimized most of all class levels. However, other social classes seem to be disproportionately victimized by certain crimes. Upper-class persons (the highest income category above $10,000) are most victimized by larceny, malicious mischief or arson, and consumer fraud. Middle-class persons ($6,000–$9,999) appear most victimized by auto offenses. On the whole, however, social class does not appear a promising variable for understanding crime victimization.

Race. Two racial categories were used by the NORC survey, white and non-white. At all levels of income, non-whites have higher rates of vicitimization for serious crimes against the person compared to whites. Property crimes show a more complex relationship to both race and income. Among lower income groups (under $6,000 per year) non-whites are only very slightly more likely to be victims of property crimes than whites, while the wealthier black is considerably more likely to have property stolen.

The fear of the black man as the major source of crime was not justified by the Commission data. Eighty-eight per cent of crimes committed against whites are committed by white offenders; 81 per cent of crimes committed against blacks are committed by black offenders. Thus, blacks are more likely to be victimized by whites than are whites by blacks.

Sex. NORC findings indicate that males in both races are more likely to be the victims of crime, with the following exceptions noted: forcible rape in both races, robbery in the case of non-whites, aggravated assault in the case of non-whites, larceny in the case of non-whites (both under and over $50), simple assault in the case of non-whites, other sex offenses in both races, and family offenses in both races. Thus, by inference the following crimes typically involve a male victim: homicide, burglary, vehicle theft, auto offenses, malicious mischief or arson, counterfeiting or forgery, fraud and consumer fraud.

Age. In general, adults in the middle age groups (20–29, 30–39, 40–49) are the most victimized by Part I and Part II offenses. Certain age and sex groups appear to be especially susceptible to certain types of offenses. Females between the ages of 20 and 29 appear highly vulnerable to forcible rape, robbery, simple assault, fraud, and other sex offenses, while males of that age group are disproportionately victimized by aggravated assault and simple assault, males age 30–39 family offense, and males 40–49 counterfeiting or forgery.

Implications of victimization by category studies   The theories of crime described above make no comment on such categorical differences as those between regions, sex, and age groups. These theories would probably hold crime to be greatest among those categories with least opportunity for success and/or highest aspirations. Thus we might predict crime to be highest in the South—the poorest region in the United States; in the inner city; in the lower class; and among underprivileged minority groups. Crime theories discussed above cannot account for age and sex differences. Interestingly enough, it is found that crime is highest in the West (the "land of opportunity") and lowest in the South. Not all crimes are concentrated in the inner city. Petty theft and vandalism are more often found in the suburbs, and white-collar crimes and fraud are scattered throughout the city. Similarly, certain crimes are equally divided by class level: namely, crimes against property. It is also nonconfirmatory that blacks, though more often victims of crime than whites, are more likely to be victimized by whites than vice versa.

Distribution of offenders among certain social categories   Perhaps the bulk of research in crime and delinquency has concerned the distribution of offenders among certain social categories, mainly social class, sex, age, race, nativity, and area. These distributions have implications for the major crime theories that were reviewed above.

Social class. A number of studies have shown the distribution of crime and delinquency by socio-economic class. Studies in ecology have shown that arrests for most crimes are disproportionately concentrated in the inner-city slums. Because police records usually contain no social class data, it is difficult to study SES differences directly from police records. However, the several studies that have delved into the social class backgrounds of offenders have consistently yielded the finding that the delinquency and crime reflected in official records overwhelmingly centers in the lower or working classes.[44]

It has been argued that these studies, because they are based on official records, may reflect biases toward lower-class people on the part of the police, courts, and other agencies of law enforcement. Recently, a number of self-report studies of crime and delinquency have shown that middle- and upper-class youth have commited just as many offenses as lower-class.[45] These inconsistencies have not yet been reconciled, and the controversy goes on between advocates of official *versus* unofficial reports as a basis for study. Even exponents of official statistics acknowledge that crime and delinquency are likely to occur in all income groups. Quite possibly it will be found that although crime in general can be found at all social-class levels, certain types of crime—e.g., robbery, burglary, and family crimes, as in victimization surveys—are more highly concentrated among lower-class people, other types, such as fraud and white-collar crime are upper-class offenses, while still other offenses, especially delinquency of teens, are equally distributed at all social-class levels.

Sex. As judged by arrests, males commit many more crimes and acts of delinquency than females. The ratio of eight men to one woman in the UCR has held constant over the years. These ratios were primarily for adults. Among youths, the ratio for males as compared to females is closer to six to one, according to Children's Bureau statistics. As in the case of findings on social class and crime, it is debatable whether these findings are due to greater criminality among men or due to greater proneness of men to arrest. Recent self-report studies, however, corroborate the official statistics on this point. Boys commit more offenses in virtually every category.[46] There are variations, however, in the ratios, depending on the criminal act—that is, for some crimes, women more closely rival men. For such crimes as burglary, auto theft, robbery, manslaughter, assault, possession of weapons, drunk driving, drunkenness, vagrancy, and gambling, men far outnumber women. However, for a few offense categories—larceny, forgery, counterfeiting, aggravated assault, murder, narcotic law violation, disorderly conduct, and sex offenses, women more closely resemble men in police statistics, with ratios of about five to one. Self-report techniques show girls are highest in such delinquencies as ungovernability, running away, and sex offenses. There is a trend, however, toward greater involvement of females in more areas of crime. Women are increasingly becoming involved in cases of embezzlement and forgery. They are also involved as associated with men in many cases of property crimes, although they are rarely charged. Thus, while the statistical picture is more convincing for males as compared to females, there is no assurance that it will remain so.

Age. Although all types of crimes are committed by persons of all ages, there is a much greater probability of young persons being arrested for the most serious felonies. Some types of crimes, such as auto theft, burglary, and larceny are committed predominantly by teenagers (under 20). Two other offenses, robbery and forcible rape, are committed by persons under 25 years of age. Some serious crimes are, of course, characteristic of persons over 25 years of age. These include criminal homicide, aggravated assault, narcotics, alcohol and gambling violations, vagrancy, murder, and white collar and professional crime. Thus, age cannot be used as criterion of seriousness in crime. Just as many serious crimes characterize young offenders as old, and the young may actually be underrepresented in FBI statistics, due to the fact that juveniles are often not fingerprinted or their fingerprints are not always reported to the FBI. Characteristically, young people commit more serious but less skilled property offenses, while the old are more often guilty of crimes of violence, crimes against public order, and more skilled property offenses.

Race. Statistically speaking, non-whites have a sizably greater proneness to arrest than whites. This applies in both arrest and convict statistics. FBI statistics indicated about 22 per cent of arrests are of non-white persons, while *National Prisoner Statistics* indicate 29 per cent are black, despite a population of approximately 10 per cent black. While self-report data is not available on race *per se,* the author's studies comparing responses of youths from predominantly black high schools in Watts, Los Angeles, indicates that black–white differences in delinquency are not as great as official statistics indicate. This finding would seem to indicate, as has been alleged by criminologists for years, that black persons are discriminated against by the agencies of law enforcement — the police, courts, and even corrections — as they are in other areas of our society.

While the black–white differences are not as great as traditionally assumed, on certain crimes the differences between black and white crime rates are especially pronounced, indicating a higher prevalence among blacks. Especially noteworthy are such crimes as homicide, assault, carrying and possessing weapons, receiving or buying stolen property, gambling, and liquor laws. On the other hand, in certain types of crime, blacks are strikingly close to whites in rates of offense (which possibly indicates a lower prevalence among blacks, if biasing of police and courts is held constant). These include driving while intoxicated, auto theft, forgery and counterfeiting, sex offenses, drunkenness, embezzlement, and fraud.

Nationality as a factor in crime. One would ordinarily expect that foreign-born immigrants would have higher rates of crime than native Americans. Immigrants are disproportionately male, usually of lower-class origin seeking greater opportunities, ignorant of the law in this country, and forced to crowd into urban slums. In fact this belief may have been the basis of many of our stringent immigration laws in this country. However, FBI statistics and statistics compiled by the National Commission on Law Observance and Enforcement indicate that the native-born American actually exceeds the foreign-born in rates of crime. In part, as a study by Taft indicated, this was due to the disproportion of older adults in the immigrant population. Also, the generalization does not hold true of all immigrant groups. Immigrants of Mexican, Greek, and Italian descent have higher rates than the native born. Generally, crime involvement of immigrants from southern and eastern Europe is larger than for the immigrants from northern and western Europe, as judged by commitments to penal institutions.[47] This is even more true when corrected for age differentials between the foreign born and native born.

These generalizations hold true only of crime. Statistics on juvenile delinquency of the foreign born are not available because the foreign born are usually over juvenile court age.

Area variations. Area variations can be studied from a variety of points of view, including intracity variations, rural–urban variations, state-by-state variations, and regional variations.

Probably the most widely studied variations are those crime variations taking place within a city. The main body of findings surrounds the concentric zone theory of the Chicago school of sociology. Students of Burgess and Park, including Faris and Dunham, Shaw and McKay, Thrasher, and Zorbaugh, did extensive studies of the variation of a variety of forms of deviant behavior according to their distribution by concentric zones. Although the early studies used numerous zones, these were later simplified into five concentric zones: Zone I, the central business district; Zone II, the slum area or zone in transition; Zone III, zone of working men's homes—two- and three-family flats or dwellings; Zone IV, an area of single family dwellings or residential zone; and Zone V, the suburban or commutation area.

Briefly, a wide gamut of deviant behavior was located, by studying police, hospital, and other official records, in Zones I and II. Conventional crime, delinquency, mental illness in general and schizophrenia in particular, suicide, prostitution, vagrancy, dependency, illegitimacy, infant mortality, and high death rates were found all highly concentrated in these two areas. With the exceptions of manic-depressive psychosis, white-collar crime, and gambling and prostitution, all of the above problems decreased as one moved from Zones I and II out toward the periphery of the concentric circles. Manic-depressive psychosis was found dispersed evenly throughout the zones. White-collar crime was found more prevalent in Zones IV and V of the city. Gambling and prostitution were prevalent not only in Zone II, but sometimes beyond the surburban fringe. Thus, the findings on concentric zones more or less corroborate findings on social-class differentials in crime as shown in official police records. The validity of these findings, as far as official records are concerned, has not been widely disputed. However, a recent self-report study of delinquency has indicated that delinquency is more highly dispersed throughout the city than is shown in police and other official records.[48]

City size also plays a role in the determination of official crime rates. Most crimes show a continuous progression in rates as size of city increases.

Implication of offender-by-category data   Most crime theories depend upon "official" data that indicate that most offenders come from lower-class backgrounds. The SES studies are inconsistent on this point. A controversy goes on between those who believe in official statistics, which support the lower-class hypothesis, and those who advocate the use of self-report and non-official statistics, which generally bring to light a high incidence of "hidden" middle- and upper-class delinquency. Criminal offenders tend to vary by categories quite unrelated to SES, that is, by age and sex. Males in both official and self-report data commit more crimes. Major crime is more often an offense of the young than the old. Studies of race and nativity as factors in crime fail to confirm traditional crime theories which would view underprivileged minority group status as contributory to crime. While blacks have higher official crimes rates than whites, self-report study casts doubt on this finding. Also, blacks are not higher in all forms of official crime than whites. Contrary to the theories and lay public opinion, immigrants actually have lower crime rates than native Americans. While area studies using official reports have shown most forms of deviancy to be concentrated in the inner-city slum, notable exceptions exist—white-collar crime, manic-depressive psychosis, gambling, and prostitution. Also, self-report study challenges this finding. Thus, offender-by-category studies have given no clear mandate to the traditional crime theories.

TRENDS IN CRIME

What is the extent of crime in the United States? This is not an easy question to answer. The current public view is that crime is increasing and that this indicates a gloomy prognosis for society. However, can we assume crime is increasing and can we jump from this assumption to conclusions about decadence, delinquent society, or a "sick society"? Furthermore, does this justify a return to some less complex stage of societal development as some have advocated? Is our society headed on a collision course as far as crime is concerned? These questions can only be answered through studying crime from several points of view. Are the crimes committed in the United States generally of a serious nature such as to threaten the survival of society? Are the rates of these serious crimes increasing in the United States? How does the United States stand as compared with other countries of the world, especially as far as serious crime is concerned? Most important, what can we expect for the future in America? Some of these questions can be answered by looking at trends in crime in the United States. Others require comparative cross-cultural analysis of the United States as compared with other societies. The next section will deal with the former—trends in crime in the United States. Subsequently, we shall look at what cross-cultural data is available.

Unlike some European countries, which have maintained national statistics on crime for more than a century and a quarter, the United States has maintained national crime statistics only since 1930.[49] Since that year, the FBI Uniform Crime Report have shown a phenomenal increase in crime rates. This trend has applied to serious crimes and crimes in general, and has been constant except for a decline during the early war years, when large numbers of young men were recruited into the armed forces. However, for a variety of reasons, the FBI statistics could not be considered at all reliable until 1958 (the year UCR published a special issue explaining changes in crime classification). Rural regions were slow in coming into the system. Another problem was that the urban poor increasingly in recent years have sought police protection and reported crimes that before would have gone unreported.

Probably most important has been the trend toward professionalization of the police, which has led to more efficient enforcement of laws and better record-keeping and reporting. Thus, in some cases the phenomenal increase in "rates" of crime have been little more than a statistical artifact. For example, in 1953 Philadelphia reported a 70 per cent increase in index crimes plus negligent manslaughter and larceny over $50. This increase was due to a new city administration that discovered that crime records had for years minimized the amount of crime in the city. An even more fantastic change occurred in New York. Following a survey by police expert Bruce Smith which uncovered many instances of failure to report (local precincts would hold back complaints because detectives feared that the reporting of large numbers of unsolved burglaries would provoke shakeups), all precinct numbers were taken out of the New York City telephone book, and any person wishing to report a crime had to call the central station. In the year following the change, assaults rose 200 per cent, robberies 400 per cent, and burglaries 1,300 per cent over 1948 figures.[50] Recently, other cities have undergone vast increases in crimes reported due to similar changes in police practices.

Other changes have also influenced the FBI statistics. Insurance coverage has increased, and thus people may be more inclined now to report crime because many believe it necessary to report a criminal event in order to collect from insurance companies. Classification changes by local police also may have had some effect in increase rates of reported crime.

Based on UCR statistics alone, it is difficult to conclude much about trends in crime. There is some evidence that certain serious crimes are decreasing in relative frequency or rate. UCR statistics since 1958 in fact show a minor decrease in willful homicide, despite the changes in reporting procedure noted above. Bell notes that although there has been an increase in crime in large cities and small towns, cities between 10,000 and 250,000 population showed decreases in crime between 1940 and 1953. Certain cities—for instance, Portland and Seattle—showed decreases in overall crime during this period, despite population increases.[51] Another study by Powell noted that crimes of violence increased from 1830 to the 1870's in Buffalo, declined steadily until the turn of the century, rose again until 1918, then receded to the pre-Civil War level by 1940.[52]

What is to be made of these various and conflicting statistics? Bell has proposed that there is a "myth of crime waves." He believes the reason we believe so devotedly that crime is increasing is in part "yellow journalism" and in part the vested interests of law-enforcement agencies in crime. For example, he cites as example the statistic of one in four of seventeen-year-old youths being "arrested" in 1957 published by the California Youth Authority:

> One reason, perhaps, why the California Youth Authority released its reckless statistic is that it hoped, by shocking the public, to mobilize pressure for an increased appropriation at the next session of the legislature. Such "inflation" of crime is not an uncommon feature of law enforcement in the United States today.[53]

Bell cites evidence that there has been greater control over organized crime, over corruption of law enforcement agencies, and over labor racketeering. There is greater evidence of a decline in violence in the streets over the past 30 or 40 years. The difference between now and then is that now Americans have a greater exposure to vicarious violence through television, radio, and other mass media. Thus, Bell asks, "Do we then have a crime wave or a 'crime reporting' wave?"

The President's Commission has analyzed the UCR statistics since 1960. Looking at offenses known to the police for the period 1960–1965, rates for willful homicide and forcible rape have remained relatively constant. Rates for robbery and aggravated assault have risen moderately, while rates for property crimes of burglary, larceny of $50 and over, and motor vehicle theft have risen rapidly in that period. These changes are at least proportional to changes shown by arrest records.

For other serious but non-index offenses, rates follow a much more checkered pattern. Arrest rates rose 13 per cent for simple assault, 13 per cent for embezzlement and fraud, and 36 per cent for narcotics violations, while the rates for gambling declined 24 per cent and for drunkenness 11 per cent.

Factors indicating an increase in crime   It has been noted that certain social categories are disproportionately prone to certain types of crime or to crime in general—such as the young for serious property offenses, and adults for crimes of violence and crimes against public order. What changes have taken place in the population in this country? What trends do those changes indicate?

First, there has been an increase of young people. Thus, we have noted a strong trend in the direction of increasing burglary, major larceny, and auto theft—typically offenses of the young people. The increase in the composition of young people seems to confirm the trend shown in FBI statistics.

There has been an increase in urbanization, a trend which would conceivably indicate an increase in crime generally. But, concurrently, there has been an increase in affluence, or a decrease in the lower-class segment of our population, which has traditionally been blamed for most serious crime. Perhaps these are to some extent countervailing trends. The social-class changes, however, point additionally to changes in the nature of crime. White-collar crime should be increasing among adults. Auto theft, malicious mischief, and petty theft among the young should also be increasing, as these are typically middle-class delinquencies. In the next section, we shall attempt to weigh and balance these trends and statistics on crime to produce a picture of the United States today as seen vis-à-vis other societies of the world and as compared to its own past. As a preview of what is to come, it will be shown that the United States appears to be at a stage in which violence, both political and social, is on the decrease, while utilitarian crimes are on the increase. Along with this trend, there may also be a greater tendency toward "escapist" types of crimes, as well as other forms of disorder.

CRIME IN THE UNITED STATES: AN ASSESSMENT

Statistics indicate that crimes against property are extensive and appear to be increasing in the United States. There is evidence that forms of property crimes are prevalent at all class levels.

Statistics on crimes of violence indicate that perhaps the extent of violent crime in America is overstated and also that when the bias of official records is taken into account, there is reason to believe that crimes of violence (especially willful homicide, forcible rape, robbery, and aggravated assault) appear to be on the decrease.

Though the statistics are not clear-cut on this point, there is some evidence of an increase in "escapist" crimes, especially drug addiction and drug abuse. Drunkenness arrests have declined somewhat, but perhaps this indicates a change in law enforcement policy.

Looking at theories of crime, we have noted that certain classic theories have been rejected or ignored by American theorists: the geographical, the biological, and the utilitarian. American crime theory has developed essentially from two classic approaches: the theory of economic determinism, and the theory of imitation. In sum, these theories have attributed our crime problem to the inequitable distribution of status and economic rewards in capitalistic society and the learning and transmission of deviant patterns from generation to generation. In these theories, there has been a relative neglect of statistics on trends or cross-cultural comparisons of crime. If crime, especially crime against property, is increasing in the United States, there should be an increase in the conditions specified in these theories—that is, stratification gaps or barriers, and increased communication among deviants. However, these conditions do not appear to be increasing. Indeed, the number of lower-class people appears to be decreasing, and there is a burgeoning middle class. This, in turn, would increase the difficulty of communication among subcultural deviants, as their cohorts may be moving socially and geographically. Because traditional social theories of crime fail to fit the trends as well as recent evidence as to the prevalence of crime in the middle class, new theories are developing. As was shown, Bloch and Niederhoffer recognize the existence of delinquent gangs in both middle- and lower-class neighborhoods. A whole new line of theories has been developed to explain the "spread" of delinquency to the middle class. These theories will be discussed in Chapter 6. In explaining the emergence of middle-class delinquency, these theories begin to account for the increasing trend in property crime in modern society. Crime may be traced to excessive leisure, to mass media, to peer group, to "anomie of success," and the like.

Thus, we have a rough picture of the trend in property crime in America. This picture is to some extent corroborated by cross-cultural studies of delinquency and crime. Although reliable cross-cultural statistics on crime and delinquency do not exist, impressions can be drawn from recent studies. Cavan and Cavan have attempted to summarize studies of 14 prominent societies of the world.[54] There are essentially four different types of societies. In *folk villages,* such as the traditional Eskimo and the Mexican *barrio,* crime and delinquency is noticeably absent, with the exception of certain crimes of violence (such as murder of a wife's seducer among the Eskimo). In *villages in transition* (among the Eskimos, the Tepoztlan in Mexico, and in India), there is evidence of an increase in crime and delinquency, including excessive drinking, sexual promiscuity, and petty thievery. In the *transitional city* such as exists in India and Mexico, delinquency and crime increases in the urban slums where crime is instrumental to survival. The highest rates of delinquency and crime exist in the *industrialized cities* in the West, including the United States, France, West Germany, the Netherlands, Belgium, and Sweden. Despite this increase in crime and delinquency with modernity, Cavan and Cavan feel that one area of crime — violence, injuries, and murder — has been decreasing.

> Without any statistical proof, the impression gained was that physical injuries and murders occurred more often, and with less provocation, in the past than at present.[55]

While recognizing that any portrayal of trends is based upon impressionistic statistical evidence, perhaps a trend and cross-cultural portrait can be deduced from the theory of social organization developed earlier in this book. In terms of Merton's schema, societies of the world may be viewed in terms of five possible behavior patterns: conformity, rebellion, innovation, ritualism, and retreatism. These five types were related to other typologies in Chapter 4. Using Cavan's framework described in the previous chapter, "true conformity" in Merton's sense is relatively limited in contemporary society in transition. We have argued that deviancy is an index and instrument of social change. It will be seen in the chapter on white-collar crime that criminality and also juvenile delinquency pervade middle- as well as lower-class sectors of our society. Few if any are capable of escaping deviancy altogether, in part because certain forms of "deviancy" in terms of traditional standards are considered "conformity" in terms of present standards. Also, some people may deliberately violate a rule they feel is wrong. In modern society there is, to a greater or lesser degree, a choice of either neurotic endurance of frustration, or delinquency. Paul Goodman has expressed this well:

> Thwarted, or starved, in the important objects proper to young capacities, the boys and young men naturally find or invent deviant

objects for themselves; this is the beautiful shaping power of our human nature. But on the other hand, the young men who conform to the dominant society become for the most part apathetic, disappointed, cynical, and wasted.[56]

GENERAL THEORETICAL FRAMEWORK

In terms of our theoretical framework, we should expect that in the oligarchic or totalitarian societies (such as contemporary Communist societies) deviancy would be directed more toward the retreatist pole, implying higher rates of mental disorder, suicide, drug addiction, and alcoholism. Needless to say, statistics on this would be difficult to gather because of the tight control over such information in Communist states. However, contemporary capitalism, because of its utilitarian basis, would be polarized near the innovation—rebellion end of the continuum. Primitive society is marginal to the deviancy continuum, behavior being almost exclusively in the zone of "conformity." In between primitive and capitalist contemporary society would lie the emergent or transitional nations. These nations witness widespread rebellion against traditional customs and elites, and thus are characterized by high rates of violence and increasing rates of crime generally. However, compared to contemporary capitalist society, property crimes are relatively low, and confined to lower-class people. In the capitalist state, there is a shift of focus away from rebellious crimes of violence and toward innovative acts oriented at the acquisition or enjoyment of abundant economic goods, services, and resources. The general relationship between deviancy and level (form) of societal organization is portrayed in Figure 5–1. This portrait would explain the apparent anomalies in the crime trends—such as increases of theft, decrease of stable rates of murder.

One difficulty, however, exists with the application of this typology. It appears to be an effective device for describing past and present societies. But it excludes future or utopian societies. That is, there is no reason to believe that a "middle ground" society will not emerge in between capitalism and Communism. To project a "utopian" society we must ask what conditions are absent in all large-scale societies. Our theoretical framework will be useful in indicating those conditions. This discussion will concern the conclusion of this book.

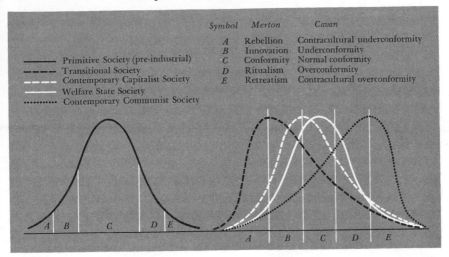

Symbol	Merton	Cavan
A	Rebellion	Contracultural underconformity
B	Innovation	Underconformity
C	Conformity	Normal conformity
D	Ritualism	Overconformity
E	Retreatism	Contracultural overconformity

Primitive Society (pre-industrial)
Transitional Society
Contemporary Capitalist Society
Welfare State Society
Contemporary Communist Society

Figure 5–1.   Deviancy as related to level of social organization

With this theoretical–typological framework in mind, let us take a look at some cross-cultural data to determine if this scheme stands the test of empirical data. According to this framework, we should expect crimes of violence (rebellion) to decrease in accord with the industrialization of society but retreatest disorders (suicide, mental disorder, and alcoholism) to increase as the curve of deviancy moves toward the right on our chart. At the close of this chapter, we shall examine the evidence accrued relevant to theories discussed above.

CROSS-CULTURAL APPLICATIONS

The theories of deviancy discussed in the present chapter and the disorganization and anomie theories discussed in Chapter 3 make certain assumptions which can be examined in the light of cross-cultural data. Current disorganization theory carries the assumption that modern society is more disorganized than previous society. This assumption can be tested if we can derive first an index of "modernity" or industrialization and then correlate this index with a second index of societal instability. Another assumption of current deviancy theory is that most deviancy can be traced to material and economic deprivation, especially if combined with unlimited aspirations. We should expect in accord with this assumption that transitional societies, those in the process of industrialization, would engender the widest variety of deviancy types, in that these societies have the greatest material deprivation, which may be compared with the conspicuous wealth of countries like the United States and those of Western Europe. Along with this assumption, there is the implicit view that deviancy is a unidimensional variable, that as disorganization increases, all (or most) forms of deviancy increase concurrently.

The theory and typology developed above departs from these assumptions to some extent. According to the theoretical model, transitional society is characterized by what has been termed "acute disorganization"[57] as a major form of deviancy. This extreme disorganization appears to decline in contemporary society and deviancy settles into less disruptive forms. As compared with folk society or primitive society, contemporary society appears unstable, but as compared with transitional society (probably far more prevalent than folk society *per se*) contemporary society seems somewhat more stable. If our theories of deviancy and disorganization hold true, we should expect deviancy generally to decline. However, according to our model this would not appear to be the case. Only violence decreases (or at least fails to increase as in our trend data above); other forms of deviancy (innovative, ritualistic, retreatistic) appear to increase. Thus, it appears that much deviancy may increase as society becomes more industrialized and thus more "wealthy." It is also projected that deviancy is not a unidimensional variable. As society changes from a transitional society to a full-scale industrial society certain forms of deviancy increase while others decrease.

In the next section it will be shown that our conclusions are borne out by cross-cultural data. Our cross-cultural investigation will, of course, be limited by what data are available. Available data are limited largely to transitional societies, capitalist societies, and welfare states. For totalitarian societies, data are not generally available. Thus, inquiry will be limited to the development from transitional society to contemporary capitalist or welfare society, which process we shall term "industrialization." Index data are available on industrialization, political stability, homicide, suicide, neurosis, and alcoholism. Our investigation will be confined to these variables. The criterion of political stability may be used to test whether or not contemporary society is more or less stable than transitional society. Homicide is one of the deviant acts that was included in the "rebellion" type in the empirical typology of Chapter 4. Variation in homicide will thus bear upon the hypothesized relation between industrialization and declining violence. Suicide, neurosis, and alcoholism have been pictured as ritualist or retreatist disorders. Thus, in terms of the above theoretical model and available data, the following hypotheses can be stated for cross-cultural test.

1. *The higher the industrialization, the greater the political stability.* This hypothesis contrasts with the disorganization theory assumption that previous society was more organized than the present society.

2. *The higher the industrialization, the less the rate of homicide.* Disorganization theories posit a one-to-one relationship between the development of modern mass or disorganized society and deviancy. However, our transitional model posits that homicide actually declines in contemporary society as compared with transitional society.

3. *The higher the industrialization, the greater the rate of suicide.* It is implied above that modern society is actually somewhat more stably organized than transitional society. However, this does not free modern society from deviant behavior. Certain forms of "retreatist" disorder may result from the decline in group conflict, which carries with it a decline in in-group solidarity which ordinarily would protect an individual from subjective malaise. This point will be discussed more fully below.

4. *The higher the industrialization, the greater the rate of neurosis.* The curve of deviant behavior moves in the direction of both ritualism and retreatism in contemporary society. It has been suggested above that ritualism is a useful type in understanding neurosis.

5. *The higher the industrialization, the greater the rate of alcoholism.* Alcoholism should similarily correlate, although perhaps not as well as the latter two variables, because not all forms of alcohol involvement are individualistic pursuits.

Measurement of cross-cultural variables   Variables to be measured include "modernity" or industrialization, political stability, homicide, suicide, neurosis, and alcoholism. The first two have been measured by previous investigators. The second two are given directly in the United Nations *Demographic Yearbook,* and the last two may be indirectly measured by data drawn from the *Yearbook.*

Industrialization as here defined refers to the extensiveness of the development of specialization and the division of labor within a society. It has been shown that Durkheim viewed it in terms of the "progressive preponderance of organic solidarity." Marsh has developed an empirical index of this concept which he calls "social differentiation."[58] What Marsh calls "social differentiation" we call industrialization. Marsh built an index of industrialization upon Murdock's World Ethnographic Sample of 467 societies. Murdock's earlier index combined scores for population size and for social stratification yielding a range of scores from 0 to 7. Marsh added an additional 98 societies to this list to make a total of 565 societies. He also added two indicators of differentiation in order to distinguish more fully the broad spectrum of national societies: (1) percentage of males in each society who are in nonagricultural occupations, and (2) gross energy consumption in megawatt-hours per capita for one year. The two indicators were combined into a single index by z-scores. Because Murdock's index was earlier designed primarily as a way of comparing primitive societies, the latter two indicators form the major component in Marsh's scale for contemporary or non-primitive nations. Both of these are quite clearly indices of industrialization.

Political instability is a variable which has recently been operationalized by Feierabend and Feierabend.[59] A Guttman scale of political instability was developed by Nesvold following the earlier work of the Feierabends.[60] Nesvold's index for 82 nations is based on observation of instances of violent political instability for the period 1948–61. The data for the Nesvold index were specific instances of overt social aggression such as civil wars, riots, mass executions, and guerrilla warfare, and less violent events such as general strikes, suicides of political leaders, martial law, and falls of cabinets. These instances were drawn from two sources: (1) The *Yearbook of the Encyclopaedia Britannica,* and (2) *Deadline Data on World Affairs.* The index consists of Guttman scale scores constructed from twelve separate political events classed into four scale types by factor analysis. The coefficient of reproducibility varied between 0.94 and 0.97, depending upon the time period being considered for scale purposes. Because Nesvold's index refers to a wide variety of events occuring in society at large and because it focuses upon intergroup conflict, it seems an adequate index of social disorganization, which has been defined in Chapter 3 as referring to "conflict between functions" and "disruption of functional relations."

Indices of homicide, suicide, neurosis, and alcoholism are drawn from the *Demographic Yearbook* for 1965.[61] The year 1965 was selected because this was the most recent year at the time of compilation and because the assumption behind the Marsh and Nesvold indices is that predictions can be made from them to present behavior. While the homicide and suicide rates are stated as such in the *Yearbook*, the indices of neurosis and alcoholism are indirect. Neurosis is measured by the rates of death resulting from ulcer while alcoholism is measured by rates of death from cirrhosis of the liver. The logic behind this link is that both neurosis and alcoholism have been measured by these indirect indices. The duodenal ulcer is one among several psychophysiologic or psychosomatic disorders that result from stress.[62] Studies have shown that psychosomatic complaints are actually the best index of neurosis. The twelve-item scale developed by the Army Neuropsychiatric Adjunct to screen mentally ill draftees consists entirely of psychosomatic complaints, including reference to upset stomach indicative of possible ulcer.[63] Death rate from ulcers would therefore form a crude indicator of neurosis. Such a measure, however, has the limitation that it probably excludes a large proportion of the population who are neurotics (and who do not die from ulcers). Findings using this index, though the only cross-cultural index available for a large number of nations, can only be tentative.

Death from cirrhosis of the liver is also an indirect measure of alcoholism, or at least excessive alcohol consumption. Although there is some evidence that cirrhosis of the liver is due to diet deficiencies associated with excessive alcohol consumption, irregardless, cirrhosis of the liver is commonly associated with alcoholism or inebriety.[64]

Based on these methodological assumptions, we may make cross-cultural comparisons and correlations. The data for these comparisons are given in Table 5–2. Since data have been compiled from different sources, statistics were not available for some coun-

TABLE 5-2 Cross-cultural rates on independent and dependent variables by country

Country	Political instability	Neurosis	Alcohol abuse	Suicide	Homicide	Industrialization
Australia	5	5.8	4.9	14.5	1.6	72.7
Austria	5	9.9	25.2	22.8	1.0	51.3
Belgium	14	5.2	9.8	14.0	0.7	74.5
Brazil	28	4.1	12.2	14.2	10.8	26.3
Bulgaria	– –	4.9	4.7	8.7	2.1	23.0
Burma	50	10.6	15.9	2.9	16.7	19.2
Canada	7	5.1	6.4	8.2	1.3	89.9
Ceylon	43	1.4	4.8	11.6	3.2	28.8
Chile	40	3.5	37.3	3.0	2.3	40.6
China, Republic of (Taiwan)	6	8.8	12.7	19.1	1.4	32.4
Colombia	80	5.6	4.6	4.8	25.5	24.8
Costa Rica	24	2.5	6.6	3.0	3.5	24.1
Czechoslovakia	– –	4.1	9.3	21.3	1.1	65.5
Denmark	3	7.1	7.7	19.1	0.8	55.7
Dominican Republic	32	0.9	8.3	1.0	2.1	23.5
Ecuador	21	2.3	3.7	0.6	5.2	23.5
Finland	6	4.5	3.5	19.8	2.2	47.5
France	97	3.0	31.7	14.9	0.8	57.5
Germany (W)	8	6.4	20.7	19.3	1.2	68.4
Greece	22	4.7	15.9	3.2	1.2	31.0
Guatemala	– –	1.5	8.6	3.0	14.0	17.1
Hungary	– –	6.0	8.7	28.6	1.7	36.8
Iceland	3	2.7	2.1	9.0	0.5	52.2
Ireland	1	7.2	2.7	2.0	0.6	42.7
India	76	1.8	10.3	0.5	2.2	20.3
Israel	5	3.8	4.6	5.0	– – –	48.0
Italy	32	6.6	21.3	5.3	1.1	41.3
Japan	27	9.6	10.1	14.9	1.5	41.5
Jordan	34	1.5	1.3	0.3	2.4	16.1
Luxembourg	0	4.1	26.8	9.4	0.6	70.8
Mexico	36	4.8	20.0	1.8	22.0	29.3
Netherlands	1	4.0	4.0	6.5	0.4	58.0
New Zealand	5	5.6	2.9	8.0	1.4	58.0
Nicaragua	44	1.4	4.9	1.0	26.0	16.7
Norway	4	2.9	3.7	8.0	0.7	55.2
Panama	37	2.5	2.8	5.3	7.3	26.9
Peru	48	1.6	5.6	1.4	2.1	23.0
Philippines	26	7.9	3.2	0.6	2.3	20.9
Poland	– –	5.8	5.8	8.4	1.0	45.8
Portugal	29	9.0	29.4	9.5	1.2	29.6
Spain	58	6.3	17.4	4.9	0.1	31.4
Sweden	4	8.4	5.7	18.5	0.8	62.7
Switzerland	6	6.2	14.8	16.8	0.7	51.6
U.A.R. (Egypt)	40	1.5	0.4	0.1	4.1	23.9
United Kingdom	21	– – –	– – –	11.2	0.6	84.6
United States	30	5.7	12.1	10.8	5.1	109.4
Uruguay	18	4.8	7.5	12.2	4.8	39.7

NOTE: Low scores indicate low political instability

tries on either the dependent or independent variables. If too much data was missing on a given country, that country was excluded from analysis.

Results of cross-cultural analysis In accord with the above analysis, industrialization is inversely related to political instability and homicide rates and directly related to suicide, neurosis, and alcohol abuse, as shown in Table 5–3. As expected from the crudity

TABLE 5-3 Intercorrelation matrix

Variable	x_1	x_2	x_3	x_4	x_5	x_6
x_1 Industrialization	– –	−0.44	−0.40	0.48	0.24	0.13
x_2 Political instability	– –	– –	0.42	−0.39	−0.27	0.23
x_3 Homicide	– –	– –	– –	−0.34	−0.12	−0.07
x_4 Suicide	– –	– –	– –	– –	0.45	0.17
x_5 Neurosis	– –	– –	– –	– –	– –	0.29
x_6 Alcoholism	– –	– –	– –	– –	– –	– –

of measurement, homicide, suicide, and instability correlated better (a moderate order correlation) than do neurosis and alcohol abuse. It is significant that although the latter two are low-order correlates, they are in the expected direction. Also significant is the fact that instability and homicide are positive correlates, and so are suicide, neurosis, and alcohol abuse, indicating the presence of two separate common factors. This supports the polarity of rebellion (instability and homicide) on the one hand and ritualism-retreat (suicide, neurosis, and alcohol abuse) on the other. Further light is cast on the hypotheses by Tables 5–4, 5–5, and 5–6. These tables show the actual countries in a cross-tabulation between industrialization and the dependent variables political instability, homicide, and suicide (neurosis and alcohol abuse were excluded from this detailed analysis due to their lower-order correlation with industrialization). In these tables there appears to be a clear polarity between the West European and Scandinavian countries, on the one hand, and the Latin American countries on the other. The former are highly industrialized capitalist countries or welfare states, while the latter are transitional countries. The transitional countries are politically unstable, high in homicide, and low in suicide. The opposite its true of the contemporary capitalist–welfare state countries.

TABLE 5-4 Industrialization as related to political instability

	Low Industralization	*High Industrialization*	
Low Political Instability	Ecuador Greece Taiwan Uruguay	Australia Austria Belgium Canada Denmark Finland Iceland Ireland Israel Luxembourg Netherlands New Zealand Norway Sweden Switzerland United Kingdom West Germany	
	number: 4	number: 17	total: 21
High Political Instability	Brazil Burma Ceylon Chile Colombia Costa Rica Dominican Republic Guatemala India Jordan Mexico Nicaragua Panama Peru Philippines Portugal Spain U.A.R.	France Italy Japan United States	
	number: 18 total: 22 $Q = -.901$	number: 4 total: 21	total: 22 grand total: 43

NOTE: Four Communist countries—Bulgaria, Czechoslovakia, Poland and Hungary—were excluded, as Nesvold found they did not scale, and therefore contributed errors to her total scale.

TABLE 5-5   Industrialization   as   related   to   homicide

	Low *Industrialization*	*High* *Industrialization*	
Low *Homicide.* *Rate*	Greece Portugal Spain Taiwan	Austria Belgium Canada Czechoslovakia Denmark France Iceland Ireland Italy Luxembourg Netherlands New Zealand Norway Poland Sweden Switzerland United Kingdom West Germany	
	number: 4	number: 18	total: 22
High *Homicide* *Rate*	Brazil Bulgaria Burma Ceylon Chile Colombia Costa Rica Dominican Republic Ecuador Guatemala Hungary India Jordan Mexico Nicaragua Panama Peru Philippines U.A.R. Uruguay	Australia Finland Japan United States	
	number: 20	number: 4	total: 24
	total: 24	total: 22	grand total: 46
	$Q = -.915$		

NOTE: Israel reported no data on homicide.

TABLE 5-6 # Industrialization as related to suicide

	Low Industrialization	High Industrialization	
	Burma		
	Chile		
	Colombia	Canada	
	Costa Rica	Ireland	
	Dominican Republic	Israel	
	Ecuador	Italy	
	Greece	Netherlands	
Low	Guatemala	New Zealand	
Suicide	India	Norway	
Rate	Jordan		
	Mexico		
	Nicaragua		
	Panama		
	Peru		
	Philippines		
	Spain		
	U.A.R.		
	number: 17	number: 7	total: 24
	Brazil	Australia	
	Bulgaria	Austria	
	Ceylon	Belgium	
	Hungary	Czechoslovakia	
	Portugal	Denmark	
	Taiwan	Finland	
	Uruguay	France	
High		Iceland	
Suicide		Japan	
Rate		Luxembourg	
		Poland	
		Sweden	
		Switzerland	
		United Kingdom	
		United States	
		West Germany	
	number: 7	number: 16	total: 23
	total: 24	total: 23	grand total: 47
	$Q = .695$		

Summary and conclusion

In assessing theories of deviancy, both historical and contemporary, the major line of criticism throughout the present chapter has been the "particularistic" nature of these theories. That is, either they are based on a limited set of data which excludes from consideration a large portion of the deviant population, or they select a particular segment of the deviancy phenomenon for focus, overgeneralizing to larger areas of deviancy. Earlier theories were developed largely through observation by physicians of patients or inmates in prisons. Because these factors lacked statistical control for social class, they stressed factors now known to be class bound, such as physical abnormality, I.Q., and even family disorganization. Thus, social class would explain both the biological or psychological problems and deviancy, the predicted outcome. Logically, then, current social theories of deviancy stress social class as the "true" explanation of deviancy, in reaction to these earlier theories. However, there is currently a lack of agreement as to the bearing of social class on different types of deviancy. Certainly lack of opportunity does not explain middle-class delinquency or white-collar crime. We may also add that these theories, though reckoning with the high prevalence of official deviancy in the lower class, are not set up to explain the extensiveness of deviancy in all sectors of our society or the increasing trend toward deviancy despite the burgeoning expansion of the middle class and decline of the lower class. Furthermore, these theories are not stated such as to apply cross-culturally. An examination of available cross-cultural data reveals that, contrary to current social class theories of deviancy, (1) major forms of deviancy are probably more prevalent in the "wealthy" countries where there is greatest opportunity, (2) deviancy is not a unidimensional variable (an assumption of social disorganization theory). Actually, there is no current theory of deviancy that meets our criterion of "universalism"—that is, taking into account all available prevalence, trend, and cross-cultural data, as well as drawing assumptions from larger theories of society. The foregoing will be a brief outline of such a theory drawn from the general theory (Chapters 1 and 2), incorporating all types of deviancy (Chapter 4) and reckoning with previous deviancy and disorganization theory (Chapters 3 and 5) as well as all available deviancy data so as to account for the variety of deviancy types both cross-culturally and intraculturally.

INSTITUTIONAL THEORY OF DEVIANCY

The above theories of deviancy have been criticized as being in various ways particularistic, in the sense that they are ahistorical, narrowly empirical, not cross-culturally valid, and not linked with general theory, but derived from the immediate experience of the theorist. Current sociological theories are largely class theories of deviancy that focus upon social class as the primary explanatory variable. Our theory does not exclude class entirely from consideration, but incorporates a concept of class that is more relevant than the ones used in the deviancy theories. Deviancy theories use the concept of class in the tradition of American stratification theory. Classes are categories of people who have similar income, occupation, and education levels in larger society. In our theory, however, classes are groups of people within specific institutional contexts. People spend a large proportion of their waking hours within such specific institutional contexts. For example, children spend eight to ten hours a day in school. Employed men and women spend the same hours in a work-setting. It seems logical, therefore, that men, women, and children should evaluate and rank themselves in terms of their positions in those institutional group contexts. Dahrendorf has suggested that Marx's concept of class can be effectively redefined in this way:

> By *social class* shall be understood such organized or unorganized collectivities of individuals as share manifest or latent interests arising from and related to the authority structure of imperatively coordinated associations.[65]

Dahrendorf's focus on "imperatively coordinated associations," Weber's term for what today is termed formal or complex organizations, suggests another important consideration: organizational context. The theory of organizations states that behavior may be viewed as varying in terms of the structural of organizational settings. We should expect deviancy to be widespread in some organizational settings and absent in others.

In explaining deviancy, both in a given society and cross-culturally, it is therefore necessary to take into account three considerations: (1) positions of individuals within organizational settings, (2) various types of organizational settings, and (3) the prevalence of both position and type of organization. In terms of this theory, other group differences within the society are secondary and possibly derived from positional and organizational differences in deviancy. Take, for example, social-class differences. We should expect unskilled laborers within a large assembly-line industry to have certain alienative attitudes and become involved in deviant behavior. However, skilled workers in a craft occupation, intrinsically oriented with respect to their work, would be satisfied with their work and would not become involved in deviancy. Both, in class theory terms, would be "lower class" occupations, that is, "blue collar."

The theory being developed here may be termed the "institutional theory of deviancy," because it places a primacy of importance on participation in institutions, that is, formal or complex organizations (to be defined in Chapter 6). There are essentially three steps in applying this theory to any organization (or society): (1) Place the organization in terms of its organizational type (to be discussed below) or, in the case of a whole society, in terms of the predominant form of organization found within that society. (2) Fit the appropriate curve of conforming and deviant behavior (A, B, D, C, or E)—see Figure 5–1—such that certain predictions can be made about modal behavior and normal deviates. (3) Incorporate certain secondary hypotheses about individuals who are excluded from that organization (or society) and who may aspire to membership or identify with the organization or who relate in other ways to the organization—outsiders (such as pledges in a fraternity, dropouts in high school, persons not accepted for employment in a firm, peer group social isolates, and the like).

Although the topic of formal organizational typologies and deviancy will be discussed in great detail in the following chapter, the general theory and typology on which the formal organizational typology is based can be discussed generally in this chapter. This general discussion will be useful in presenting an alternative to the theories of deviancy discussed in this and previous chapters and in showing the more general application of the theory to all social groups. That is, although the focal point for this theory is variability of behavior between institutions or organizations, the same theory can be applied to larger groups (collectivies and societies) and to smaller groups (work groups, gangs, subcultures, communities, and families). The theory probably works best when applied to complex organizations, because they command the greater part of a person's day, but can be used just as validly if an informal organization (such as a criminal group) commands an equal part of a person's allegiance. Actually this is the reverse of conventional deviancy theory which focuses upon noninstitutional or illegitimate groups in explaining deviancy.

In Chapter 2, it was shown that the major theories of society utilize essentially five types in analysis of societal development: communal society, anomic society, pluralistic society, oligarchic society, and totalitarian society. Of these, three are the most frequent in looking at the world societies of today and, as will be shown in the next chapter, in viewing organizations within society. These are anomic, plural, and oligarchic forms of organization. These will be discussed in the next chapter as utilitarian, normative, and coercive forms respectively (Etzioni's analysis). For now, it will be sufficient to see how these three types can be used in comparative analysis generally. That is, we shall discuss each general type briefly and suggest examples of societal, organizational, or other group contexts that would fit the given type. This will yield immediate insight as to the kinds of deviant behaviors that should be expected predominantly in those group settings. We have already looked at the cross-cultural variates in deviancy in developing our general theory. In foregoing chapters we shall look at smaller group contexts, including formal organizations such as industrial, business, professional, and other adult work-settings, schools, churches, and the like; informal group settings such as work groups in industry, child peer groups, and neighborhoods; and also quasi-formal, illegitimate groups such as organized criminal groups, professional criminal groups, and delinquent gangs. Thus, later chapters will give us a fairly detailed analysis of deviancy as seen in various institutional and group settings. Our present effort will be to develop a general picture of what is to come. Let us proceed to examine each of the three types.

Anomic organization   Briefly, this type of organization is characterized by excessive intergroup conflict; breakdown in the normative structure and social control; weakness of government; loss of sharedness of meanings, values, and beliefs; and unceasing change. The modal behavior type is the "bohemian" or in Merton's terms "innovation" as a mode of adaptation. This behavior refers to such traits as unscrupulousness, self-interestedness, calculativeness, exploitativeness, market orientation, cosmopolitanism, and the like. In extreme forms of anomic organization (acute anomie) we should expect an emphasis upon violence (rebellion), while in less extreme forms (mild anomie) we should expect the emphasis to change to theft and other pecuniary crimes (innovation). We have seen that this appears to fit transitional society (acute anomie) such as some rapidly developing Latin American societies and contemporary capitalist society (mild anomie) such as the United States. In the former there is an emphasis on violence, while in the latter upon pecuniary crime. Within American society, we should find the same form of organization and behavior in business and industry. Parallel to societal organization, violence as a typical form of deviance would be an emphasis upon and outgrowth of participation in blue-collar industries, while pecuniary crime would characteristically result for participation in white-collar industry. White-collar crime is a characteristic offense for white-collar industry and business, while assault and other violent crimes are characteristic offenses for blue-collar industry (not necessarily assaults committed on the job, but that growing directly or indirectly from the structure of work resulting in barroom brawls, knifings, union gang violence, or indirectly from family fights largely relating to problems of work and the like).

For students, school is the counterpart of work in terms of behavior corollaries. The probability of delinquent behavior depends upon the structure of school organization. In anomic school settings, we should find high rates of delinquency. These are schools that have, for various reasons, lost control over student participants. In later chapters it will be shown that control will vary with such factors as the amount of conflict within the adult community from which the school draws (for example, interracial conflict and inter-class conflict), with the effectiveness of school officials, and with the orientation of the school (business, trades, college prep, and the like). Of these three, the first is probably the most important. A school placed in an anomic setting will crystalize the development of delinquency and in fact may create anomie in the community through promoting intergroup contact (and possibly conflict). Interestingly, a high-delinquency school may actually have a high proportion of upper- and middle-class students. This may explain some of the anomalies of the self-report findings discussed above.

The concept of anomic organization also seems to fit various illegitimate quasi-formal or informal settings, mainly violent gangs, professional gangs, and organized criminal groups. In this context, violent gangs grow out of a very loose gesellschaft neighborhood context where the criminal and conventional groups are in conflict. Violent gang behavior implies rebellion against both criminal and conventional norms. Although the professional criminal has usually been seen as part of a very tight knit group, recent research indicates that professional crime grows out of very loose and nonbinding group ties. One professional criminal, therefore, may victimize another. Organized criminal groups tend to be part of a dual structure that emphasizes in-group loyalty, on the one hand, and a predatory attitude toward other members of society, on the other hand. The organized criminal group is properly characterized, therefore, as anomic-oligarchic (dual structure) in organizational structure. This terminological usage will be made clear in the next chapter.

Other group settings will be elaborated in chapters to come. These examples will suffice to show the utility of application of group theory in case of anomic organization.

Oligarchic organization   This is the polar opposite of anomic organization, in the sense that through the domination of one group over the organization, overt deviation is severely restricted. Rigid philistinism results. Individuals conform to the norms unwillingly or despite the realization that their personal goals will be thwarted by that conformity. Merton terms this adaptation "ritualism," and if carried to extreme degrees "retreatism." This is the appropriate model for the analysis of contemporary Communist societies. Although data are lacking on these societies, we should expect relatively high rates of neurotic and psychotic behavior, alcoholism, suicide, and other instances of ritualism-retreat.

Within our own society, there are various organizations which fit this model, including prisons, mental hospitals, military organizations, and concentration camps (politely termed "relocation centers" during World War II). Studies indicate that these settings are conducive to "adaptive" forms of deviancy (such as homosexuality) and to development of secondary adjustment or satisfaction with minor rewards (such as ritualism). Other studies indicate various forms of withdrawal (schizophrenia and suicide) in extreme settings (solitary confinement in prison, concentration camp settings). Other than in these settings, it is difficult to find examples of such groups within our own society because, as indicated above, the predominant emphasis in our society is upon the anomic form of organization and innovative deviancy.

Pluralistic organization   Pluralistic society is characterized by a balance between the above two extremes. Government is neither too strong nor too weak. Freedom is maximized for all, in that there is an optimal amount of social control. This means that creative conformity is maximized in this society. For the individual, there is freedom to experiment in either direction of deviancy, as long as behavior does not become too extreme. In terms of Figure 5–1, contemporary welfare state countries, mainly the Scandinavian bloc countries, have achieved this balance. This does not mean that these countries are free of deviancy. In these countries, ritualism and retreatism (as in the case of suicide) appears to be more a problem than in contemporary capitalistic society. Also, innovative-rebellious behavior is more rampant than in the Communist bloc. However, it can be said that these countries have an optimal amount of deviancy at both poles. The total amount of deviancy is probably less than in the other societies, and deviancy does not take the extreme forms that it takes in other countries. This probably also means that deviancy is least disruptive and detrimental and is more likely to be functional, in the sense that it leads to meaningful and orderly change (thus expanding the range of conforming behavior) both in the structure of these societies and in the outlook on deviancy. These societies, thus, are not ideal in the sense of a utopian absense of deviancy, but they are ideal in the sense of "society in transition."

Nonorganizational forms of deviancy   Some forms of deviancy (notably mental disorder, suicide, alcoholism, and ethnic intolerance) are explained not by participation in various organizational settings, but by exclusion from those settings or continuous rejection and rebuff within those settings. This may be a form of group repression and may be viewed in a sense as a form of coercion as in the oligarchic setting. However, because these forms result from exclusion from organizational settings, it becomes more difficult to explain them in terms of any specific institutional settings. Inasmuch as class, race, sex, religion, and other such qualities may become the basis for exclusion, these factors are the best means of explaining these forms of deviancy. It is appropriate, therefore, to look at these problems in terms of the individual's position in larger society rather than in terms of particular organizational contexts when we are dealing with ritualist-retreatist problems. A later chapter in the book will have just such an emphasis. It will be revealed there that there is considerable substantiation for this view in empirical data. For example, both official and unofficial data indicate that mental disorder may meaningfully be viewed in terms of socio-economic class standing *per se*.

Institutional contexts of deviancy

If our goal is to understand deviancy fully, we must realize that it is insufficient to view it merely as a product of larger social organization or as differentially distributed among various social categories. These factors, it will be shown, are secondary. Although a worker may conceive of himself as "working class," his primary identification is his position in the particular organization for which he works or spends the plurality of his waking hours. Deviancy must be seen in terms of its specific organizational contexts. This topic has been explored by students of "social organization"; they study both formal and informal organizations.

Development of the theory of organizations

One of the central purposes of this book has been to show the relationship between the study of deviant behavior and other specialized areas of sociology. In Chapters 1 and 2, the relationship between the study of deviancy and general sociological theory was explored. In Chapter 3, three perspectives on deviance

Notes for this chapter are on pages 385–387.

were discussed and this discussion included one approach—mass society theory—which has not previously been related to the study of deviancy. If this can be done, the study of deviance can be related to the study of collective behavior. In Chapters 4 and 5, insights drawn from previous chapters are applied in terms of current studies of deviancy. In Chapter 5 it is suggested that the current lack of agreement and absence of empirical support for existing theories of deviancy may be due to their "particularism." This means that not only do the theories fail to take into account available deviancy data both for our nation and the world, but these theories are also particularistic in the sense that they are not systematically related to any of the general theories discussed in Chapters 1 and 2.

When this relationship is made, it is seen that deviancy must be viewed within a comparative group context rather than in terms of isolated social problems. Furthermore, it is suggested that perhaps the most important of all group contexts are organizations—that is, formal or complex organizations. From the sociological point of view, these have the greatest impact on the individual's behavior, because he spends most of his time in such organizations. Other organizations or organizational settings (national society, the neighborhood, play groups, and the family) may also have a great impact on the individual. Whether those settings exert a primary impact depends upon the amount of involvement of individuals in those groups. The juvenile gang, the professional criminal group, or the family may command the greatest allegiance of some individuals but not others. These settings will be explored in later chapters of the book. However, in keeping with the logical sequence of the book, from larger to smaller group settings, the present chapter will be concerned with formal organizational settings (bureaucratic settings). What we learn from this study will be applicable to some extent to smaller organizational settings. Thus, in the foregoing chapter, still another area of sociology, the study of organizations, will be related to the study of deviance.

Within the area of social organization, there have been a number of attempts at classifying social organization. However, these are relatively recent. For a long time this field was plagued by a dichotomy between generalized statements about social organization, on the one hand, and particular studies of social organization, on the other. This may be because for a long time the field paid acknowledgements to Weber's classic discussion of "bureaucracy."

WEBER'S BUREAUCRACY

The modern study of social organization began with Weber's extensive study of bureaucracy. Although he paid much attention to general theoretical classification of types of rationality and types of authority, for Weber bureaucracy is a singular phenomenon, and it had singular consequences for personality in what is termed the "bureaucratic personality." Weber felt that a number of characteristics were universal to all bureaucracies: (1) *hierarchicalization* or vertical structure of positions, (2) *task specialization,* the distribution of tasks among various positions and the development of spheres of influence, (3) more or less stable *rules* of office defining member obligations, (4) the *office* or "bureau" characterized by continual function and the "files"—written records regarding administrative decisions, actions, and rulings, (5) *impersonality* in the selection of officials and conduct of general activity, (6) large size, and (7) "efficiency" and rationality.[1]

BUREAUCRATIC PERSONALITY

Weber and, more recently, Robert K. Merton have discussed the types of personality that emerge from this singular bureaucratic context. Merton emphasizes the dysfunctions and limitations of this personality, citing Veblen's concept of "trained incapacity" and Dewey's idea of "occupational psychosis" as descriptive concepts. The bureaucratic personality characteristics stem from the structure of bureaucracy. (1) Hierarchalization produces a high level of *status anxiety, discipline obedience,* and *conscientiousness,* among subordinates in a bureaucracy. (2) Task specialization gives rise to rationality and discipline. (3) Emphasis upon conformity to rules of office gives rise to *ritualism, conservativism,* and *goal displacement* (adaptation in which instrumental values become terminal). (4) Emphasis upon impersonality gives rise to a *matter-of-fact* attitude in interpersonal relationships.[2]

BUREAUCRACY AS A VARIABLE

The more recent emphasis in the study of social organization has shifted from the belief that bureaucracy is a single phenomenon to attempts at classifying a variety of bureaucracies. These typologies are based on the variation that can occur within bureaucracy.

(1) The degree of all the "universal" characteristics may vary (that is, the degree of hierarchalization, task specialization, and the like). (2) The extent of commitment of individuals within a bureaucracy may vary, only the most committed fitting the bureaucratic personality type. (3) Based upon Weber's own analysis, different writers have emphasized that there are different types of rationality that form the basis for bureaucracy. (4) There are correspondingly differentials in power and authority relationships.

TYPES OF BUREAUCRATIC ORGANIZATION

A number of typologies based on a single criterion or set of criteria have been developed in the study of formal organization. Most of these, as in the case of deviancy typologies discussed above, may be classified as "nominal typologies." Nominal typologies imply that there are distinctions between types of organizations but that the types are not part of any ordinal ranking. Other typologies, however, have some degree of ordinality and may serve as a basis of regrouping the other typologies.

Nominal typologies Gouldner has suggested a typology of organization focusing upon the *rules* and the way they are used, including: (1) the organizational level that initiates the rules, (2) the nature of values of the organizational level that legitimate the rules, (3) the nature of values of the organizational level in violation of rule enforcement, (4) the types of normative explanation given for deviance from rules, and (5) the variations in effects of rules on the statuses of members of organizations.

In a *mock bureaucracy,* all the apparatus of bureaucracy exists (rules, hierarchy, office, files, and the like), but on a day-to-day basis the rules and the apparatus are ignored, due to the influence of the tight informal group. With regard to the five criterion: (1) rules are imposed by an outside unit, (2) rules are not legitimated by values of any organizational level, (3) rule enforcement violates the values of both elites and non-elites in the bureaucracy, (4) deviation is explained in highly individualistic terms (such as uncontrollable needs), and (5) deviation is status-enhancing.

By contrast, in *representative* or *democratic* bureaucracies there exist all the characteristics of bureaucracy and the rules are accepted as seen in these five criterion: (1) the rules are initiated at all levels, (2) the levels legitimate the rules in terms of their own values, (3) rule enforcement does not violate the values of any level, (4) deviance is explained as ignorance or accident, and (5) deviance impairs the status of both elites and non-elites.

Lastly, *punishment-centered bureaucracy* is characterized by arbitrary imposition of rules from above and unwilling adherence by subordinates (as in prisons and mental hospitals): (1) rules are initiated by the head man or top-level management, (2) the higher-level officers legitimate rules in terms of their own values and the lower participants define the rules as illegitimate in terms of own interests and values, (3) enforcement violates the values of lower-level groups, (4) deviancy is expected and is deliberate, not rationalized, and (5) deviation may lead to status gain for lower-ranking members.[3]

Another typology, based upon the social characteristics of those who run the administrative apparatus, has been developed by Fritz Marx. (1) *Guardian bureaucracy* is run by persons who represent a state ideology. (2) *Caste bureaucracy* is run by persons who occupy the highest caste of bureaucracy, such as a caste of educated people. (3) *Patronage bureaucracy* is run by those with highest commitment to party or purpose. (4) *Merit bureaucracy* is run by those measured by objective standards to be most competent.[4]

Talcott Parsons has formulated still another typology, based upon his "AGIL paradigm." Organizations are characterized in terms of their primary value or goal orientation, including: (1) *adaptation* or orientation toward economic production, (2) *goal attainment,* orientation toward political goals, (3) *integration,* oriented toward integration, and (4) *social control,* oriented toward maintenance of personnel through coercion, inducement, or therapy.[5]

The last of the nominal typologies, that of Blau and Scott, is based upon a *cui bono* or "who benefits" distinction. (1) In *mutual-benefit associations,* the rank-and-file benefit, the central organizational problem being the maintenance of internal democracy *vis-à-vis* apathy and the oligarchical structure. (2) In *owner-management benefit* organizations, the central problem is maximizing efficiency primarily and work satisfaction secondarily. (3) In *service organizations, "public in contact," or client centered organizations,* the central problem is the conflict between service and formalities of administrative procedure. Lastly, (4) in *commonweal* organizations that serve the public-at-large, the central problem is the development of democratic mechanisms that can be controlled by the public-at-large.[6]

Ordinal typologies Two closely related ordinal typologies of organizations may be cited. Franz Neuman distinguishes three types of *commitment* —(1) ideological, (2) material, and (3) fear— based upon three corresponding methods used by elites: (1) persuasion, (2) material benefit, and (3) use of force.[7] Similarly, Etzioni distinguished basically three types of compliance relationships, relationships based upon types of power or sanction predominant in an organization and the orientation of lower-level participants. (1) In *coercive organizations* (such as prisons and concentration camps) physical sanctions are dominant, and members are negative and alienative in orientation. (2) In *utilitarian organizations* (such as businesses and industries), remunerative or material sanctions are dominant and members are calculative, a quasi-negative or quasi-positive orientation. Last, in *normative organizations* (such as churches, universities, and ideological political parties), symbolic sanctions predominate and member orientation is positive and moralistic.[8]

TABLE 6-1   Paradigm for organizational analysis

	TYPE OF COMPLIANCE RELATIONSHIP		
	Coercive	*Utilitarian*	*Normative*
Power-means manipulated	Physical sanctions	Material sanctions	Symbolic sanctions
Orientation of subordinate actor	Alienative	Calculative	Moral

SOURCE: Amitai Etzioni, *A Comparative Analysis of Complex Organizations* (New York: The Free Press, 1961).

Synthesis Etzioni's typology contains the highest degree of ordinality, thus making possible the grouping of other typologies from one end of the continuum to the other. This synthesis is given in the following paradigm, which lists typologies under the appropriate Etzioni type.

Gouldner's typology is quite analogous to Etzioni's. In *mock bureaucracy*, members maintain no sense of moral commitment to the rules of bureaucracy and are thus calculative in Etzioni's terms.

TABLE 6-2   Cross-classification of organizational typologies

Author		Typology	
[Etzioni]	[Normative]	[Utilitarian]	[Coercive]
Gouldner	Representative	Mock	Punishment-centered
Marx	Guardian, patronage	Merit	Caste bureaucracy
Parsons	Integration	Adaptation Goal attainment	Social control
Blau–Scott	Mutual benefit, commonweal	Owner– management, service organization	

This contrasts with the high moral commitment to rules in *representative* bureaucracy. In *punishment-centered* bureaucracies, rules are imposed arbitrarily on unwilling (alienative) subordinates.

Fritz Marx's typology also seems analogous. Etzioni describes coercive organizations as having caste echelon levels (caste bureaucracy). As in Fritz Marx's *guardian* and *patronage* types, in Etzioni's normative organization there is an emphasis on high or ideological commitment. Last, in *merit* bureaucracy, evaluation takes place by impersonal standards; therefore, participants tend to be neither positively nor negatively involved, or in Parson's terms "affectively neutral" (calculative).

Etzioni uses much of Parsons' language in his analysis. It seems logical, therefore, to draw a connection between Parsons' and Etzioni's framework. Parson's *social control* type bears a strong relation to Etzioni's coercive compliance, in that in both there is an emphasis on maintaining control, conceivably implying the ultimate necessity of coercive sanction. *Adaptation,* like utilitarian compliance, refers to business and industrial bureaucracy. *Goal attainment* would also fit the utilitarian typology, in that Parsons is referring to government bureaucracies which Etzioni designates utilitarian. In *integrative* systems, priority is given to voluntary compliance with norms governing action, as in Etzioni's normative organization.

The Blau–Scott typology seems to fit only two of Etzioni's types. No doubt a *cui bono* typology necessarily excludes coercive settings, in that in a sense there is no real benefit to anybody within these settings. The two most democratic or normative settings are the *mutual-benefit* and *commonweal* types. The mass is benefited by and thus complies with bureaucratic rule. The *owner-management* and *service* types are profit-oriented thus similar to Etzioni's utilitarian organization.

Etzioni's typology has been selected for more detailed presentation in this chapter for three reasons. (1) It contains the greatest degree of ordinality and thus lends itself better to comparative analysis, especially where organizations cannot be fitted into any one typology and must be labeled a dual or quasi-type. (2) It relates explicitly to general theories of social organization discussed above. Thus, coercive compliance is the small scale equivalent of oligarchy or totalitarianism; utilitarian compliance of anomic or multipartite organization; and normative compliance of pluralistic organization. This will be discussed further below. (3) Etzioni's typology contains an explicit link with deviance typologies discussed above. Calculative compliance of utilitarian organization is conducive to innovative adaptation. Alienative compliance should correlate with ritualistic adaptation. Moral compliance is favorable to creative conformity.

In our subsequent discussions of Etzioni's types, the resemblance to other typologies of formal organization discussed above should be borne in mind. We shall also seek a tie to various types of authority relations in the following discussion.

TYPES OF AUTHORITY RELATIONSHIPS

Etzioni's emphasis upon "compliance," with its subconcepts of power basis and subordinate orientation, has traditionally been discussed under the rubric of authority and authority relationships, primarily by Weber, but also by Barnard. Weber defines *authority* not as objective but rather as subjective. He believes authority is the "probability that certain specific commands will be obeyed," and obedience is traced to peer constraint rather than the action of a superior. This Weber clearly distinguished from *power,* which he defined as the "probability that the actor can carry out his will despite resistance." Thus, to Weber the essence of authority was that it was *voluntary,* while power was independent of the volition of the actors involved.[9]

Chester I. Barnard focuses upon this voluntary nature of authority in his definition of authority as the "character of a communication (order) in formal organization by virtue of which it is accepted by a contributor or 'member' of the organization as governing the action he contributes . . . the decision as to whether an order has authority or not lies with the person to whom it is addressed, and does not reside in 'persons of authority' or those who issue the orders." In order for an order to be accepted as authoritative, four conditions have to be met: (1) it must be understood, (2) the receiver must believe it consistent with organization policy, (3) it must be seen as compatible with his personal interest, and (4) he must be physically and mentally able to comply with it. Orders are obeyed because: (1) they usually comply with the four conditions, (2) they lie within the "zone of indifference" of orders "clearly acceptable" without conscious questioning, and (3) the informal group maintains social control to maintain the zone of indifference.[10]

Basing his action on these considerations, Barnard dichotomizes authority into two types: (1) *authority of position* —which is that due to the advantage of position rather than to superior ability, and (2) *authority of leadership* —which is that due to superior knowledge, understanding, and ability regardless of position.

Similarly, Weber gives a more detailed analysis of authority, dividing it into three types: charismatic, traditional, and legal.[11] Each of the three types of authority can be distinguished in terms of its basis. *Charismatic authority* is based upon the belief of its followers in the supernatural powers of the leader. *Traditional authority* is based upon the sanctity of tradition within a sacred, eternal, and inviolate social order. *Legal authority* is based upon belief in the supremacy of the law.

Charismatic authority is based upon affectual rationality, arises in times of crisis, and is radical or revolutionary, existing outside of the institutional order. It is antithetical to bureaucracy, in that there is no hierarchy, no formal rules or law, no salary but income derived from booty, and the like. Because charisma implies magical powers, failure may be devastating for the charismatic leader and may contribute to his downfall. However, charisma may also disappear through "routinization of charisma" or conversion to more traditional forms of authority. This may arise under one or a combination of conditions: (1) the material interests of followers become their dominant concern, (2) the leader's material interests become paramount to him, (3) the old leader disappears, leading to a crisis of succession, or (4) the group obtains its revolutionary goal.

With the routinization of charisma comes traditional authority, typically characterized by the hereditary leader or one ordained by supernatural power. There are three subtypes of traditional authority. In *patriarchal authority,* leadership is direct and personal, but limited by sacred tradition or informal contract. In *patrimonial authority,* there is need for indirect control via associations and subordinate leaders due to larger size of organization. Lastly, the final phase of *feudalism* involves a contractual relationship between ruler and serf.

With the formation of contractual relationships, legal authority first begins to emerge. In its highest form, legal authority involves the emergence of the state and of bureaucracy characterized by continuous official business, written rules and duties, separation of ownership from control, and unappropriated office. Legal authority is the antithesis of charismatic.

Taxonomy for comparative analysis of organizations

We have seen that the various typologies of complex organizations could be subsumed under Etzioni's three types of compliance: coercive, utilitarian, and normative. However, the usefulness of Etzioni's typology does not stop there. Let us examine the typology in more detail. It will be shown that the typology is rooted or derivable, directly or indirectly, from the "classic" typology drawn from social theory developed in Chapter 2. It can also be shown that the typology subsumes the types of authority described by Weber, and Barnard.

We have seen in Chapter 2 that, using DeGré's typology, modern societies can be classed into essentially three types: oligarchic (or totalitarian, if concentration of power is extreme), pluralistic or democratic, and anomic. Etzioni similarly classifies smaller scale, complex organizations into three analogous types: coercive, normative, and utilitarian.

As in Etzioni's coercive organizations, in oligarchies or totalitarian states there is an exclusive reliance upon repressive, violent, physical punishment as a means of ensuring compliance. Another feature in common is the caste-like nature of organizational structure. In the oligarchic setting, a rigid philistine adaptation takes place, just as in coercive organization there is an alienative orientation and ritualist modes of orientation.

In anomic organization, there is a characteristic absence of common values and emphasis upon exchange value, paralleling the calculative orientation of utilitarian organization. It will be shown that our constructive typology suggests certain features not discussed by Etzioni, such as conflict between functions, ineffective government or management, absence of effective regulation, and constant change. In anomic organization, the fluid bohemian personality dominates, paralleling the innovative adaptation expected in utilitarian organization according to the following discussion.

Pluralistic organization is related to normative organization, also by inference. In pluralistic organization, government and regulation are effective because they are based on a balance of restitutive and repressive sanctions. There is a heavy reliance upon persuasion and negotiation between various groups, paralleling the symbolic sanction of Etzioni's normative organization. There is also a high common value orientation which parallels the positive moral commitment of Etzioni's normative type. Thus, there should be a relationship between the creative man adaptation and the conformity adaptation that will be postulated for normative organization.

Etzioni's typology also can be used to synthesize the various typologies of authority. Etzioni's analysis differs, however, with the types of authority in that it is broader, referring to types of *compliance relationships*. That is, Etzioni recognizes that some types of complex organizations are stable and yet do not have legitimate authority as described by Weber.

The relationship between Weber's and Barnard's types of authority and Etzioni's compliance types may be seen in the following paradigm (Table 6–3), as related by the general theory categories.

TABLE 6–3 Cross-classification of theoretical typologies and types of authority

Author	*Oligarchic organization*	*Anomic organization*	*Pluralistic organization*	
Etzioni	Coercive compliance relation	Utilitarian compliance relation	Normative compliance relation	
Weber		Legal authority	Traditional authority	Charismatic authority
Barnard			Authority of position	Authority of leadership

The major forms of bureaucracy are found under legal authority and in capitalist Western societies. These are business and industrial bureaucracies, which Etzioni terms utilitarian settings. It will
be shown, however, that Etzioni finds the sphere of bureaucracy to
be broader than Weber conceived it. Both Weber's traditional authority and charismatic authority may be found within normative
compliance bureaucracies. The paradigm shows the absence of a
counterpart of coercive compliance in Weber's analysis. This no
doubt is due to Weber's focus upon legitimate authority. Coercive
authority is not seen as legitimate by subordinates. This is Weber's
omission rather than Etzioni's exaggeration, because prisons and
mental hospitals are certainly bureaucratic settings.

The paradigm also shows that although Barnard's typology is
similar to Weber's, Barnard's focus upon legitimate authority forces
both of his types into the normative compliance typology.

Lastly, it should be noted that Etzioni takes into account the
distinctions *within* the normative compliance relationship. What
Weber terms "charismatic leadership" and what Barnard calls "authority of leadership" Etzioni terms "social normative power," while
"traditional authority" and "authority of position" are termed a
pure normative power in Etzioni's analysis. Thus, Etzioni's typology
is indeed all-inclusive of authority types.

Let us now look at Etzioni's analysis in more detail. Etzioni, as
has been shown, conceives of four types of compliance relationships,
distinguished by the type of power[12] and power-means manipulated
as well as by the orientation of the subordinated actor. In *normative
compliance relationships,* there is a primary emphasis upon the
exercise of normative power, that which rests upon allocation of
symbolic rewards and deprivations. There are two subtypes of normative power, based upon the types of symbolic rewards and
punishments manipulated. *Pure normative power* is based upon the
manipulation of *prestige, esteem,* and *ritualistic symbols,* while
social normative power is based upon the allocation and manipulation of *acceptance and positive response.* Pure normative power
is more frequent in vertical relations (in which actors are of different
rank) and is exercised directly down a hierarchy, while social power
is more common in horizontal relations (in which actors are of equal
rank—that is, informal relations) and is exercised through the
group. Pure normative power is based upon norm-internalization
and identification with authority, while social normative power is

based upon sensitivity to pressures of primary groups. In normative compliance relationships, the involvement of subordinated actors is positive, deferential, and even emotional, and may be classified as "moral" involvement. Examples include members of an ideological political party, parishioners in a church, and devoted adherents of a cause.

In *utilitarian compliance relationships,* remunerative power or power of control of material resources and rewards is the primary type of power. Subordinated actors are typically calculative in their orientation, which means they are either negative or positively oriented but of low emotional intensity (that is, affective-neutrality). Examples include clients, customers, and employees.

In *coercive* compliance, the predominant type of power used is coercive, implying the threat of physical sanctions (pain, deformity, death, frustration of vital needs). In this setting, subordinated actors are typically alienative in their orientation, meaning that they are intensely negative or hostile, in the sense of hostility toward a foreigner or alien. This adaptation typically characterizes inmates in a prison or mental hospital.

The scheme is not an absolute one but Etzioni conceives of the three types of power as being exercised in varying degrees by most organizations. However, generally one or another is emphasized, because if two types of power are exercised simultaneously, they tend to neutralize one another. Because of this relativity, there are not three but nine possible types of compliance, three of these more effective than the other six and empirically more frequent: numbers 1, 5, and 9 in Table 6–4.

TABLE 6-4 **Kinds of power by kinds of involvement of subordinates**

KINDS OF POWER	KINDS OF INVOLVEMENT		
	Alienative	*Calculative*	*Moral*
Coercive	1	2	3
Remunerative	4	5	6
Normative	7	8	9

Etzioni's *dynamic hypothesis* states that organizations tend to shift their compliance structure to these three types, and resist factors pushing them away.

Etzioni's three types of effective compliance—coercive, utilitarian, and normative—are not merely categorical types, but imply degrees or magnitude, as seen in Table 6–5. Coercive organizations involve the least participation of lower-ranking members, while normative organizations imply the most. Coercive organizations, however, involve the most subordination and normative organizations the least subordination of lower-ranking members. Last, in coercive organizations, elites are assigned the least legitimacy while in normative organizations they are assigned the most legitimacy.

TABLE 6–5   Correlates   of   compliance   relationships

	TYPE OF COMPLIANCE RELATIONSHIP		
	Coercive	*Utilitarian*	*Normative*
Subordinate participation	Least	Medial	Most
Subordination of members	Most	Medial	Least
Legitimacy of elites	Least	Medial	Most

Analytical classification

Each of the settings—coercive, utilitarian, and normative—contains variations in degree of characteristics. That is, we can find differences between coercive organizations as to degree of coercion and alienation. We can find differences between utilitarian organizations as to extent of use of remuneration or material sanction and extent of calculative orientation and extent of alienation. Similarly, normative organizations can be classified in terms of degrees of symbolic sanction and moral orientation.

COERCIVE ORGANIZATIONAL SETTINGS

These, again, are organizations characterized by coercion as a major means of control over lower participants and by high alienation of most lower participants. Examples include concentration camps, prisoner-of-war camps, prisons, traditional "correctional institutions," custodial mental hospitals, "relocation centers," and coercive unions. The major organization task of such organizations is "keeping inmates in," or custody, and "keeping inmates disciplined."

These organizations, however, are not equally coercive and equally alienative, but instead vary in degrees of these characteristics, as shown in Table 6–6.

TABLE 6–6 Organization classified by degree of coercion and alienation

Least Coercive and Alienative			*Most Coercive and Alienative*	
Coercive union	Relocation camps	Delinquency correctional institutions Custodial mental hospitals	Regular prisons	Concentration camps

These organizational settings vary from left to right in terms of degrees of coercion and alienation, the least coercive and alienative being coercive unions increasing as we move to the right of the table. The one exception is the case of concentration camps, where an interesting phenomenon occurs. Here, prolonged and extreme exposure to coercion leads to conversion, or identifying with the aggressor, accepting his norms, and deflecting alienation onto scapegoats, such as new inmates.

Among these various coercive settings, there are three basic types: concentration camps, prisons, and correctional institutions. These are defined separately. *Concentration camps* are organizations that serve specifically as tools of mass murder. The term *prison* is a general term referring specifically to organizations that serve merely to detain persons. This term applies to conventional prisons but also to some mental hospitals, homes for the aged, relocation centers, and forced labor camps. The term *"correctional institution"* refers to an organization that combines detention and rehabilitation. Another variable in this analysis is the degree of *amalgamation* of inmates and organizational elites. In the more coercive settings, inmates form a separate subsystem apart from the staff, while in less coercive settings there is an amalgamation of staff and inmates.

TABLE 6–7 Organizations classified by degree of separation of elites and subordinates

Amalgamation				*Separation*
Coercive unions	Relocation centers	Correctional institutions	Prisons	Concentration camps

Thus, in more coercive settings, a sharp *"caste-like"* separation of inmates from staff emerges, implying minimum interaction, when interaction would breach the "caste taboo." Informal leadership becomes separate from formal leadership, in that the inmate subculture develops its own leaders ("right guys") whose behavior displays "conspicuous defiance" of official norms and values and who defy sanctions of the staff. In the most coercive settings, work assignments are made arbitrarily by prison staff and food, shelter, and clothing are held or withdrawn arbitrarily or in accord with compliance. Certain inmate types develop to counter this tendency. These *inmate types* serve in reallocating goods and services as well as jobs. The "merchants" perform the former service and the "fixers" reallocate jobs and living quarters.

In the most coercive settings, the middle-of-the-roaders are termed "rats" or "stoolies," but paradoxically their function is to make for acceptance of the outlook, norms, and values of subjects by the power-holders, not the reverse. This is shown by the fact that middle-of-the-roaders may be leaders in the less coercive settings. For example, in the relocation centers, there is a relative degree of cooperation among inmates and guards, use of collective bargaining, and efforts at self-control among inmates.

UTILITARIAN ORGANIZATIONAL SETTINGS

Utilitarian settings are those characterized by remuneration as a major means of control and by calculative involvement of subordinated actors. Etzioni points out that these are ordinarily termed "industries." There are three subtypes distinguished by the characteristics of lower participants in those organizational settings. These actually represent status categories, and statements made about a given type of industry apply to a lesser degree to its social class. The lowest of these is "blue-collar" industries, including factories and mines. Next come "white-collar" industries, primarily offices. Last are professional industries. Each of these subtypes contains rank-ordered status categories. As we look up the ranks, we see increasing normative control and decreasing remunerative control and alienation. Thus, within blue-collar industries, the most alienative and most oriented toward pay rather than prestige or other symbolic rewards are the unskilled workers, followed by semi-skilled and skilled in that order, increasingly normatively controlled.

Studies indicate that unskilled workers will take a more frustrating assembly-line job for a pay increase. The same applies among white-collar workers. The lowest are the clerks, salesgirls, and tellers, who are the most alienative and calculative and the least "moral" in their orientation. Next come supervisory clerks or private secretaries, who have a closer contact with management, and are more normatively oriented. Finally, semi-professionals, such as engineers and laboratory technicians, are more normatively controlled than the other two white-collar categories, but are less normatively controlled than full-fledged professionals. Professional industries, including research organizations, planning firms, and the like, are primarily normative and secondarily utilitarian in characteristic compliance. Table 6–8 summarizes the relationship between remunerative—normative control and type of industry.

TABLE 6–8 Subordinate actor orientation by type of industry

MOST CALCULATIVE, ALIENATIVE						MOST NORMATIVE, MORAL
←						→
Blue Collar				*White Collar*		*Professional*
Unskilled	Semi-skilled	Skilled	Clerks Salesgirls Tellers	Supervising clerks Private secretaries	Semi-professionals	

NORMATIVE ORGANIZATIONAL SETTINGS

In normative settings, normative power is the major means of control, lower-ranking members of the organization are highly committed, and compliance rests upon internalization of directives that are accepted as legitimate. The major means of control include leadership, rituals, manipulation of social and prestige symbols, and resocialization.

There are nine major normative organizational types, although only five are pure normative types—religious organizations, ideological political organizations, general hospitals, universities, and voluntary associations. In schools and therapeutic mental hospitals, normative sanctions are primary but coercion is an important secondary power-base. In professional organizations, remuneration proves to be an important secondary power-base. Social movements are difficult to analyze, as they do not constitute true organizations; however, the core organization of social movements would seem to be predominantly normative.

DUAL COMPLIANCE STRUCTURES

As has been noted, when two types of power are exercised simultaneously, they tend to cancel out each other or neutralize each other, making for ineffectiveness in an organization. However, certain types of organizations are both effective and dual in structure. They are such due to the development of special mechanisms for reducing the waste of power resources. One example of this is *temporal segregation* of the exercise of the different power-means. This is illustrated by wartime combat military units. Combat units rely heavily upon normative power (leadership, rituals, for instance) in that remunerative sanction would not be adequate to the risks required. However, when these sanctions fail, for example when soldiers retreat when ordered not to do so, coercive sanctions may be used, such as shooting at retreating troops. Thus the two types of sanctions are segregated in time, permitting both to be used. Similarly, labor unions may resort to coercion in times of crisis to prevent strikebreaking or cooperation with management. While labor unions may be of various dual or pure types, coercive–utilitarian, coercive social, social, and coercive, the majority of unions are utilitarian–normative dual types.

COMPLIANCE OF HIGHER PARTICIPANTS

While Etzioni's analysis is confined largely to the compliance of subordinates, his discussion does extend to compliance of elites in his analysis of the distribution of charisma. Due to a high position in structure, elite compliance is usually moral or calculative but seldom alienative, in that leaders are expected to gain satisfaction from intrinsic symbolic rewards. In fact, in Etzioni's use of the term, *charisma* refers to the ability of an actor to exercise diffuse and intense influence over the normative orientations of other actors. Pure charisma is achieved continuously, while *routinized* is ascribed to office. Charisma and bureaucracy are both variables to be found in degrees, although charisma may be found within bureaucratic settings.

Etzioni distinguishes three basic types of elites. *Generalists* are elites who make decisions about *ends,* and thus control *expressive* activities. *Specialists* make decisions about *means,* thus controlling instrumental activities, usually one particular activity. *Segmentalists* are also instrumentally oriented, however with respect to a multi-functional sub-unit.

Charisma is not absolute, but is responsible to several *mechanisms of control,* social processes which prevent or reduce deviance, keeping charisma in its proper place. *Preventative mechanisms* protect positions from being occupied by noncharismatics or deviant charismatics. *Postfactum mechanism,* however, can handle dysfunctions which develop despite preventative measures. *Built-in* mechanisms are activities or social units serving other functions which are used for control purposes. *Segregated control mechanisms* are social units or activities which serve primarily control purposes. Preventative mechanisms are generally built-in while post factum mechanisms are generally segregated.

In these terms, there are essentially three types of charismatic structures in normative and utilitarian organizations, two of which are in normative. (Coercive organizations generally have no organizational positions in which charisma is required.) In T-structures, charisma is concentrated in top positions (such as the Ford Motor Company). In L-structures, charisma is concentrated in all line positions (such as the Catholic church). In R-structures, charisma is limited to one or more rank (such as hospitals, universities). T-structures refer to "bureaucratic" structures, that is, utilitarian organizations, while R- and L-structures are normative. R-structures imply social power among elites, while L-structures entail *pure normative* compliance.

By elites, Etzioni means a group of actors who have power. In utilitarian organizations (T-structures), middle-ranking participants are specialized elites while upper elites are generalists. The

lowest ranks are instrumental performers and are generally alienated, not toward the upper, but toward middle-ranking elites.
This conflict may be mediated by lower-ranking elites.

In R-structures—that is, universities, general hospitals, and
therapeutic mental hospitals—middle-ranking elites are generalists (usually professionals) while upper-ranking elites are specialists or segmentalists. There is extensive reliance of social power
in handling professionals.

In L-structures, all ranks are generalists rather than specialists
or segmentalists. Here, there is an extensive reliance upon preventative and post factum control. For example, novice elites may
be required to attend the organization's own educational unit or
perform practice or test assignments. After admission to the ranks,
the elite may be nullified through suspension, expulsion, or even
execution. Similar to T-structures (but not R-structure), in L-
structure, top elites have charisma over both middle- and lower-
ranking members and may use their power to settle conflicts between lower-ranking members.

Deviancy and conformity in various institutional contexts

We have seen in our comparative study of social
organization in Chapter 2 that different societies have different
organizational structures and that this implies differential behavioral outcomes for the members of those societies. Our basic
trichotomy, between anomie, pluralistic, and oligarchic organizational types, was linked to a trichotomy of behavioral or personality adaptations—bohemian, creative, and philistine adaptations.

We may expand the Thomas–Znaniecki behavioral typology
by bringing to bear descriptions of behavior drawn from general
sociological theory. That is, references to behavior are found in
many social theories. Tönnies, for instance, sees behavior in gemeinschaft as altruistic but in gesellschaft as egoistic. Because gesellschaft fits our anomic model, one trait of the correlated bohemian
behavior would be egoism. The foregoing behavioral descriptions,
therefore, will not be limited to Thomas and Znaniecki. Because
the various characteristics are discussed by several theorists, we
shall draw freely from all without specific citation.

The *bohemian* may be generally described as one who is hostile, competitive, unscrupulous, self-interested, or egoistic, lacking in any basic stable goal-orientation, and in a constant change and turmoil.

The *philistine* personality implies withdrawal from competition or conflict, a lack of individual interest apart from devotion to duty or state, fear of violent repression, and a rigid, unchanging nature.

By contrast, the *creative* or *conforming adaptation* implies a reconciliation of these two opposite adaptations. The creative man exhibits a cooperative or tolerant attitude toward groups outside his own; maintains a balance between his own private interest and his subordination to group goals; maintains a certain amount of respect for legal sanctions and other common "rules," but on occasions finds reason for questioning the rules; and orients toward change while maintaining a common goal or destiny.

There is an almost perfect correspondence between this trichotomy of philistine, bohemian, and creative man, and Etzioni's "orientation of subordinated actors"—alienative, calculative, and moral.

The philistine is alienative in that he conforms to rigorous societal rules and laws out of fear of repression rather than through any positive commitment. We can also see, if our comparison is accurate, that the alienative adaptation implies rigid conformity to institutional or societal demands.

By contrast, the bohemian is quite clearly "calculative" in that his orientation is material and egoistic rather than altruistic, resembling the utilitarian "rational man." If our comparison is accurate, it follows that the calculative orientation implies other bohemian traits such as competitiveness, hostility, and constant change.

Lastly, the creative man is "moral" in the sense of a commitment to group values but, in a higher sense as well, in devotion to the welfare of the group through his participation in constructive change in terms of the loftiest values of society. Once again, it follows that if the creative man–moral orientation analogy is appropriate, moral orientation implies other creative man traits such as cooperation, benevolence, change orientation, and the like.

We have not yet incorporated all areas of theory covered in the early part of this book. We have left out for a while the section dealing with anomie, disorganization, and mass society theory. We saw that this section culminated with Merton's discussion of "types of adaptation" to anomie, including conformity, innovation, ritualism, retreatism, and rebellion. In Chapter 4 it was shown that Merton's typology suffices as an adequate and useful constructive typology of deviancy. A congruence was shown between Merton's typology and existing psychological and social typologies of deviancy. One clarification drawn from the other typologies was that "conformity" is never a purely nondeviant type in a changing society. Even the conformist violates some norms and in doing so may contribute to needed social changes. This was verified by an empirically based typology of delinquent and criminal behavior.

We will be able to show a tie to these types of adaptation and the schemes discussed above. Though Merton's analysis is helpful in both institutional and societal contexts, it was shown that the alienation approaches discussed in the chapter on mass society largely lacked the institutional applicability that will be attributed to Merton's types, that the meanings of alienation are various and often confused, and that few attempts have been made to apply typologies of alienation in specific contexts. Thus, alienation has been treated as a problem for both "mass society" and "totalitarian society." Little attempt has been made to deliniate in the mass society literature which types of alienation should plague mass society and which types totalitarian society. Therefore, it would seem that Etzioni's discussion is instructive to mass society theory, rather than the other way around. Mass society, as analogous to utilitarian settings, would imply "calculative orientation" of members—that is, "market orientation," "self estrangement," "reification," "normlessness," and the like. Totalitarian society could be more typically characterized by Etzioni's alienative response, and lower-ranking members of these societies would feel powerless, isolated, and meaningless. We shall not attempt to work all the variants of alienation into discussion of organizational deviance, because Etzioni's simple trichotomy seems to be an excellent summary statement of what could be done with alienation variables. However, in the case of Merton's typology of adaptations, our analysis can be enhanced through utilizing his terms of analysis.

APPLICATION OF MERTON'S TYPES

A three-way tie can be drawn between Merton's types, Etzioni's analysis, and the Thomas–Znaniecki model.

Philistinism is represented in Merton's types by two concepts— ritualism and retreatism. The ritualist rejects or scales down his lofty aspirations so that he may conform to the institutional means. The retreatist neither makes an attempt to seek commonly accepted goals nor conforms to institutional means. The ritualist probably best illustrates philistinism in the sense of rigidly, conservatism, unchangingness, and, as described in "bureaucratic personality," departmentalization and specialization. Retreatism fits the philistine model only in the sense of rigidity and unchangingness; however, the retreatist is a behavioral nonconformist. In Etzioni's terms both adaptations would be alienative, retreatism being the most alienative. In terms of Seeman's alienation types the distinction between ritualism and retreatism would be one of generality of alienation. The bureaucratic ritualist might feel alienated in the sense of powerlessness and meaninglessness, but not isolation, normlessness, or self-estrangement, while the retreatist might feel alienated in all senses of the term alienation.

Bohemian adaptation is a general type that would include Merton's innovation and rebellion. Innovation implies rejection of institutionalized means and emphasis (or over-emphasis) upon adherence to shared goals of success. Rebellion implies the development of a new system of means and goals which is alternative to and conflicts with the dominant system. It should be stressed that some forms of "innovation" are more properly labelled creative man adaptation in the Thomas–Znaniecki sense. However, if the deviancy is labelled such by society and/or does not relate to any stable life organization, an innovative adaptation could be treated as bohemianism. Rebellion would seem to befit more closely the bohemian adaptation in the sense of rejection of traditional schemes, although while the bohemian never really settles on one scheme, the rebel in Merton's sense may develop an acceptable one. Certainly Merton's types can be easily associated with Etzioni's "calculative orientation." The innovation adaptation implies the use of efficiency means to obtain the desirable end of pecuniary success (a material end, as in Etzioni). The rebellion adaptation is not as easy to link with calculative orientation; however, operationally it will be shown that the alternative system institutionalized may exist within the same organizational setting as the calculative based innovation.

It hardly seems necessary to explain the link between Merton's "conformity," Thomas and Znaniecki's "creative man," and Etzioni's "moral orientation." With moral compliance comes a creative willing attitude toward conformative compliance.

INSTITUTIONS AS OPPORTUNITY STRUCTURES

Cloward and Ohlin, following Merton's analysis, have characterized various neighborhood settings as contexts for one of three different subcultures.[13] In criminally organized lower-class neighborhoods, the innovative criminal subculture arises, implying the presence of illegitimate "opportunity structures." In disorganized lower-class neighborhoods in which the criminal and legitimate sector are at odds with one-another, the conflict subculture arises due to the absence of illegitimate opportunities. Other neighborhoods are characterized as "unorganized" rather than disorganized, due to the inability of juveniles to participate in either legitimate or illegitimate opportunities and to the lack of conflict subcultures.

This kind of application of Merton's schema—innovation represented by criminal subcultures, rebellion by conflict subcultures, and retreatism by retreatist subcultures—fits even more readily in the case of complex organizations. In such organizations access to legitimate or illegitimate opportunity structures is carefully controlled and maintained through organization policy.

Normative organization structures may be conceived of as controlling access to legitimate means. Such organizations are the route to achievement through conformity to both institutional means and success goals. Individual adaptation should be creative and conforming in these settings, due to the presence of such opportunities. By contrast, coercive settings represent an enforced absence of such opportunities. The traditional prison and custodial mental hospital are designed primarily for custody of patients and seldom for rehabilitation or therapy, which might be conceived as legitimate opportunities. In both settings, the duration of incarceration is characterized by a lack of *immediate* legitimate or illegitimate opportunities; however, prison may be distinguished from an asylum in that it provides *future* illegitimate opportunities.

We may propose that though in both settings philistinism is (that is, ritualism and retreatism are) the typical adaptation of inmates, release is followed by innovation in the case of the prisoner, but continued philistinism in the case of the mental patient. Furthermore, the promise of future illegitimate opportunities may be heartening for the prisoner, which promise is not offered to the mental patient. We will note, however, as in Etzioni's analysis, that in extremely coercive settings, such as concentration camps, innovative practices—for example, corroboration and conversion— may emerge as a means of survival.

Again, as noted in Etzioni's analysis, the lower one's position is in a coercive organizational structure, the greater his chances of adoption of the more retreatist rather than ritualist stance. For example, prisoners of war who lacked any leadership qualities were found to submit to apathetic suicide in the POW camps in North Korea during the Korean war. Studies have shown that solitary confinement may lead to the mental deterioration of in- mates who are otherwise isolated within the inmate subculture.

By contrast to coercive settings, in utilitarian settings, one may find opportunities for creative conformity among top-echelon occupations, but as we descend the organizational hierarchy there is a greater tendency toward innovation–rebellion. We will note within retail and industrial settings that instances of "white collar crime" epitomize the innovative orientation and that similar oc- cupational crimes occur at all levels of the utilitarian organiza- tion hierarchy. It must also be noted, however, that there is a ten- dency for blue-collar workers, who for the most part are barred from mobility, to adopt a rebel stance in developing a somewhat subversive informal group which controls production and en- courages non-institutional behavior. Throughout the analysis of utilitarian organizations, it can be seen that these organizations, due to the material basis of compliance and calculative member orientations, can contain to some extent illegitimate opportunity structures. Studies of white-collar crime and other forms of occu- pational crime indicate that such norms are passed on as part of normal socialization into informal work-group norms.

It should be noted that the preceding analysis assumes a societal goal orientation as a basis for comparative analysis. In nearly all organizational settings, participants take a conforming orientation toward organizational goals; but in doing so, they may deviate from societal goal proscriptions. For example, conformity to an institu- tional goal of "keeping inmates in" may mean giving up a number of goals endorsed by larger society—pecuniary success, heterosexual relations, power, and so on.

Similarly, we are assuming for comparative purposes the institutionalized means sanctioned by society at large (although there may be less difference between societal and organization adherence in this criterion in terms of Merton's anomie theory). A person may in fact be acting upon directives of an organization and through such conformity deviating from the point of view of our analysis. If we can use societal means and goals as a basis for comparative analysis, organizations may be compared in terms of typifying certain deviant modes of behavior, as is shown in Table 6–9 below. This will be illustrated by drawing from studies of formal organizations in the pages to come. Later in the book, this same line of analysis will be applied to less formally organized group settings.

TABLE 6–9   Deviant and conforming modes of behavior by organizational type

| | ORGANIZATIONAL SETTING | | |
	Coercive	*Utilitarian*	*Normative*
Etzioni	Alienative	Calculative	Moral
Thomas–Znaniecki	Philistine	Bohemian	Creative man
Merton	Retreatism/ Ritualism	Rebellion/ Innovation	Conformity

DEVIANCY IN UTILITARIAN INSTITUTIONAL SETTINGS

The major framework of this book is the institutional context of deviant behavior. This perspective differs somewhat from those offered in traditional theories of crime and other forms of social pathology. Deviancy is seen as varying primarily with institutional context, and secondarily with other sociological variables such as socio-economic status, race, sex, and religion. Individuals who participate in utilitarian institutions will be oriented in the direction of innovative or rebellious deviation, while involvement in coercive institutional settings is conducive to "escapist" adaptations such as ritualism or retreatism. The rationale of this theory involves the concept of self-conception. Individuals conceive of themselves primarily in terms of their institutional affiliations, and secondarily in terms of more remote categories such as social class, sex, and age group. Race appears to be an exception to the rule, however, because of the large unemployment of black Americans in our society, making institutional affiliation apparently secondary. While this perspective is somewhat in contrast with traditional theories of deviancy, we shall see that it helps to explain certain anomalies and emphases of recent studies. Thus, we would expect criminality to be lower among clergymen than among businessmen, among college professors than among accountants, among ascetic Rabbis than among prosperous industrialists.

White-collar crime   One of the anomalies to be explained is the observation of surprisingly high rates of what Edwin H. Sutherland has termed "white collar crime."[14] White-collar crime (we prefer to hyphenate the term) is defined as "crime committed by a person of respectability and high social status in the course of his occupation."[15] Thus, we will see that white-collar crime lends itself well to institutional analysis. The definition excludes so-called street crimes, such as burglary, robbery or aggravated assault, which are not generally committed by persons of means. Such crimes include violation of antitrust laws, food and drug laws, safety and health laws, business licensing laws, housing codes, and a multitude of other regulatory statutes.

Sutherland, though not able to adduce much proof of his thesis from official sources such as FBI Uniform Crime Reports, was able to codify some rather impressive findings. He investigated decisions of courts and regulatory commissions under the antitrust, false advertising, patent, copyright, and labor laws as applied to corporations. He found that during a 45-year period, 980 adverse decisions had been rendered against 70 of our largest corporations. Every one of the 70 corporations had a decision against it, and the average number was 14.0. Ninety-eight per cent of the 70 corporations had at least four adverse decisions. About 60 per cent of the 70 corporations had been convicted by criminal courts. They averaged approximately four convictions each. As far as cost is concerned, white-collar crimes collectively are estimated to exceed ordinary crime.

It is interesting that nearly all of the examples given of white-collar crime occur in the context of utilitarian settings: business and industry. Sutherland's polemic emphasis should not obscure the existence of "white-collar crimes" by employees of lower rank in companies and retail establishments. An article in *Life* magazine has portrayed the broad gamut of employee cheating, theft, fraud, and other areas of criminality in retail establishments.[16] These acts range from fudging on records by managers, to theft of goods by delivery men. The *Reader's Digest* staff in 1941 sought to document occupational crime in several occupations involving retail trade and service, including automobile garages, radio-repair shops, and watch-repair shops. Investigators for the magazine disconnected a coil wire in an automobile, a relatively easily diagnosed problem, and then took the automobile to 347 garages in 48 states. Of these, 129 garages immediately noted the trouble, and either charged nothing or a nominal fee for the work. The remainder — 63 per cent of the garages — overcharged, inserted unnecessary parts, charged for work not done or for parts not needed, or took like action. Similarly, a radio in excellent working condition was taken to repair shops after one of the tubes had been loosened. Of 304 shops, 109 honestly identified the obvious difficulty, but the rest (almost two-thirds) treated the job as a substantial repair problem. Finally, the investigators loosened the small screw that fastens the winding wheel on a watch, and then requested a number of shops to repair it. In almost half of the cases the jewelers charged for cleaning work not performed, and for parts not needed or used.[17]

To say that deviancy exists at all levels of utilitarian organizations is not to say that crimes are identical. Upper-status businessmen and industrial leaders, when they commit crime, commit, in Lemerts' terms, relatively invisible acts, covert, secretive, arising from middle-class values. Thus, upper-status offenders may conceive of their acts as instrumental to status goals or as means of solving money problems. By contrast, lower-status acts may reflect an orientation toward duping the customer, being "smart," or perhaps even acting "tough" in Miller's terms.

In terms of our organizational theory of deviancy, it is no coincidence that Sutherland found crime prevalent in utilitarian settings of business and industry. Both lower- and higher-status participants in these settings pursue pecuniary rewards as a primary goal. It is in these structural settings that there is the greatest strain toward anomie, in Merton's sense of the term, in the sense of "innovation" — overemphasis on goals combined with deemphasis of institutionalized means. At the lower-status levels of utilitarian bureaucratic settings, theft activities may be more overt and defiant thus indicating a greater tendency toward "rebellion" as a mode of orientation.

Just as business and industrial settings may provide a culture for the growth of deviant adaptations, certain types of school structures may provide for "white-collar delinquency." This idea may shed some light on the current controversy concerning underreported delinquent behavior in middle-class neighborhoods.

White-collar delinquency   Traditional approaches to crime and delinquency assume that crime and delinquency are an inverse variant of social class; and in American sociology this assumption remained unshaken by negative evidence for decades, primarily because studies have relied heavily upon official records as sources of data on crime. As early as 1943, however, Porterfield,[18] using an anonymous questionnaire, reported surprisingly few differences between 337 college students and 2,049 alleged juvenile court delinquents, and found no relation between parent income and offenses in pre-college days, for the college sample. He explained higher frequencies reported by juvenile court delinquents as due to progressive segregation, cumulative frustration, and multiplying barriers to basic needs of court youngsters—that is, due to the court experience itself rather than social class differences *per se*. Since Porterfield's early work, a multitude of investigators have reported little or no relation between parental or personal socio-economic status and criminality-delinquency as measured by anonymous self-report questionnaires.[19] The consistency in these findings is so great that they cannot be dismissed as an artifact of a particular research setting or method, even though acceptance or partial acceptance of them might call for a major revision in traditional social class theories of crime and delinquency. The conscientious student of crime must at least consider alternatives in explaining crime and delinquency.

These anonymous self-report findings have not met with universal approval by criminologists. Indeed, the most tolerant position, even among authors of self-report studies, is to acknowledge that middle-class delinquency is more prevalent than traditionally believed. Few, however, have failed to add that middle-class delinquency is not as serious as the same type of lower-class delinquency. Typical middle-class delinquent acts, according to this view, include such peer oriented acts as drinking, drag-racing, speeding, sex practices, truancy, gambling, petty theft, fist fighting, and vandalism (all misdemeanors if committed by adults). Similarly, existing explanations assume, implicitly or explicitly, lower-class origin of delinquent actions. Such explanations include the upward diffusion of working-class values via the mass media; weakening of the middle-class deferred gratification pattern, making middle-class youngsters more like traditional lower-class; difficulty of middle-class sons in matching their father's achievements; lack of community services in middle-class neighborhoods; development of communication since World War II; and upward mobility of lower-class families into middle-class.[20]

In the context of the framework developed here, this separation of lower- and middle-class delinquency applies mainly among youngsters whose parents are employed in utilitarian institutional settings. Parent deviant orientations as well as values become reflected in adolescent versions of deviancy. Thus, the father who openly acknowledges duplicity in business dealings or income tax evasion may find his son engaging in cheating in school, falsification of identification, and petty theft. However, there is reason to believe that even traditionally lower-class forms of delinquency may be highly prevalent in the middle class (including, for example, gang fighting, carrying concealed weapons, auto theft, and narcotics). This observation is based upon our organizational theory of deviancy, which states that juvenile delinquency itself is institution-bound. That is, delinquency can only be understood in terms of specific institutional contexts, in particular in terms of local school or local area settings.

Schools may be classified in terms of our theoretical categories anomic, pluralistic, oligarchic, or in organizational terms utilitarian, normative, and coercive. Delinquency should be highest in the anomic–utilitarian settings where we expect conditions of group conflict–calculative orientation. This is congruent with innovative and rebellious orientations usually linked with delinquency. There is no basis for distinguishing public schools in terms of organizational purpose or compliance structure, because public schools are supposedly the same in this respect. However, we can differentiate schools in terms of the presence or absence of the structural bases of group conflict or organizational anomie, which would provide an index of utilitarian compliance structure. If a school is populated with heterogeneous groups, we have the structural bases of group conflict. Contrary to social class theories of delinquency, this holds regardless of socio-economic level of school areas. Thus, delinquency is an outgrowth of participation in school settings in which there is excessive diversity of socio-economic groups engendering group conflict.

We may hypothesize that the greater the heterogeneity of a school attendance area, the higher the rate of self-reported delinquency. A tentative test of this hypothesis was done using data drawn from a self-report delinquency study conducted in Los Angeles and Long Beach, California. Data were taken on nonprobability samples of high school boys and girls in Long Beach and Los Angeles.[21] In this study, heterogeneity referred specifically to socio-economic heterogeneity. Heterogeneity was compared to two "traditional" correlates of delinquency—area status and area racial segregation—and self-reported delinquency was compared to official delinquency on all of these variables.[22]

The results are shown in Tables 6–10 and 6–11. In Table 6–10, scores on both independent and dependent variables are given for the seven high schools in our sample. In Table 6–11, intercorrelations are given for these measures. These indicate that heterogeneity is highly correlated with self-reported delinquency but not with

TABLE 6–10   Self-reported delinquency (males only) as related to high school of attendance, with data for selected census tract variables

Levels of Self-reporting Delinquency	HIGH SCHOOL ATTENDANCE AREA						
	Poly L.B.	*Wilson* L.B.	*Jordan* L.B.	*HS#1* L.A.	*HS#2* L.A.	*HS#3* L.A.	*Millkn.* L.B.
Higher	80.0	52.1	75.0	40.0	40.0	34.4	31.5
Lower	20.0	47.9	25.0	60.0	60.0	65.6	68.5
Totals	100.0	100.0	100.0	100.0	100.0	100.0	100.0
$N =$	(15)	(48)	(4)	(15)	(35)	(32)	(105)
SOCIO-ECONOMIC HETEROGENEITY							
	18.3	11.9	11.2	10.6	10.	8.1	4.3
MEAN SOCIO-ECONOMIC LEVEL							
	61.4	79.9	62.0	41.9	44.8	34.3	81.4
MEAN SEGREGATION LEVEL							
	17.2	6.8	4.4	89.3	66.1	83.9	5.0
602 SERIES PETITION RATES							
	18.3	14.8	10.5	26.3	40.5	21.5	4.8

TABLE 6–11 Correlations for the seven field study high schools (males only) between independent variables (socio-economic heterogeneity, social status level, and segregation level) and dependent variables (self-reported delinquency and 602 series petition rates)

	Self-reported Delinquency	*602 Series Petitions*
Socio-economic heterogeneity	0.96**	0.00
Social status level	—0.08	0.81*
Segregation level	—0.20	0.93**

*p = 0.05
**p = 0.01

official delinquency. The opposite is true using the traditional independent variables, social status and segregation. If we accept self-report findings this suggests a bias in officially reported delinquency against lower status and underprivileged ethnic groups, as earlier suggested by Porterfield. At the same time these findings give us tentative support for our school area organization theory specified above and help to explain the anomalous findings as to middle-class delinquency in that middle-class schools can be just as heterogeneous as lower-class schools.

The link between heterogeneity of a school area and delinquency seems logical enough. Certainly diversity creates the classic situation of disorganization or anomie discussed in Chapter 3. One may wonder why the school attendance area is stressed as such an important unit of analysis. Briefly, it is because the school for a youngster is as important a reference group as the work setting is for adults. A youngster thinks of himself in terms of the social system of the school. In highly heterogeneous school areas, there is intergroup conflict in the community, leading to a breakdown in social control. The informal system becomes separate from the formal system of the high school, becoming an autonomous adolescent social system. Participation, particularly at the lower status level of this system may be conducive to delinquency. It is this lower stratum group which opposes another dominant group with whom it conflicts. The school thus becomes a battle-ground for latent or manifest conflicts within its environing community. The development of adolescent social systems will be discussed more fully in a later chapter dealing with informal group settings for deviancy.

DEVIANCY IN COERCIVE INSTITUTIONAL SETTINGS

Deviant behavior is best understood in terms of its organizational context. This has been the basic premise of this book. It has been proposed that much behavior of a criminal or delinquent nature can be viewed as an outcome of participation in utilitarian organizational settings, that is, in industries and businesses. This analysis is derived from Etzioni's analysis of organizations. While Etzioni's focus is primarily upon the features of organizational structure, and secondarily upon the behavior of participants resulting from this structure, our focus has been the reverse. We are attempting to view deviant behavior in terms of organizational context.

Etzioni's analysis of behavior in coercive organizational settings is limited basically to the descriptive term "alienative." We have seen in the chapter on mass society that the word alienation has various meanings: powerlessness, normlessness, meaninglessness, isolation, self-estrangement, reification, loneliness, and the like. It would seem, however, that in the coercive institutional setting, Etzioni means all of these senses, with the important qualification that these are passively felt and not acted upon aggressively. Within the confines of a coercive setting, alienative feelings cannot be acted upon to any significant degree and must be endured patiently, as the alternative to compliance is physical punishment. Some, of course, may choose this alternative; however, we shall see that it is far more common for a person to elect the alternative of adapting and adjusting. Thus, deviant types appropriate to coercive settings are Merton's ritualism and retreatism. Ritualism would be more typical of mildly coercive or quasi-coercive settings (such as nunneries, totalitarian political groups, and relocation camps).[23] Retreatism as well as ritualism becomes prevalent in the more coercive settings (custodial mental hospitals and prisons). However, under the most extreme conditions, as in concentration camps, inmates are faced with basically two alternatives: retreatism and probable death, or innovative adaptation for survival purposes.

Organizational settings may be viewed as analogous to subcultures, as described by Cloward and Ohlin. Utilitarian settings are "subcultures" in which there is high access to illegitimate opportunity structures with relatively low emphasis upon adherence to institutional means. In coercive settings, by contrast the opposite situation exists. Low access to private and shared goals exists among inmates by virtue of relative absence of legitimate or illegitimate opportunities. Inmate behavior, therefore, resembles that of a "retreatist" subculture, or even more likely a "ritualist" subculture.

Thus, behavior may be labeled deviant though quite typical in these various institutional settings in terms of societal goals or institutional means.

Ritualism in quasi-coercive settings   Not all coercive settings are purely coercive but may tend strongly toward other compliance structures.

Four settings may be cited as examples of quasi-coercive settings: the Japanese factory, the nunnery, the totalitarian political group, and the "relocation camp." Each of these areas of studies illustrates the development of ritualist subcultures among inmates.

Abegglen's empirical study[24] illustrates the adjustments made by employees in a rather unusual work situation. The Japanese factory, according to Abegglen, offers many benefits to its workers: yearly bonuses, various allowances, a welfare program, and—most important—life tenure. However, there is one major disadvantage. Once a worker is placed in one of two categories—wage-earning labor or management—upon being hired, there is no mobility between categories. That is, there is a kind of quasi-caste system existing in the Japanese factory. As a result, while laborers remain extremely loyal to their employer through life, their productivity is relatively low by United States standards.

Low productivity is one form of ritualism. The individual does not aspire to higher production due to a lack of incentive. In another quasi-coercive setting, the nunnery, ritualism takes a different form. While in the Japanese factory some coercion is found in the caste system of worker-management relations, in the nunnery, mild coercion is found in the manipulation of food and the absence of ordinarily normal rewards such as heterosexual relations, absence of stimulating forms of recreation, and presence of austerity of life.

Monica Baldwin's book *I Leap Over the Wall*[25] describes life in a nunnery and the experiences of a person who had left the nunnery. After 28 years in a convent, Miss Baldwin left the convent in 1941 for a secular life. She recounts the austerity of convent life, but reflects throughout her book an inability to meet the demands of secular life. She is at times overwhelmed by what she conceives as immoral behavior of people she meets. Secular life was generally a strain for her and her life goal became a "cottage in the clouds" in which to settle down. Her experience indicates the scaling-down of normal aspirations that occurs as a result of the experience of life in a convent setting.

Totalitarian political parties illustrate a kind of ritualistic adherence of subordinates in another way. Selznick describes the structure of the Communist party as quasi-coercive.[26] Though the appeal to individual members is ideological, party structure is undemocratic. The party hierarchy is elected, but not democratically. A single slate of candidates is chosen by technical analysis and simply rubber-stamped by the membership—that is, there is a plebiscite. Criticism is only allowed of the general party, not of particular officials. Resulting behavior has two facets, *insulation* and *absorption,* each a kind of deprivation. Insulation refers to the isolation of the individual member from such ties as home, family, and job. Absorption refers to domination over thought process by the party. Both of these processes are certainly conducive to ritualist involvement.

In still another quasi-coercive setting, the ritualist subculture may be seen developing. American "relocation camps" for Japanese-Americans during World War II and Communist Koreans during the Korean War have been described in these terms. Leighton describes the adaptation of the Japanese to Poston Relocation Center during World War II.[27] Despite the coercion of physical confinement, Poston policy emphasized the rights of aliens and the desirability of democratic self-management. Despite hurried preparation of the camp, the administration of Poston attempted to develop economic opportunities and wholesome community life for the evacuees. The effect of this semi-coercive treatment was the toleration of frustration and the emergence of self-government among the evacuees, a government which managed to gain certain privileges through an inmate strike.

A similar situation is described in White's research study, *The Captives of Korea.*[28] The American camp studied (Pusan) was run according to Geneva rules. Prisoners were fed rations equal to that of the soldiers who captured them. They were not forced into giving confessions and were allowed to develop a chain of command among themselves. The results of this treatment were surprising. At the conclusion of the war, 100,000 out of 171,000 refused repatriation (compared to 20 Americans out of 12,000).

In the above illustration, a number of instances of "reluctant conformity" or ritualism have been described in various quasi-coercive settings. In the Japanese factory ritualism is shown by low productivity. In the nunnery, it is shown by the loss of capacity for enjoyment of secular life. Participation in a totalitarian party is characterized by a deprivation of social ties. The relocation camp encompasses adjustment to frustration through self-rule. The unusual example of the Korean captives shows that the extent of frustration of inmates depends largely upon previously acquired aspirations, rewards, and values, and that what might be ritualist behavior in a coercive setting may prove to be willing conformity.

EMERGENCE OF RETREATIST SUBCULTURE IN COERCIVE SETTINGS

As stated above, Etzioni has described extensively the coercive setting from the point of view of organizational structure. Our interest is in behavior, resulting from this structure, which has been extensively discussed in the empirical literature—especially studies of prisons and custodial mental hospitals. Concentration camps will be discussed below as illustrative of extreme coercion.

Studies of custodial mental hospitals have indicated the presence of coercive organizational features and techniques of treatment of mental patients. Goffman's account of such organizational settings is probably the best available source.[29] Custodial mental hospitals have several coercive features. They are "total institutions" in that work, sleep, and play occur in the same location, under a single authority, in company of others. The incoming patient is subjected to a highly degrading "stripping process" divesting him of all previous status and relegating him to the role

of child. Once admitted, the patient is subject to a caste-like hierarchy and echelon and an unusually cruel privilege system in which
the patient must sacrifice much to achieve small rewards.

Patient reaction to this coercive regime clearly illustrates a
trend toward greater and greater retreatism. The patient undergoes four stages of adaptation. The first stage of *situational withdrawal,* the patient is aware only of his own body blocking out the
surrounding environment. This is followed by *rebellion* or *in-
transigency,* which is met by severe reprisals by the hospital staff.
Subsequently a *colonization* stage occurs, during which the patient
learns to accept the deprivations of the hospital experience (that
is, ritualism). Last is the *conversion stage,* during which the patient
accepts the staff image of self (a negative self-image) and ceases
attempts to assert individuality or to obtain normal rewards (that
is, retreatism). Experienced patients adopt "secondary adjustment
techniques" or "make do's" for working the system, acquiring
favorable work assignments, and obtaining contraband goods.
While there is an innovation component in these techniques, in the
larger context, they would more appropriately be termed ritualist
forms and they are oriented at minor privilege and reward and not
primary roles which could only be obtained through release and
freedom.

While Goffman's analysis is no doubt unmatched in portraying
the coercive effects of state mental hospitalization, numerous
other works have been done on the subject. Belknap[30] has shown
how control by attendants and the ward system in a large Southern
state mental hospital has led to retreatist behavior among a large
number of patients. The maintenance of a stable and functioning
organization is disproportionately vested in the nurses, attendants,
and even the patients themselves. The hospital is divided into
four formal and six actual levels. Level I includes the superin-
tendent, clinical director, staff physicians, and dentists. Level II
includes primarily the professional group such as social workers,
nurses, and miscellaneous therapists. Level III consists of the
attendants, stratified by such prestige categories as sex, seniority,
reputation, and personal ability. Level IV formally consists of the
patients—informally organized, however, into three groups:
(*a*) the *privileged,* or those who work on the ward, (*b*) those of
limited privilege, or those generally neither cooperative nor un-
cooperative, and (*c*) those *without privilege,* or those considered

dangerous, listless, withdrawn, or disturbed. Placement of patients is done following admission. The fate of the incoming patient depends on the operation of the ward status system. If he is lucid at the time of his placement in the ward situation (level 6), he may move upward in the internal system through levels 5 and 4. Incoming patients who are unable to accurately perceive the situation achieve either slow upward mobility or permanent low status in level 6.

Such permanent placement lowers the likelihood of consistent attention by attendants and ultimately the professional personnel. Both the attendants and the patients are likely eventually to label the patient as "incurable" and may offer resistance to future mobility. The patients in level 4 are likely to regard themselves as mentally sound and think of the patients below as "crazy people." Few personal associations between level 4 and level 5 of the patients structure result. Belknap showed that the patients rather than the attendants or the doctor within level 4 actually determined the ultimate upward mobility in the ward for the majority of patients and thus the eventual discharge from the hospital. In essence, the levels with the most authority, prestige, and training are the farthest removed from the patient population in terms of individual contact. Thus, as a result of the caste-like stratification within the ward system, leaving becomes very difficult for most of the patients. Due to long custodial care, the patient becomes "desocialized," and often his outside relationships become severed.

This desocialization process has been the theme of much of the literature on mental hospitalization. Hardt and Feinhandler[31] found, in accord with Hollingshead's earlier work[32] that the social class level of a patient is inversely related to the risk of continuous long-run hospitalization. Thus, there is evidence of a reactive influence of hospital upon mental patient. Even more relevant, Dunham and Weinberg[33] found a highly stratified ward system hospital which served as a repressive influence upon patients at Columbus State Mental Hospital. They found the development of opposing employee and inmate subcultures, the employee emphasizing "norms of control" and the inmate emphasizing "norms of accommodation." The central values of inmates, in order of importance, are: (1) going home, (2) residence on certain types of wards, (3) the attentions of doctors, (4) certain jobs within the hospital system, and (5) the good will of the attendants. Dunham and Weinberg find that the central orientation of the hopeful wards is "going home," while on the chronic wards it is "making the best of hospital life." Generally they found that returnees had spent a considerably longer time in the hospital than discharged patients. Thus, there is both objective and subjective adaptation of ritualism (adaptation to secondary reward values, such as the good will of the attendants) rather than primary values (such as "going home"). They found that patients on the disturbed wards were characterized by an "inner preoccupation with conflict," which might indicate a retreatist adaptation (relinquishment of both primary and secondary goals of the hospital).

Prisons as Coercive Settings. Although the lower-ranking participants in traditional prisons presumably have deviated behaviorally in a different way from that of mental patients, we shall see that their treatment within the traditional prison setting is much the same as the treatment of mental patients in asylums, with much the same results as far as their behavior goes *within* the prison setting. A major premise of traditional institutions is that, in order to minimize the danger to both the institutional staff and the community, security should be regarded as the dominant goal. Mechanical security measures are instituted, including the building of high walls or fences around prisons, construction of gun-towers, the searching of inmates as they pass through certain checkpoints, pass systems to account for inmate movement, and counts at regular intervals. The objective of custody is met quite effectively, as few prisoners escape and those who do usually are quickly apprehended. All of these measures, of course, serve to deprive prisoners of reward values regarded as primary in society-at-large. Heterosexual relations are absent; all status symbols are removed as inmates wear prison issue, march in groups, and are identified by number; mail is censored; visiting is limited and closely supervised; and privacy is virtually nonexistent. Isolated, punitive, and regimented, the traditional prison and many juvenile training schools develop a monolithic society, caste-like and resistive to change.

In response to this system of deprivation, an inmate subculture develops whose primary function is to maximize for prisoners whatever secondary reward values can be obtained. Status within this inmate system is determined largely by degree of effort in pursuit of inmate values. At the very top of the inmate group are the "politicians" or "big shots," those who have not only earned respect among their fellows but also have developed rapport with the staff. These tend to be persons with extensive institutional experience, who have been tested in interactions with other inmates sufficiently that they are neither readily "pushed around" by their fellows nor distrusted as "stool pigeons." They have also been tested sufficiently by the staff to be assigned jobs in offices or other locations where they can communicate readily with staff and often have access to institutional records. Because of their possession of "inside" information and their access to the staff, they can command considerable deference from other inmates. However, they can also convince inmates that they generally work for their interest through manipulating the staff. They are thus the leadership in the inmate caste, and the middlemen between the staff and inmates.

Beneath the "politicians" in status are the great mass of inmates, often called "right guys" or "straights." Although some of these will ultimately be elevated to politician status, they generally avoid overtures toward staff members for fear of being labeled "fink" or "squealer." In inmate society, squealers share the lowest stratum with sex offenders, the physically weak and immature, and the mentally disordered and retarded.

Aggressive inmates often are distrusted, and sometimes are feared, by staff and inmates alike, and thus do not as often as might be expected occupy a high position in the inmate society. Their tendency toward violence rather than manipulation imperils both the stability of the institution and the maintenance of reciprocal relationships between staff and inmates.

The favored adaptation among prisoners is reluctant conformity in pursuit of secondary reward values (that is, ritualism). Included among these secondary rewards are homosexual relations (taking the place of heterosexual relations), reassignment to a more favorable prison job, and access to certain minor physical gratifications such as cigarettes, candy, and reading material. Although, in view of the behavioral nature of criminals as compared with mental patients, retreatism seems unlikely, there have been instances of the relinquishment of hope, contentment with prison life in preference to freedom, and separation from reality in response to the threat of coercive sanction.

Concentration Camps as Extreme Coercive Settings. There is evidence that within the setting of extremely coercive concentration camps, innovation is rivaled closely by retreatism as an adaptation to incarceration. Three settings have been studied to a greater or lesser extent: (1) the German concentration camps of World War II, (2) Andersonville, and (3) North Korean POW camps during the Korean War.

The German concentration camps were set up under Hitler's regime for the humiliation and extermination of resisters and "inferior races."[34] They served to segregate and eliminate opposition, create slave labor and provide experimental guinea pigs, and provide training ground for future SS officers. At the top position in each camp was a commandant in charge of administrative and duty officers and guards, all of whom had the power of life and death over any inmate. Kogon describes the SS as cultural misfits who were given free play of their instincts toward the prisoners, and in return received rewards for their excessive brutality.

The new inmate, after having been subjected to degradation and humiliation, followed one of several mental paths. If the stress was too much for him, he would break physically and mentally, displaying psychotic behavior. Another adaptation was conversion, in which the prisoner became a trusted inmate who could be entrusted with such jobs as guard, orderly, or foreman. Both of these adaptations imply a repudiation of outside role and self-identification and of withdrawal from pursuit of primary or secondary values—that is, they imply retreatism. On the other hand, the prisoner could rise above the urge to succumb. Three forms of adjustment were common: being a "lone wolf," having group allegiance, and forming bonds with those of the same political beliefs. The underground at Buchenwald enabled the inmate to survive. Organized by the "big shots," it succeeded in saving many from death, increasing prisoner solidarity, and eventually corrupting and controlling enough SS to make the end easier when the Allies came. This survival adaptation indicates innovation as a mode of adaptation.

Of interest is the fact that a concentration camp similar to Buchenwald was developed in the United States. The physical and organizational conditions described by McElroy in his descriptive account of *Andersonville*,[35] a Southern POW camp during the Civil War, parallel those of German concentration camps. The physical conditions at Andersonville were oppressive. At its largest, there were 35,000 prisoners in the stockade, an area of only thirteen acres. Food, shelter, clothing, and medical care were absent or extremely insufficient. In part due to crowding, the camp was filthy and the death rate from disease was extremely high.

Soon after imprisonment, many of the men attempted to escape by scaling the stockade during the night. This attempt proved ineffective, however, because one of the prisoners had informed the Confederates of the escapees' intentions. In response to the prisoners' attempts, the Rebels constructed a Dead Line twenty feet from the stockade, which if touched would bring about immediate death by shooting. After this, escape efforts were restricted to tunneling under the stockade. These attempts were rarely successful, and when a tunneling prisoner was caught he was chained to a steel ball for the duration of his imprisonment.

In addition to these coercive actions by the prison staff, the organization of the inmate subsystem sharply limited prisoner activity. The inmate subsystem could only be characterized as disorganized or anomic. Prisoners had no self-government. The rule was "every man for himself" and justice was frontier justice. One group called the Raiders composed of 200 New Yorkers made nightly raids on the rest of the camp, stealing anything that would be valuable in trading with the guards. They in turn received favors by informing to the guards. A small group tried to overthrow the Raiders, but was unsuccessful due to a lack of organization. New soldiers were constantly arriving, and gambling was extensive as a possible means of gaining money and articles for trading. There was no attempt to share, as most items were too valuable just to give away. Eventually the Raiders were overcome by a group of 150 called the Regulators.

Due to these various factors—the Dead Line, the constant conflict between prisoners, concern over primary needs, and the informant system—men eventually lost the desire to try to escape, and the rates of insanity, death, and disease were extremely high. These forms of behavior are firm evidence of retreatism.

The conditions in the North Korean POW camps were strikingly similar to those of America's Andersonville. When captured, the American soldiers were subjected to severe physical and mental stresses. They were collected in large groups and marched north. There was no medicine for the wounded. Food was unpalatable and insufficient. Clothing was scarce and the winter weather was severe. Shelter was inadequate and overcrowded.[36] As in the other cases shown above, the prisoners exhibited very little organization among themselves. Each was competing with the other for essentials of life. Huts were overcrowded. Disease was rife. Lines of authority were broken. Escape attempts proved futile. Morale was lessened appreciably by false reports by the Chinese of United Nations defeats and losses.

Under these circumstances, prisoner behavior had all the markings of retreatist adaptation. Goals became increasingly short-run. The men became increasingly apathetic, developing a slow, plodding gait, called by one man a "prisoners' shuffle." They developed food fantasies about the good meals they had had in the past. In the face of extreme conditions of disease, many died— though, in the opinion of many, some of whom were doctors who survived the experience, many more died than was warranted by mere physical conditions. Men retreated further into themselves, refused what little food was available, would not exercise, and finally lay down as if waiting to die. These men were reported sane and clear of mind, but seemed willing to accept the prospect of death rather than to continue fighting a severely frustrating and depriving environment. In some cases, "therapy" consisted of kicking a man until he was mad enough to get up and fight.

Upon arrival at a POW camp, men were subjected to informal and formal group control, which later was termed "brainwashing" because of its presumed effect on personality. Although this much-publicized control had overstated effects upon the personalities of American soldiers, there was indeed some tendency toward what Goffman terms "conversion." The central feature of Chinese camp control was the nearly total destruction of the prisoners' formal and informal group structure based on segregation by race, nationality, and rank. The Chinese were then able to take over leadership of the POW groups through substituting their own leaders, by preventing any kind of group meeting, by fomenting mutual distrust among the men, and by obtaining information from informers. All mail was censored, and usually only bad news was delivered. If a man did not receive any mail, this was used as evidence by the Chinese that loved ones had abandoned him.

Conversion to Communism was encouraged by physical rewards such as extra food and medicine, in addition to nonmaterial rewards of privilege and status. Resistance, on the other hand, was countered by threats of death, non-repatriation, reprisal against family, torture, decreases in food and medicine, and imprisonment. Few of these except imprisonment was consistently used, and chronic resistance was usually handled by transferring a prisoner to a so-called "reactionary" camp. Collaboration was highest among those who were most likely to be sympathetic toward Communism, those who had chronically occupied a low-status position in this society. However, chronic collaboration only occurred in 10 to 15 per cent of the cases. In very few cases, however, was there a personal change of belief, but merely behavioral compliance such as writing and broadcasting propaganda, giving false confessions, informing on fellow POW's, and the like.

It is interesting that the *conversion* response occurred, because conversion represents an innovative response to the situation. That is, prisoners utilized illegitimate means to obtain their own goals, in Merton's terms, the technically most efficient means to goal attainment. However, in the North Korean POW camps, the vast majority of prisoners adopted a ritualistic-retreatistic stance, which the men termed "playing it cool," consisting of physical and emotional withdrawal from the whole environment, an attitude of watching and waiting, rather than hoping and planning.

Summary and conclusion

In Chapter 5 an organizational model for the study of deviancy was developed. The major premise of this model is that people evaluate the self in terms of their position and relationships within relatively small-scale organizations. For most people, this refers to the more-or-less legitimate formal organizations in which they spend their lives day after day—for example, work and school as formal organizational settings. Deviant behavior occurs in these settings and can be understood in terms of formal organizational structure. For individuals who do not participate in formal organizations (such as the unemployed and juvenile school dropouts), deviant behavior can be understood in terms of the subcultural organizations in which they participate (this topic will be discussed in more detail below).

The present chapter was concerned with developing a typology of formal organizations and of corresponding forms of deviant (or conforming) behavior. The earliest systematic discussion of formal organization was that of Weber who outlined the characteristics of bureaucracy in detail. However, Weber seemed to ignore variations in bureaucratic organization. Because of this tendency toward overgeneralization, recent approaches to the study of formal organization have stressed variation in bureaucratic organization, that is, types of formal organization. There has been a proliferation of typologies, including those of Gouldner, Fritz Marx, Parsons, Blau-Scott, and Etzioni. Of these, Etzioni's is the most adequate for purposes of this text for several reasons: (1) it ties in closely with the trichotomy of theoretical types developed in Chapter 2 of this text: anomic, pluralistic, and oligarchic, (2) it seems adequate as a constructive typology synthesizing the various typologies developed herein, (3) it subsumes in its meaning Weber's types of authority, thus insuring continuity with his thinking on bureaucracy, and (4) it contains explicit reference to behavioral adaptation (which other typologies of formal organization lack). As Table 6–12 shows, Etzioni's typology permits the development of a "grand synthesis" of organizational and behavioral typologies, characteristics, and empirical findings. Table 6–12, a review of the contents of this chapter, includes a summary of behavioral and organizational typologies, giving their characteristics, and examples of each.

TABLE 6–12 Cross-classification of organizational and behavioral typologies

GENERAL ORGANIZATIONAL TYPOLOGY

Etzioni	utilitarian	normative	coercive
Gouldner	mock	representative	punishment centered
F. Marx	merit	guardian/patronage	caste
Parsons	adaptation/goal attainment	integrative	social control
Blau–Scott	owner-management/ service	mutual benefit/ commonweal	
Weber	legal authority ("bureaucracy")	traditional authority/ charismatic authority	

SUMMARY OF ORGANIZATIONAL CHARACTERISTICS

	Anomic	*Pluralistic*	*Oligarchic*
Etzioni	material sanction	symbolic sanction	physical sanction
Gouldner	rules are ignored	rules accepted	rules imposed arbitrarily
F. Marx	leader selection by objective standards	leaders: those ideologically committed	leaders occupy highest caste

Table 6–12 (Continued)

Parsons	political or economic goals	integrative goals	custodial goals
Blau–Scott	public-in-contact benefits; owner–management benefit	rank-and-file benefit; public-at-large benefits	
Weber	based upon belief in supremacy of law	based on belief in supernatural powers of leader, or sanctity of tradition	

ORIENTATION OF SUBORDINATES

Thomas–Znaniecki	bohemian	creative man	philistine
Merton	rebellion–innovation	conformity	ritualism–retreatism
Etzioni	calculative	moral	alienative

SUMMARY OF BEHAVIORAL CHARACTERISTICS

Thomas–Znaniecki	competitiveness	cooperativeness	withdrawal
	hostility	tolerance	apathy and rigidity
	unscrupulousness	scrupulousness	anxiety
	egotism	self- and group-centered	altruism
	radicalness	moderateness	conservatism
Merton	end justifies means	ends and means in balance	means as ends in themselves
Etzioni	neutral: neither positive nor negative	positive or favorable orientation	negative or unfavorable orientation

EXAMPLES OF ORGANIZATIONS

"industries" /blue collar	religious organizations ideological political organizations	concentration camps POW camps; prisons
white collar professional/	general hospitals universities voluntary organizations	correctional institutions custodial mental hospitals "relocation centers" coercive unions

EXAMPLES OF BEHAVIORAL ADAPTATIONS
(DRAWN FROM EMPIRICAL STUDIES)

white collar crime and delinquency		suicide mental disorder low productivity satisfaction with secondary rewards low social contact identification

Noninstitutional contexts of deviancy

7

In Chapter 6, three types of formal organizations were discussed as varied settings for deviant or conforming behavior. Utilitarian organization, the first, is closely allied with the general theoretical type, anomic organization. The second, coercive organization, is related to oligarchic organization. Lastly, normative organization is the formal organizational counterpart of pluralistic organization. It was proposed that innovative and rebellious behavior would be found mainly in utilitarian organizations and that ritualism and retreatism would be found in coercive organizations. Normative organizations are conducive to widespread conforming behavior.

If the organizational theory of deviancy were restricted to formal organizational settings, however, it would exclude from consideration most of the major forms of deviancy. Fortunately, there is no reason why our analysis should be so restricted. Many noninstitutional forms of deviancy are organized. (*Note:* The term "noninstitutional" here refers to informal or non-formal settings of deviancy. It does not mean "institutions" in the sense of—for example—the government or the family.) There is a clear màndate in the literature for viewing crime and delinquency in this manner. Our analy-

Notes for this chapter are on pages 387–389.

sis, in this sense, follows upon Sutherland's proclamation that crime is learned in intimate association.[1]

The structure of criminal groups has been variously described in the literature on crime. Such groups have been portrayed as gangs, mobs, rackets, syndicates, cartels, subcultures, and near-groups—all terms suggesting variation in social organization. In the present chapter we shall have occasion to look at these various group structures in the light of our organizational analysis. We should expect that criminal groups should take the form of utilitarian organization or possibly a utilitarian-coercive dual type. In viewing criminal groups in this way, new light may be shed on criminal behavior that takes place within these organizational contexts. Predictions can be made that may instigate a search for new facts about such behavior. It will be proposed, for example, that professional crime approximates the pure utilitarian type, while organized crime takes a dual utilitarian-coercive form. This formulation calls into question traditional theories of professional crime, which blur its description with that of organized crime.

Most of the literature on deviant organizational structure pertains to crime and delinquency. Using our organizational framework, let us now look at this literature.

Criminal organization

Textbooks on crime include several types of criminal organization. Two major forms of criminal organization are professional crime and organized crime, which will be discussed at length here. Organized vice and related forms of criminal organization will be discussed briefly.

PROFESSIONAL CRIME

In terms of the typology of deviancy and the theoretical framework developed in this text, the professional criminal would be seen as working within a utilitarian compliance structure—that is he is calculatively involved and oriented toward predominantly material reward values. Traditional studies of the professional criminal by Sutherland, Maurer and others seem to contradict this characterization. These early studies led to the view that the professional criminal was involved in a mutually binding system of norms, consensually understood and voluntarily obeyed, or obeyed because of fear of sanction. That is, traditional studies have led to the belief that the professional criminal is involved in a normative or normative-coercive compliance structure. Very recently, more thorough study by the President's Crime Commission has led to a reversal of this traditional thinking. The Crime Commission model of professional crime is, it will be shown, much more in line with the utilitarian compliance model than is the traditional image of the professional criminal.

Traditional theories of professional crime   Prevailing knowledge of professional crime stems primarily from a relatively limited literature composed mainly of case studies. The first of these, Sutherland's classic, *The Professional Thief,*[2] was published in 1937 and describes the life of a thief in the period between 1905 and 1925. Besides case studies, the majority of work has been done on particular types of criminal activity normally engaged in by professionals, including confidence game operation,[3] pickpocketing,[4] professional robbery and burglary,[5] and receiving stolen goods.[6] Beyond this, little has been done in estimating the extent or trend of professional crime.[7] Moreover, the caricature of the professional criminal has been drawn primarily from anecdotal and case-study accounts. Thus there has been virtually no attempt to test suppositions made from these accounts and their interpretations.

The tendency has been to follow Sutherland's distinction between professional and other types of remunerative crime:

> The term "professional" when applied to a criminal refers to the following things: the pursuit of crime as a regular day-by-day occupation, the development in that occupation, and status among criminals. The professional criminal is differentiated from the occasional criminal, the amateur criminal, the unskilled and careless criminal.[8]

Professional crime, in terms of this definition, includes such activities as pickpocketing, shoplifting, sneak-thieving from stores, banks, and offices, stealing from jewelry stores by substituting inferior jewelry for valuable pieces, stealing from hotel rooms, forgery, and extortion.[9] The portrait of the professional criminal emerging from this definition is well summarized by Cavan:

The professional criminal has at least seven distinguishing marks that, taken together, differentiate him from other types of criminals. (1) The professional criminal gets his living primarily or solely by the commission of crime. . . . (2) His crimes are almost without exception financial in nature; crimes of violence are secondary to financial crimes. (3) The professional criminal has acquired the skills necessary to commit one or several related types of crime, and he tends to specialize in a particular type of crime. (4) The professional criminal organizes his life around his criminal speciality and subordinates other phases of his life to his money-making activities. (5) The professional criminal usually works alone or in a small group of two to four fellow technicians. . . . (6) Although professional criminals may work in one city for a number of years, they usually find safety by moving from city to city. . . . (7) The professional criminal is an accepted member of the criminal world to which he looks for social status and approval and to whose disapproval and reproofs he responds.[10]

Thus, the professional criminal is seen as belonging to a tightly knit subcultural organization—the criminal underworld—as shown by the distinctive language or argot of professional criminals, the existence of elaborate special techniques and skills transmitted through the group, and by the existence of a distinctive set of codes of the underworld, such as mutual honesty and secrecy with regard to groups activities. The professional criminal is seen as typically associating with a "mob" that interlocks with other mobs, conveys criminal skills, and supports the code of honesty and secrecy with the threat of dismissal, ostracism, or death. The professional criminal in this view is seen as developing a criminal philosophy justifying his actions and preventing remorse and regret, thus solidifying the criminal role and criminal self-concept. "Professional thieves have in common acquaintances, congeniality, sympathy, understandings, agreements, rules, codes of behavior, and language."[11]

In comparison with other offenders, an extremely high degree of consensus exists among professional criminals. Professional criminals develop common attitudes toward themselves, toward their crimes, and toward their common enemy, the police. These common attitudes include the support of other thieves in order to overcome the ostracism of conventional society. Other thieves help the individual to find solace and rationalizations for his behavior. The group gives him a cultural situation in which to carry on his social existence and a group of values held in common by all thieves. More specifically, the relationships among professional criminals are characterized by a "code of honor." In a sense this corresponds to the code of ethics and standards governing conduct in the more respectable professions. A professional thief, for example, is always punctual about his obligations and appointments. He must never "squeal" on another member of the profession. In fact, a professional thief will endure severe punishment rather than inform on another. There is considerable agreement on this rule, for it is supported by loyalty and identification with other thieves. It is also supported by certain motives of self-interest, including loss of prestige, danger of reprisal, and the difficulty of finding other thieves with whom to work if one fails to live up to the code of honor among them.[12]

Revised view of professional crime   Recently, The President's Commission on Law Enforcement and Administration of Justice attempted the most rigorous study of professional crime ever done. The Commission sponsored a pilot field-research study in four cities—Atlanta, Chicago, New York, and San Francisco—during the summer of 1966. The Commission consultants talked to police, district attorneys, and professional criminals themselves in these cities. The consultants spent the balance of their time in the field (about 10 to 15 days each) locating and talking with professional criminals. The number of criminals interviewed varied from a low of eight in one city (Chicago) to 19 in another (San Francisco), with a total of 50 being interviewed. About two-thirds of the total number were in jail or prison at the time of their interviews. Although the sample is small, it is large compared to previous studies.

In conducting its study the Commission defined professional crime as "crime committed for personal economic gain by individuals whose major source of income is from criminal pursuits and who spend the majority of their working time in illegal enterprises."[13] The Commission referred to crime as an occupation rather than a specialized skilled pursuit, as defined by Sutherland. Thus, the definition does not separate professional crime from occasional crime, amateur crime, and the like. However, the Commission points out that the original definition of professional crime is somewhat vague and almost inherently includes other categories of crime. The skills of professional criminals may vary from the superb skill of the big-time jewel thief to the semi-skill of the petty thief. Furthermore, it is impossible to distinguish between crimes as to professionality in official statistics. It is difficult in practice to distinguish a professional's work from that of an amateur. Also, the types of crime professionals are involved in vary from time to time (for instance, bank robbery is no longer a favored offense due to increasing risk). The Commission pointed out that the focus of the early theories of professional crime was upon certain *types of* professional *criminals,* rather than professional *crime per se* —and, in particular, on high-status, successful professional criminals. The Commission was aware, however, that it was indeed possible that its findings result from differences in definition and that traditional statements may hold in the case of the highly skilled, successful professional criminal.

These preliminary statements were necessary because the Commission's findings were by-and-large a reversal of traditional allegations about professional crime. The Commission-sponsored study found that professional criminals tended to be generalists (rather than specialists), to operate in a variety of loose associations with other professionals, and to exhibit no particular loyalty to their fellows. The typical professional is a small-time operator. His preoccupation is the "hustle," which means moving around the bars and being seen; it means asking "what's up." It means "connecting" in the morning with two others who have a burglary set up for the evening, calling a man you know to see if he wants to buy 10 stolen alpaca sweaters at $5 each, and scouting the streets for an easy victim. It means being versatile: passing checks, rolling a drunk, driving for a stickup, boosting a car, burglarizing a store. It is a planless kind of existence, but with a purpose—to make as much money as can be made each day, no holds barred.

Early studies by Sutherland and Maurer stressed that professional criminals enjoy a sense of identity and solidarity and work within a set of well-defined norms and codes of loyalty, helpfulness, and honesty in dealing with one another. The Commission-sponsored study however, found that only the more successful professionals could be so characterized. It found that the associations or gangs which run-of-the-mill professionals form to commit their crimes tend to be unstable, and that this instability results in part from the diversity of their activities. There is an absence of ethical codes. Few interviewed seemed to feel bound to any "no ratting" rule. Typically they appeared to take it for granted that others would do whatever necessary to protect themselves—to avoid imprisonment or reduce a sentence—and that they, therefore, should do likewise. Further, criminals expected to be cheated by their colleagues, or by most colleagues. Many of those interviewed reported having been cheated by fences and even by their partners in a particular venture. Victimization of one professional group by another is apparently also fairly common, limited only by fear of reprisal. One prominant example is the usurious interest rates paid by the professional criminal to the loan shark.

Social organization of professional crime   The findings of the President's Commission appear to have more empirical validity than those of the largely impressionistic studies that preceded it, and they seem to be more in accord with the larger theoretical framework developed earlier in this text. Compared to organized crime, professional crime may been seen as operating within a larger utilitarian organization of criminals and their victims. Professional criminals are calculatively involved in a very loose, anomic associational network and are motivated predominantly by remunerative rewards. By contrast, it will be shown that organized crime implies coercive threat of physical punishment and a generally alienative compliance of subordinates and the public-at-large who are involved in the organization of organized crime. Professional criminals tend to avoid violence at all costs, but violence is the typical means of gaining compliance by organized criminal groups. Generally the victims of professional criminals comply because of some remunerative incentive (in confidence operation, sale of stolen goods, and various kinds of fraud). Inevitably remuneration is the objective for the professional criminal, while the subordinate in organized crime may be merely avoiding punishment. Though professional criminals sometimes kill, it is almost always for money, and usually as a service to organized crime.

Thus, the distinction between organized crime and professional crime is not merely one of degree of skill, size, or organization, or of duration of the criminal task, as implied by traditional theories. Rather it is a basic one of organizational context and, once understanding this context, we can predict much about the two types of behavior. Professional crime seems to imply a utilitarian noninstitutional organizational framework, while organized crime, it will be shown, implies a dual utilitarian-coercive compliance structure.

ORGANIZED CRIME

While studies of professional crime are rather scant and the studies are inconsistent, organized crime has been studied extensively by criminologists and by government agencies. Thus, there are generally agreed characteristics of organized crime. These have been summarized by Clinard.

> The characteristic features of organized crime are these:
>
> 1. Hierarchy involving a system of specifically defined relationships with mutual obligations and privileges.
> 2. Not confined by political or geographic boundaries. Intracity or intercity; intra- or interstate.
> 3. Dependence upon
>   *a.* the use of force and violence to maintain internal discipline and restrain competition;
>   *b.* the securing and maintaining of permanent immunity from interference from law enforcement and other agencies of government.
> 4. Criminals operating for large financial gains and specializing in one or more combinations of enterprises which fall in the area of moral problems where public opinion is divided.
> 5. Striving for either monopolistic control or establishment of spheres of influence between or among different organizations.[14]

It can be seen from these characteristics that organized crime tends toward the oligarchic-coercive pattern described above. Clinard, in fact, has characterized organized crime by its *feudal structure,* with all-powerful "lords of the underworld" having the allegiance of several underloads who, in turn, have a variety of subordinate henchmen varying from lieutenants to what might be termed "serfs."[15] This feudal analogy supports the oligarchic-coercive characterization because one of the types listed under oligarchy is feudalism (Sjoberg) and because caste hierarchy is part of Etzioni's characterization of coercive organization. More recently, the President's Commission has pinpointed this structure to 24 exclusively Italian groups operating as criminal cartels in large cities across the nation. In individual cities, the local core group may be called the "outfit," the "syndicate," or the "mob." These 24 groups work with and control other racket groups, whose leaders are of various ethnic derivations. In addition, the thousands of employees who perform the street-level functions of organized crime's gambling, usury, and other illegal activities represent a cross-section of the

Nation's population groups.[16] Each of the 24 groups is known as a "family," with membership varying from as few as 20 men to as many as 700. The organization, as a whole (previously known as the Mafia) is known as La Cosa Nostra. Each family in the organization is headed by one man, the "boss," whose primary functions are maintaining order and maximizing profits. His authority in all matters relating to his family is absolute. Beneath each boss is an "underboss," the vice-president or deputy director of the family. He collects information for the boss; he relays messages to him and passes his instructions down to his own underlings. On the same level as the underboss, but operating in a staff capacity, is the *consigliere,* who is a counselor, or adviser. He gives advice to family members, including the boss and underboss, and thereby enjoys considerable influence and power. Below the level of the underboss are the *caporegime,* some of whom serve as buffers between the top members of the family and the lower-echelon personnel. To maintain their insulation from the police, the leaders of the hierarchy (particularly the boss) avoid direct communication with the workers. The caporegime fulfills the buffer capacity. Other caporegime serve as chiefs of operating units. The lowest-level "members" of a family are the *soldati,* the soldiers or "button" men who report to the caporegime. A soldier may operate a particular illicit enterprise—such as a loan-sharking operation, a dice game, a lottery, a bookmaking operation, a smuggling operation—or he may "own" the enterprise and pay a portion of its profit to the organization, in return for the right to operate. Beneath the soldiers in the hierarchy are large numbers of employees and commission agents who are not members of the family and are not necessarily of Italian descent. These are the people who do most of the actual work in the various enterprises. They have no buffers or other insulation from law enforcement. They take bets, drive trucks, answer telephones, sell narcotics, tend the stills, work in the legitimate businesses.

This oligarchic line organization is reflected in the typical mode of operations of organized crime. Especially important in this regard are the "enforcers," whose duty is to maintain organizational integrity by arranging for the maiming or killing of recalcitrant members. There is a rigid code of conduct requiring members not to interfere with the leader's interests and not to seek protection from the police. They should be "standup guys" who go to prison in order that the bosses may amass fortunes. The code gives the leaders exploitative authoritarian power over everyone in the organization. Loyalty, honor, respect, absolute obedience— these are inculcated in family members through ritualistic initiation and customs within the organization, through material rewards, and through violence. Though the underlings are forbidden to "inform" to the outside world, the family boss learns of deviance within the organization through an elaborate system of internal informants.

Thus, as in coercive formal organizations, the basic sanction is threat of punishment and the orientation of subordinates is alienative, fearful, and in Merton's terms, ritualistic. However, organized crime does not rely exclusively upon coercive sanction. Probably the major reason for joining an organized criminal syndicate would be the promise of material reward. For relatives of high-ranking Italians, normative rewards may also come into play. The best characterization, however, is probably dual coercive–utilitarian compliance. Members are motivated by fear of punishment and desire for material reward. The coercive, "feudal" nature of organized crime probably accounts for its stability and resistance to law enforcement (see Sjoberg's discussion of the stability of feudalism in Chapter 2). Certainly professional criminals are easier to apprehend and convict than top-ranking organized criminals.

VICE AND RELATED DEVIANCY

The approach taken in this text is that most forms of crime are organized and that social organizational structure has an important bearing on the nature of criminal activity. This approach differs somewhat from that used in current crime and deviancy texts, in that it is closer to a pure sociological approach. Current crime and deviancy texts tend to call upon a variety of casual factors—physiological, psychological, ecological, and the like—to explain crime. Many of these texts are not really sociological at all, but potpourri eclectic. This may be stated as a general criticism of crime and deviancy studies in sociology. There is a sparcity of group-structural studies to draw upon. However, aside from studies of organized and professional crime, there are a few studies of vice and related deviancy which bring to bear structural factors. These include studies of homosexuals, prostitutes, inebriates, and narcotics users. The greatest amount of group structure research has been done with respect to juvenile delinquency. These studies will be covered in a later section of this chapter. The foregoing discussion of vice and related deviancy, however, will round out the adult crime picture, including most forms of group-based adult crime. Unorganized forms of crime will be discussed briefly in the next chapter.

Our approach so far has been to view deviant behavior as a role played within particular organization settings. White-collar crime, for example, is a product of participation in utilitarian settings—that is, businesses and industries—because these settings are especially conducive to anomie in Merton's sense of the terms, elevation of success-goals to the exclusion of legitimate means. Participation in organized and professional criminal groups has somewhat the same effect, in that there is a primary commitment to remunerative goals and secondary or tertiary commitment to normative or symbolic goals. The term vice generally refers to a degrading or debasing habit that enslaves the individual, causing harm to himself but only incidentally to others. Generally where there is vice, there is *negotiated exchange*. Bredemeier and Toby have noted that this principle, the idea that the individual is expected to secure what he needs and wants from others by contracting a mutually advantageous arrangement,[17] is at once one of the governing principles of American society and a motivating factor behind vice and other criminal behavior.

Money is very much involved in most vice activity, and thus most of such relationships can be characterized as utilitarian compliance structures. Violence is involved only when one of the parties to the relationship attempts to deviate from the utilitarian model. A prostitute will attempt to roll her customer only if he fails to provide the remuneration promised. Similarly, a "punk" will assault a "queer" only if the queer fails to provide compensation. Violence will break out in a barroom only if there is an extreme violation of barroom norms. The drug addict will result to violent means of obtaining "bread" only if nonviolent means fail.

One limitation of our group-structure analysis, it may be said, is that it fails to account for the individual's motivation to join such groups or for the creation of such groups. This topic will be discussed later. But briefly, we can trace such groups and their participants to the structure of larger society. Organized crime is made possible largely because of a widespread tolerance of and interest in what organized crime offers, mainly gambling, narcotics, and vice. More specifically, the services of prostitutes and homosexuals may be employed by those most involved in legitimate utilitarian structures as an extension of the principle of negotiated exchange. Other group structures may be havens for those who fail to or lack a the desire to gain access to legitimate utilitarian institutional settings—such as dope rings and skid row alcohol groups. For the present, it may be fruitful to discuss the four vice areas upon which group-structure research has been done: homosexuals, prostitutes, inebriates, and narcotics users.

Homosexuals   Possibly because it is a sensitive area in which to do research, very little work has been done on homosexuality. Limiting the topic to the social organization of homosexuals, the field is even more limited. Probably the best study of the homosexual community was done in Canada.[18] Another study was done as part of a larger study of boys in Nashville, Tennessee.[19] Our analysis will draw extensively from these two sources as they serve as good illustrations of utilitarian-anomic organization of the homosexual community, showing such processes as conflict, rivalry, and negotiated exchange within the community.

The homosexual is broadly defined, a person who has had sexual relations with his own sex. This definition is in fact extremely broad, as it includes as much as 37 per cent of the total male population, according to the Kinsey report. There are, of course, various types and degrees of homosexuality. For some there may have been the only one homosexual encounter, while for others homosexuality is the exclusive means of sexual gratification. Kinsey estimated that 4 per cent of adult males are exclusively homosexual throughout their adult lives. There are various types of homosexuals as suggested by such terms as "butches," "queens," and "punks," which homosexuals use. The core of homosexual society consists of the overt homosexuals who are relatively unsecretive in their activities and inclinations. They are not concerned about the danger of being exposed. These homosexuals, easily recognizable by outsiders, congregate in public places: certain bars, restaurants, and the like. More numerous, however, are the covert or secretive homosexuals. While overt homosexuals retreat from the demands of society and renounce societal goals, covert homosexuals hesitate to risk exposure by being seen in the company of known homosexuals.

An interesting sidelight has to do with occupational affiliations of homosexuals. Overt homosexuals generally are from utilitarian occupations, business, industry, or service occupations; covert homosexuals may be drawn from professions as well as utilitarian occupations. One might hypothesize that the more normatively based professions do not tolerate homosexuality, as it does not comply with their moral orientation of compliance, and contrariwise that utilitarian occupations are more congruent with deviant sex adaptation, in that the individual's private life is irrelevant to the exchange functions he performs. As homosexuals ascend the status ladder in business, however, it becomes more and more necessary to conceal their homosexual activity. Etzioni, it may be remembered, finds managerial positions more normative in compliance than lower-level posts.

Because overt homosexuals are excluded from the professions and from top-level business positions, there develops a built-in conflict within the homosexual community. The covert homosexual, who is generally better educated and of higher occupational status, looks down on the other, and is sometimes hostile toward him because of the possibility of public exposure which the overt homosexual threatens.

Homosexuals generally develop cliques of the same status levels within which sex relations do not take place, perhaps because of norms something like the incest norms found in larger society. These cliques are generally more solidary than the sexual associations outside, but even within the clique there is evidence of hostility and sexual rivalry based upon the narration of exploits. The formation of these cliques, however, lays the foundation of the anomic-utilitarian relations that develop within the homosexual community at large. First, this means that covert homosexuals must seek out strangers for sexual gratification, and generally these may be overt homosexuals because they are easier to locate. This precipitates conflict based upon covert-overt homosexual class differences. Another source of sexual gratification, however, may be the adolescent male hustler who demands money in exchange for sex relations. The adult male client pays a delinquent boy prostitute a sum of money in order to be allowed to act as a fellator. The adolescent hustler does not consider himself a homosexual and maintains his belief by strict compliance with certain norms. The relationship must be strictly as a way of making money, never for sexual gratification. The sexual transaction must be limited to mouth-genital fellation, and no other sex acts are tolerated. It is an affectively neutral relationship. Violence is not used except in cases where the homosexual does not conform to the norms.

In sum, the homosexual group structure displays all of the markings of an anomic–utilitarian compliance relationship. Homosexual relations are generally impersonal, pervaded with conflict and rivalry, and often mercenary. That these factors are correlated with homosexuality is more than coincidental. In terms of our framework, these organizational features help to provide an opportunity for homosexual experience and to maintain homosexual patterns of behavior—that is, to "create" homosexuality. The clique patterns of homosexuals indicate that normative compliance is largely incompatible with homosexual sexual behavior and it is necessary to separate the two.

Prostitution   A hasty examination of prostitution would lead one to conclude (1) that prostitution is traced largely to early childhood experiences involving either parental rejection or divorce (or both), (2) that the prostitute, while maintaining an affectively neutral attitude toward customers, is immersed in a subculture of rather close affiliations with fellow workers, including other prostitutes and procurers, and (3) that the prostitute follows a fairly orderly "career" in deviance.

While family background may be important as a predisposing factor in prostitution, it does not explain prostitution. Nevertheless, this has been the prevailing explanation of prostitution:

> Twentieth-century theorizing concerning this occupational group has employed, almost exclusively, a Freudian psychiatric model. The prostitute has thus been variously described as masochistic, of infantile mentality, unable to form mature interpersonal relationships, regressed, emotionally dangerous to males and as normal as the average woman.[20]

These psychological causes may be important but are not sufficient causes of the continued pursuit of prostitution. There are, no doubt, countless individuals who have such motivation who never become prostitutes, perhaps because of moral training or because the opportunity never presents itself, or because of mere pragmatic fear of consequences—psychological, biological, and social. There must be some initial contact with the idea of prostitution and some degree of socialization to the techniques of prostitution in order for one to become involved in systematic prostitution behavior. These initial contacts may be termed precipitating factors. In addition, we should not ignore pattern maintaining factors, those that keep the person involved in prostitution on a semi-permanent basis. Our thesis will be that maintenance factors are found in the group structure(s) surrounding prostitute activity.

What is the nature of this group structure? A common view is that the prostitute is enclosed in a subcultural web or relatively intimate and binding relations with her co-workers. This view holds that the prostitute learns a fairly tight code which defines customers as "squares" to be exploited and which defines colleagues as honest and helpful. It holds, further, that prostitution is therapeutic and helpful and should not be stigmatized, thus protecting the prostitute's self-image against reproach and stigma. This theoretical code increases in-group solidarity and makes it possible to exploit the customer-outsider.[21] Studies, however, indicate that no such normative loyalty exists among prostitutes and their colleagues. On the contrary, their attitudes toward each other are quite similar to their attitudes toward customers. No doubt prostitutes generally exhibit a calculative, exploitative attitude toward their clients, in part based upon their family background experience but also based upon advice of other prostitutes and the teaching of experience in which the girl may have been exploited without compensation. Thus, the prostitute will demand money, often in advance of the sex act, and exact payment using violence with the help of a pimp. Prostitutes may develop the cynical attitude that man is corrupt, an attitude which is confirmed when the married man betrays his wife or when the moralist betrays his publically stated values. An unnecessary interaction with a customer is frowned upon, and the prostitutes are encouraged not to experience sexual orgasm with their clients. That is, the relation must be affectively neutral.

There is considerable evidence, however, that the prostitute "code of ethics" is not applicable in practice. Prostitutes are not always hostile and manipulative toward their clients. More interesting, however, there appears to be little loyalty between prostitutes and their relations with one another are perhaps as calculative and manipulating as relations with their "tricks" or "johns." Bryan found that when prostitutes were asked to rate the people with whom they came in contact, they rate themselves significantly more worthwhile than colleagues. Interestingly, the prostitute did not rate men-in-general, women-in-general, or "johns" on a lower level than herself. Only call girls were rated as being significantly less worthwhile than the self.[22] In the same study, respondents interviewed frequently mentioned that they had been robbed, conned, or otherwise exploited by their call-girl friends. Furthermore, they indicated that their relationships with other call girls were marked by interpersonal conflict, disloyalties, and mutual exploitation.

Even more in contrast with the normative conception of the prostitute subculture is the career involvement of the prostitute. One is tempted to draw an analogy between becoming a prostitute and pursuing any other professional career. The prostitute is inducted into prostitution by a girlfriend who is a prostitute or by a boyfriend who is a pimp. She then may receive several months of intensive training by the pimp or by a prostitute girl trainer. She then develops client contacts, which she maintains after her training. According to this normative conception, the prostitute becomes increasingly committed to the prostitute code and loyal to the pimp and other prostitutes. The pimp is usually her common-law husband or lover.

This normative career image has been questioned on several grounds. First, prostitutes generally come from family backgrounds in which there was intensive conflict between parents. The girl will subsequently develop no real sexual identification and will be unfamiliar with her proper role in the heterosexual relationship:

> In all of their interpersonal relations the girls shifted constantly between an obvious, surface type of ingratiating behavior and a deeply hostile, aggressive behavior. With their lovers they attempted to ingratiate themselves by giving them large portions of their income. At the same time, they frequently acted in an aggressive, hostile manner, calling them pimps and trying to degrade them in other ways.[23]

It has been pointed out above that her relations with other prostitutes is characterized by rivalry and conflict; thus, other prostitutes provide no stable basis for contact. Another objection to the career idea is that prostitution is generally a short career. Physical attraction is a prime consideration in continuance and youth tends to be at a premium. Thus, most prostitutes are under 29 years of age and the modal age falls between 21 and 25.[24]

The fact that call girls may serve an apprenticeship under another call girl or a pimp seems to contradict the idea of rivalry, as this would seem to imply cooperative behavior and the sharing of information and of clients. No doubt, in some cases a genuine friendship may develop between trainer and trainee. However, self-interest cannot be dismissed as a basis of the relationship. The female trainer, who generally has more customers than she can handle by herself, actually profits economically from the relationship. She receives forty to fifty per cent of the total price agreed upon in the contract negotiated by the trainer and the customer. In addition to the profit of fee-splitting, the call-girl trainer is able to maintain a business relationship with her customer when she herself is not available or desirous of serving the customer. Also, the financial gains may be much greater for the trainer, because she may employ several girls at once.

Another non-career aspect of the prostitute is her career mobility. The status of the prostitute is generally determined by her class background before entering prostitution, the class status of her patrons, her age, and her general attractiveness. Two of these factors, age and attractiveness, are affected by length of career. The highest status category is the call girl, often drawn from middle- or upper-class backgrounds, the lowest is the brothel prostitute, and in between is the lone solicitor or street-walker. The call girl caters to upper- or middle-class men, the brothel prostitute to lower-class men, while the street walker may draw a variety of clientele. With increasing age and decline in physical attractiveness, even the call girl may decline in status to the lowest brothel prostitute. This is especially likely if she becomes a drug user or addict. Thus, downward mobility is almost inevitable for the prostitute. This may be one reason for the high rate of suicide and suicide attempts among prostitutes.[25]

In sum, the prostitute is enmeshed not in a normative subculture but in a rather anomic and utilitarian network of relations, not only with her customers but also with her co-workers. The primary sanction is renumerative and the typical orientation is calculative. Based on her family background, the prostitute has a rather calculative "affectively neutral" attitude toward people in general. However, this is not alone the cause of her prostitution. Upon entrance to prostitution, she is exploited by her female trainer or her pimp. She is exploited by her customers. Even other prostitutes will con her or steal from her. Thus she develops a normless, calculative attitude which helps to sustain her involvement in prostitution. It is no coincidence that the secondary occupations of prostitutes almost invariably are in utilitarian organizational settings. Lemert found the most typical occupation of prostitutes is waitress, with domestic service second, followed by maid and factory worker, these comprising 50 per cent of his sample of 1,825 females arrested for prostitution in Los Angeles in 1948. The remaining were miscellaneous occupations, mainly utilitarian, housewife, and unemployed.[26] As in the case of homosexuality, it is possible that these occupations have a greater tolerance for prostitution, but in addition, it seems likely that these occupations provide an atmosphere which is comparatively favorable to prostitution, based upon the calculative orientation of subordinate actors.

Inebriety   Drinking behavior illustrates group processes similar to others discussed above, although to some extent there are unique group processes involved in drinking behavior. Uniqueness of group structure in the case of any given form of deviancy should not be overemphasized, however, because there is much overlap in group activity. Prostitutes, for example, may become involved in excessive drinking, in drug abuse, and even in homosexual behavior. Drinking behavior seems to be linked with many forms of deviancy. The President's Crime Commission found that professional criminals spend much of their time hustling in bars and trying to determine where the action is. Prostitutes and homosexuals also congregate in bars, meeting acquaintances and making contacts. Taverns are a common meeting ground for the criminal. It should prove interesting to note the features of the group setting of drinking, because it may throw light on the origin of other forms of deviancy.

Drinking groups and drinking settings may be characterized by their anonymity, superficiality of social relations, and impersonality. Participants may falsify their identity or play imaginary roles. They generally think of each other in terms of stereotypes rather than in terms of "total personality." There is extreme tolerance of difference and deviancy as compared with conventional settings, and whatever sanctions are used are "restitutive sanctions."

Very often, there is a kind of "false personalization"[27] — that is, a pretending to act friendly to people who are strangers, combined with negotiated exchange, where very often it is friendliness itself that is exchanged for money (as in the case of the B-girl). All of these features point to a kind of *gesellschaft* organization, what we have referred to as anomic-utilitarian organization. These features are illustrated by two recent studies of drinking groups, one of tavern drinking groups[28] and the other of street drinking groups, specifically "winos."[29] While done on two different types of drinking groups, these studies portray the drinking groups similarly. Both studies were done by participant observation. Cavan's study of tavern behavior was carried on from the Spring of 1962 through the early part of 1965 in approximately one hundred bars in San Francisco. Rooney's study of "winos" was based on the experiences of living in Skid Row for one to two weeks at a time in Stockton, Sacramento, and Fresno, California. Both studies provide rich illustrations of the above characteristics of drinking behavior.

There is evidence of structured situations of drinking. Drinking is not merely the isolated behavior of a wino who gets a bottle and drinks it himself, nor are participants in a tavern isolated from each other. Rooney found that Skid Row drinkers manifest consistent efforts to structure situations so as to involve interpersonal contact and some degree of emotional reinforcement. Cavan found that public drinking places are "open regions" where those who are present, acquainted or not, have the right to engage others in conversational interaction and the duty to reciprocate overtures of sociability. In fact, she found that in a bar a person had to make a concerted effort to avoid interaction. He had to sit in a particular posture, minimizing the amount of physical space he takes up at the bar. He must sit "with his forearms either resting on the edge of the bar, or flat on the bar before him, his upper torso hunched slightly forward over the bar, with all of his drinking accoutrements contained within the area before him. The area delimited by the inner sides of his arms defines his visual focus as well."[30]

Although this description of drinking settings conveys the impression that they would be the ideal place for a person who desires intimate social contact, this is not the case. Barroom contacts may be very short-lived. The tentative and superficial character of bar conversation is reinforced by the expectation that the meeting will be circumscribed in time and space. Moreover, there is a kind of enforced anonymity. Participants are not obliged to recognize one another and typically refrain from showing any recognition in future encounters. Winos, similarly, form "bottle groups," groups that share the same bottle after contributing to its purchase, with relative strangers, and that these groups disband as soon as the bottle is finished and their participants may never see each other again. Though the group drinking experience is the only situation in which a Skid Row wino receives personal recognition and affectional response, these groups do not develop strong feelings of group solidarity for two reasons: The boundaries of the cliques are seldom defined, and almost any individual can join; also, the focus is an instrumental goal—the alcohol—rather than an expressive goal, such as getting to know each other personally.

In both drinking settings, participants may take advantage of the fact that there is no way of proving or disproving their claims to former identity. Skid Row winos exchange ego-boasting rationalizations, retell past experiences, offer boastful stories of their accomplishments, and reaffirm their status as "good men." Patrons in taverns sever themselves from their biographies in a number of ways. They seldom mention their surname, their line of work, or their political or ideological beliefs. They may also exercise the liberty to prefabricate an entire life for themselves with little likelihood that it will be later exposed, as they will rarely if ever encounter other patrons outside the bar (and if so, recollection of acquaintance will be suppressed or denied). Whatever knowledge is gained of patrons is generally of a stereotypical kind. "Patrons may come to be labeled 'the guy who always makes out with the chicks,' 'the big spender,' 'Arnie, who always has a bag of jokes,' and the like."[31]

We might speculate that in the most extremely anomic settings, in Durkheim's sense, actors utilize restitutive sanctions and minimize repressive sanction. This appears to be the case in drinking groups where there is extreme tolerance of differences and deviancy, and whatever sanctions occur are generally intended to restore equilibrium of social interaction. Cavan finds that barroom settings are conducive to a latitude of behavior greater than that permitted in many other public settings. A variety of self-indulgent and otherwise improper acts can be engaged in. These include acts of violence, if short and quickly over, which may be ignored once they have happened. Heterosexual petting and necking may occur unnoticed, though in full view of others present. The exception is homosexual bars, where legal restrictions are greater. *Faux-pas* may be committed with equanimity and loss of motor control may carry little disapprobation. Rooney notes the extreme openness of bottle groups to membership, indicating a certain amount of tolerance. Though blacks are often excluded from Skid Row "flop-houses" with the approval of white residents of the area, blacks are unequivocally admitted to membership in bottle groups. No willing black is refused membership in a bottle group if he has the cash, and he appears to be accorded the same degree of accept-ance as the white members.

Probably the most striking feature of drinking relations is the prevalence of negotiated exchange and false personalization. The overriding consideration in wino groups is the individual pursuit of alcohol as a goal. The primary purpose of grouping is not friend-ship but, in a very material sense, economic gain. Poverty-stricken winos are faced with an economic dilemma, for they can purchase little wine with the small sums they beg or earn by odd jobs. The "bottle gang" is a corporate answer to this dilemma. A number of individuals pool their capital for a common goal. Each member is a stockholder and the leader is in a sense chairman of the board. The corporation is dissolved when the bottle is emptied. Each man is allowed two gulps from the bottle, and one of the members is certain to protest and to grab the bottle if one member defaults. Although each man contributes differently and receives the same amount, a man is expected to reciprocate in the long run. Thus, relations are only in a very marginal sense communal.

Of course, bars are, as discussed above, the traditional mar-ket places for services and commodities of various kinds:

> Other than liquor, perhaps the commodity most frequently han-dled in the public drinking place is sex, on either a commercial or noncommercial basis. But there are also bars that deal in narcotics, stimulant drugs, gambling, stolen merchandise, and a variety of other illicit goods.[32]

B-girls, prostitutes, and male hustlers may utilize the facilities of a public drinking place as a work setting. On the other hand, bars may be often used as the location for a "pickup" which itself may have no obvious financial basis, but which may involve un-anticipated expense. Unlike the pickup, the B-girl may engage in flirtatious sociability, but only in exchange for a form of financial remuneration. The patron purchases a drink for the B-girl. The drink usually will cost him at least twice its price at the bar. The bartender makes note of the purchase and later compensates the B-girl. Prostitutes are, of course, available for sexual purposes at many bars, and generally the services of a prostitute may be obtained much more quickly and in a more business-like manner than may the attention of a pickup.

Drinking settings are the focal point for many forms of deviancy. It may be that the lowering of inhibitions that results from the sheer physical effect of the alcohol may be a contributory factor in the causation of various forms of deviancy. It may also be said that the calculative orientations of the various deviants who populate the tavern or other drinking groups account for the fairly anomic nature of this group setting.

Drug abuse   One of the most potent criticisms of Merton's anomie theory has been issued by Lindesmith and Gagnon.[33] They attack Merton's concept of retreatism in reference to the problem of drug addiction. Retreatism is a solution to the conflict problems of anomie which involves abandonment of both the success goal and legitimate means to its pursuit. Ultimately this results in continuous attempts at escape. Merton claimed this adaptation would refer to "some of the adaptive activities of psychotics, autists, pariahs, outcasts, vagrants, vagabonds, tramps, chronic drunkards, and drug addicts."[34]

Lindesmith and Gagnon's critique is important because, as can be seen in the above quote, retreatism includes many of the problems discussed above. Certainly inebriety is included, and perhaps prostitution and homosexuality may imply a kind of withdrawal from the endless struggle for success.

Briefly, their argument is that retreatism is not the appropriate description of drug addiction, as the drug addict inevitably becomes actively involved in the pursuit of money to support his habit and thus is involved in criminal or innovative behavior, rather than retreatism. They further suggest that drug addicts actively pursue the goal of pecuniary success because such success would insure a constant support for their drug habit:

> If it is conservatively estimated that there are 5,000 addicts at large on the streets of Chicago each day, and that each of them steals only $25 worth of goods per day, this would mean that addicts would

in one year steal goods to the value of $45 million. From this one might reasonably argue that addicts are quite successful criminals. . . . In the context of American control policies, the use of drugs, and especially the use of opiates, does not provide an escape from the requirements of society, but instead plunges the newly recruited addict into an abrasive contact with the world, which he could not have anticipated. Ordinarily his first and greatest problem is his pressing need for money. If one asks him about his aspirations, he is likely to place more rather than less emphasis upon the success goal, for, if he could attain it, he would enjoy it doubly. . . . By the same token, the addict does not renounce the means, legitimate or illegitimate, of making money. . . . The paradox anomie theory faces is that while opiates can be used for retreatist motives, they are used in this way primarily by those who are not addicted to them. . . . It would appear that marihuana would be a more potent retreatist and addicting drug than opiates, because its euphoric effects persist and are not counteracted by withdrawal distress and the host of evil consequences that ordinarily beset the opiate addict.[35]

The focus in this quote is upon the activist orientation of the drug addict. The drug addict seeks money in order to sustain his habit, and is likely to use criminal means because legitimate means are closed to him. This is particularly so after he has become fully addicted to a drug. In the larger sense of the term, however, this activism is not incompatible with "retreatism." In fact, one of the criticisms directed to Merton's SS and A paradigm is that it contains no reference to "activity versus passivity" as a variable.[36] That is to say, the category "retreatism" is neutral with regard to activism or passivity. As Lindesmith and Gagnon define retreatism, it refers to complete withdrawal from all competitive and market relations. But this is not Merton's meaning. Merton merely holds to a repudiation of cultural success goals and institutional means.

The problem is largely one of definition and system referent. For Merton, the actor is operating within larger society, while for Lindesmith and Gagnon, he is working within a smaller system of relations. That is, it is possible that both Merton's analysis and Lindesmith and Gagnon's characterization may be true: the drug addict may be retreatist *vis-à-vis* the goals of larger society, but innovative with respect to a smaller social system; he may steal, but only to obtain money for drugs, not to obtain "success" and its prerequisites. In fact, drug addicts explicitly reject success as a goal, and this rejection is part of their larger repudiation of the major values of society. It is evident that drug addicts are not frugal but rather that they are hedonistic. They are innovative only in that they are calculatively involved in a subsystem whose common goal orientation refers to drugs. Thus, in the larger sense, in Merton's sense, drug addicts are retreatist, rejective of both societal goals and institutional means. But in the subsystem sense, they are innovative in their selection of illegitimate means to obtain a shared goal. In the next few pages we shall attempt to corroborate this view, drawing from empirical studies on the topic of drug use. This discussion will include not just addiction, but also the larger topic of drug abuse, which includes marihuana.

Drug Abuse as Retreatism. Even Lindesmith and Gagnon acknowledge the fact that drugs may be initially taken for retreatist purposes. Contrary to Lindesmith and Gagnon's argument, it appears that the use of marihuana may be ritualistic while heroin is retreatist. Winick finds that marihuana use was common among jazz musicians that that their reasons for smoking marihuana were generally recreation, relaxation, and tension release, offsetting the stress and tension of constant mobility and "one-nighter" dance or night club dates.[37] Winick suggests that marihuana may be helpful in adapting to periodic unemployment, thus implying that it may be reflective of the "underprivileged" portion of the jazz musician in our society. This "adaptation" would seem to imply ritualism, in Merton's sense of scaling down lofty aspirations while conforming to legitimate means of success. (Winick also found that jazz musicians seldom engaged in any other form of deviancy than marihuana use.)

On the other hand, the heroin user appears to have a clear-cut rejective orientation toward American values, particularly "success," as it is usually defined (acquisition of wealth, high social position, conspicuous possessions). This rejective orientation is tied with a rejection of legitimate means, and both are indicated by the addict's alienative jargon and value system. Finestone has described this system of jargon and values based on a study of 50 black male users of heroin in Chicago.[38] The drug addict is never content with the conventional word for even the most commonplace objects. He uses "pad" for house, "pecks" for food, "flicks" for movies, and the like. The word he uses is more concrete or earthier than the conventional word such as to reveal an attitude of subtle ridicule toward common usage. Finestone notes that two themes are central, those

of the "hustle" and the "kick,"[39] and that these are in direct antithesis to two of the central values of the dominant culture, the paramount important of the occupation for the male in our society, and
the importance of regulating conduct in terms of its future consequences. Certainly, adherence to both of these conventional
values—work and future orientation—is necessary to success in the
general sense of the term. Finestone goes even so far as to suggest
that the black drug addict, through his jargon and values, is unconsciously adhering to the earlier "Uncle Tom" patterns of accommodation to dominant white society.

Drug Abuse as Innovative. With regard to the smaller social
system immediately surrounding the drug user, it appears that
innovation is an appropriate description of behavior. Once again,
in Etzioni's terms, the drug-user is calculatively involved with
his fellows, often exploiting them or others in his immediate environment in order to obtain a consensually recognized goal, drugs.
That is, the drug addict social system may be described as "utilitarian." The young drug-user identifies with an elite group, the
society of "cats." He eschews the use of force and violence as a technique for achieving his ends or for settling problematic situations.
He achieves his goals through manipulative techniques, his wits,
and his conversational ability. He gets what he wants through persuasion and ingratiation and uses the other fellow by deliberately
outwitting him. The drug addict is thus calculatively involved in
his relations. The ideal role is that of pimp, to be supported by
exploitation and manipulation of a woman.

The link between marihuana and jazz music is interesting in
this context, because the structure of both the jazz group and jazz
itself is very loose.

> Improvisation is a central element in jazz and it is possible that
> there are certain personality characteristics which attract the jazz
> musician to a field in which it is not necessary to follow a score literally,
> but in which hovering around the reality of the beat of the music is a
> desirable quality.[40]

It is also interesting to note that the major setting for jazz music
is the tavern, night club, or barroom, which we have previously
described as utilitarian in organization.

In describing other forms of deviancy above, it was noted that
the utilitarian organization of deviant groups helps to maintain

the pattern of deviancy. The deviancy is itself a response to group structure. Homosexuality and prostitution generally entail an exploitative impersonal and remunerative relationship between persons. By virtue of their involvement in Skid Row groups and tavern behavior, "winos" and other inebriates obtain goals not directly available elsewhere. The study of drug addiction indicates that group structure may also be conducive to relapse and recidivism. Because group structure is more loose in the drug group than in conventional groups, the drug group may be attractive to the individual who is unable to adjust to the demands placed upon him by conventional groups.

Group settings of juvenile delinquency

From the earliest systematic study of juvenile gangs to the present there has been a change in the face of gang theory. The most prominent juvenile gang theories were developed on the basis of field studies done principally in Chicago and other Eastern big cities. These theories, we shall see, viewed gangs as relatively integrated groups arising primarily in lower-class neighborhoods. Because these theories were based upon findings drawn on older established cities and/or based on studies done some time ago, we shall call these "traditional gang theories." A large group of new theories of the adolescent group has since developed, largely on the basis of studies done in the less established Western cities. Based upon the new findings and theories, older theories have been called into question. It will be interesting to note that as in the study of professional crime, the shift in emphasis has been away from the "normative image" of adolescent gangs toward the "utilitarian image" of adolescent groups, from an image of gangs as well-integrated to an image of gangs as highly unstable groups.

TRADITIONAL THEORIES OF JUVENILE DELINQUENT GANG ORGANIZATION

The theme of the integrated nature of gang organization was set some forty years ago by Thrasher,[41] although the major works on types of gang organization were done recently.

Thrasher studied over one thousand juvenile gangs largely consisting of youths of foreign-born parentage in Chicago. Though Thrasher stressed that gang structure varied widely, there were certain common features in all gangs. He argued that we may view the gang as a primary group exhibiting such primary group features as cooperative behavior—harmony and mutual aid; *esprit de corps*—subordination of the individual to group control and consensus; solidarity based on consensus within a group; and the development of a "gang code" reflecting in part certain human virtues taught by association with fellow members. The reason that gang membership was conducive to gang delinquency was because the tight integration into the youthful gang brought with it an alienation from foreign-born parents and from other adolescent gangs, an alienation which often resulted in conflict. Because of Thrasher's work gangs came to be viewed as well integrated groups.

This integrated gang structure is paramount in Cohen's work. In *Delinquent Boys,*[42] Cohen viewed the gang as a kind of closed system or "subculture" which provides a well-integrated set of values to which a lower-class youngster can become committed (and act in terms of) and thus resolve his status problems. Cohen proposed that lower-class youngsters are often ambivalent because they are exposed to middle-class success values, primarily in school, but lack the means of obtaining them. They resolve this ambivalence by entering the delinquent subculture, which is a repudiation of middle-class standards. Thus, gang behavior, is nonutilitarian, malicious, and negativistic in reaction to middle-class values, and hedonistic and autonomous in resistance to authority. Although Cohen did not delineate which lower-class boys would select the delinquent pattern rather than the "college boy" or "stable corner boy responses" (both non-delinquent), we may infer that it is the most status deprived and/or most exposed to middle-class values who adopt the gang delinquent pattern.

Cohen's theory underwent extensive criticism, in part because it was recognized that other forms of delinquent gangs existed[43] and in part because the idea that gang delinquency was exclusive to lower-class neighborhoods was challenged.[44] Probably as a result of this criticism, Cohen revised his view of gang delinquency to include not one but five types of gang subcultures.[45] These included (1) the *parent-male subculture,* (2) the *conflict-oriented gang,* (3) the *drug-addict subculture,* (4) the *semi-professional theft subculture,* and (5) the *middle-class delinquent gang.*

All five of these gangs or subcultures are conceived of as well-integrated gang structures, with a value system that members were obliged to accept. The *parent-male subculture,* called "parent" because it was the basic core model as discussed in *Delinquent Boys,* referred to the small, lower-class gang of status-deprived boys who respond to middle-class values in a kind of reaction formation asserting values opposite of middle-class values—nonutilitarian, negativistic, malicious, and the like. The *conflict-oriented* gang was seen as a highly organized group which attacked not the middle-class but other gangs, defending its "rep" and "turf" in gang "rumbles." The *drug-addict subculture* consisted of still another possible group formation, composed of "cats" characterized by a particular value system, jargon, dress, and use of drugs as a means of escape. Interestingly, although Cohen and Short posited the drug-addict subculture as a highly integrated group, in his later research Short could find little or no evidence of the existence of such groups.[46] The *semi-professional theft subculture* differed from the above in that it was utilitarian, systematic, and pecuniary, using strong-arm methods to obtain its means and selling rather than destroying stolen merchandise. This category seemed to be a concession that such a thing as "innovation" in Merton's sense of the term existed in the lower class. The last category, the *middle-class delinquent gang,* allowed for the possibility of middle-class delinquency, although clearly the majority of gang delinquency and delinquent types was still decidedly lower-class. The middle-class delinquent gang expressed such emphases as deliberate courting of danger, and playboy attitudes toward liquor, sex, and automobiles.

Subsequent to Cohen's formulation of gang types, Cloward and Ohlin developed a typology of gang behavior differing with Cohen and Short's typology in incorporating differentials in neighborhood organization. Cloward and Ohlin,[47] call to attention the possibility of differentials in neighborhood organization. Although they suggested fewer types, Cloward and Ohlin's typology was quite similar to Cohen and Short's. There were three basic types: (1) *criminal gangs,* (2) *conflict gangs,* and (3) *retreatist gangs. Criminal gangs* are oriented toward illegal income and status appropriation and develop in areas integrated around adult criminal patterns. Major forms of delinquency included theft, extortion, and related instrumental acts. *Conflict gangs* are oriented toward acquisition of status by illegitimate means and arise in disorganized neighborhoods, those in which criminal models are unavailable due to a conflict between the adult conventional and criminal sectors. Major forms of delinquency were violence and vandalism. *Retreatist gangs,* those involved in illicit drug and sensual experience, arise in neighborhoods in which neither legitimate nor illegitimate opportunities are available. It should be noted that all of Cloward and Ohlin's gang types were lower-class types and there was no statement about differences in gang organization according to type in Cloward and Ohlin's analysis.

REFOCUSING GANG THEORY

This "subcultural" view of delinquent groups found in Cohen and Short's as well as Cloward and Ohlin's gang typologies has been called into question on several counts. Yablonsky argues that delinquent gangs are not well-integrated groups as the term "gang" implies, but rather they are comparatively disorganized "near-groups" whose major characteristics are diffuse role-definitions, limited cohesion, impermanence, minimum consensus on norms, shifting memberships, disturbed leadership, and limited definition of membership expectations.[48] Likewise, Matza has attacked the notion of subculture as implying a "hard deterministic" concept of the delinquent as perfectly constrained by an ethical code which makes his misdeeds mandatory. Matza views the norms of the delinquent group not as inescapably binding upon the individual delinquent, but rather as based upon shared misunderstandings within the delinquent group and the individual status anxiety of the member who does not want to reveal his ambivalence with regard to conventional beliefs *versus* delinquent beliefs. Thus the delinquent *drifts* between conforming and delinquent behavior based upon a situation of *anomie* or conflict of values in his social field.[49]

Based on these objections to traditional gang theory as well as the objections to the lower-class slant of traditional typologies, a number of new theories and typologies of the delinquent group have developed. These typologies shift the emphasis away from the "normative" conception of the gang to one approximating the "utilitarian" model of social organization.

One theory emerging is what might be called "youth culture theory." This theory states that juvenile delinquency results not so much from participation in a given subculture or gang as it does from involvement in a rather loosely defined subculture of youth, the "youth culture," organized only in the sense of opposition to adult values and in expressively alienated youth roles such as "hood," "beat," "bohemian," and "Joe College."[50] This theory holds that delinquency does not arise from a response to frustration but rather it arises from the absence of meaningful goals to strive for. Delinquents are alienated in the sense of lacking group goals, thus, implying loose cohesion of the delinquent group (as group goals are generally thought of as requisite to group cohesion).

Another new approach arising from the controversy may be termed the "theory of adolescent society" or "adolescent social system theory." This theory holds that delinquent behavior results from exclusion from the more highly organized high school campus "leading crowd" and from participation in less organized deviant subgroups in a high school social system.[51] More specifically, delinquency results from participation in an "insider" social stratification system which arises autonomous from the adult social system in middle-class, urban, industrialized, large school districts.[52] The juvenile delinquent is a participant in a lower strata within the insider stratification system and much of his delinquency can be interpreted in terms of illicit market relations in which interpersonal status and power are the goals that delinquent groups vie for.

The family as an organizational setting

Thus far in this chapter we have looked at group structures that are conducive to criminal behavior. We have examined the group contexts of professional crime, organized crime, homosexual behavior, prostitution, inebriety, and drug abuse. These topics cover most forms of crime, and appropriately so, because our organizational theory of deviancy holds that crime is largely the result of group participation, while other forms of deviancy, mainly mental disorder, suicide, and intergroup prejudice, are traceable to isolation from group participation or the threat of such isolation.

The family is a peculiar group setting, however, in that variations in family organization can bring about variations in deviancy from one end of the deviancy spectrum to the other. This peculiarity is traced to two factors. For some of its participants the family is a "total institution." For the mother and very young children, "work, sleep, and play may take place in the same place." Thus, behavior of those participants will vary only insofar as family structure varies. Probably the most important basis of this peculiarity, however, is that the family is a group in which relations may approach intimacy not found in other groups in Western Society. That is, members of our urban nuclear families depend upon their families for emotional needs that ordinarily are not met in other groups. Family structure largely determines to what extent those emotional needs will be met. If they are not met in the family, the person must look elsewhere. The outcome of his quest may involve some form of deviancy. If he is successful in finding outside affiliations he may become involved in criminal behavior. If he is unsuccessful, he may suffer prolonged neurosis or eventual psychotic breakdown.

TYPOLOGY OF FAMILY ORGANIZATION

Based on a study of current literature on the family, there are four basic forms of family organization, which we may term mechanical, organic, forced, and anomic, using Durkheim's terms.[53] Each is conducive to certain forms of deviancy or conformity.

Mechanical solidarity Characterized by fewness of mutual obligations, looseness of ties, instability in crisis, simple division of labor, and weak boundaries with other organizations in society, mechanically solidary nuclear families are generally merged into larger extended families to which the members may be as closely related or more closely related than to the other nuclear family members. The extended family, in turn, is integrated on a primary group level with other groups in society.

The purest form of mechanical solidarity known to anthropologists, the "band" is integrated basically upon family ties.

> Kinship ties, structured in their nature by marriage rules, are the integrating mechanism in band societies. The social bodies, the parts of the society, the differentiation of persons into statuses . . . are all familial. . . . Social differentiation makes parts and statuses in the society that exist irrespective of the particular personnel who fill them. In band society all of these are familistic differentiations; every person is one or another kind of consanguinal or affinal relative.[54]

Generally, these families are matrilinial in organization, although this is based primarily upon the mother's relation to children in socialization and rearing.[55] However, this does not imply a strong position of dominance of the mother over the family, as urban people would understand matriarchy.

Max Gluckman has described a mechanically solidary family existing among the Neur,[56] a pastoral tribe of the upper Nile River in East Africa. Gluckman points to the existance of estrangement in the family due to the extension of ties to wider kinship groupings which ties are important in building the cohesion of the larger society. Family organization is matriarchal, as shown by the female inheritance rights—mainly of cattle. A child may have many fathers among the Nuer. The child grows up with many affectionate ties, ties which he plays off against one another and thus is released from any effective control by the nuclear family.

Forced division of labor   Groups characterized by forced division of labor, it is recalled, are characteristically overorganized for a given stage of development. The various functions or roles are excessively regulated or regimented. Members are assigned tasks inappropriate to abilities or interests. Lower-ranking members lack "equality in external conditions of conflict." As "archaic forms of society," they are characterized by repressive law, unduly low social differentiation, inappropriate influence on the collective conscience, and instability in crisis, if the crisis results from internal conflict.

Duvall[57] has provided an excellent description of such families which she terms the "traditional family structure" as contrasted with the "developmental or democratic family pattern" in American society. (discussed below)

The traditional family structure is characterized by strict autocratic control by the parents (usually the father), and discipline is based upon authority—irrational authority—with instant unquestioning obedience expected. The father is characterized by the following traits: (1) he knows what the child "should" be, so he does not seek to understand the child as an individual; (2) he is interested only in activities which he determines are his responsibility for the child's "good"; (3) he places emphasis on giving things and doing things for the child; (4) is interested in the child's accepting and attaining goals set by him, the father; (5) finds satisfaction in the child's owing him a debt which can be repayed by the child's obedience and by bringing honor to the family by achieving goals established by the father; and (6) feels that parenthood is a duty which is forced on him as a biological function.[58]

The mother of a traditionally oriented family: (1) keeps house; (2) takes care of the child physically; (3) trains the child to regularity; (4) imposes discipline; and (5) makes the child good (obedient, moral, religious).[59]

Organic solidarity   Organic solidarity typifies the most advanced form of society and refers to such characteristics as interdependence of self-interest regulated by collective interest (that is, collective conscience), a high division of labor (differentiation of roles, each member playing a different role), high development of individual conscience, a moderator role of government, the use of restitutive sanctions oriented toward a return in state rather than repression, and stability in the midst of a crisis. Duvall gives a perfect description of such families, which she calls democratic or developmental families. This family is characterized by its flexibility, and emphasis on individual self-development.

The father exhibits the following attitudes: (1) the father and the child are both individuals; (2) the father seeks to understand the child and himself; (3) he concerns himself with all activities and needs of the child; (4) he places emphasis on the growth of the child and himself; (5) he is interested in the child's determining and attaining his own goals (moderator); (6) he finds satisfaction in the child's becoming a mature individual; and (7) he feels that parenthood is a privilege which he has chosen to assume.[60]

The mother: (1) trains for self-reliance and citizenship; (2) sees to the emotional well-being of the family; (3) helps the child develop socially; (4) provides for the child's mental growth; (5) guides with understanding; and (6) relates herself in a love capacity.[61]

The organically solidary marriage is one in which each individual offers a service complementary to the other. There is a strong tendency for each person to play a unique role in the group. A couple with organic solidarity are able to adapt to situationally induced role demands that might cause disorganization and divorce in a traditional family. Such marriages have a more fundamental attachment than mere formal contract and thus a greater security in the marriage. Each feels needed by the other. Neither feels nonreciprocity. They are both inclined to be tolerant, to overlook disagreements rather than make issues of them. Conflict is not viewed as disorganizing, but as being merely on the surface of an abiding relationship.

Anomic division of labor   Anomic societies, it is recalled, are characterized by conflict between functions or roles, without regulation from specialized government, based on orientation toward similar goals or values. Anomie typically follows a period of forced division of labor and may be necessary to "break out" the various functions which have not emerged but should have, based on the state of societal development.

In our society, many families are characterized by anomic division of labor, based upon the breakdown of the traditional family and the emergence of the democratic or developmental family. This is shown in the high rates of divorce in American society. Approximately one marriage in four ends in divorce. Based upon this trend, divorce laws have become more liberal. Today divorce is given freely and is oriented at restitution or return in state.

Divorce is based upon a lack of consensus between two spouses as to the functions of each and the roles and rules appropriate to role-integration. Difficulties are viewed as disruptive of the marriage and separation tends to follow even the slightest conflict. Among divorced couples, individualism is high for both the man and woman. They are more ego-centered and rigid, while the happily married are more out-going and adaptable.[62]

Changes in the relations of the sexes are in part traced to the movement for female emancipation. Women are no longer content to preserve their marriage at all costs. Women who were once content to endure cruelty or immorality on the part of their husbands under forced division of labor in marriage are now rebelling. They expect a more equal status and function in marriage. They expect more than the domestic housewife role bestowed by tradition. Our increasing divorce rate does not necessarily mean that there are more unhappy marriages. It may simply indicate that more people who are unhappily married seek divorce than before because they find less reason to stay married.

THE FAMILY IN TRANSITION

The family may be viewed optimistically as in a process of transition from a previous form, the traditional family, to a future form, the democratic family. Deviant behavior may be viewed in part as a product of this transition.

Before urbanization, two thirds of all the families lived on farms as a self-supporting unit. Many of the major functions now delegated to other institutions, including economic, religious, educational, and recreational functions, were the exclusive domain of the family. The father worked the land and took care of the needs of the family. Traditionally a dominating person, he maintained control over his children by means of arbitrary authority. Because children had few outside contacts, they naturally tended to copy the patterns of their parents in later marriage. The boy learned to be a man, a husband, and a father mainly through having lived in a family headed by a man. A girl learned the duties of the woman, wife, and mother by close contact with her mother. During the day the boy would help his father with the chores and they were close companions. When the family did something like going into town, they did it together. The family was a close unit and they depended on each other for their welfare.

Effects of urbanism   During the late nineteenth century, farm people increasingly sought employment in the city. An urban job provided security not dependent upon climate and offered a higher standard of living for the family. However, urban living destroyed the boundary surrounding a family. The father spent much of the day away from home for long hours at work. The child seldom if ever observed his father at work (sometimes he didn't even know what his father did for a living). Because the child was no longer vocationally trained by his father, the family sent him to school where he could train for a trade or profession. The father's inclinations notwithstanding, the son might come to seek another occupation than what the father did.

In the urban setting, the children associate less and less with the family, based in part on access to other non-family associations, and in part on the void created by the absence of the father in his work. Boys may seek the companionship of older boys as father surrogates, as adult male surrogates are absent. This attraction to older boys in part formed the basis of the development of gangs. Younger boys follow and support older boys passively in various delinquent activities, intrigued by the knowledge of fun through illegitimate activities.

Sheldon and Eleanor Glueck, in their controlled study of 500 reform school delinquents, found that the delinquents gravitated toward older boys as well as toward other delinquents.[63] Redl, in his psychoanalytic theory of gang delinquency, has suggested that the basis of gang formation is desire on the part of gang members for a "father image."[64]

What with the father being so often either remote or absent, many American families may be characterized as matriarchal. As a result, the urban family is favorable for the socialization of the girl child but not the boy. This may explain why the American male matures later than the female. In the family and in grade school, the boy is surrounded by female role models. However, a boy is always encouraged to act like a man. His father encourages him to fight back against a bully. Peer group culture carries masculinity norms down from traditional culture. A boy will be teased by his peers for acting like a sissy, even though he may have had no other identifications. The American male child can be seen as seeking masculine identification. Such identifications appear to him as anti-female. The masculine person is one who contrasts most with females. Females are passive; he must be active. Females are kind; he must be cruel. Females are artistic; he must be mechanical. Females are good; he must be bad.

The "ideal" male, following this analysis, is the active, cruel, criminal mechanic. Because of their fear of being submerged by female norms and values, boys growing up become hostile toward women in a kind of "reaction formation" against sissy, feminine, mother identification. These bad-boy impulses may be mobilized in gang delinquency, race violence, minute men activities, or war, based on limited legitimate means of aggression.[65]

The American male may come into marriage with these hostile aggressive attitudes toward women. He thus reverts to the tradition-minded father-type, in a situation in which it is inappropriate. The son can't and doesn't want to follow in his father's footsteps. The wife may not like his cruelty nor does she feel she has to put up with it because of alternatives to marriage available to her. The marriage may therefore go through a period of anomie for years. The wife may rebel against the "domestic servant role." She may seek the "glamour role" or "aesthetic role," each of which may reduce her total contact with her children and husband. She may come into conflict with her husband at every contact. They may decide to avoid each other, either physically through individual pursuits, or psychologically through seldom speaking to each other—namely, psychological divorce.

Many American families are characterized by psychological divorce. There may be little agreement over basic values or the division of labor. But conflict seldom occurs due to psychological isolation. This psychological divorce is justified as being "for the sake of the children."

Based in part upon wives' alienation from their husbands, and upon a decline in function for wives, there has been an increase in working wives. Women today make up one third of our labor force. Over half of all women are in our labor force at a single moment, and of these, three fourths of them are married and have children. The Gluecks found many more of the delinquents had mothers who worked than non-delinquents.

It is based upon the breakdown of the family that gang delinquency comes to exist. There would be no credence to differential association theory if the family served as an effective social unit.

Increasing delinquency In part, the increasing delinquency is traced to the emergence of the gang as an alternative to the anomic family. However, these statistics also reflect the increasing influence of the courts and the police as socializing agents. In small, mechanically solidary communities, informal rather than formal agencies are used. Twenty years ago if boys took a car for a "joy ride" or hitchhiked to another town, or "swiped apples from the corner grocery store," it was considered a boyish prank, part of growing up, and the boys were punished by informal sanctions, mainly by their parents. Today such acts are classed as misdemeanors and subject to police action. The burden of punishment has been taken off the parents and given to the state.

Family organization and mental illness We have seen that the "anomic" urban family results from a conflict between parental role conceptions. The father may adhere to a traditional role conception while the mother may seek a more developmental role. Under some conditions, however, one or both parents may adhere to the traditional pattern and this becomes the established family pattern. While the unstable anomic pattern may lead to juvenile delinquency as children seek affection in extra familial gang contacts, the stable traditional pattern may lead to problems of an opposite nature, that is, various degrees of mental illness. The literature on mental illness stresses the authoritarian, traditional family structure as a major cause.

The various mental health disciplines are in basic agreement with respect to the importance of family experiences in the etiology of mental illness. Although differences between disciplines occur in terms of the issue of priority—that is, early experiences such as "infant trauma" *versus* later experiences of adjustment in adolescence—the notion of intra-family conflict is basic to most approaches: psychiatric, psychological, anthropological, sociological.

For Freud and his followers, the conflict between the ego-super-ego and the id was based upon the conflict between father and son within the family. The Oedipus complex is based upon sexual repression of a son's sexual orientation toward the mother, with the father seen as a barrier to that gratification. Neo-Freudians agree that the pattern of conflict occurs in the family. However, they disagree that the conflict is based on the mother as a sex goal. Malinowski[66] argues that the conflict is the conflict for authority. In Western society, the patriarchal family places the father in a dominant position and the son in a submissive position, leading to resentment of the father's dominant position and general privileges. Among the Trobriand Islanders of New Guinea, this resentment is directed toward the mother's brother who is given authority over the child in that society.

Erich Fromm[67] adds to this analysis by asserting that not only does the child resent the authority, but he also fears it, is anxious about being punished, when such authority is irrational authority. This is the authority of an authoritarian father or mother forcing the child to give up his individuality (his "I") and yield to parental demands. Prohibition of sexual impulses is merely a means of making the child submit. To Fromm, the family plays an important role in "breaking" the individual so that he will submit to irrational authority in other institutional settings. Fromm sees American society, and society in general, as dependent upon irrational authority for its maintainence.

In *The Sane Society,* Fromm characterizes American society as pervaded by anonymous, irrational authority.[68] The basic adaptation of individuals in our society, says Fromm, is "adjustment," a conformity and basic alienation which Fromm equates with mental disorder. The individual's "I" is repressed, leading to retreatism or

ritualism, neurosis or psychosis, based upon a basic fear of authority which is instilled in childhood by the authoritarian parent.
Fromm takes the position that if a person is alienated he is insane.
If a large number of persons are alienated, it is possible for a whole
society to be characterized as insane. Fromm's approach is probably
more a polemic against his perception of rigidity of social organization than a rigorous scientific account. Fromm acknowledges that
an alternative to neurosis is rebellion against such authority, although he claims that few choose this alternative.

By contrast, Arnold Green[69] argues that "avoidance techniques"
may prevent neurosis. Green recounts that in the Polish-industrial
community of his childhood, the typical father was authoritarian
and yet his children avoided damage to the "core of self" through
avoidance techniques. On the other hand, among middle-class authoritarian familes, a youngster is unable to avoid parental suppres-
sion, due to awesome threat of withdrawal of love (which is more
extreme in actuality than any threat of physical punishment) and
consequently chooses absolute conformity to parental demands,
leading to submersion of his basic self in *personality absorption*
in which the child is shaped in the parents' image. The child wishes
to rebel but cannot due to immense anxiety. Middle-class parents
adopt personality absorption based upon basic ambivalence to the
child due to their mobility aspirations, hedonistic orientations, and
a need for privacy which the child interferes with.

The basic orientation of the family studies has been directed
toward the authoritarian family. While the authoritarian family
is held accountable for mental disorder, the *laissez-faire* or anomic
family is held accountable for problems of delinquency. The former,
using the terms of Durkheim, is a kind of "forced division of labor"
in which regulation is not in accord with abilities, and individual
members are prevented from "equality in conditions of conflict."
In the latter there is too much conflict, preventing the working
together and preventing passing on sufficient regulation effectively.

Summary and conclusion

This chapter has involved an examination of a variety
of deviant group settings. Could the chapter be reread in reverse

order, we could perhaps trace the life process of a given deviant person. We could suggest possible family backgrounds, peer involvements, and subsequent deviant group-affiliations. In so doing we could propose a "sequential model" for purposes of understanding various forms of deviancy and thus provide an explanation of these forms. However, such an enterprise would not only be highly speculative and unverified, but it would also be contrary to the lessons taught by our study of deviancy. One lesson clearly taught is that the most substantiated and current portrayals of most criminal deviancy indicate that *most criminal and delinquent groups are loosely organized, following the "anomie-utilitarian" pattern described earlier in this text,* and about the only clearly reliable statements we can make about most criminal deviates is that they have anomic group backgrounds in family, school, and work.

As for the explanatory task of predicting particular forms of deviancy outcomes — such as, homosexual behavior — from the group history of an individual, the very term "anomie" seems to contradict that such a task can be done. Just as Matza suggests that delinquents may "drift" in and out of delinquency, criminal deviates may drift from one form of criminal deviation to another. We have seen that prostitutes may often engage in homosexual activity for pay, that their pimps may be drug addicts or pushers, that professional criminals are frequent bar patrons, and that bar patrons may be involved in a spectrum of deviant activity. Parenthetically it may be added that all of these forms of deviancy are supported by "anomic-utilitarian" group structure. All of this seems to corroborate futher the central theme of this book; that various forms of deviancy cannot be viewed *in abstracto* but rather that many forms of deviancy may be the result of similar or the same group structures.

Thus, our conclusions about deviancy yield an approach that is somewhat opposed to a "hard determinist" sociological point of view. One's group background will affect his inclination toward criminal or conforming patterns of conduct. We know that social-class background will correlate with deviancy, in that working-class occupations are exclusively within "utilitarian-anomic" settings and are thus conducive to "utiliarian-anomic" extravocational group involvements. We can then apply sociological theory to smaller group settings to predict deviancy outcomes. However, particular forms of deviancy do not appear to have unique group structures. The particular form of adaptation within these group settings are determined by personality and hereditary factors which are beyond the domain of our analysis. This does not mean, however, that our sociological approach is useless—that it lacks the potentiality for providing a basis for prediction and control of deviancy problems. In fact, because the most immediate "cause" of criminal deviancy is the group structure that surrounds it, deviancy is more responsive to changes in that group structure. That is, we may best hope to change the criminal deviate by altering the group structures he intimately participates in or by involving him in alternative group structures. This is more practical and effective than attempting to alter his perceptions of previous group experiences. The topic of altering deviant group structure will be discussed at great length in the final chapter of this book.

Unorganized forms
of deviancy

Most of the forms of deviancy we have examined are organized and fit the theory of differential organizational participation fairly well. These forms, largely criminal, result from a history of participation in deviant group settings, mostly of the anomic-utilitarian type. Deviancy types applicable to these organized settings are innovation or rebellion in Merton's terms, bohemianism in the terms of Thomas and Znaniecki, underconformity or contracultural underconformity in Cavan's terms, and career crime in Clinard's terms.

A complete deviancy picture cannot be drawn without some discussion of unorganized forms of deviancy. In a way, this sounds contrary to the theory of differential organizational participation, if the theory is taken to mean that all deviation results from participation in some immediate reference group. This is not the intent of the theory, however. While type of group membership is one dimension to be explored, degree of participation is another dimension which can be incorporated within the theory. That is, certain forms of deviancy — such as mental disorder, suicide, and prejudice — can be explained in terms of alienation or isolation from various types

8

Notes for this chapter are on pages 389–391.

of groups. Certain forms of neurosis and psychosis are often traced to parental overprotection, enforced solitude, or lack of ability to fit into neighborhood peer groups. Schizophrenia has often been portrayed as due to maternal overprotection from neighborhood gangs. Some forms of suicide may result from isolation or fear of isolation, particularly in terms of business reversal or bankruptcy. While all of this is very speculative, at least it is shown that there is room for unorganized forms of deviancy within the theory of differential organizational participation. To apply this theory, the theorist would first examine a particular group setting, such as the delinquent gangs described above as "utilitarian" in organizational structure. One would then examine the deviant patterns resulting from exclusion or isolation from such groups when, in fact, the individual seeks membership. Unorganized deviancy could be seen as the converse of organized deviancy — for instance, the "retreatist" rejects the means and ends of society-at-large, but lacks the group affiliations to instrument a new normative system (rebellion).

Unlike the types of deviancy discussed above, then, the forms of deviancy discussed in this chapter involve isolation, alienation, or fear of such isolation or alienation from interpersonal group association. We may expect that these problems would be the opposite of those discussed above in other respects as well. Typical deviancy patterns discussed in this chapter will be of the ritualist or retreatist type in Merton's terms, the philistine type in Thomas and Znaniecki's scheme, "overconformity" or contracultural overconformity in Cavan's typology, and a noncareer deviancy in Clinard's classification. Three basic types will be discussed from this point of view: mental disorder, suicide, and prejudice. Two other types that have been classified retreatist adaptations will be discussed — drug addiction and inebriety — even though these types have been discussed above in terms of group contexts. These two types of deviancy are possible in both an organized and unorganized type. It is quite conceivable that many inebriates and drug addicts are without significant group association and thus should be discussed as unorganized deviancy. Both types have been portrayed in terms of "double failure" — that is, the deviant's failure to gain membership in either legitimate or illegitimate groups. Furthermore, these forms may be retreatist in terms of society-at-large even though they may have some group contact basis, and thus they should be discussed along with the other retreatist types in this chapter.

The forms of deviancy discussed in this chapter are unique in still another basic way. With such problems as white-collar crime, organized crime, professional crime, homosexuality, and the like, discussed in the previous chapter, we argued that the primary cause of the deviation was the type of group to which the individual belonged, normative, utilitarian, or coercive, and that larger social structure was secondary. However, with the problems discussed in this chapter, inasmuch as these problems imply isolation from legitimate and/or illegitimate groups, the individual is directly exposed to the social structure of a large society without intervening groups that which might serve as a basis for the protection of his self-concept through rationalization. Thus, with mental disorder, suicide, and the like, we can more directly impute their cause to the social structure rather than the group structure and would be more inclined to predict that there would be true differentials in these forms of deviancy according to social class position. It is to these problems that social stratification theory is most relevant (and whose study has contributed the most to social stratification theory).

With criminal forms of deviation, social class theories are less applicable and require the most clarification because of the factor of intervening groups. There may indeed be a relation between social class and group participation. For example, it may very well be that lower socio-economic groups tend to be less well organized than middle- or upper-class groups, and therefore more inclined to foster criminal deviancy. Various factors—lower education, limited socialization, lack of knowledge of organizational procedure, poor leadership, and the like—seem to indicate the likelihood that lower-class groups are not well integrated. However, this premise is not specified or made clear in current deviancy theories such as those of anomie or status deprivation. Two other theories are just as plausible: that in a capitalist society such as ours, anomic groups are prevalent at all socio-economic levels; and that perhaps the working class is highly organized in opposition to capitalist exploitation (labor unions, informal work groups, and the like). This theory would hold, as does Sutherland's theory of white-collar crime, that it is not so much the amount of criminal deviancy but rather the kind of deviancy that varies by social class, the lower class being inclined toward official, conventional, blue-collar crime and middle- and upper-class people being involved in unrecorded white-collar crime.

Mental illness

CONCEPT

The field of mental health–mental disorder encompasses a myriad of conflicting definitions, corresponding to various approaches. Orthodox Freudian psychiatrists define mental health in terms of freedom from sexual repression. Neo-Freudians, like Horney and Fromm, define it in terms of freedom, not in particular from sexual repression but from authority and authoritarian restraint. Anthropologists may define mental illness as deviation from a statistical norm, usually the mode, implying that mental illness is not an absolute phenomenon but that it is relative to norms. Clinical psychologists view mental health as freedom from "stress" produced by a variety of factors: economic, occupational, racial discrimination, as well as family difficulties. Sociologists, on the other hand, may tend to play down "personality factors" in favor of role and role conflict as essential to problems of mental health and mental disorder. The lay public may adhere to still another conception of mental health as eccentric, unpredictable, and even violent behavior. Indeed, the variety of definitions and emphases reflects the current state social disorganization or anomie within the mental health professions. That is, various mental health disciplines have not developed a division of labor with respect to the study of mental disorder. They consequently explain the same social phenomenon using different terms, concepts, and definitions, each pursuing separately the same common goal, some more successfully than others.

In a very direct sense the concept of anomie seems applicable. The mental health professions are in conflict, for economic status in terms of foundation and government support, for academic recognition and esteem, as well as for self-satisfaction of explaining a social phenomenon in terms of one's own value perspectives. It is possible that this incapacity of the mental health professions to provide a "united front" explains the often noted lack of sophistication of the lay public in terms of the findings of the mental health professions. This is especially unfortunate in light of the fact that a good proportion of people employed to treat or control mental illness— psychiatric attendants, nurses, police—are considerably influenced by the stereotypes of insanity passed on in popular culture. Arriving at an adequate definition of terms is especially important in the field of mental disorder. A clear concept of mental illness is an important starting point.

Mental illness is closely related to the concept of personality disorganization—which may be defined as a disruption of role relationships in pursuit of a person's life goals. Although personality disorganization may result from exterior causes—such as some environmental crisis—mental illness implies that a given role disruption results from within the individual, not necessarily related to exterior environment. The immediate conflict of selves is the basic cause of mental disorder, though this may be a byproduct of some previous environmental crisis. Mental illness is defined as a disruption of the capacity for role relationships in pursuit of reward values typical of persons in a given subculture—implying inner conflict or "conflict of selves."

It can be seen that in all cases the basic criterion of "self-conflict" is crucial to the concept of mental illness developed here. The selves said to be conflicting are, in the words of Mead, the "I" and the "me."[1] The "I" or active self is distinct from the "me" or passive self that is acted upon. The "me" is the internalized attitudes of others toward self and toward group activities. The "I" and "me" are separated for purposes of analysis because they often are in conflict with each other. When an individual acts impulsively, the "I" controls behavior and the "me" is absent. On the other hand, when a person consults tradition and custom in determining his behavior, the "me" determines behavior. (The distinction between the "me" and "I" in Mead's work is roughly parallel to Freud's distinction between the ego–super ego and the id, though marked differences exist between Mead's and Freud's general theories.) It can be seen that the "me" predominates under the condition of perfect mechanical solidarity, in Durkheim's terms, while the "I" is more an expression of one's unique characteristics rather than one's culture, and becomes more important under the condition of organic solidarity.

It may be pointed out that this definition does not separate mental disorder from many if not most cases of juvenile delinquency or criminality which imply both disruption of role relationships and inner conflict. This suggests the need for further limitation of our definition.

We may conceptualize delinquent behavior as traced to overt

conflict between the "me" and the "I" and mental illness as covert conflict between the "me" and the "I". For example, when a person expresses aggressive or sexual impulses (the "I") overtly contrary to what he has been taught as proper behavior (the "me"), the person is deemed a delinquent. On the other hand, when a person has these impulses and is either incapable or prevented from expressing them, he may, if observed by a psychiatrist, be deemed a neurotic or psychotic.

It may be observed that in both cases impulses exist that contrast or conflict with what one has been taught is appropriate behavior. In folk societies, it is pointed out by anthropologists, culture shapes even one's basic impulses, thus precluding a conflict between impulse and custom. It is thus only in more advanced industrialized societies that widespread problems of mental disorder occur. Other things equal, we can expect mental disorder to prevail under a condition of forced division of labor where the "I" is suppressed, while problems of delinquency will prevail under the condition of anomic division of labor, both being reduced under organic solidarity.

TYPOLOGY

It is as difficult to formulate a typology of mental illness as it is of delinquency and crime. A number of studies have shown the difficulty psychiatrists have in making consistent diagnoses, and placing individuals into detailed psychiatric categories.[2] For this reason, we shall direct our attention toward the basic distinction between normal, neurotic, and impaired. This distinction may prove fruitful in relation to our general typology of deviation. It may be recalled that a distinction has been made between "heinous" contracultural criminal offenses (those involving "subterranean" value orientation) and those classified as "normal" or innovative delinquency (oriented toward dominant values). Both the innovator and the rebel reject institutional norms of society.

In the case of mental disorder, the individual may maintain subterranean orientations in the sense of a covert "I" conflicting with internalized dominant value orientations, however, the individual is so incapable of pursuing them that he is believed to reject them. The neurotic is capable of maintaining a behavioral facade, adhering to institutional means (ritualism), while the psychotic is not (retreatism). Both, however, maintain orientations at odds with what they have been taught as right. For example, a basic value of our society is "activity and work,"[3] according to Robin Williams. A person may dislike activity and work, unknown even to himself, and may come to participate passively (ritualism) or to become a passive nonparticipant (retreatism). He may experience anxiety because of a discrepancy between what he secretly wants to do, play ("I"), and what he feels he ought to do, work ("me"). If a person behaves as such with respect to a number of basic values, he will be deemed psychotic or neurotic. On the other hand, if the person is capable of admitting to himself that he dislikes activity and work, rejects both and seeks play, he will be deemed a delinquent, or at best a vagrant (that is, a rebel).

It follows that many neurotics are potential delinquents. If a neurotic can be made to realize his hidden value orientations—such as thrills, kicks, sadism, and the like—he may be converted to a delinquent if he can be made to reject his "me" and act on impulse. In the process, however, the person experiences guilt and anxiety because of the powerful influence of the "me"—that is, the individual has been taught to believe that such impulses are wrong.

PEER GROUP ORGANIZATION AND MENTAL ILLNESS

In American society, whose basic norms, values, and standards are undergoing change, youth in general and peer groups in particular are an instrument of that social change. While the old and the young share basic values—a functional prerequisite of society—the young come to question some traditional values. Through contact with his peer group, a youngster may develop normative values in conflict with those of his parents. If in that conflict he rebels against family control, peer group norms and values will determine behavior. If, on the other hand, the family is successful in shutting off the youngster from the influence of the peer group, through prohibition, geographical mobility, or through alienating the youngster from the peer group, the youngster's "I" will be submerged by the norms and values of his parents. If, however, the youngster maintains latent allegiance to peer group norms and values or unconsciously desires peer group contact, he will be neurotic for these suppressed impulses will provide a constant source of dissatisfaction.

A number of studies have traced mental disorder—expecially schizophrenia, predominantly a "youth" mental disorder—to this alienation from peer group ties or isolation. Faris[4] characterizes the schizophrenic as a "shut in" or seclusive personality. His physical separation from sympathic social contacts leads to eccentricity, illogicality, inappropriateness of emotions, hallucinations, and delusions so characteristic of schizophrenics as youngsters. Such persons have a history of rejection by peer group either due to physical unattractiveness or overconventionality of parentally imposed standards, or both.

In another article, Dunham[5] describes such catatonic traits as self-consciousness, timidity, cautiousness, an inferiority complex, and inhibition as traced to seclusiveness from informal contacts based in part upon ignorance of subjects of common knowledge to teenagers and overconformity to adult standards: obedient, honest, moral, economically insecure, studious, intropunitive.

Weinberg[6] agrees with Faris and Dunham, finding among a sample of 53 catatonics ignorance of interpersonal techniques (especially the techniques of handling the opposite sex) and relatively low peer group contact is traced to a tremendously domineering mother who prevented association with peers. Weinberg finds, however, that catatonics are not complete recluses and that they participate on a limited basis in peer group relations; however, they have very unsatisfying relations with their peers in the sense of "isolation in association," such as a jilting or exploitation in courtship. Later marriage was broken, due to mother's dominance. In *Society and Personality Disorders*,[7] Weinberg contends that schizophrenia entails the breakdown of previously effective neurotic defenses, often due to dissatisfaction with the "isolation-in-association" relationship. Similarly, Hollingshead, Ellis and Kirby[8] find a social mobility orientation among schizophrenics, stating that actual schizophrenic breakdown accompanies the completion of education and the realization that it did not confer the personal and emotional gratifications sought after.

Kohn and Clausen[9] find that schizophrenics as compared with a control group actually did not differ in terms of group (formal or informal) association. In fact, schizophrenics may be compulsive "joiners," but are isolated in associations or alienated from friends, or in marriage psychologically divorced.

Although this brief review of studies of schizophrenia does not cover all forms of mental disorder, it is illustrative. Schizophrenia has received the most attention in the empirical literature, primarily because it is the largest category of mental disorder. Schizophrenia accounts for about one-fourth of the first admissions to mental hospitals and one-third of all readmissions.[10] This figure is quite large considering that a high percentage of mental hospital admissions are "non-functional" or organic psychoses. The two other major forms of functional or non-organic psychosis, manic-depressive disorder and involutional psychosis, combined amount to 12 per cent of first admissions or about 6 per cent each.[11] Furthermore, there is considerable evidence that, though these two categories differ somewhat in symptomatology from schizophrenia, the main etiological difference is the age of the patient. That is to say, although the factor of social isolation seems to play a main role in all three disorders; the behavioral outcome may be different, possibly because of the patient's age. For schizophrenics, the average age of first admission is in the early thirties. For manic-depressives the average is about forty. But for involutional psychotics, the average age is fifty-five.[12] That is, schizophrenia is a disorder of young adulthood, manic depression a disorder of middle age, and involutional psychosis a disorder of old age. All three disorders are outcomes of interpersonal stress. While the schizophrenic has peer group difficulties, the manic-depressive may experience rejection by relatives or work associates. The involutional psychotic faces the rejection of retirement and gradual withdrawal from social interaction. Childhood background cannot be ignored as a factor in these disorders. The evidence indicates that like the parents of schizophrenics, those of the manic-depressives tend to be "traditional" parents, emphasizing moral training, discipline, overconscientiousness, overmeticulousness, narrow social interests, perfectionism, and the like.[13] Evidentally, the parents of schizophrenics are more severe, precipitating the onset of an earlier illness.

In all of these forms of psychosis we find three basic factors: age, parental background, and social isolation. All three disorders are revelatory of coercive traditional family backgrounds and subsequent peer, family, and work isolation. It seems likely that, in accord with our model, one follows from the other. That is, there is a relationship between (1) the individual's attempt to conform to the strict standards of an authoritarian parent, and (2) later interpersonal isolation. The normative system to which the individual conforms is not in accord with that of his close interpersonal associates. Nevertheless, in order to gain the respect and admiration of associates, the individual strives even more to conform to traditional standards. This contracultural overconformity may be motivated by the desire for reminiscent parent approval or by the feeling that once a person has "made his mark," his fellows will certainly realize their previous impression of him was mistaken. However, psychotic breakdown will occur if the individual finds evidence that such is not the case, as in his expulsion from a group.

One may wonder to what extent these same generalizations apply to the neuroses. While the psychoses are characterized by the term retreatism, implying resignation from overt participation in society's normative system and isolation from group participation, we have characterized the neuroses by the term ritualism, implying that the individual partially accepts society's normative structure and participates to some extent in groups. Psychosis and neurosis should, however, be conceptualized as separate ways of adapting, just as retreatism and ritualism are separate "modes of adaptation." However, there are interesting similarities in the backgrounds of psychotics and neurotics. The parental background of neurotics is similar to that of psychotics: a traditional father or mother. Parents instill unrealistic levels of aspiration and a lack of self-acceptance. When the individual fails to live up to these high ideals, he may suffer from "break of compensation" and use of neurotic defense mechanisms. Of course, the Freudian approach to neurosis emphasizes the excessively rigid childhood moral training (also characteristic of traditional parents).[14]

AMERICAN SOCIAL STRUCTURE AND MENTAL ILLNESS

So far in this chapter we have argued that mental disorder and other social problems contrast with the criminal forms of deviancy discussed in Chapter 7, insofar as they result from isolation from participation in organized groups. Criminal deviation results from participation in particular forms of groups. Because criminal deviation may depend upon access to participation in criminal groups, social-class membership may be secondary to group membership as an etiological factor. These intervening groups complicate the sociological explanation of criminal deviancy, as it is not established that there is any relationship between socio-economic status and the prevalence of utilitarian–anomic groups. In fact, in a capitalist society these groups would be prevalent at all class levels. There is reason to believe that upper- and middle-class people may be as much or more concerned about money, a remunerative sanction, as lower-class people; therefore, utilitarian groups may be even more prevalent in the upper and middle class.

When a form of deviancy, as with mental disorder, is traced to isolation from group participation, however, there is a more direct relation between socio-economic status and that form of deviancy. For one thing, there is considerable evidence that a group's participation is directly related to socio-economic level; the higher one's social status the greater his participation. Based upon this finding, there is reason to believe that mental illness, which is correlated with social participation, would correlate with socio-economic status; the higher the socio-economic status, the lesser the mental disorder. The lower-class individual, when isolated from social contact, may suffer the greatest frustration and anxiety (that is, anomie) of all members of society, because he lacks the group supports that could help him to rationalize or serve as an alternative to success in the larger socio-economic order. Thus, it seems that anomie theory would work best with a problem like mental disorder, as the individual is confronted directly by the larger social structure of society as portrayed in anomie theory.

Unlike the studies of criminal deviancy we have cited, studies of mental disorder consistently show an inverse relation between the seriousness and prevalence of mental disorder, on the one hand, and socio-economic status on the other. In examining these studies it should be noted that this observation holds both when official statistics and when unofficial data are used as a criterion of mental disorder. Hollingshead and Redlich[15] found schizophrenia ten times more prevalent among the lowest social class (class V) than among the highest social class (class I) in New Haven, Connecticut. Faris and Dunham[16] found schizophrenic disorders concentrated in zones I and II, heavily populated by unskilled laborers and the unemployed—that is, by lower-class people. One exception, however, was manic–depressive disorder, found more evenly distributed throughout the city.

These findings, unlike traditional findings on delinquency, are probably not due to overrepresentation of lower-class persons among mental hospital patients. Hollingshead and Redlich found only the lowest social class overrepresented in the mental hospital, which did not account for class V's higher prevalence of schizophrenia when rates were computed per 100,000 population. Nor are such findings due to reliance upon official records which may be biased toward certain social groups. A large-scale study of the prevalence of mental health in Manhattan,[17] involving a large sample of 1,660 adults in the 20 to 59 age-range using home questionnaire data, confirmed the finding that mental disorders were both more prevalent and more serious in the lower class. The midtown Manhattan findings correspond quite closely with those of the New Haven study. While there were almost five times as many in the lowest socio-economic strata diagnosed "impaired" as compared with the highest socio-economic strata, there were six times as many diagnosed "well" in the highest socio-economic stratum. These differences were traced to a contrast between the open opportunities doctrine of our society and the meager career accomplishments of lower-class persons, leading in many to a immobilization, in accord with the anomie theory explanation.[18]

Just as extreme mental disease can be said to be more prevalent among the lower classes, it has been found more prevalent among other underprivileged groups, a fact which provides further support for the anomie explanation of mental disorder. Holding social class constant, Malzberg found blacks higher in dementia praecox, general paresis, and alcoholic psychosis than whites, though lower in old-age psychoses: involutional, and senile and manic depression.[19] Interestingly, most neuroses have frequently been found more prevalent among middle than lower classes.[20] Analogously, less disadvantaged minority groups have a higher proportion of neurosis as a characteristic mental disease. Several studies have shown Jews to be higher in neurosis though lower in psychosis than the general population.[21]

The common underlying explanation emerging from social organization theory is that the more extreme repression of lower-class people via economic and social discrimination producing socio-economic failure leads to the more incapacitating forms of psychosis and neurosis. Economic insecurity more often characterized middle-class persons associated with non-incapacitating forms of psychosis—namely, manic–depressive psychoses—and neurosis. One would expect retreatist disorders to be more prevalent among lower-class persons, based upon essentially three factors: (1) anomia, a sense of hopelessness based upon economic failure and subsequent rejection of legitimate avenues to achievement of economic goals; (2) more basically, a repression of self, based upon the authoritarian family pattern found more frequently among lower-class persons (sociologically described as a rigid adherence to the "me" aspect of self as a means of salvaging some degree of individuality); and (3) lower informal and formal social contact. Among middle-class people, neurotic conformity is sometimes required even though there may be minimal commitment to values, or even though success may be only minor. Upper-class persons, on the other hand, are freed from economic worries, and consequently the impulsive self (the "I") is free to emerge in the open *vis-a-vis* dominant values which are available.

In any society characteristically "oligarchic" or "quasi-caste" in nature (which types have been linked above with Merton's anomie theory) we may expect differentials in sanity according to place in society. The oppressed will in the short run react to this state of overorganization by means of submission and retreat, while in a truly open class society or democratic social order, where achievement corresponds to ability, success values and rewards are allocated according to social class, making for stability and general state of satisfaction with attainments. All members of society participate in social organization actively, receiving from it in gradations according to their ability. Those of lesser abilities do not suffer despair, and are glad to receive what they earn by their efforts. Creative potentialities (the "I") are developed to the greatest degree, because the social order incorporates only relevant criteria for the assignment of persons to various status levels.

In sum, problems of mental illness are intimately related to the nature of social organization. If widespread conflict exists between social classes, as in anomie, mental illness is "acted out" in overt conflict and thus is minimized as a problem; while in "forced division of labor," mental illness exists without outlet and consequently with little hope of reduction.

Suicide

CONCEPT

Sociological definitions of suicide vary somewhat with the lay concept. While most laymen define suicide simply as self-inflicted death, sociologists have stressed that suicide refers to a broader phenomenon, including "the intentional takings of one's life or the failure when possible to save one's life when death threatens."[22] Similarly, Durkheim defined suicide as "all cases of death resulting directly or indirectly from a positive or negative act of the victim himself, which he knows will produce the result."[23] Thus, sociologically, it is possible for suicide to occur where the cause is some external force or person, such as loss of life in battle due to courageous action where the probability of death is great. In fact, some psychiatrists go so far as to assert that true accidental death in humans rarely occurs, but is caused by unconscious self-aggression in the form of a "death wish." Thus a person killed in an auto race would be considered an accidental death by the lay public but a suicide by a psychiatrist.

The distinction between suicide and accident is often an arbitrary one. A person who takes an overdose of sleeping pills realizes that the probability of death is high; but so does a person who goes skin-diving in shark-infested waters or who drives at a high speed while intoxicated. The sleeping-pill death may be more consciously induced than the violent sport accident, but both are highly probable suicides. Indeed, the sleeping pill may not be a true suicide attempt, in the sense that the person may be trying to teach someone a lesson and does not really expect to die before being rescued.

TYPOLOGY

Psychiatrists believe that in many cases the method a person chooses to end his life is an important clue to the reason he found life unbearable.[24] They say that such an individual unconsciously chooses a method symbolic of the subconscious problems and motives that led to his suicide.

The methods chosen by some people to kill themselves are extremely strange and varied. Menninger says:

> I have well-authenticated cases in which men or women have committed suicide by hanging themselves, or taking poison, in the tops of high trees; by throwing themselves upon swiftly revolving circular saws; by exploding dynamite in their mouths; by thrusting red-hot pokers down their throats; by hugging red-hot stoves; by stripping themselves naked and allowing themselves to freeze to death on winter snowdrifts out of doors, or on piles of ice in refrigerator cars; by lacerating their throats on barbed wire fences; by drowning themselves head

downward in barrels; by suffocating themselves head downward in chimneys; by diving into white-hot coke ovens; by throwing themselves into craters of volcanoes; by shooting themselves with ingenious combinations of a rifle and a sewing machine; by strangling themselves with their hair; by swallowing poisonous spiders; by piercing their hearts with corkscrews and darning needles; by hanging themselves with grapevines; by cutting their throats with handsaws and sheep-shears; by swallowing strips of underclothing and buckles of suspenders; by forcing teams of horses to tear their heads off; by drowning themselves in vats of soft soap; by plunging into retorts of molten glass; by jumping into slaughterhouse tanks of blood; by decapitation with homemade guillotines; and by self-crucifixion.[25]

While most of these spectacular suicides indicate a violent intropunitive hatred of self with a desire to punish self or others for misdeeds, some indicate an apathetic desire to put oneself out of misery. The former is termed *anomic suicide*, and is characterized by irritation, disgust, and violent recriminations against either life or one particular person. The latter is termed *egoistic suicide*, and is characterized by apathy, indolent melancholy, and self-compliance. We are still lacking a term for the type of suicide inflicted by some exterior force or agent. Such suicides are carried out not to punish or relieve self, but to benefit the group. *Altruistic suicide* is characterized by energy of passion or will, calm feeling of duty, mystical enthusiam, and peaceful courage.[26]

In analyzing any given instance of suicide, it is rarely possible to label it a pure instance of one type. This is because each type of suicide, as will be shown, arises in a different organizational context. Just as social organization is seldom pure or ideal typical, suicides often are of mixed types.

SOCIAL ORGANIZATION AND SUICIDE

In many instances of suicide, it is difficult to trace the act to the nature of group organization. One is even tempted to resort to astrological explanations. For instance, it has been observed that the largest proportion of suicides for men occur on Monday, for women on Sunday. It would seem that colder, gloomier days of Winter would cause a marked increase in the number of suicides. But Spring, when nature seems to come alive, is the suicide season. More people kill themselves in Spring than at any other time of the year.

In the United States and most of Europe, April is the peak month, followed by May and March.

Émile Durkheim examined various non-sociological explanations of suicide: psychopathology, the effect of race and heredity, the process of imitation and cosmic factors such as humidity, temperature, the amount of sunlight. In each case, he argued convincingly that the phenomenon under consideration is not the determinant but either merely an index in underlying changes in social organization, or a noncorrelated factor altogether.

> Each social group really has a collective inclination for the act, quite its own, and the source of all individual inclination, rather than their result. It is made up of the currents of egoism, altruism or anomy running through the society under consideration with the tendencies to languorous melancholy, active renunciation or exasperated weariness derivative from these currents. These tendencies of the whole social body, by affecting individuals, cause them to commit suicide.[27]

Durkheim was not always explicit on the subject of social organizational correlates of the different types of suicide. One can infer, however, that altruistic suicide, as it is attributed to excessive group integration, is linked with the abnormal form of forced division of labor, while anomic suicide and egoistic suicide, both of which are linked to insufficient group integration or excessive intra-group functional conflict, are both linked to anomic division of labor. Both mechanical and organic solidarity are described by Durkheim as having an appropriate degree of integration for their stage of development, and therefore, the two polar types of abnormal solidarity should implicitly or explicitly be the focal point of Durkheim's suicide.

It is noteworthy that two of these types are traced to anomic group organization and one to oligarchic structure. The former, anomic organization, characterizes occidental countries of today and is relevant to our frame of analysis. Thus, in accord with the thesis of this chapter, suicide is for the most part traced to isolation from group contact (egoistic suicide) and insufficient group integration, or to fear of rejection and possible isolation-in-association (anomic suicide) and intragroup conflict. Egoistic suicide seems to characterize todays capitalist society or welfare state, while anomic suicide characterizes transitional countries. However, oddly enough, egoistic suicide appears to be greatest in countries with greatest organic solidarity, as was explained in Chapter 5, and, though we have no data to show this, it would be most likely in totalitarian countries, based on greater atomization of groups. Thus, suicide appears to be inversely related to the solidarity and intimacy of subgroups in a society. In contemporary society, such intimacy and solidarity appears to be declining and the suicide rate is rising. Thus, the most "anomic" transitional countries of Latin America appear to have relatively low suicide rates, as local community and other intimate subgroups are still strong in those societies.

At any rate, with suicide as with mental disorder, the behavior is traced to isolation from groups, such that the individual is directly exposed to the social structure of larger society. We should therefore expect suicide to vary with such macrosocial factors as socio-economic status, age, sex, and the like. Also, we should expect Merton's anomic theory to be useful and relevant. The term "anomie" is traced, in fact, to Durkheim's discussion of suicide, and anomie has been researched fruitfully using the Mertonian macrosocial variables. Suicide differs from mental disorder insofar as suicide generally results from sudden disruption of one's normative framework, while mental disorder implies a more-or-less chronic or gradual disruption. One may speculate that suicide is a means of avoiding mental disorder and resulting humiliation. Both problems, however, may be seen within the context of contracultural overconformity and retreatism. The suicide victim may think of himself as a tragic martyr performing a noble or self-sacrificing act to maintain his dignity in another person's eyes. The schizophrenic may have used every means to win the approval of another person before his schizophrenic retreat.

In the following pages, suicide will be discussed largely in terms of these macrosocial factors. It will be shown that though suicide is somewhat differently related to larger social structure than is mental disorder, the larger social structure is of primary relevance.

Forced division of labor and altruistic suicide   No doubt suicides have been found among folk or primitive societies, societies which closely resemble Durkheim's mechanical solidarity. For example, the Kwakiutl Indians of Canada are quite familiar with this practice. Among the Kwakiutl, suicide may often result from failure to maintain status in accordance with the property consciousness of these people.[28] However, among many primitive societies— for instance, the Australian aborigines, African Bushmen, and Hottentots—there is little or no awareness of the practice of suicide.[29] Other primitive societies, such as the Andaman Islanders and the people of the Caroline Islands, were unfamiliar with suicide until the practice was introduced by Europeans. In fact, most major instances of altruistic suicide are drawn not from small-scale, primitive societies, but from large-scale societies characterized by an archaic caste-like division of labor—that is, a forced division of labor. As under mechanical solidarity, the individual is directly related to society, and behavior is determined largely by tradition and by edict of central authority. But unlike mechanical solidarity, power is concentrated and society is organized on a large-scale, formalized, structured basis. Such societies are over-organized, monolithic, and totalitarian.

It is among castes or caste-like societies that better known suicide practices are found. In caste-oriented India, the *sutee* is practiced among widows of high-caste persons, giving passport to nirvana by atoning for the sins of the husband and giving social distinction for the relatives and children. Among the Japanese Samurais, whose principal objective was successful and faithful service to the emperor, who was considered divine in origin, the practice of suicide developed for those who could not perform this service. The Kamikazes sacrificed themselves in battle, again out of devotion to the emperor.[30] The practice of *jushi,* in which followers and servants killed themselves after the death of their chief, was practiced among the Ashantis, a West African kingdom state. During wartime, altruistic suicides increase. Durkheim traced this in large part to the excessive integration of the armed services, essentially oriented around a caste-like social organization of ranks.

Where altruistic suicide occurs, the society's scale of values places individual welfare or individual life low in priority. In true mechanical solidarity, there is little distinction between the fate of an individual and the fate of a group, for power is diffuse. As such, there is less tendency to ask any given individual to make the sacrifice of his life, and greater tendency, when necessity demands, to call upon the collectivity, including its leaders, to rise up against opposition.

Anomie and suicide   While the more usual practices of suicide are classified as altruistic, by far the most common to Western society are anomic suicide and egoistic suicide. Both are prevalent in a society or sub-society going through a period of anomie. It is anomic and egoistic suicides that comprise the official records on suicide. Altruistic suicides occurring in modern society may be classed as battle casualities, and murders (where a person, fighting for a "cause," is killed). Therefore, the records that have been kept on suicide should reflect egoistic and anomic suicide, and not altruistic suicide rates.

Examining these records down through history, it is seen that suicide rates vary as a society's social integration varies. It is known that although suicide rates had been only moderate during the Golden Age of Greece, that Greece suffered high suicide rates after its decline in power, and that during this period it suffered a confusion of customs and moral codes, and individuation symptomatic of anomie. Similarly, in Rome, during the period of the fall of the Republic there was a period of anomie, and suicide rates greatly increased.

We know that Europe during the Middle Ages was characterized by stability of social organization, and there was very little suicide, while during the Renaissance, again characterized by individuation and normative dissensus, rates of suicide greatly increased. Similarly, rates of suicide have markedly increased in contemporary urban civilization over the previously rural-based society.[31]

In the United States, the suicide rates seem to fluctuate as social integration fluctuates. During four great periods of economic crisis—1908, 1923, 1929–33, and 1937—suicide rates, especially among white males (though not females) increased. During the Great Depression, suicide rates among white men almost doubled as compared to the previous low period.[32] During periods of war (World War I, World War II, and the Korean War), suicide rates in the United States fell appreciably, indicating firmer, more stable social organization.

Statistics consistently bear out the proposition that suicide declines as social integration increases. On almost every social characteristic, more integrated groups invariably have lower rates of suicide than do the less integrated. (1) The Catholic rate of suicide is noticeably less than the Protestant or Jewish rates. One Protestant faith which has an even lower rate of suicide than do Catholics is the Mormons. The reason for the lower Mormon rate is the well-organized community surrounding this religion, giving members a feeling of belonging. The reason for the higher rates among Protestants in general is the greater emphasis upon individual conscience inherent in that faith, while Catholicism is characterized by high organization, control of thought due to Church law, and access to the confessional as a relief for feelings of guilt. (2) Married indi-

TABLE 8-1   Suicide and social disorganization (correlation of social factors)

The Social Situation	Type of Social Organization	Prevalent Attitudes	Amount of Suicide
Greece before decline	Stable	State more important than individual	Moderate
Greece: decline of power	Confusion of customs and moral codes	Individual	Greatly increased
Rome before fall of the Republic	Stable	State more important than individual	Moderate
Rome: period of fall of the Republic	Confusion of customs and moral codes	Individual	Greatly increased
Middle Ages	Stable	Individual belonged to God	Very little
Temporary Crisis in the Middle Ages, as plagues, harassing of witches, etc.	Conflict, inability to control the situation		Increase in the groups involved
Renaissance	Confusion of customs and moral codes	Individual	Greatly increased
Preliterate villages	Stable	Social needs supersede individual needs	Very little
Orient (until recently)	Stable	Social needs supersede individual needs	Very little, except when dictated by social custom
Contemporary cities	Confusion of customs and moral codes	Individual	High suicide rates
Religious communities	Stable	Individual belongs to god, social needs take precedence	Very little
Rural communities	Stable	Tendency towards attitudes of the religious community	Very little

SOURCE: Ruth S. Cavan, *Suicide* (Chicago: University of Chicago Press, 1928), p. 106.

viduals have less tendency to commit suicide than do the divorced, widowed, and unmarried. Childless families have a greater tendency toward suicide than established families with children. It seems reasonable to conclude that married people have a stronger social organizational context than do unmarried people. Non-married groups are by contrast anomic. (3) Male rates are higher than female rates, except among adolescents from 15 to 19 years of age, when female rates are higher than male suicide rates. This may be traced to the greater individual responsibility placed upon men, and greater subculturalization among women than men, although statistics may merely reflect greater success at suicide among males. (4) Old people (55 and over) are more often successful at suicide than young people. The higher suicide may reflect the low integration of old people, who have lost contact with family, whose integration into work groups may wane, and whose group contacts may be weak and purposeless. (5) Whites have higher rates than blacks. However, blacks in the North have higher rates than blacks in the South. In both cases, it seems likely that suicide is associated with low integration. Some studies have indicated a higher degree of subcultural integration among blacks, which integration declines as they move from the South to the North. (6) There have always been higher rates in urban than in rural areas. (7) The high rates of suicide in poorer sections of the city reflect instability and disorganization rather than poverty *per se*. Although rates of suicide are high in the poor areas—the zone of transition and central business district—so is the heterogeneity and disorganization of these zones. If neighborhood organization could be held constant, the wealthier neighborhoods could possibly be higher in rates of suicide.

SOCIAL STRUCTURE AND SUICIDE

Although suicide appears to have a relation to larger social structure, the relation is a confusing one. Suicide appears to be lower in cohesive groups such as countries at war, Catholics, married people, and females. On the other hand, it appears to increase as countries become industrialized, and thus, in Durkheim's sense "organically solidary." Suicide seems to be prevalent among both the very poor and the very rich and less so among the moderately wealthy. Some hypotheses about social structure and suicide might be proposed to explain these anomalies. The more highly industrialized countries become, the less the cohesion of subgroups and the less the number of cohesive subgroups; thus, the greater the suicide. Within the more suicide-prone, industrialized countries, the individuals most inclined toward suicide are those most isolated and/or those for whom rejection has occurred suddenly. Of course, individuals suddenly excluded from intimate groups (family, church, community) are likely candidates for suicide. We would find individuals who are socio-economically very mobile, either upward or downward, in the category of suicide-prone persons. A sudden rise to wealth may lead to estrangement from intimate groups, just as sudden depression. Durkheim noted this in his explanation of anomic suicide, but stressed the individual's psychological feelings of "goallessness" and/or despair (anomie). Although these attitudes may figure into the explanation of suicide, the isolation and rejection with regard to intimate groups is the primary factor, because such group supports can compensate for such feelings of anomia. The individual must bear these feelings alone, and thus is directly exposed to the reality of his position in society's social structure.

Intergroup prejudice

Intergroup prejudice, although conceptually distinct from mental illness and suicide, can be traced to some of the same social factors. Social isolation appears to play a significant role in the development of prejudice, just as it does with mental illness and suicide. We cannot intelligently discuss prejudice, however, until we first define the concept.

CONCEPT

As popularly used, the term prejudice may be equivocally used to mean "good taste" or rational judgment. This kind of prejudice is not problematic, but in fact is probably necessary to the survival of society. The kind of concern here is a much more negative form. A clue to this negative meaning is found in the Latin origin of the term prejudice: *prejudicum* (a preceding judgment). In Latin, the *prejudicum* was a judicial examination in Rome held prior to a trial as a way of determining the social status of the would-be-litigants. This implies that the case would be decided not in terms of the merits of the case alone but on the basis of the ascribed characteristics of the litigants. The term prejudice today is defined differently by different authors, but all are definitions related to the word's origin.

Several authors have defined prejudice basically as an unmodifiable attitude. Ackerman and Jahoda define prejudice as a categorical generalization based on inadequate data, without regard for individual differences, fulfilling a specific irrational function for the bearer.[33] Allport and Kramer define prejudice as a pre-existing attitude so strong and inflexible that it seriously distorts perception and judgment.[34] Simpson and Yinger define prejudice as "an emotional, rigid attitude toward a group of people."[35] Two writers have focused on intergroup conflict or value difference in their definition of prejudice. Robin Williams, Jr., defines prejudice as negative attitude toward groups one has contact with based on value differences.[36] Similarly, Oliver Cox defines prejudice as a social attitude propagated among the public by an exploiting class for the purpose of stigmatizing some group as inferior so that that group may be exploited.[37]

TYPOLOGY

In the various definitions discussed above there are two basic ways of defining prejudice. In the first sense, a person is prejudiced against some group because he holds some value which he fears that group might destroy. For instance, a landlord may fear that if minority groups live in his dwellings, members of the majority group would move out and thus he would lose money. He may himself live in an integrated neighborhood, and thus he is prejudiced in one sense but not in another. In the second sense of the term prejudice, a person might hold general attitudes about minority groups or one particular minority group which are based on no particular value difference, which are rigid and unchanging, and which are based on inadequate data. It is this second type of prejudice which will be of concern in the following discussion. This form is far more problematic than value-based prejudice, insofar as it is rigid and unchanging.

Authoritarian personality   The second form of prejudice is particularly relevant to our frame of analysis because it has been linked with a personality syndrome called the authoritarian personality, and the authoritarian personality as it is described in the literature has many of the markings of contracultural overconformity. The study of the authoritarian personality was begun after World War II by Frenkel-Brunswik and Sanford,[38] in order to discover what type of personality was conducive to the anti-Semitism that had been so much a part of the Nazi movement in Germany. The authors applied an anonymous scale on anti-Semitism to 24 university of California men and 76 women. Eight women who scored highest in anti-Semitism and the eight who scored lowest were then interviewed at length. Among the many characteristics which were linked to anti-Semitism, two were outstanding: a kind of philistine conformity to convention, and a sense of social isolation. All of the eight girls high in anti-Semitism said they liked their parents, and subscribed to statements indicating obedience to authority, were conservative, and were from socially mobile, ethnocentric families. They also showed a great deal of "social anxiety." Those high in anti-Semitism were found to have a conformist, rigid attitude toward middle-class standards.

Studies of correlates of authoritarianism corroborated the idea of contracultural overconformity. The F-scale (authoritarian) has been correlated with numerous variables. Authoritarianism has been found inversely correlated with age; that is, older people are more inclined toward authoritarianism. It has been found inversely correlated with education: the more the education the less the authoritarianism. It has also been found highly correlated with anomia, which Srole defined as a sense of self-to-other belongingness.[39]

These findings seem to indicate that, in accord with our framework, the authoritarian personality is more prevalent among the old and less educated, both of which tend to be conservative and conventional groups, and among those who feel isolated and alone. Other studies focusing particularly on social class and social mobility amplify this exclusion image of the prejudiced person. Prejudice has been found strongly related to downward social mobility.[40] Authoritarian personality is found to be particularly prevalent among lower-class people.[41] These two findings lend further evidence that prejudiced people are isolated from group contacts because group isolation is directly related to downward social mobility and inversely to socio-economic status.

What conclusions can be made about prejudice as compared to other problems discussed in this chapter? Like both mental disorder and suicide, it apparently is related to isolation and rejection or the fear of isolation and rejection. The prejudiced person overconforms to what he perceives as the conventional norm of group superiority and the defense of middle-class values. Are prejudiced people more often neurotic or psychotic than others? Apparently not. The F-scale was applied to a group of patients in a mental hospital and the scores were in the middle range. It is quite conceivable that prejudice may be "functional" for personality in the sense that through projection the individual can ward off guilt over failure and reduce anxiety. This may explain the apparent rigidity of prejudice. Without prejudice, the prejudiced person might otherwise suffer psychotic breakdown. However, if this projection of guilt onto minority groups becomes extreme, breakdown may occur in the form of paranoia. Thus, as compared to the prejudiced personality, mental disorder and suicide involve a failure to project guilt and anxiety onto out-groups.

Drug and alcohol abuse

As indicated in Chapter 7, there is some doubt as to whether drug and alcohol abuse represent true retreatist problems. In Chapter 7, it was shown that with respect to subgroup participation, the drug addict and inebriate may in fact be calculative or innovative rather than retreatistic, but that Merton's portrayal of these two problems as retreatistic *vis-a-vis* larger society was probably accurate. However, the concept of the calculative inebriate or drug user is still open to question. There is some evidence that drug users and inebriates form practically no group affiliations. While in Chapter 7, we have examined the group context of certain types of drug addicts and inebriates (which was portrayed as very unstable and loose in structure), in the foregoing pages we shall shift the emphasis to the evidence that drug users and inebriates lack group contacts. In the final analysis, we shall be able to rank-order these two forms of deviancy as somewhere between mental disorder and the juvenile "near group" adaptation.

If the organization of modern American society were to be described as approaching the "organic" or "pluralistic" ideal, we can see a framework for the prediction of changing forms of deviancy. In the above framework, innovation in Merton's sense should be the predominant pattern of deviancy. However, we should also predict an increase in "ritualist" and "retreatist" forms of deviancy. In Merton's theory, these modes of adaptation include such phenomena as drug addiction, inebriety, mental disorder, and suicide. We would expect these patterns to be increasingly prevalent in modern industrial society, based upon the theoretical framework. But how can they be explained in the light of the apparent cohesiveness of pluralistic society? Although it is necessary to examine each disorder separately to answer this question, in general it can be shown that these disorders are those of "outsiders"—those who do not fit into the industrial division of labor or those who feel estranged from that system. These are people who perceive society at large as unfair, unjust, and coercive, who feel alienated from it, and resort to either the expedient of unwilling conformity (ritualism), as in some neurotic disorders, or, who may withdraw entirely from the system (retreatism), becoming "critics-at-large."

There is reasonable validity to the argument that drug abuse as a form of "deviancy" is largely created by our legal system.[42] Lindesmith and Gagnon, have shown that the various narcotic substances outlawed in the United States—especially the opiates, marihuana, peyote, and the like—are legal in other countries and in fact were legal in the past in the U.S. "There seems little reason to doubt that, in terms of the available definitions of deviant behavior, a substantial part of marihuana and opiate use in the world today cannot be viewed as deviant behavior."[43] Lindesmith and Gagnon even argue that this may jeopardize Merton's anomie theory: "Since the theory of anomie is proposed as a theory of deviance, and since some drug use is not deviant, the theory can hardly be relevant to the nondeviant portion."[44]

In answer to this criticism, two points may be made. First, these categories of drugs are defined today in various Western societies, including our own, as deviance, and that definition may very well be appropriate in terms of present-day society. Second, and probably more important, the form itself may not be defined by individuals within a society as deviant; however, in terms of our frame of analysis, their behavior and beliefs may reflect deviance. For example, in the case of ritualism, if individuals will confess that they have not been able to achieve their goals and that they have dampened their aspirations, we can categorize their behavior as ritualistic, whether or not they think of themselves as "deviant."

In the United States, the use, possession, and sale of certain forms of drugs have been defined as illegal. These drugs can best be categorized as addictive *versus* nonaddictive drugs. It is here that a distinction can be made between ritualistic and retreatistic drug use. There is ample evidence that marihuana, peyote, LSD, and other hallucinogenics are non-addictive drugs, while primary addictive drugs include opium and opium derivatives: morphine and heroin. One may deduce that the marihuana user may take marihuana for the purpose of release of tension, or experience of pleasure, as a means of adaptation to limited goal attainment. By contrast, the addictive drug-user makes a commitment to nonadaptation. Thus the addictive drug-user makes certain retreatist commitments. These are seen in the process of becoming an addict. A person must first take an addictive drug, experience withdrawal distress, seek the drug for relief, take more, experience relief, and, lastly, conceive of himself as an addict.[45] The initial motivation for taking a drug may be an escapist motive. Finestone has argued that the "kick" is a continuing motive of the drug addict whose whole life style is dominated by a quest for unusual existential pleasures such as abnormal sexuality, progressive jazz, and, of course, heroin.[46] This orientation toward the "kick" is in a sense retreatist in that it implies a rejection of conventional values of work, success orientation, rationality, and the like. The drug addict is escaping from the world of work into a world of the immediate impulse. It has been shown that one of the greatest difficulties of drug addicts in kicking the habit is that even after treatment or therapy, the addict may experience the frustrations of everyday life of work or unemployment as a kind of "withdrawal distress" thus triggering a need for drugs, which is very strong conditioned response.

Lindesmith and Gagnon pose still other arguments which are problematic for Merton's anomie theory. They argue basically that access to drugs rather than anomie explains differentials in rates of drug use. They find that during the last century, drug use was high among "respectable females" and low among the young and the urban, and Negro slum dwellers, while the reverse is true today. They posit that this change is not due to changes in rates of anomie but basically due to the fact that legislation has made the opiates illegal, closing all access to the drugs to all but those who have access to illegal means.

> The general nature of the addicted population of any nation can be most easily predicted from a knowledge of the type of control policy in use. Control by prohibition and police suppression seems to be regularly associated with a concentration of addiction among young, urban males of the lower or criminal classes who also have the easiest access to illicit sources of supply.[47]

Lindesmith and Gagnon cite evidence that shows doctors to be high in addiction, and argue that this is still further evidence in favor of the access-availability hypothesis. They further argue, in contrast to the "double failure hypothesis" and the idea of retreatism as applied to drug addiction, that the drug addict must steal a great deal in order to sustain his habit and therefore is actively involved in crime. "As the drug is continued after the initial trial, it is used progressively less for its euphoric effect, which diminishes and virtually disappears, and more and more for the purpose of staving off withdrawal symptoms."[48]

These criticisms can be met, we believe, by our previous analysis. We have argued that those most inclined toward retreatism are those who are "outsiders" who cannot find a place in our industrial system or cannot gain entry into that system. What groups are these? Today we are primarily referring to the urban slum Negro and to youth in general. It is interesting to note that in the last century the major group in this regard was "respectable females" who were bound by custom and tradition to a traditional domestic role, and that it was not until the 1920's, with the Woman's Suffrage movement, that women gained entry into the occupational system. By contrast, in the past century, educational requirements for most jobs were not high, thus making for easy entry into the occupational system by youth and at least for access to manual labor employment by Negroes. Today, however, with a highly complex technology, high school education (an exception during the last century) is a bare minimum to qualify for employment, and college is increasingly becoming required for many jobs. Thus, we find that the two groups who are lacking in education, youth and urban Negroes, are the ones who do not gain entry into the system. The basis for anomie has in fact changed during the last century. As for physicians, one can fairly well concede that their addiction cannot be traced to anomie, as they are highly successful group. However, it should be added that they are nearly always discussed as a highly extraordinary group and that certainly availability of drugs cannot be discounted entirely as an important factor in addiction.

Finally, it should be pointed out that drug addicts may procure money through other means than traditional theft: burglary, larceny, robbery, and so on. Finestone has pointed out that drug addicts reject violent means and prefer the use of wit in obtaining money. Their major source of money is via the role of pimp, or through confidence activities. It should be added that studies have not substantiated the belief that drug addicts are responsible for even a minority of crimes against property. The hypothesis that drug addiction is for the most part a retreatist mode of adaptation therefore remains worthy of inquiry. If the drug user has euphoria or escape as an objective of his drug use, we have an operational form of deviancy. There is reason to believe that drug addicts are "outsiders" who do not maintain legitimate employment nor do they systematically engage in deviant "occupations," but they gain the money necessary to maintaining their habit through dependency on some employed person, as in the role of pimps.

INEBRIETY, ALCOHOLISM, AND RETREATISM

Drunkenness and excessive social drinking are prevalent in American society. Estimates of the number of alcoholics in the United States range all the way from less than 750,000 to more than 6,000,000. Actually, this disagreement may be one of classification—that is, what constitutes an alcoholic as opposed to a "social drinker." However, there is no doubt that the use of alcohol is highly prevalent in American society. This holds true when one examines police statistics on drunkenness. Two million arrests in 1965—one of every three arrests in America—were for the offense of public drunkenness.[49]

In trying to reach fairly exact figures, Jellinek has worked out a formula which takes into consideration several different factors: ". . . the number of deaths from cirrhosis of the liver, admissions to mental hospitals of alcoholic psychotics, arrests for drunkenness, admissions to general hospitals for diseases associated with chronic alcoholism, reports of deaths from alcohol, and so on."[50] Based on experience carefully weighted against limited field surveys, this formula would indicate that there are between four and five million alcoholics in the United States.

TYPES OF ALCOHOLIC DRINKING

There is a tremendous variability as to what constitutes problem drinking and what constitutes alcoholism, as pointed out above. Part of this problem is due to the fact that drinking behavior may progress through stages of progressive seriousness. In fact it is estimated that alcoholism in our culture typically evolves over a period of 15 to 20 years of excessive drinking for its full development.[51]

Retreatism   We will begin with the most severe category of drunkenness: alcoholism. Alcoholism traditionally has been portrayed in terms much akin to Merton's "retreatism"—namely, in terms of deterioration of social relationships, isolation, and failure and consequent withdrawal:

> The repeated allusions in the clinical literature to oral dependence, frustrated dependency strivings, and deep unconscious conflict over the gratification of dependency needs suggest, in the concepts of Parsons, a fundamentally ambivalent motivational structure in which the "alienation component" is dominant and the underlying motivation is one of "a need to avoid giving way to the dependency need at almost any cost." Coupled with a long-run disposition to passivity, this points to the pattern of "withdrawal" which, in Parson's paradigm, is the motivational equivalent of Merton's retreatism.[52]

Generally, alcoholism is defined in terms of escapism from life's problems and responsibilities, again indicative of retreatism. The following definition is representative:

> An alcoholic may be described as a person who is unable to have a satisfying life without the use of alcohol; the person who is unable to face the demands or responsibilities of life without an increasing dependency on alcohol; as the person who is basically insecure and unhappy, seeking to relieve the pain of living through the use of alcohol.[53]

Ritualism   Ritualism, as discussed here, does not refer to the ritualistic consumption of alcohol, as in Christian Communion, drinking bouts in primitive societies, and the like. Rather, ritualism here refers to the use of alcohol as a means of conformity and adjustment to a situation of frustration of success goal-aspirations. This is differentiated from retreatist and alcoholic drinking in that it does not ordinarily interfere with one's social relationships or work performance, and in fact may facilitate such roles. This is generally referred to as "social drinking" or even "excessive social drinking" depending primarily upon the extent of such drinking behavior. However, such drinking can easily shade in the direction of retreatist behavior, for example, if an individual begins to show up at work or at important social gatherings under the influence of alcohol. Nor does our analysis imply that release of anxiety or tension or inhibition is the only motivation for alcohol consumption. Some people drink because they like the taste of certain alcoholic beverages, perhaps in conjunction with appropriate food, even though avoiding if possible the feeling of drunkenness. Others may drink because of social pressure, even though not enjoying the taste of alcohol and perhaps intensely disliking alcoholism. If drinking is done for purposes other than escape or tension release, in fact if for ritual purposes, drinking behavior in Merton's scheme may be compatible with a conformist adaptation.

Because neither ritualist nor conformist drinking are of great concern publically, the most important distinction can be made between social drinking and alcoholism (the ritualist *versus* the retreatist adaptation). Once again (as in the distinction between normal and contracultural criminality), the distinction is made in terms of dysfunctionality of a person's behavior in our industrial system. In a complex industrial society, each person is assigned many roles, in his home and family, in his occupation, and in the community. Because our society is characterized by specialization and a high level of interdependence, we depend upon each individual to fulfill his many roles and responsibilities for the society to maintain its structure and organization. This is in contrast to the simple society where such interdependence is much less (as in the humorous caricature of the "town drunk"), and therefore drunkenness on the part of the individual does not leave a harmful affect on the social structure. When an individual becomes an alcoholic in a complex society, he can no longer properly fulfill his roles, and his home as well as the society becomes disorganized. Therefore it can be shown that there is a relationship between alcoholism and both personal dependency, which can better be termed idiosyncratic susceptability, and stage of societal development.

TABLE 8-2 Drinking susceptibility and level of society

LEVEL OF SOCIETY	IDIOSYNCRATIC SUSCEPTIBILITY	
	Strong	*Weak*
Simple	"Town drunk"	Friendly fellow
Complex	Alcoholic	Social drinker

Summary and conclusion

Several different social problems have been discussed in terms of the same basic underlying causes: isolation from group affiliations, parental coerciveness, and socio-economic standing. Behaviorally, these disorders were viewed in terms of overconformity and retreatism as varying results of these situational factors. We would expect that in all of these forms of deviancy, including mental disorder, suicide, prejudice, and drug and alcohol abuse, there is a background of parental coercion, rejection or isolation from meaningful group affiliations, and possibly socio-economic failure or its anticipation.

Though these problems may well have the same underlying causes, they are not synonymous adaptations. They may be understood as adaptations varying with the degree of parental coerciveness, of isolation, and of socio-economic failure. We may rank-order these disorders in terms of the degree of severity of these conditions. Neurosis and prejudice probably occur under conditions of the least coerciveness, isolation, and failure of the problems discussed here. Neurotics and prejudiced people probably have marginal group ties, maintain a position of limited occupational success, and have suffered only mildly coercive parental backgrounds. These may be viewed as ritualist adaptations and mild overconformity to conventional values.

Although excessive social drinking and the use of non-addicting drugs may well be conformative adaptation, the use of addicting drugs and addiction to alcohol are probably more retreatistic adaptations, implying greater coerciveness of parental backgrounds, greater isolation, and more limited occupational opportunity. In a sense, there is overconformity in these adaptations. The alcoholic and the drug addict do not attempt to knock down barriers to success either through legitimate of illegitimate means. Even more likely, however, drug addicts and alcoholics at one time may have attempted to conform to parental expectations and having failed, may have resorted to alcohol or drugs as a form of guilt neutralization.

We should expect most parental coercion, and/or isolation, and/or socio-economic failure in the case of the psychotic, and psychosis may be viewed as an extreme form of retreatism and overconformity. The psychotic may not conform to public standards, but in a twisted way may indeed conform to parental expectations, say through regression to a childhood period of acceptance. Psychosis may also be the outcome of a prolonged period of striving to conform to parental standards.

Suicide differs from all of these problems insofar as it results from a sudden change in the three conditions specified, parental coercion, isolation, or failure. Although admittedly our framework is very tentative and speculative, it can serve as a point of departure for further inquiry.

Conclusion: The goal of social transition

9

The task of this text has been to show a unity between general sociological theory and the study of social disorganization and deviant behavior. In Chapters 1 and 2, and outline was presented of the major images of society that are based upon large-scale theories of major social thinkers of the past and present. The outcome of this analysis was a constructive typology which incorporated most of these major images of society into one scheme. Five basic types of social organization were suggested: atomistic or communal society, multipartite or anomic society, pluralistic or democratic society, oligarchic society, and totalitarian society. Both the communal and totalitarian extremes could be eliminated for purposes of understanding the present-day large-scale societies of the West. In Chapter 3, early and recent theories of disorganization were discussed and the disorganization school was historically linked to the multipartite view of society. Though the term "disorganization" has passed from vogue because of heavy criticism, similar theoretical assumptions appear in current-day anomie and mass society theory.

This prevailing "gesellschaft" view of modern social organization found in current deviancy theory exists without any apparent concern or interest in alternative images of social organization.

Notes for this chapter are on pages 391–392.

For instance, some nondeviancy writers insist that modern society is oligarchic in organizational structure, others insist it is pluralistic. Even if it could be proven that American society is purely anomic, the examination of alternative images would yield insight as to the nature of other societies, subsystems within American society, and perhaps future organizational phases of American society.

In Chapter 4, there was a shift in focus away from the organization of society to the nature of deviancy. Several different schemes for classifying deviancy were examined and a constructive typology was developed using Merton's and Cavan's types as primary categories for deviancy analysis. A tentative empirical rank-ordering of deviant acts based on survey results was presented.

In Chapter 5, various well-known theories of deviancy are examined. These theories, as well as the disorganization theories of Chapter 3, are examined in the light of existing incidence, trend, and cross-cultural data on deviancy. These data indicate, on the one hand, that the belief that modernization brings violence and group disintegration appears to be in error. Violence appears to be declining in the modern West as a whole as compared to the transitional societies of Latin America. On the other hand, innovative acts appear to be increasing in prevalence throughout all sectors of society. We may foresee a decline in the trend as society approaches the ideal of pluralism exemplified by Scandinavian countries. Pluralism is not without its disadvantages. Apparently, suicide, mental disorder, and other retreatist modes of behavior are more problematic in pluralistic countries than in the less stable capitalist or transitional societies. As to the state of American society, the conclusion of Chapter 5 is that it is comparatively stable; however, it is neither purely anomic nor pluralistic, but has characteristics of both, implying that the United States is indeed a society in transition. Organizational analysis can tell us something about the goal of that transition, which is the topic of this chapter.

In Chapter 5, we have also attempted to cast doubt upon a number of deviancy theories. For example, theories that trace deviancy to poverty or relative poverty are questioned by our finding that wealthy countries apparently have higher rates of certain forms of deviancy, such as theft and suicide. Also, new field data highlight the extensiveness of middle-class involvement in certain forms of deviancy, such as white-collar crime. Our analysis would be vacantly negative and incomplete if it extended only to questioning old theories.

In Chapters 6 to 8, a new theory of deviancy is developed, termed the theory of differential organizational participation. Borrowing some knowledge from the theory of political pluralism, we propose that in a society such as our own, individuals are not related directly to the "external system" of social organization but are related indirectly through the medium of intermediary groups. That is, it is inaccurate to portray the deviant as one who by himself meditates about the corruptness of society and consequently plots for himself a career in crime. Rather, these beliefs and rationalizations are learned through contact with other deviants.

This accepted, the next question one must answer is: Where in the social structure do we find such deviant groups which provide such antisocial beliefs and careers? Traditional theories would point an accusing finger at the inner-city slum. Such groups would arise as a result of frustration and despair. However, a such simple answer, though grounded in common sense as well as in the psychological theory of frustration-aggression, lack the benefit of the study of social organization. Rephrasing the question in sociological terms: What is the nature of deviant group organization, under what conditions does such group organization flourish, and where in the social structure of larger society do we find such groups? For the answers we may look to the theory of complex or formal organizations.

Analysis of a variety of typologies of complex organization results in a constructive typology of three basic organizational types: coercive, normative, and utilitarian. These three bear a striking similarity to the three general organizational types discovered in Chapter 2: oligarchic, pluralistic, and anomic. Also, parallel forms of behavior are manifest. The general deviancy typology of retreatism-ritualism, conformity, innovation-rebellion is paralleled by the complex organizational counterpart of alienative, moral, and calculative behavior.

In brief, we should expect most innovation-rebellion forms of deviancy to occur in utilitarian settings, while ritualist-retreat adaptation would be situated in coercive settings. In a capitalist-industrial society, utilitarian group settings occur at all socioeconomic levels; thus, we might expect crime and delinquency in various forms at all socio-economic levels. True coercive settings are not prevalent in a society such as ours, but where they exist there is evidence of ritualist and retreatist modes of behavior.

While Chapter 6 was concerned with deviancy that developed in formal, institutional, "legitimate" group settings, Chapter 7 applied the same group theory to informal or noninstitutional groups. The lesson of Chapter 6 is that most forms of criminal deviancy would be expected to arise from utilitarian-anomic group settings. We find in Chapter 7 that the trend in crime theory has been away from the normative conception of the criminal and juvenile gang toward the idea that such groups are loosely organized, anomic, "near groups." Our theoretical framework suggests this trend.

In Chapter 8, there is a shift in emphasis away from group organized forms of deviancy to types of deviancy that result from isolation. The isolated individual is directly related to larger social organization. He must face alone the sometimes cruel consequences of his position in the stratification system of larger society. Stratification has direct bearing on these problems. We should expect that insofar as a problem is unshared or is that of an isolated individual, its prevalence would be greatest in the most underprivileged sectors of society. This applies to mental disorder, alcoholism, drug addiction, and prejudice behavior. Suicide, though a product of isolation and rejection, may violate this principle, because it results largely from sudden socio-economic and interpersonal disruption, which may be just as prevalent in the upper as lower class. But as a general statement, all of these retreatist problems are somehow tied to larger social structure rather than to intermediary group, and thus there is less confounding of explanation by these groups and explanations can be more clear-cut and simplified.

So far in our analysis there has been little if any attention to social amelioration, to the "curing" of social problems. In fact, we have stated that some problems of deviancy can actually be functional in leading to necessary and beneficial reforms. However, a *laissez-faire* attitude toward deviancy is not the intent of this point. Deviancy is often painful and undesirable for both the deviants and possible victims. What is not suggested is ways of controlling deviancy *per se,* for particular forms of deviancy are merely symptoms of social maladjustment. What is suggested is the direction of social change. At each level of social organization, society-at-large, complex organization, informal group, and the like, we may propose the ideal that may be striven for through responsible action. There is no proof to the theory that utopian organization is inevitable. Therefore, it is reasonable to suggest directions for leadership effort. So in the foregoing chapter, we shall point to the direction of change for achievement of "ideal" organization at various social levels. The only validity for these suggestions, however, is that which arises from the study of social theory and current society. What we say remains to be tested and should provide a foundation for action research.

Utopian society

Although the nature of utopian society has always been a favorite topic of novelists, sociologists have retreated from utopian analysis. This reluctance to venture an opinion as to what is the ideal society is perhaps based on the anti-scientific, value-laden nature of the task. This sociological reticence is unfortunate, however, because sociologists, with their knowledge of comparative social organization, are probably in the best position to discuss utopian society. Perhaps social scientists view utopian analysis as silly and naive, but this view is questionable, especially for those who study social problems, deviancy, and social disorganization. Our concept of social problems, deviancy, and social disorganization depends very heavily upon what our concept of ideal or utopian society is. For instance, if utopian society involves absolute sexual freedom, then many forms of sex deviancy would not be defined as such.

CONCEPTS OF UTOPIA

If we want to talk about the concept of utopia, we must turn to literature.

As early as the fifth century B.C., Plato developed his concept of the ideal state in *The Republic*.[1] In Plato's ideal state, society would be divided into three quasi-castes: the elder Philosopher-Guardians, the governing body who rule the state; the Auxiliaries, who provide military protection for the state; and the Workers, the husbandmen and other providers of food, clothing, and other useful materials. Each class would do its own business without interfering with the tasks of the other classes. All citizens would be educated to music and gymnastics, and assignment to one of the three classes would be dependent upon performance in these two capacities.

Plato's ideal state depended upon abolition of the family and socialization of all children as wards of the state. By contrast, in Sir Thomas More's *Utopia,* the family was the basic unit of the state.[2] First published in 1516, Utopia was written in response to social injustices of the time of Henry VII in England. Utopia — a small, isolated island kingdom founded by King Utopus — was a communal society in which princes were representatives of patriarchial, elected family headmen. Thus, utopia was a pure democracy in which all goods were communally owned and in which every citizen worked. Sir Thomas proposed that the result would be the elimination of vice and violence; the establishment of religious toleration; and the eradication of capital punishment for crime in favor of slavery.

While Plato's and More's ideal societies may have been utopian concepts for their time, in terms of contemporary society and our theoretical analysis, they seem like provincial folk societies whose major limitations include lack of adaptability to external change, lack of integration with other societies, and repression of individual differences and freedom. Perhaps, because of this earlier conception of utopia, present-day utopian novels have been satirical and negatively pessimistic about the nature of such "ideal societies." Probably the most widely read of these utopian novels are Huxley's *Brave New World*[3] and Orwell's *1984.*[4]

Huxley portrays a world existing "632 after Ford." In *Brave New World,* science governs man; human beings are mass-produced in hatcheries, with large groups of identical human beings coming from a single egg to perform identical work functions. As in Plato's *Republic,* the family has been eliminated, art is stifled completely, religion is restrained, and humanistic aspects of culture are destroyed, leaving room only for a domination of science.

Like Huxley, Orwell paints a vision of a future society dominated by a totalitarian state, (in this case Big Brother), in which there are no laws to obey but there is total control of thoughts through television and other means of surveillance over citizen action and public statement.

From reading Huxley and Orwell, one gets the definite impression that "utopia" is something to be avoided at all costs. The opposite impression is given when one reads B. F. Skinner's *Walden Two.*[5] Skinner, one of the leading exponents of behavioral psychology, developed a conception of a utopian community whose code of ethics is based on the science of human behavior. As in Plato's *Republic* there are three classes—Planners, Managers, and Workers—to which Skinner adds a fourth: Scientists. The Planners direct behavior, based upon scientific principles of human behavior, which principles are subject to change through experimentation. Planners are not elected, but earn their positions through demonstrating their merit, as in a merit bureaucratic system. Planners, however, do not become despotic because wealth is divided equally and all are required to perform some physical labor, and consequently status and power differentials between leader and follower are not great. Also as in Plato's *Republic,* children are raised in nurseries, but parents are allowed to visit their children. As result of this planning, crime, mental disorder, suicide and other social problems are eliminated insofar as neurotic emotions of excessive anger, jealousy, deprivation, and the like are eliminated through self-control conditioning and minimization of situational frustration. In this atmosphere, art, music, literature and other intellectual pursuits flourish, although there is no leisure class.

Though one may take issue with particular aspects of Skinner's scheme, Skinner's appears to be the most carefully contrived ideal society. Interestingly, what Skinner developed bears close resemblance to a current-day existing, successful experimental society, the kibbutzim of Israel. Sociologically, Skinner's scheme also suffers the limitations of the kibbutzim, which we shall examine shortly.

WHY UTOPIAN EXPERIMENTS FAIL

Communal experiments have been attempted again and again throughout history, but most have failed. From the point of view of our theoretical analysis, we can see why such experiments fail. Their social organization is not suitable for application to large-scale society, and the members of these groups refuse to follow the rigid regime required of members of these societies. When communalism is applied as a basis for large-scale society, it usually results in totalitarianism. National Socialism thrived in the anomic

Germany of its time primarily because it offered a return to *gemein-schaft*—to a communal form of existence. But without totalitarian central control, communalism, because it entails individual relation to society without intervening groups, would degenerate into war of all against all. Communist countries throughout the world rely upon dictatorial central control, the official ideology being that threats from capitalist countries make such control necessary. However, organizationally, it can be seen that such control is a requisite to stability when communalism is applied to large-scale society.

On the other hand, the prospect of "organic solidarity," "positivist society," "pluralism," and the like, which are large-scale counterparts of communal utopia in social theory, may not bring with it all the utopian benefits forseen by adherents. Durkheim, in his later writings, saw the need for community that was lacking in large-scale societies. One form of suicide prevalent in large-scale societies—egoistic suicide—he found traced to lack of integration of the victim into society, especially with respect to affective relations. In *The Division of Labor,* Durkheim did not deal with the diverse effects that accompany the division of labor, and in fact he dismissed these as only occurring in abnormal circumstances—the anomic division of labor. Only in *Suicide* does Durkheim see the necessity of communal life.

> What is needed, holds Durkheim, are new kinds of intermediary groups which can regulate the specialized occupational life of modern men. He advances a plan for the development of communal or corporate organization among people working in the same occupation and industries. Men in the same segment of the economy will understand each other's problems well enough to respond to them flexibly. They can establish a viable group life which can exercise effective moral control over all the participants on the basis of intimate knowledge. These occupational corporations were to be represented in a national assembly, with employers and employees each having a separate representation. The number of representatives for each was to be determined by the importance that public opinion assign to their group. The corporations are to be organized on a national basis, coextensive with the national development of the modern economy. They are to maintain carefully their independence of the state.[6]

This "utopian plan" was anti-utopian in the sense that there were no plausible mechanisms for instituting it. However, it was an answer to both the Marxian and the Comtean versions of utopia.

What Durkheim seems to have been attempting was a synthesis of Marxist and Comtean views.

We have been able to see in the years since Durkheim that this corporate community does not spring forth automatically, but we can see the present period as one of change. However, the focus of our analysis is not merely upon the results of change from folk to urban society, nor is it appropriate to categorize our society as mass society (even though there are some elements of mass society in our own), as our social organization is a really very cohesive one. The major change of our time is the development of communal organizations within our larger pluralistic organizational setting. Within our larger society, individuals who are most satisfied and least inclined toward suicide, mental disorder, and other retreatist pathologies are those who are tied to intermediary organizations. The family is one such organizational tie, in the broader sense of the term, but it is also important that the person be linked to larger groups.

Looking at the development of intermediary group life during the past century, it is evident that not all of these are "corporate groups." The first of these "communal reforms" were carried out by organized labor. Labor unions today provide a basis for consensus where no such community existed in the past. As C. W. Mills has pointed out, however, the vast majority of white-collar workers have no such occupational identification. Nevertheless, there is ample evidence that participation in voluntary organizations is directly related to socio-economic position.

Certainly it can be said that there are many categories of individuals in our society who are not integrated into communal group life: the chronically unemployed, the vagrant, the divorced, certain highly successful people whose success has cut them off from communal ties, and students. Social progress entails bringing the advantages of communal participation to these individuals. However, this does not necessarily involve corporate communities, as Durkheim stated. It has been shown in the case of the Japanese factory system that corporate communities are not always compatible with productivity and allocation of tasks according to ability. Corporate community might mean the destruction of job mobility, in that if individuals are paternalistically protected by the corporation, they are satisfied with their place in life and do not seek to expand their range of abilities. The problem, then is not providing corporate shelters for individuals but that of making various opportunity structures available to all persons through communal association.

In MacIver's terms, what is needed is the development of a full range of associations in congruence with the full range of interests and aptitudes. Presently, those groups most prone to anomia— students, unorganized intellectuals, the chronically unemployed, and the like—are those with no group association to represent their interest. It should be pointed out that such groups are emerging. In Los Angeles, for example, an organization for divorcees called "Parents Without Partners" has been somewhat successful in helping divorcees make a satisfactory adjustment. Alcoholics Anonymous for chronic drinkers and Synanon for drug addicts have reported success with those who seek communal membership. The emergence of student reform groups on college and universities through the country, while terrifying to members of the established adult community, are somewhat promising in the sense of providing the basis for the forthcoming organization of students. It was pointed out that during the now famed "revolt at Berkeley," there were no admissions to the Berkeley student medical center for psychiatric disorders.

In every case we have described, the organizations are just beginning to reach out and become a major interest-group, and it may be some time before it can be said that every interest finds its representation. In today's society, it is somewhat true that the individual with the dissident view is the one with no friends, no associations. However, those who do find communal association manage to counter anomia. Those who do not (and this may be a large percentage) may go on every day expressing dissident views and being rejected, or keeping such views private and thus feeling to some extent thwarted.

INTEGRATION OF COMMUNAL AND PLURALISTIC
SOCIETY IN ISRAEL

The lack of communal association is perhaps such a glaring need in modern society that possibly the only way the ideal society could be rapidly developed is through starting at the ground level, organizing society along lines of relatively complex division of labor, while at the same time providing for communal association for the members of society. This is to some extent what has happened in Israel. Israel is a country with relatively great occupational differentiation for a country of its size, and yet, it incorporates a system of communal association, including the kibbutzim, the workers' settlements, and a combination of the two groups called Moshar Shittufu. There are over 300 kibbutzim (collective agricultural settlements) in Israel as well as workers' settlements and combined kibbutzim and workers' settlements. While the kibbutzim represent only 5 per cent of the population, their importance exceeds their numbers as far as Israel is concerned. The ideals of the kibbutzim are those which brought Israel into being. The kibbutzim provide the most distinguished leaders of the country. Most important, they are the model for future Israel.[7]

The Israeli communes are an answer to the problems of loneliness and despair which accompany life in modern society. Although the kibbutzim are still autonomous agricultural units, there are tendencies in the direction of larger organization. We can predict specialization and division of labor to emerge between the kibbutzim as they serve a larger role in Israeli society. However, for purposes of describing what appears to be an emergent "ideal society," it should be helpful to describe life in the kibbutz and then to project how the kibbutzim may one day form a larger societal organization that incorporates both advantages of communal solidarity, on the one hand, and recriprocal organic solidarity, on the other hand.

The kibbutzim are collective agricultural settlements organized very closely around the paramount socialist axiom: "To each according to his needs; from each according to his abilities." The kibbutzim are organized structurally along lines very similar to those of most folk or communal societies. Kibbutzim are relatively small. All property is owned collectively. There is no exploitation of labor. All major decisions are made by the entire community in biweekly town meetings. Officials are democratically appointed to carry out policy determined at the meeting and to administer the various economic and social institutions of the kibbutz. Their tenure of office is brief (never more than three years), a feature that prevents the rise of a leadership caste, and an entrenched bureaucracy. There is a remarkable congruence between social norms and behavior of members of the kibbutzim. Although the kibbutzim oppose the introduction of industry into their economy, they have a diversified agriculture: dairy, field crops, vegetable gardens, fishery, fruit orchards, flocks, poultry, and fodder. Agriculture is also highly rationalized and mechanized, producing a prosperous agricultural economy.

Unlike folk people, however, the people of the kibbutzim are enlightened, intellectual, cosmopolitan:

> Kiryat Yedidim is not a village of peasants either in fact or in its self-image. On both scores the members of the kibbutz comprise a landed intelligentsia. In the fields one hears discussions not only of crops and machinery, but of books and music, of politics and literature. At the end of the working day, the interest of a chaver may turn to a class in English, a lecture in genetics, a chamber-music concert, a discussion of politics, a dramatic performance.[8]

Though the people of the kibbutz seek community and consensus as a primary value, they appear to have no desire to give up the values of a participant society which they brought with them from various parts of Europe. It is quite clear that their purposes is to develop a society which combines both:

> As a kibbutz, Kiryat Yedidim is not only an agricultural village. As a kibbutz it perceives itself as the vanguard of man's quest for the ideal society, part of the shock troops in the future social revolution. The kibbutz, together with the urban proletariat with whom it identifies, will—it is hoped—bring socialism and, ultimately, the classless society to the entire country. These political convictions, stemming from an avowedly Marxist ideology, have led Kiryat Yedidim to join with other kibbutzim of like mind in a large kibbutz federation. In turn, the Federation has joined with urban workers of similar political persuasion to form a political party.[9]

The general goal of the kibbutz movement in Israel appears to be the development of a true associational society. Such a society contrasts with American society primarily in that all individuals would be assured of membership in a communal group, which might also be an association representing the interest of that individual. In our own society, associations are usually not communal groups, but rather they are a loose collectivity of members who may never even see each other, let alone provide a basis for affectual relations with one another. While the reorganization of society along lines of the kibbutz would solve many of the problems of modern society, there is some evidence that certain "total institutional" aspects of the communes are undesirable to members. Crises are occurring in the kibbutzim, crises based primarily upon the desire for privacy.

Women, especially, are dissatisfied with the amount of work required of them in the commune, work from which they were supposedly liberated when put on an equal status with men. Many women are finding they are not happy being enamcipated from their own homes. The hard physical labor has been a strain on them. They feel insecure with their marriages since in the kibbutz these may be terminated when love is no longer present, and many women feel resentful because of separations from their children who are raised in nurseries in the kibbutz. Thus, there is once again a tendency toward establishing the family as a separate institution from economic life.

If the family becomes a separate institution, as it inevitably has in the evolution of society almost everywhere, we can expect that Israel may evolve closer to a true associational society rather than a complex of segmental communes. However, based upon the original design of the society, the essence of the complex merged with simple equilibrium might still be maintained.

TOWARD UTOPIA IN CONTEMPORARY SOCIETY

The model for utopia in contemporary society does not appear to be found either in primitive communal society or in contemporary pluralism. Both forms of social equilibrium produce a strain on the members of society. Communal poeple although grateful for the intimacy which community brings, suffer from restrictions on personal freedom. In pluralist society, personal freedom of choice is limitless but at the cost of loss of community affectionate ties. The ideal model for contemporary society would be a combination of both plural and communal extremes. Conceivably these are not incompatible, but can be incorporated within the same society. Thus, subgroups of society may be communally organized, but each subgroup could be integrated into a larger division of labor. Once agriculture becomes fairly automated, a community may become somewhat specialized without losing its autonomy and without defeating the principle that "everybody works" and the principle of collective ownership of property.

Another way of reducing strain would be to make communal cooperation voluntary, optional, and selective. A couple could, for example, raise their children in a cooperative nursery but establish a private dwelling to live in. Or some families, desirous of providing maximal emotional and intellectual stimulation for their children, may prefer to raise their children in a nuclear family setting, but may desire to participate in cooperative living, agriculture, health care, and the like. This flexibility is incorporated to some extent in some the utopias described above. Plato suggests the need for a leadership class of intelligentsia, as well as a military and a working class. Skinner gives a scientific class of planners a primary position in affecting necessary changes. The Israeli kibbutzim abide by a principle of the moral duty to perform manual labor, but members comprise a landed intelligentsia. But the direction of social change in these communal utopias is toward merging of communal and associational ideals.

Ideal organization of smaller institutions

It has been suggested that the framework developed in this text implies that the ideal society is one composed of democratically run "communal associations," themselves organized on a larger societal level based upon democratic government and interdependence of interests. In this section, based upon a survey of examples of such groups, a description of the ideal communal association within such societies will be given.

Etzioni's ideal organization appears to combine a pure and social normative compliance structure. This is ideal in the sense of adherence of followers, voluntary loyalty to authority, least use of coercive sanction, highest participation of members, and the like. For such organizations to be general to society presupposes, however, a certain level of societal development. It presupposes that it is not necessary to have institutions whose main purpose is to incarcarate or maintain custody for large masses of individuals—that is, coercive institutions. It presupposes either that industrial production is fully automated or that there is a form of collectivization of economic resources. The former is a solution of capitalist countries while the latter is the ideal of Communist countries. Thus, the ideal institution is one whose purpose is primarily the development of symbolic culture and allocation of symbolic rewards, but at the same time allocating acceptance and positive response by intimate group association. Present-day examples include some churches, some professional organizations, some trade unions, and some universities. Demographic trends indicate that more and more people are seeking and achieving occupations in such organizations. In addition, there is a significant trend toward "professionalization" in other areas of endeavor, for example, in police work, business, and industry. Thus, the ideal organization of the future can be constructed from present-day examples.

Although the domain of our analysis includes churches and universities, it would be well in this section to consider examples of organizational settings that deviate in that they are usually not normative in compliance structure (pluralistic, and the like). Usually labor unions are coercive or utilitarian settings; however, in Lipset, Trow and Coleman's study of the International Telegraphers Union we see a "deviant case" of pluralism, democracy in a labor union. While the traditional mental hospital is custodial and coercive in compliance structure, the therapeutic mental hospital, as Maxwell Jones describes it, offers new hope that mental patients can be most effectively treated in a normative setting. Although juvenile delinquents are usually treated in a custodial quasi-authoritarian manner, Shaw shows that in Red Hill School, delinquency can be effectively treated permissively and through democratic means. These suffice only as a few examples of countless new organizational settings, but serve well to illustrate the type of organizations our society might strive to develop in the future.

NORMATIVE ORIENTATION OF THE PRINTING TRADE

It has been shown that skilled, semi-skilled, and unskilled workers are controlled by utilitarian power, attracted by remunerative incentives, calculative in their involvement in work, and increasingly alienative in lower ranks (that is, unskilled workers). These orientations and relationships are in part due to the work setting of workers and in part traced to the nature of labor unionism.

The major theme of socialist thinking historically has been the exploitation of labor in industrial settings and the consequent alienation of labor. Blauner has clarified this Marxist theme by showing that alienation does not apply to all workers, but primarily unskilled workers and secondarily semi-skilled workers,[10] Blauner found the workers in an auto assembly plant (unskilled) alienated in four senses: powerlessness, meaninglessness, isolation, and self-estrangement. In the textile industry (semi-skilled workers) there was pervasive powerlessness and meaninglessness but the community atmosphere of the mill town in which the industry was studied permitted satisfaction with work in a situation where freedom, control, and self-expression was lacking, and providing a feeling of belongingness rather than isolation. By contrast, in the printing trades, there was no evidence of any forms of alienation, this lack being based upon a craft tradition and a high degree of worker control which provided a basis of job security, community integration, self-expression, and esteem. In addition to submitting to an alienating work setting, manual workers may also have to hold membership in an oligarchical labor union. Most labor unions have oligarchical rather than democratic leadership.

The International Telegraphers Union and the printing trade serves as an exception to the traditional pattern described above, and because it has been pointed out that the future of the labor market lies in skilled rather than unskilled or semiskilled labor, the ITU may serve as a model for the future of labor-management relations. In part, the current predominance of oligarchical labor unions may be due to the past history of crisis in labor-management relations. Huberman has shown that labor-management relations have gone through a three stage history: (1) the early period of prohibition, (2) a period of toleration by management, and (3) the present period of recognition by management.[11] In a period in which there is markedly reduced conflict between labor and management, the tightly-structured, oligarchical leadership is no longer needed to respond to crisis situations.

When we consider the power of the ITU, we see that there is no opportunity for management to exploit individual laborers nor, for that matter, union leaders. Neither management nor union administration is allowed direct control over men in the shop. Because of a high pay scale and a craft tradition in addition to social gratifications surrounding work, there is no evidence of alienation and workers are intrinsically rather than extrinsically oriented with regard to the rewards of work.

Lipset, Trow, and Coleman have described the organization of the ITU as democratic or pluralistic, characterized by the institutionalization of opposition in the structure of the union.[12] The ITU is unique in that it has a two-party system, active for 50 years. Its members are highly paid and exercise power, express ideas, and build potential opposition through a network of voluntary social organizations, both formal and informal groups, and an extravocational social system. It is these groups which provide the basis for democracy in the ITU for they mediate between workers and management (both union and business), providing a basis for "grass roots" support and/or opposition.

NORMATIVE ORGANIZATION IN A REFORM SCHOOL

The traditional juvenile correction facility has been hotly criticized by criminologists for aggravating the juvenile delinquency problem by providing a meeting place and training ground for future criminals and by subjecting youngsters to a coercive, hostile environment which will confirm attitudes of hatred and hostility toward legitimate society. Red Hill School, in England, is a striking exception to this pattern. This experimental school has proved highly successful in resocializing delinquents in a permissive, democratic setting.[13]

Red Hill School was founded in 1934 as a new approach to delinquency. It is a privately owned boarding school for the education and psychological treatment of maladjusted boys of high intelligence. The boys living there range from 11 to 16 years of age. The student enrollment is 55. The boys are referred to Red Hill by education authorities throughout the country and many have been through the juvenile courts or are on probation. Red Hill accepts only boys with intelligence quotients of 130 or higher. The problems of the boys are various. Some of the boys are neurotics, thieves, sexual deviants, habitual truants, and the like who have all been diagnosed as delinquent and maladjusted.

The staff at Red Hill includes 11 teachers, a matron and her assistant, a secretary, 13 custodial workers, and the director, the aforementioned Otto L. Shaw. There are nine governors of the school who have legal responsibility for the ownership and maintenance of the school. The boys are not kept in the school by means of force. If the boys absolutely do not want to stay at Red Hill after having the opportunity to talk to other boys and a counselor or members of the staff, they can be returned to the custody of their parents, relatives, or someone approved by the education authorities. These cases are very rare. Boys may also go to town any time or visit with parents and relatives many times during the year.

There is absolutely no corporal punishment at Red Hill. Social control and discipline is not absent, however, and it is through self-government that the boys learn the purpose of nondelinquent behavior. The major expression of self-government is the *community meeting*. This occurs every two weeks. Almost every boy serves on a committee. Examples include the Food and Hygiene, Sports, Social, Library, Maintenance and Decorations, Hobbies Council, and Music committees. Committee heads make up the community meeting. This form of government helps develop a sense of responsibility in the boys. Although adult staff members are present at the meetings and sometimes try to guide decisions in a proper direction without trying to appear superior, only the students enjoy voting power and once the community meeting has made a decision it can never be overruled by the staff. Thus, it is through establishing a democracy in miniature (pure normative power) that a successful method of handling delinquency has been developed:

> During the years, about 300 students have passed through the school. Six former pupils have died, and we have failed to keep contact with six others. Of the remainder, we regard as radically cured on a permanent basis, 67 per cent of the pupils. Twenty-one per cent have been improved. Two per cent have not really qualified for the label of improvement, but are certainly not failures. With 10 per cent of the children we have failed.[14]

This would seem to be an extremely low rate of failure when compared to that of the more traditional correctional center.

Two similar programs have developed in the United States, the Highfields Project[15] in New Jersey, and the Provo Experiment in Delinquency Rehabilitation,[16] using the technique of *guided group interaction*. The basic difference between these two projects is that the Highfields boys live at Highfields while the Provo boys live at home, attending guided group interaction sessions at the end of each work day. Basically, other features are the same. Both projects handle small groups of boys (about 20 at a time) for short-term care (three to four months). Both are "walk away" institutions with no fences, no guards, and generally few formal rules, and a lack of emphasis upon inmate-staff deference. Thus, the boys live in an atmosphere of freedom which allows the opportunity to deviate (and suffer the consequences). The primary feature of these two settings is that rehabilitation and therapy is not done by staff psychologists, counselors, or social workers, but it is done by the boys themselves. Guided group interaction sessions are held in small groups (six-person maximum) and each group is told that no member may be released from the program until each member of the group has reformed his attitudes along conventional lines. This group treatment uses the principle of "retroflexive reformation" which Cressey proposed as an effective means of rehabilitation.

> A group in which criminal A joins with some non-criminals to change criminal B is probably most effective in changing criminal A, not B; in order to change criminal B, criminal A must necessarily share the values of the anticriminal members.[17]

Even more important, this method encourages the development of normative social power in a pure normative compliance structure and thus corresponds to ideal organizational structure. In terms of recidivism as a criterion of success, these two settings appear to resemble Red Hill School. Recidivism rates were found to be half those of boys admitted to a more conventional reform school, and somewhat lower than boys released on probation.

DEVELOPMENT OF A THERAPEUTIC COMMUNITY

As we have seen, the traditional mental hospital as described by Goffman, Dunham, Weinberg, and others is viewed by patients as a coercive setting and a highly ineffective one in treating mental patients from the point of view of recovery. For this reason, there has been a trend toward out-patient care and community methods of treatment of mental patients. Both of these are used to some extent in the Industrial Neurosis Unit of the Belmont Hospital in England, as described by Jones.[18] The Industrial Neurosis Unit is an experimental attempt to develop and study community methods of treatment of mental patients in an institutional setting. The function of the unit was to study the problem of the chronic, unemployed neurotic and to help him overcome his problem through living in the therapeutic community setting. Only selected patients are accepted on the unit. If an applicant sends a full psychiatric report on his problem and if, to the unit staff, the case represents a psychiatric problem and employment difficulties, it will be accepted. Neurotics and persons with character disorders made up the majority of the population on the unit. The community is staffed by four psychiatrists, one psychologist, two psychiatric social workers, two disablement resettlement officers of the Ministry of Labor, five occupational instructors, one research technician, and a total nursing staff of about twenty. Because the units have only one hundred beds, this represents a higher number of personnel than one would find in most hospital units for mental patients in the United States.

There is an emphasis on vocational rehabilitation and guidance in the program at Belmont. Patients are required to work the major portion of their day in either industrial workshops within the unit or in selected jobs in neighboring communities. The aim is not to keep the patient busy, or to train him for a new vocation when he is discharged, but to approximate as nearly as possible the kinds of situations he will be forced to cope with and adjust to when he is returned to the working force in society.

Community meetings take up the other major portion of the day for the patients on the unit. These are mandatory meetings for all and this is where the patients are expected to bring out their problems, discuss, and eventually resolve them. All patients and staff members take part in the community meeting, and no one has more authority to speak his opinions or complaints than any other member. Patients interpret, support, and suggest solutions to the problems of other patients, and often, through this experience, gain insight into their own problems. On some days vocational rehabilitation films from the Ministry of Labor are shown and on Friday a psychodrama is produced, followed by open discussion. Patients then write, produce, and explain psychodramas in terms of their own personal lives. The remainder of the day is spent on the unit in recreation, and for some patients, free hours in the nearby community. Meal times are set by the staff, as are the hours to arise in the morning and retire at night. Patients also participate daily in cleaning up the ward and keeping their own area of the unit neat and attractive.

The role relationships of the staff and patients are significant in characterizing the therapeutic community. The relationship among staff members is not highly stratified. All work within the staff is done on a team basis, with the opinion of each member being as important as the next. All final decisions are made by final majority rule. Staff–patient relationships are more inclusive and less structured than in custodial mental hospitals. The nurse's role is threefold—authoritative, social, and therapeutic—the emphasis being placed upon the therapy role. Her major task is to transmit and represent the culture and temper of the therapeutic community of the patients. The doctor does not play the conventional, white-coat professional role, but he functions not only as a supporting and interpreting figure, but also a friend to the patient. The patient's role is to absorb the culture of the unit, and thereby become a valuable therapeutic tool with respect to other patients.

How successful was the Neurosis Unit? Follow-up studies were done through unannounced meetings: social workers calling at the home of the former patient six months after discharge. Through interviewing the patients and members of his family she rated his adjustment success in the family situation and in working on the job. Through a composite of many factors considered, the psychiatric social worker rated 61 per cent of those interviewed in the Good, Very Good, and Fair classes of adjustment and her estimate of their labor value on the labor market showed that 41 per cent were employable and another 25 per cent were employable under sheltered conditions. Thirty-seven per cent had made a good or very good social adjustment, while 67 per cent had made a fair social adjustment or better. The follow-up study showed that those patients who were most successful were those most involved in the many aspects of the therapeutic community. These figures represent a relatively high success rate when it is seen that the patients had not responded to any treatment previously and were previously chronic unemployed.

This serves as still another example of how community treatment can be efficacious in resolving many of the dilemmas created by present-day institutions.

PORTRAIT OF THE IDEAL INSTITUTION

The few examples of democratic, normative institutional settings given above serve to provide a model for progressive effort. The general perspective of this analysis has been that participation in normative settings can reduce anomia, whether it can be the "anomia of success" or of despair. The result of such participation is the elimination of feelings of isolation, loneliness, powerlessness, and the like among workers. It can reduce hostility among delinquents. On the other hand, such participation can lead to a "reality orientation" among neurotics. The purpose of such organizations might be to provide a basis for therapy of the lonely or discontent, or, on the other hand, a basis for development of social rather than antisocial feelings among delinquents.

Although the details involved in every organization are different, it is interesting to note that the common denominators of normative power, democracy, organic solidarity, pluralism, and the like, combined with normative social power or communal organization, characterizes all progressive and ideal settings, in line with the projected ideal society discussed in the first part of this chapter. Ultimately, if members of society are all involved in moral communities, there will be no need for special institutions set apart to treat people with problems either of a psychic or social nature.

Toward neighborhood organization

As in the previous sections, the focus here will not be upon neighborhoods usually considered to be organized, namely middle-class and upper-class neighborhoods, but upon those usually portrayed in the literature as disorganized or "malorganized."

Neighborhood disorganization was a major concern of Faris, Queen, Elliott and others of the earlier school of social disorganization. Shaw and McKay, Faris and Dunham, Zorbach, Thrasher, and others of the early Chicago school used the social disorganization framework to explain juvenile delinquency, mental disorder, suicide, alcoholism, and various other disorders. This framework linked poverty and disorganization as a one-to-one relationship. W. F. Whyte, however, challenged that framework. He found through participant observation (as opposed to the official record analysis characteristic of earlier studies) in an Italian community that the slum was not really disorganized at all but may be seen as a highly interrelated system constituted by political machine, businesses, and the rackets. The portrait of the slum that emerges from Whyte's study seems to be the other extreme of disorganization—one of rigid, hierarchical organization. One could use the concept of oligarchy to project certain patterns of behavior that emerge in

Whyte's street-corner society—rigid conformity to the code of the group, patriarchal leadership, controlled violence, and the like.

Emerging from these different studies of low-income neighborhoods is the idea that there may be different types of slum neighborhoods. Cloward and Ohlin suggest there may be three types: criminal-organized, disorganized, and unorganized, from which arise criminal, conflict, and retreatist subcultures respectively. However, the idea that lower-class neighborhoods can be organized along relatively conventional lines is a new idea which has not received much attention from social pathologists. This, in fact, is the theme of a recent book by Herbert J. Gans, *The Urban Villagers.*[19] Gans shows that it is indeed possible to have a slum neighborhood which is organized in a way consistent with the idea of normative social power and communal organization.

Gans conducted a participants-observation study of an inner-city Boston neighborhood called the West End. Gans was interested in testing the prevailing assumption of city planners that low-income people's problems were caused by their living in a slum, and that they lived a way of life that was a deviant form of the middle-class one—born of deprivation and lack of access to a better standard of living. Gans concludes that the West Enders were not frustrated seekers of middle-class values and that their way of life constituted a distinct and independent working-class subculture. Most of the West Enders' relationships are with peers, among people of the same sex, age, and life-cycle status. This peer group remains for life. The West End family system is an "expanded family" more open than the middle-class nuclear family but not as inclusive as the extended family of primitive societies. Families are adult-centered, rather than child-centered as the middle-class family or adult-directed as the upper-middle class. West Enders are "person-oriented" rather than "object-oriented" (in Etzioni's terms oriented toward acceptance and positive response rather than calculative). West Enders can only be individuals *within* the peer group, and paradoxically the group cannot work together for a common goal. The peer group life is a "spirited competition of individuals jockeying for respect, power, and status." West Enders are poorly related to the "outside world." Work and education are seen only as means to ends. The caretakers (service-oriented, market-oriented, and missionary) are not needed by the West Enders, because they have their own social system and culture and can take care of themselves.

They have no interest in state or federal government. They are not "brainwashed" by the mass media in selection of consumer goods, but select only that which enhances their peer-group life.

What are the behavioral results of this type of social structure? Although all of Merton's types of deviancy are found in the West End, there is little or no innovation—that is, professional criminal activity. The predominant deviancy is of a ritualist variety—for example, social drinking as a means of coping with life problems. However, the West End cannot be portrayed as a deviant community, as far as its own values and norms of behavior are concerned, but only as regards the values of middle-class society.

FROM ALCOHOL TO ASSOCIATION AS A NORMATIVE ORGANIZATION

Alcoholics Anonymous is not an organization in the conventional sense of the word; thus, it can be discussed here as noninstitutional group behavior.[20] There are no fees or dues. The only requirement for membership is an honest desire to stop drinking.

Though AA is not allied with any particular faith, sect, or denomination, clearly its purpose is to treat alcoholism through reestablishing the moral community which the alcoholic seeks. The seeking person must be convinced of "the need for moral inventory, confession of personality defects, restitution to those harmed, helpfulness to others, and the necessity of belief in an dependence upon God." The unity of AA is derived from its members through their common plight with alcoholism. AA is attempting to prove that one alcoholic could affect another as no non-alcoholic could, and that through strenuous work, one alcoholic is vital to the permanent recovery of the other. AA has been highly successful both in reuniting homes and in helping alcoholics to maintain normal employment.

Democracy in a small group

The general goal of organizations, both formal and informal, institutional and noninstitutional, has been to apply the principles of pluralistic or democratic organization to smaller settings. This has been suggested in the case of society-at-large, industry, schools, mental institutions, juvenile gangs, neighborhoods, and the like. So far, our analysis has been largely sociological. However, in this and subsequent sections, we will be applying the same principles to social-psychological and psychological phenomena. It should be noted, however, that we are dealing on a different level of analysis. The ideal power relationship in a small group is normative, not pure but social-normative power.

There is some evidence that there has been a general shift away from authoritarian-led groups to democratic groups, referring to styles of leadership. A study by Lippitt and White points out the advantages of "democratic" leadership over such alternative forms as "authoritarian" and *"laissez-faire."*[21] The study was done under the direction of psychologist Kurt Lewin. For their study, Lippitt and White created activity clubs of five youngsters each, matched for IQ, popularity, physical setting and equipment, activity interests, activity content, and leadership. The children worked on craft projects under the direction of adult leaders who were thoroughly briefed as to the style of leadership they were to adopt. Leaders were rotated among the groups, each leader adopting each role, so that the effects of leader personality would be randomized.

The three types of leadership can be compared primarily with regard to who makes decisions and assignments, and whether or not the leader remains aloof, praises or not praises, defined his standards of praise. In the authoritarian role, the leader makes all decisions about policy and procedure and in detail makes all assignments of activity tasks and companions. He remains aloof from the group and keeps his standards of praise to himself. By contrast, in the *laissez-faire* role the group alone makes all decisions and assignments, and the leader merely supplies information and materials when requested and acts friendly rather than "stand-offish," never praising or evaluating in any way. The *democratic* role represents a compromise of these two extremes. Decisions and assignments are made by the group but with the guidance of the leader. Each is free to work with whomever he or she chooses. The leader praises or criticizes but makes clear the basis for his praise and criticism. The leader is a group member in spirit but does not do much of the work.

It was found that each of the three styles of leaderships evoked significantly different styles of group behavior. When the groups were led by democratic leadership, interpersonal relations and relations with the leader exhibited little aggression, and when frustrated these groups attacked the source of frustration (for example, a hostile stranger in the room) rather than displace aggression on to out-group scapegoats. More individual differences were shown, and yet there were more requests for attention from club members, indicating group mindedness. Productivity was not as high as in autocracy, but the level of productivity was not dependent upon the leader's presence in the room.

By contrast, the groups under *laissez-faire* leadership were low in productivity. They were highly aggressive toward club members and to the leader and were lacking in individual differences. In fact, through the emergence of leadership among the boys, productivity rapidly increased when the adult leader was not in the room.

In some ways, the autocratic led groups were similar to the *laissez-faire*. They were aggressive toward fellow club members, in one case aggressive toward the leader, and low in individual differences. However, most authoritarian groups were apathetic in response to their leader, highly dependant upon him, and constantly demanding in attention from him. The apathetic authoritarian groups tended to scapegoat out-groups and accept and internalize unjust criticism from an adult stranger in the clubroom. These groups were, however, the most productive of all, but their productivity was dependent upon the presence of the leader in the room.

When the group leadership changed from authoritarian to democratic or *laissez-faire,* the previously apathetic groups indulged in "outbursts of horseplay" between the members on the first day of their transitions to a *laissez-faire* and a democratic group situation. This need to "blow off" disappeared with more meetings in the freer atmosphere.[22]

It can be seen that, except with regard to the criterion of supervised productivity, the democratic group had a number of advantages as compared with the other groups. As DeGré's analysis would suggest, freedom was maximized in the democratic groups in that greatest individual differences could be displayed there. There was greater solidarity and morale among the democratic-led groups, less mutual or leader directed aggression, and greater "intrinsic gratification" from work. Furthermore, there was a healthy opposition to unjust arbitrary authority in the democratic group. The *laissez-faire* appears to have no advantages over the others, while the authoritarian group benefits only from greater work productivity.

From traditional to developmental childrearing

Childrearing and family organization have changed rapidly in the past century, as indicated in a previous chapter. In the nineteenth century, children were expected to obey authority with instant, unquestioning obedience. Children were looked upon as "conceived in sin and born in iniquity." Training was primarily directed toward "uprooting the evil in human nature," and parents often "whaled the devil" out of children. Such practices as whipping, shutting in dark closets, and depriving of food were frequent. Such practices were in part related to demands placed upon the family under frontier conditions. It was necessary for children to perform tasks expected of them in order that the family survive under frontier conditions.

However, childrearing practices have gone through a series of progressive changes. If the nineteenth-century attitude toward the child was hostility, the intervening period might be characterized by its "affective neutrality." In the 1920's, John B. Watson emphasized the necessity of "objectivity" and the "scientific approach to the child." Watson recommended kissing the child on the forehead, if at all; shaking hands with the child in the morning; never hugging, kissing or letting the child sit on your lap. In the 1930's, objectivity reached its zenith with great emphasis on the importance of routine, habit formation—that is, "adherence without deviation to regular habits for sleeping, eating, and toileting beginning in early infancy." Today, however, there is a strong movement toward emotional involvement and affection toward children, a movement which gained its impetus first in the 1940's when Gessell and colleagues Sheviakov, Redl, Baruch, Hymes, and Spock advocated acceptance of the child and his feelings without shame, guilt, or feelings of failure. Spock's *The Common Sense Book of Baby and Child Care* became the young mother's "bible" as permissive, "enjoy your youngster" attitudes toward children became widely accepted.

The present emerging era may best be described by what Duvall terms "developmental childrearing."[23] It represents a movement away from coercion and in the direction of social normative power in the family, democracy in the family, and the like. Duvall did a study of 433 mothers who were asked two questions, "What are five things a good mother does?" and "What are five things a good child does?" The responses were grouped into twelve categories for conceptions of "a good mother," and thirteen categories for "a good child." Analyzing these groupings, Duvall observed that one type is predominantly traditional in conceptual content:

> What a good mother traditionally expected of herself, usually in terms of what she was supposed to do to and for her family and children, were recognized as traditional conceptions of motherhood. What used to be expected of a child, usually in terms of behaving in ways that please adults, were seen as traditional conceptions of the good child. Traditional conceptions of both the good mother and the good child tended to be somewhat static, rigid, and specific behavioral expectancies.[24]

An alternative to the traditional mother and child role is found in the developmental model:

> A nontraditional, emergent type of conception, on the other hand, was recognized as dynamic, flexible, and growth-promoting. Its emphasis was upon the development of the person rather than on any specific form or type of behavior.[25]

The traditional child is characterized by cleanness and neatness, obedience, pleasantness to adults, respect for property, religiousness, productivity, and cooperativeness in the family. By contrast, the developmental conception child entails health and wellbeing, cooperativeness, contentment, affection, initiative, and growth potential of the child. The traditional mother is a good housekeeper, takes care of her child physically, trains her child to regularity, disciplines the child, and makes the child "good." By contrast, the developmental mother trains for self-reliance and citizenship, sees to emotional well-being, helps the child socially, provides for the child's mental growth, guides with understanding, related lovingly to child, and is a calm, cheerful, and growing person.

Another study portrays the traditional as compared with the developmental father.[26] The traditional father is a strong individual, always right; he "knows" what the child "should" be so does not seek to understand the child as an individual; is interested only in activities he determines are for the child's "good," emphasizes giving things to and doing things for the child; sets the child's goals; finds satisfaction in the child's owing the father a debt which can be repaid through obedience; and feels parenthood is an imposed duty. By contrast, the developmental father feels the child is an individual; seeks to understand the child; is concerned with all activities of the child; stresses growth of the child; helps the child set his own goals; gains satisfaction in the child becoming a mature individual; and feels that parenthood is a privilege which he has chosen to assume.

It is interesting that Duvall makes no reference in her analysis to the *laissez-faire,* "disorganized," or anomic situation of family life, which has been shown as one of the possible organizational types in every organization discussed in this book. In fact, she may not distinguish between the *laissez-faire* and the democratic parent. Developmentally reared children, as she portrays them, have the run of the house. Parents should "childproof" their living rooms, making them "invulnerable to the boisterousness" of children and should not mind when property is damaged by children. Perhaps, this emphasis upon permissiveness in childrearing is a reaction to the long-standing traditional pattern which Duvall sees as having characterized the American family. But our analysis would indicate an equally dangerous shift to *laissez-faire* childrearing practices.

Application to personality

Although personality is and has been a marginal topic in this text, it is interesting to note the parallel work that has been done by psychologists and psychiatrists. The sociological emphasis we have focused upon stands in opposition to these personality approaches. Merton's types of adaptations, for example, are by design not personality types. The same person might in different situations take different forms of adaptation. It is less clear in Thomas and Znaniecki's analysis if the philistine–bohemian–creative man types are personality or adaptation types.

There is at least some evidence that personality types will emerge corresponding to these types of adaptation. Psychoanalytic literature is replete with discussions of such types. Adorno, *et al.,* have extensively documented "The Authoritarian Personality" which seems to follow consistently a philistine or ritualist adaptation. The authoritarian personality type has been portrayed generally:

> Anti-intellectuality, a pervading sense of pessimism and lack of hope and confidence in the future; feelings of cynicism, distrust, doubt, and suspicion; a diffuse misanthropy and querulousness; a hostile and bitter outlook which verged on destructiveness; a grumbling and discontented evaluation of their current status; a rigid, somewhat dogmatic style of thinking; a lack of poise and self-assurance; and an underlying perplexity related to a feeling that something dreadful is about to happen.[27]

The authoritarian personality syndrome was studied in response to a concern over the bases of fascist personality which was largely blamed for the spirit of anti-Semitism in Europe in WWII. Because of the social importance of the authoritarian personality, it has been extensively studied; however, perhaps because other possible personality types have not been damaging or problematic—*"laissez-faire"* personality or "democratic" personality—they have not been so extensively studied. In fact there is some doubt that, though the authoritarian personality can be studied as a systematic syndrome, the democratic personality exhibits any uniformity at all. As was stated in the introduction to *The Authoritarian Personality:*

> The major concern was with the *potentially fascistic* individual, one whose structure is such as to render him particularly susceptible to anti-democratic propaganda. . . . It is one of the major findings of the present study that individuals who show extreme susceptibility to fascist propaganda have a great deal in common. . . . Individuals who are extreme in the opposite direction are much more diverse.[28]

Despite a lack of empirical work on the "democratic personality" it is possible to describe it as an "ideal type" based upon traits antithetical to authoritarism and in accord with current conceptions of ideal personality and inferentially in accord with personality descriptions in sociological theory. Parallel to our concept of the "democratic personality" would be such concepts as Riesman's "autonomous man," Roger's "self-actualizing man," Sullivan's "personification of good me," and the like. Together these divergent sources might well constitute, as I see it, the following "ideal personality":

Flexible, optimistic individual; capable of challenging the given while maintaining a sense of continuity; benevolent, tolerant, and cooperative in attitude and behavior; lacking in aggressive, hostile feelings, however, not passive in response to real threat; intrinsically oriented with regard to life activity rather than "status oriented"; oriented toward diverse groups, formal and informal; striving always not for adjustment to frustration but for attainment of higher values.

Conclusion

All too often the reader of a text such as this is left with the conclusion that, unless something is done about contemporary problems of deviancy, mass society, and disorganization, our society is bent on ultimate destruction. Although in the age of concentration camps and thermonuclear warfare the dissolution of society is indeed a possibility, the conclusion of this text is not a prophecy of doom. In a sense, despite its problems, society seems to be progressing toward newer, more acceptable forms of organization. However, at this stage of American society, we cannot take a *laissez-faire* attitude nor is it appropriate to be zealously optimistic. It will take leadership to direct our society toward pure and social normative integration, toward the combined communal and pluralist society described in the early part of this chapter. This is the responsibility with which the reader of this text is entrusted.

Notes

Chapter 1—Notes to Pages 1–8

1. This criticism of the social problems approach is made by C. W. Mills and E. M. Lemert: C. Wright Mills, "The Professional Ideology of Social Pathologists," *American Journal of Sociology*, 49 (September, 1943), pp. 165–180, and Edwin M. Lemert, *Social Pathology* (New York: McGraw-Hill, 1951), p. 7.

The authors of most texts on deviancy or social problems will no doubt object to the assertion that their text is without a theoretical framework. However, even the best of these seldom go beyond a short introductory chapter on theory, followed by a series of chapters describing individual social problems in which the theory developed in the first chapter is scarcely referred to, primarily because the volume of factual material in those chapters does not allow space for extensive theoretical analysis. Some excellent examples include Russell R. Dynes, Alfred C. Clarke, Simon Dinitz, and Iwao Ishino, *Social Problems* (New York: Oxford University Press, 1964); John F. Cuber, William F. Kenkel, and Robert A. Harper, *Problems of American Society: Values in Conflict* (New York: Holt, Rinehart and Winston, 1964); Earl Raab and Gertrude Selznick, *Major Social Problems* (New York: Harper and Row, 1959); and S. Kirson Weinburg, *Social Problems in Our Time* (Englewood Cliffs, N.J.: Prentice Hall, 1960).

2. Well known among these are R. E. L. Faris, *Social Disorganization* (New York: The Ronald Press,1955); Edwin H. Sutherland and Donald R. Cressey, *Principles of Criminology* (New York: J. B. Lippincott, 1960); Howard S. Becker, *Outsiders* (New York: The Free Press, 1963); and Marshall B. Clinard, *Sociology of Deviant Behavior* (New York: Holt, Rinehart and Winston, 1968).

3. For instance, the theories of Max Weber, Émile Durkheim, Karl Marx, Talcott Parsons, Georg Simmel, and the like.

4. Don Martindale, "Social Disorganization: The Conflict of Normative and Empirical Approaches," in Howard Becker and Alvin Boskoff, *Modern Sociological Theory* (New York: The Dryden Press, 1957), pp. 340–367.

5. Marshall B. Clinard, *Sociology of Deviant Behavior* (New York: Holt, Rinehart and Winston, 1968).

6. *Ibid.*, p. 96.

7. Lawrence K. Frank, "Society as the Patient," *American Journal of Sociology*, 42 (November, 1936), p. 335.

8. Paul Goodman, *Growing Up Absurd* (New York: Vintage Books, 1960), p. 217.

9. Herbert A. Block and Melvin Prince, *Social Crisis and Deviance: Theoretical Foundations* (New York: Random House, 1967), pp. 14–15.

10. John F. Cuber, William F. Kenkel, and Robert A. Harper, *Problems of American Society: Values in Conflict,* (New York: Holt, Rinehart and Winston, 1964), pp. 17–20.

11. Robert K. Merton, "Social Structure and Anomie," in Robert K. Merton, *Social Theory and Social Structure* (New York: The Free Press, 1957), pp. 135–136.

12. Erich Fromm, *The Sane Society* (New York: Rinehart and Company, 1955).

13. C. H. Cooley, *Human Nature and The Social Order* (New York: Scribner's, 1922).

14. Parsons' dissertation used a similar framework to analyze numerous major theories, including those of Weber, Durkheim, Pareto, and even Marx: Talcott Parsons, *The Structure of Social Action* (Glencoe, Ill.: The Free Press, 1937).

15. There is, for instance, ample evidence that the Hitler movement in Germany was popular.

> The solution offered by Hitler's group appealed to many because the flexible ideology of that group embodied a large number of popular views. . . . The energy and resourcefulness of the party organization, buttressed by popular trust in Hitler's charismatic leadership, led large numbers of people to enroll as National Socialists, confident in the ultimate success of their cause.
>
> —Theodore Abel, *The Nazi Movement* (New York: Atherton Press, 1966), p. 184.

Chapter 2

1. Weber first used the term "ideal type" to describe a type of concept with various characteristics. It is both abstract and general; it does not describe a concrete course of action but rather an ideal one. It does, however, describe "objectively possible" action. Max Weber, *The Theory of Social and Economic Organization* (New York: The Free Press, 1947), p. 13.

2. This distinction is made in Gideon Sjoberg, "Folk and Feudal Societies, *"American Journal of Sociology,* 58 (November, 1952), pp. 231–239.

3. These vary from Spencerian Social Darwinism, which posited a natural law of evolution, to the extreme activism of socialism embedded in Marx's thinking. Though these perspectives are in opposite camps on a number of important issues, they carry one very significant common assumption: that the "ideal society" can emerge from and within the context of present-day modern society. Other theoretical approaches to be covered below posit an incompatibility between large-scale organization and ideal society. It should be noted that there is no inherent correspondence between these theoretical camps and contemporary political perspectives. The evolutionary perspectives incorporate the whole range of views. It will be shown that there is similar diversity with the devolutionary and cyclical approaches. This may indicate simply that contemporary politics, at least in America, has an evolutionary slant. However, this is not to say that politics in the future will not contain the gamut of theoretical perspectives.

4. This is the thesis developed in Durkheim's first book and doctoral dissertation, *De la division du travail social* (Paris: F. Alcan, 1893), translated by George Simpson as *The Division of Labor in Society* (Glencoe, Ill.: The Free Press, 1947). Though in his later work on suicide, *Le suicide* (Paris: F. Alcan, 1897) translated by John A. Spaulding and George Simpson as *Suicide* (Glencoe, Ill.: The Free Press, 1951), Durkheim points out the prevalence of anomie in the modern world, he never really departed from a somewhat optimistic position of faith in the future. His later work, while stressing the need for reform in contemporary society, carried an overriding expectation that social reforms, such as the establishment of corporate communities, would inevitably be carried out. See, for instance, *Socialism* (New York: Collier Books, 1962).

5. Don Martindale, *The Nature and Types of Sociological Theory* (Boston: Houghton Mifflin, 1960), p. 388.

6. Max Weber, *The Theory of Social and Economic Organization,* translated by A. M. Henderson and Talcott Parsons (New York: The Free Press, 1966), pp. 115–117, 136–138.

7. H. H. Gerth and C. Wright Mills, *From Max Weber: Essays in Sociology* (New York: Oxford University Press, 1958), p. 50.

8. Robert M. MacIver, *Community* (London: MacMillan, 1927) and *Society* (New York: Farrar and Rinehart, 1949).

9. In *Community,* MacIver defines community as the most inclusive territorially based group, and associations as organizations promoting a limited number of specific interests.

10. That is, the segments are "interchangeable" groups such as families, clans, exogamous groups, and totem groups.

11. *Supra,* footnote 9.

12. R. M. MacIver, *Society, op. cit.,* p. 24.

13. An excellent translation and condensation of Comte theory is given in Talcott Parsons, *et al.* (eds.), *Theories of Society* (New York: The Free Press, 1961), pp. 1332–1342.

14. Georg W. F. Hegel, *The Philosophy of History,* translated by H. W. Johnston and L. G. Struthers (New York: Macmillan, 1929).

15. Karl Marx and Friedrich Engels, *The German Ideology* (New York: International Publishers, 1947).

16. Karl Marx and Friedrich Engels, *The Communist Manifesto* (New York: International Publishers, 1930).

17. Lewis S. Feuer (ed.), *Basic Writings on Politics and Philosophy: Karl Marx and Friedrich Engels* (New York: Doubleday, 1959), pp. 318–348.

18. It is on this point that a number of contemporary sociologists differ with Marx. It has been pointed out that social classes have not disappeared in Communist countries and that classes are no longer based upon economic considerations but instead are based on participation

in or exclusion from authority. Ralf Dahrendorf, *Class and Class Conflict in Industrial Society* (Stanford, Calif.: Stanford University Press, 1954).

19. Daniel Lerner, *The Passing of Traditional Society* (New York: The Free Press, 1958).

20. Niccolò Machiavelli, *The Prince and His Discourses,* edited by Max Lerner (New York: Modern Library, 1948).

21. The French word *rentier* connotes a person seeking security and therefore investing his savings in bonds.

22. Vilfredo Pareto, *The Mind and Society,* edited by Arthur Livingston, translated by Andrew Bongiorno and Arthur Livingston (New York: Harcourt, Brace, 1935), Vols. III and IV.

23. Pitirim Sorokin, *Social and Cultural Dynamics* (Boston: Porter Sargent, 1957), p. 639.

24. Pitirim Sorokin, *Society, Culture, and Personality* (New York: Harper, 1947).

25. In chapters to follow, it will be shown that this idea of mass society is expressed in various ways in various areas of sociology — for instance, as disorganized society, anomie, social pathology, sick society, delinquent society, insane society, and the like. We shall focus upon the close ties between these concepts rather than differences and shall contrast these concepts with theoretical alternatives presented in the present chapter.

26. John F. Cuber, William F. Kenkel, and Robert A. Harper, *Problems of American Society: Values in Conflict* (New York: Holt, Rinehart and Winston, 1964), pp. 14, 24.

27. Sigmund Freud, *Moses and Monotheism,* translated by Katherine Jones (New York: Alfred A. Knopf, 1939).

28. A. A. Brill, translator and editor, *The Basic Writings of Sigmund Freud* (New York: Modern Library, 1938).

29. Sigmund Freud, *Civilization and Its Discontents,* translated by Joan Riviere (London: Hogarth Press, 1946).

30. Sigmund Freud, *Totem and Taboo,* translated by James Strachey (New York: W. W. Norton, 1952).

31. According to Freud, the Jews were reproached not so much for killing God or Moses (the archetype of God), but more important for denying it. The Christians, by contrast, through admitting their guilt feel their sins can be forgiven and that they can be purified.

32. Ferdinand Tönnies, *Community and Society (Gemeinschaft und Gesellschaft),* translated and edited by Charles P. Loomis (New York: Harper and Row, 1957).

33. *Ibid.*

34. Generally, the term "Chicago School" refers to the early school of University of Chicago followers of Robert Park and Ernest Burgess, including Louis Wirth, Thorsten Sellin, Clifford Shaw, Henry McKay, R. E. L. Faris, R. D. McKenzie, and Herbert Blumer.

35. Robert Redfield, "The Folk Society," *American Journal of Sociology,* 52 (January, 1947), p. 293 ff.

36. Robert Redfield, *Tepoztlan: A Mexican Village* (Washington, D.C.: Carnegie Institution of Washington Publication No. 448, 1934); _____, *The Folk Culture of Yucatan* (Chicago: University of Chicago Press, 1941); _____, *Chan Kom Revisited* (Chicago: University of Chicago Press, 1950).

37. John C. McKinney, *Constructive Typology and Social Theory* (New York: Appleton-Century-Crofts, 1966), pp. 21–26.

38. McKinney distinguishes between ideal typologies, empirical typologies, and constructive typologies. *Ideal typologies,* e.g. Tönnies' gemeinschaft–gesellschaft continuum, are both abstract and general, but do not necessarily correspond to any empirical occurrence. By contrast, *empirical typologies* are constructed inductively from concrete empirical data. Empirical types do not suffice to cover all cases in hand due to some focus of the investigator, while ideal types are difficult to apply in practice to actual situations. A happy medium is found in *"constructive typology, a purposive, planned selection, abstraction, combination, and (sometimes) accentuation of a set of criteria with empirical referents that serves as a basis for comparison of empirical cases." Ibid.,* p. 3. [Italics in original.]

39. Parsons, *op. cit.* It is obvious that Parsons' categories are abstract and theoretical, but some may doubt that they have empirical referents. Most of the research in this regard is recent. For example, see the Spring, 1968 issue of *Sociological Inquiry* on empirical applications of Parsonian theory for a collection of research papers empirically applying Parsons' AGIL paradigm.

40. Émile Durkheim, *The Division of Labor, op. cit.,* pp. 353–395.

41. Durkheim uses the term "function" in various ways. "The word function is used in two quite different senses. Sometimes it suggests a system of vital movements, without reference to their consequences: at others it expresses the relation existing between these movements and corresponding needs of the organism." *Ibid.,* p. 49. While the bulk of Durkheim's "functional analysis" employs the relational definition, when Durkheim speaks of "specialization of functions" or "conflict between functions," he seems to be referring to systems, quite logically larger corporate or interest groups.

42. *Ibid.,* p. 389.

43. Howard Becker, *Through Values To Social Interpretation* (Durham, N.C.: Duke University Press, 1950). Also, see McKinney, *op. cit.,* pp. 110–113, for a summary of Becker's typology.

44. Elman Service, *Profiles in Ethnology* (New York: Harper and Row, 1963).

45. Gerald DeGré, "Freedom and Social Structure," *American Sociological Review,* 11 (October, 1946), pp. 534–536.

46. *Ibid.,* p. 529.

Chapter 3

1. Merton uses the term "middle-range" to refer to "theories intermediate to the minor working hypotheses evolved in abundance during the day-by-day routines of research, and the all-inclusive speculations comprising a master conceptual scheme from which it is hoped to derive a very large number of empirically observed uniformities of social behavior." Robert K. Merton, *Social Theory and Social Structure* (Glencoe, Ill.: The Free Press, 1957), pp. 5–6.

2. W. G. Sumner, *Folkways* (New York: Dover Publications, 1959), and Maurice R. Davie, *William Graham Sumner* (New York: Thomas Y. Crowell, 1963), pp. 23–23.

3. A. W. Small, *General Sociology: An Exposition of the Main Development in Sociological Theory from Spencer to Ratzenhoffer* (Chicago: University of Chicago Press, 1925).

4. L. F. Ward, *Dynamic Sociology,* 2 vols. (New York: D. Appleton, 1883; 2d. ed., 1897).

5. W. I. Thomas and F. Znaniecki, *The Polish Peasant in Europe and America,* 2d ed. (New York: Alfred E. Knopf, 1927).

6. *Ibid.,* p. 1130.

7. *Ibid.*

8. Charles H. Cooley, *Social Organization* (Glencoe, Ill.: The Free Press, 1956), Chapter III, p. 23.

9. Gisela J. Hinkle, "Sociology and Psychoanalysis," *Modern Social Theory,* edited by Howard Becker and Alvin Boskoff (New York: The Dryden Press, 1957), p. 60.

10. Cooley, *op. cit.*

11. C. H. Cooley, *Social Processes* (New York: Scribner and Sons, 1918), pp. 156–157.

12. Charles H. Cooley, Robert C. Angell, and Lowell J. Carr, *Introductory Sociology* (New York: Charles Scribner and Sons, 1933).

13. The list of texts with the word "disorganization" in the title includes only six texts: H. A. Bloch, *Disorganization: Personal and Social* (New York: Alfred A. Knopf, 1952); Lawrence G. Brown, *Social Pathology: Personal and Social Disorganization* (New York: F. S. Crofts and Co., 1942); Mabel A. Elliott and Francis E. Merrill, *Social Disorganization* (New York: Harper and Bros., 1950); Robert E. L. Faris, *Social Disorganization* (New York: The Ronald Press, 1955); Ernest R. Mowrer, *Disorganization: Personal and Social* (Philadelphia: J. B. Lippincott, 1942); Stuart A. Queen, *et al., Social Organization and Disorganization* (New York: Thomas Y. Crowell, 1935).

14. The only exceptions are Bloch and Faris, *supra,* footnote 13.

15. Elliott and Merrill, and Faris, *supra,* footnote 13.

16. As an illustration of the usual linking of these concepts, Clinard states in his well-known text on deviant behavior: "This book is written as a text for courses designated as 'social dis-

organization,' 'social problems,' 'social pathology,' and 'deviant behavior.'" Marshall B. Clinard, *Sociology of Deviant Behavior* (New York: Holt, Rinehart and Winston, 1963).

17. Mowrer, *supra*, footnote 13, pp. 31–32.

18. See, for example, Mowrer, *supra*, footnote 13, pp. 559 ff..

19. Elliott and Merrill, *supra*, footnote 13, pp. 39–40.

20. Robert E. Park and Ernest W. Burgess, *The City* (Chicago: University of Chicago Press, 1925).

21. Walter C. Reckless, *Vice in Chicago* (Chicago: University of Chicago Press, 1933), as quoted by Marshall B. Clinard, *Sociology of Deviant Behavior* (New York: Holt, Rinehart and Winston, 1963), p. 90.

22. Clifford Shaw, *Juvenile Delinquency in Urban Areas* (Chicago: University of Chicago Press, 1942).

23. Clifford R. Shaw and Henry D. McKay, *Social Factors in Juvenile Delinquency: Report on the Causes of Crime* (Washington, D.C.: National Commission on Law Observance and Enforcement, 1931).

24. Andrew W. Lind, "Some Ecological Patterns of Community Disorganization in Honolulu," *American Journal of Sociology,* 36:206–220 (September, 1930), Norman S. Hayner, "Criminogenic Zones in Mexico City," *American Sociological Review,* 11 (August, 1946), 428–438.

25. Ralph Kramer, "The Conceptual Status of Social Disorganization," *American Journal of Sociology,* 48 (January, 1943), p. 472.

26. *Supra,* footnote 2.

27. Ecological studies include C. I. Shaw, *supra,* footnote 22, and R. E. L. Faris and H. Warren Dunham, *Mental Disorders in Urban Areas* (Chicago: University of Chicago Press, 1939).

28. Clifford R. Shaw, *The Jack-Roller: A Delinquent Boy's Own Story* (Philadelphia: Albert Saifer, 1930), p. 74.

29. Clifford R. Shaw, *The Natural History of a Delinquent Career* (Philadelphia: Albert Saifer, 1931), pp. 53, 63.

30. R. E. L. Faris, "Reflections of Social Disorganization in the Behavior of a Schizophrenic Patient," *American Journal of Sociology,* 50 (September, 1944), pp. 134–141.

31. Paul F. Cressey, "Social Disorganization and Reorganization in Harlan County, Kentucky," *American Sociological Review,* 14 (June, 1949), pp. 389–394.

32. R. E. L. Faris, *Social Disorganization, supra,* footnote 13, pp. 53–55.

33. *Ibid.*

34. See for example, Daniel Lerner, *The Passing of Traditional Society* (New York: The Free Press, 1958) for an account of six nations: Turkey, Lebanon, Egypt, Syria, Jordan, and Iran. Another excellent source is Herbert R. Barringer *et al.* (eds.), *Social Change in Developing Areas* (Cambridge: Schenkman Publishing Company, 1965), especially Chapters 4–8 covering Algeria, Barbados, Jamaica, and Albania. These will be discussed in a later chapter.

35. J. M. van der Kroef, "Patterns of Western Influence in Indonesia," *American Sociological Review,* 17 (August, 1952) pp. 421–430, as cited in R. E. L. Faris, *op. cit.,* pp. 39–42.

36. See, for instance, John F. Cuber, "The Measurement and Significance of Institutional Disorganization," *American Journal of Sociology,* 44 (May, 1937), pp. 408–414, for an application of disorganization theory to social institutions; R. E. L. Faris summarizes his textbook approach in "Contemporary and Perspective Social Disorganization," *Sociology and Social Research,* 32 (January, 1948), pp. 679–684; Roland L. Warren shows the relevance of role theory to disorganization in, Roland L. Warren, "Social Disorganization and the Interrelationship of Cultural Roles," *American Sociological Review,* 14 (February, 1949), pp. 83–87; Ernest R. Mowrer shows the variation of various social problems with social disorganization in, Ernest R. Mowrer, "Social Crisis and Social Disorganization," *American Sociological Review,* 15 (February, 1950), pp. 60–66.

37. Herbert Blumer, "Social Disorganization and Individual Disorganization," *American Journal of Sociology,* 42 (May, 1937), pp. 871–877.

38. *Ibid.,* pp. 873, 876.

39. Louis Wirth, "Ideological Aspects of Social Disorganization," *American Sociological Review,* 5 (August, 1940), pp. 470–482.

40. *Ibid.,* p. 474.

Notes to Pages 59–72 / 374

41. Ernest R. Mowrer, "Methodological Problems in Social Disorganization," *American Sociological Review*, 6 (December, 1941), pp. 839–852.

42. Ralph Kramer, "The Conceptual Status of Social Disorganization," *American Journal of Sociology*, 48 (January, 1943), pp. 466–474.

43. William F. Whyte, "Social Organization in the Slums," *American Sociological Review*, 8 (February, 1943), pp. 34–39.

44. Harvey Zorbaugh, *The Gold Coast and the Slum* (Chicago: University of Chicago Press, 1928), pp. 198–199.

45. *Ibid.*, p. 194.

46. W. F. Whyte, *Street Corner Society* (Chicago: University of Chicago Press, 1942).

47. W. F. Whyte, *supra*, footnote 43.

48. *Ibid.*, pp. 38–39.

49. An interesting parallel has been drawn between Freud and Cooley in Gisela Hinkle, "Sociology and Psychoanalysis," in Howard Becker and Alvin Boskoff, *Modern Sociological Theory* (New York: The Dryden Press, 1957), pp. 574–603. Both Cooley and Freud postulate instincts, both view the "self" or "ego" as a mediator, and both assert the internalization of societal standards by way of "primary ideals" (Cooley) and "superego" (Freud).

50. Robert C. Angell, *The Moral Integration of American Cities*, Special Supplement, *American Journal of Sociology*, 57:1–40 (July, 1951) as cited in Elliott and Merrill, *supra*, footnote 13.

51. Herbert Hyman, *Survey Design and Analysis* (Glencoe, Ill.: The Free Press, 1955).

52. Émile Durkheim, *The Division of Labor* (New York: The Free Press, 1965).

53. For example, Gibbs equates social differentiation with anomie, which has been equated with disorganization. Jack P. Gibbs, "Suicide," in Robert Merton and Robert A. Nisbet, *Contemporary Social Problems* (New York: Harcourt, Brace and World, 1961), pp. 222–261.

54. Robert M. Marsh, *Comparative Sociology* (New York: Harcourt, Brace and World, 1967), pp. 234–235.

55. Ivo K. Feierabend and Rosalind L. Feierabend, "Aggressive Behavior Within Politics, 1948–1962. A Cross-National Study," *Journal of Conflict Resolution*, 10 (September, 1966) pp. 249–271.

56. Clinard, *supra*, footnote 16, pp. 22–29.

57. This is similar to Faris, *supra*, footnote 13.

58. *Supra*, footnote 52, p. 354.

59. Scott and Turner have argued that the contemporary anomie approach of Robert Merton which stresses the chronic pursuit of unlimited pecuniary success has little resemblance to Durkheim's anomie (disharmony of normative expectations) but has precedent in Weber's spirit of capitalism, the pursuit of gain without limit. Marvin B. Scott and Roy Turner, "Weber and the Anomie Theory of Deviance," *Sociological Quarterly*, 6 (Summer, 1965), pp. 233–240.

60. Robert K. Merton, *Social Theory and Social Structure* (New York: The Free Press, 1957), pp. 20–22.

61. Werner S. Landecker, "Types of Integration and Their Measurement," in Paul F. Lazarsfeld and Morris Rosenberg, *The Language of Social Research* (Glencoe, Ill.: The Free Press, 1955), pp. 19–27.

62. This same principle forms the basis of a current theory of compatibility in marriage, the "theory of complementary needs," which states: "In a society allowing free selection of marriage mates, each partner tends to seek within the field of eligible partners that person who most nearly satisfies his own psychological needs and who is most nearly satisfied by his own personality." Robert F. Winch, *Mate Selection: A Study of Complementary Needs* (New York: Harper and Row, 1958).

63. The survival of Israel, a small but organically solidary country, threatened by a vast but undifferentiated United Arab Republic, illustrates this point.

64. This statement suggests a sad commentary on United States involvement in South East Asia. If we, a Western, urban, organically solidary society, were to succeed in introducing our Western ideals there, we would produce chaotic disorganization of village life, making these villages even more vulnerable to invasion and infiltration.

65. Durkheim stated: "We shall call 'normal' these social conditions that are most generally

distributed, and the others 'morbid' or 'pathological.'" Emile Durkheim, *The Rules of Sociological Method* (New York: The Free Press, 1938), p. 54.

66. John Horton, "Dehumanization of Anomie and Alienation: A Problem in the Ideology of Sociology," *British Journal of Sociology,* 15 (December, 1964), pp. 283–300.

67. *Supra,* footnote 52, p. 267.

68. Alvin W. Gouldner, "Reciprocity and Autonomy in Functional Theory," in Llewellyn Gross, *Symposium on Sociological Theory* (New York: Row, Peterson, 1959), pp. 241–270.

69. *Supra,* footnote 52, p. 267.

70. John E. Nordskog, *Social Change* (New York: McGraw-Hill, 1962), pp. 44–45.

71. For instance, Émile Benoit-Smullyan stated "Durkheim, rather reluctantly, comes to rest his entire explanation upon the factor of an assumed natural increase in population. This is obviously a biologistic rather than a sociologistic type of explanation and comes closer to an outright materialism than anything in Durkheim's later work." Émile Benoit-Smullyan, "The Sociologism of Émile Durkheim and His School," Chapter IX in Harry Elmer Barnes, *An Introduction to the history of Sociology* (Chicago: University of Chicago Press, 1966), pp. 214ff.

72. Robert E. Park, Ernest W. Burgess, Roderick D. McKenzie, and Louis Wirth, *The City* (Chicago: University of Chicago Press, 1925).

73. W. F. Ogburn, *Social Change With Respect to Culture and Original Nature* (New York: B. W. Huebsch, 1922; Viking, 1927; revised edition, Viking, 1950).

74. Kenneth Keniston, "Alienation and the Decline of Utopia," *The American Scholar,* 29 (Spring, 1960), pp. 161–200.

75. Émile Durkheim, *Suicide,* translated by John A. Spaulding and George Simpson (Glencoe, Ill.: The Free Press, 1951).

76. *Ibid.,* p. 241.

77. *Ibid.,* pp. 246–249.

78. Robert K. Merton, "Social Structure and Anomie," *American Sociological Review,* 3 (October, 1938), pp. 672–682.

79. Robert K. Merton, "Social Structure and Anomie," Chapter IV in Robert K. Merton, *Social Theory and Social Structure,* (New York: The Free Press, 1957).

80. Albert K. Cohen, "The Sociology of the Deviant Act: Anomie Theory and Beyond," *American Sociological Review,* 30 (February, 1965), pp. 5–14, as quoted by Marshall B. Clinard, *Anomie and Deviant Behavior* (New York: The Free Press, 1964), p. 10.

81. *Supra,* footnote 79, pp. 672–674.

82. R. K. Merton, "Continuities in the Theory of Social Structure and Anomie," *supra,* footnote 79, p. 162.

83. *Supra,* footnote 78, pp. 673–674.

84. *Supra,* footnote 75, pp. 247–248.

85. *Supra,* footnote 79, p. 131.

86. Marvin B. Scott and Roy Turner, "Weber and the Anomic Theory of Deviance," *Sociological Quarterly,* 6 (Summer, 1965), pp. 233–234.

87. *Supra,* footnote 79, pp. 144–145.

88. *Supra,* footnote 52, pp. 375–378.

89. Constraint would only be required in the case of "rebellion." Merton has distinguished innovation, ritualism, and retreatism as "aberrant behavior," while rebellion is "non-conforming" behavior. While non-conformity is public, diffident, and altruistic, aberrant behavior is secretive, linked with a guilty belief in the legitimacy of norms violated and self-interest. (Robert K. Merton, "Social Problems and Sociological Theory," pp. 775–823, in Robert K. Merton and Robert A. Nisbet, *Contemporary Social Problems,* New York: Harcourt, Brace and World, 1966.) Constraint probably only applies to rebellion, because the other forms of deviancy are either hidden and therefore difficult to control (innovation), or oriented toward adaptation to a frustrating situation (as in ritualism and retreatism).

90. Ephraim H. Mizruchi, *Success and Opportunity: A Study of Anomie,* (New York: The Free Press, 1964), pp. 128 and 132.

91. Sebastian De Grazia, *The Political Community: A Study of Anomie* (Chicago: University of Chicago Press, 1948).

92. *Supra,* footnote 79.

93. Leo Srole, "Social Integration and Certain Corollaries, an Exploratory Study," *American Sociological Review,* 21 (December, 1956), pp. 709–716.

94. Robert K. Merton, "Anomie, Anomia, and Social Interaction: Contexts of Deviant Behavior," in M. B. Clinard, *op. cit.,* pp. 226–228.

95. *Supra,* footnote 82, p. 161.

96. R. M. MacIver, *The Ramparts We Guard* (New York: Macmillan, 1950), pp. 84–85.

97. *Supra,* footnote 93, p. 709.

98. *Supra,* footnote 91, pp. 72–74.

99. *Supra,* footnote 82, p. 163.

100. *Supra,* footnote 91, p. 25.

101. *Ibid.,* p. 73.

102. Parsons, *The Social System,* (New York: The Free Press, 1951), pp. 256–267, 321–325; Talcott Parsons, Robert F. Bales, and Edward A. Shils, *Working Papers in the Theory of Action* (Glencoe, Ill.: The Free Press, 1953), pp. 67–78.

103. *Supra,* footnote 99.

104. Albert K. Cohen, *Delinquent Boys* (Glencoe, Ill.: The Free Press, 1955), p. 36, as quoted by Merton, *supra,* footnote 82, pp. 177–178.

105. *Ibid.,* p. 178–179.

106. Albert K. Cohen, "Sociology of the Deviant Act," *American Sociological Review,* 30 (February, 1965), pp. 5–14.

107. Richard A. Cloward, "Illegitimate Means, Anomie, and Deviant Behavior," *American Sociological Review,* 24 (April, 1959), pp. 164–176; R. A. Cloward and Lloyd E. Ohlin, *Delinquency and Opportunity* (Glencoe, Ill.: The Free Press, 1960).

108. William J. Goode, "Illegitimacy, Anomie, and Cultural Penetration," *American Sociological Review,* 26 (December, 1961), pp. 910–925.

109. Elwin H. Powell, "Evolution of the American City and the Emergence of Anomie: A Culture Case Study of Buffalo, New York," *British Journal of Sociology,* 13 (June, 1962), pp. 156–168, and "Crime as a Function of Anomie," *Journal of Criminal Law, Criminology and Police Science,* 57 (June, 1966), pp. 161–171.

110. Representative studies include Bruno Bettelheim, "Individual and Mass Behavior in Extreme Situations," *Journal of Abnormal and Social Psychology,* 38 (1943), pp. 417–452; Unto Parvilahti, *Berlia's Garden: A Slave Laborer's Experience in the Soviet Utopia,* tr. by Alan Blair, (New York: E. P. Dutton, 1960); William L. White, *The Captives of Korea; Our Treatment of Theirs; Their Treatment of Ours* (New York: Scribner, 1957); and John McElroy, *This Was Andersonville* (New York: McDowell, 1957).

111. Donald R. Cressey and Witold Krassowski, "Inmate Organization and Anomie in American Prison and Soviet Labor Camps," *Social Problems,* 5 (Winter, 1957–58), pp. 217–230.

112. LaMar T. Empey, "Social Class and Occupational Aspiration: A Comparison of Absolute and Relative Measurement," *American Sociological Review,* 21 (December, 1956), pp. 703–709; Herbert H. Hyman, "The Value Systems of Different Classes: A Social Psychological Contribution to the Analysis of Stratification," in Reinhard Bendix and Seymour M. Lipset (eds.), *Class Status and Power* (Glencoe, Ill.: The Free Press, 1953), pp. 426–442; Alan B. Wilson, "Residential Segregation of Social Classes and Aspirations of High School Boys," *American Sociological Review,* 24 (December, 1959), pp. 836–845; Robert W. Winslow, "Anomie and Its Alternatives: A Self-Report Study of Delinquency," *Sociological Quarterly* (Fall, 1968), pp. 468–480.

113. *Supra,* footnote 82, p. 171.

114. The former include Hyman, *op. cit.;* Ephraim H. Mizruchi, *Success and Opportunity* (New York: The Free Press, 1964); and Winslow, *op. cit.;* while the latter include Delbert S. Elliott, "Delinquency and Perceived Opportunity," *Sociological Inquiry,* 32 (Spring, 1962), p. 227; and James F. Short, Jr., Ramon Rivera, and Ray A. Tennyson, "Perceived Opportunities, Gang Membership and Delinquency," *American Sociological Review,* 30 (February, 1965), pp. 56–67.

115. Although the number of such studies is limitless, representative works would include R. E. L. Faris and H. Warren Dunham, *Mental Disorders in Urban Areas* (Chicago: University of Chicago Press, 1939); Clifford Shaw and Henry McKay, *Delinquency Areas*

(Chicago: University of Chicago Press, 1929); and August B. Hollingshead and Frederick Redlich, *Social Class and Mental Illness* (New York; John Wiley, 1958).

116. These include Ronald L. Akers, "Socio-Economic Status and Delinquent Behavior: A Retest," *Journal of Research on Crime and Delinquency*, 1:38–46 (January, 1964); John P. Clark and Eugene P. Wenninger, "Socio-Economic Class and Area as Correlates of Illegal Behavior among Juveniles," *American Sociological Review*, 27:826–834 (December, 1962); Robert A. Dentler and Lawrence J. Monroe, "Social Correlates of Early Adolescent Theft," *American Sociological Review*, 26:733–743 (October, 1961); F. Ivan Nye, James F. Short, Jr., and Virgil J. Olson, "Socio-Economic Status and Delinquent Behavior," *American Journal of Sociology*, 63:381–389 (January, 1958); Austin L. Porterfield, "Delinquency and Its Outcome in Court and College," *American Journal of Sociology*, 49:199–208 (November, 1943); Herman Schwendinger, *The Instrumental Theory of Delinquency: A Tentative Formulation* (Ann Arbor, Mich.: University Microfilms, Inc., 1963); Arthur L. Stinchcombe, *Rebellion in High School* (Chicago: Quadrangle Books, 1964); Harwin L. Voss, "Socio-Economic Status and Reported Delinquent Behavior," *Social Problems*, 13:314–324 (Winter, 1966); James S. Wallerstein and Clement J. Wyle, "Our Law-Abiding Law-Breakers," *Probation*, 7:355–376 (April, 1947); Robert W. Winslow, *An Organizational Theory of Delinquency and Alienation* (Ann Arbor, Mich.: University Microfilms, Inc., 1966). One exception is Reiss and Rhodes's study. However, because they use juvenile court classifications along with self-report criteria, their data are not strictly comparable to these previous studies. See Albert J. Reiss, Jr., and Albert L. Rhodes, "The Distribution of Juvenile Delinquency in the Social Class Structure," *American Sociological Review*, 26:720–732 (October, 1961).

117. The Srole anomia scale includes the following five items:
— There is little use writing to public officials because they aren't really interested in the problems of the average man.
— Nowadays a person has to live pretty much for today and let tomorrow take care of itself.
— In spite of what people say, the lot of the average man is getting worse, not better.
— It's hardly fair to bring children into the world, the way things look for the future.
— These days a person doesn't really know whom he can count on.
Leo Srole, "Social Integration and its Corollaries, an Exploratory Study," *American Sociological Review*, 21 (December, 1956), pp. 709–716.

118. Wendell Bell, "Anomie, Social Isolation, and the Class Structure," *Sociometry*, 20 (June, 1957), pp. 105–116; Dorothy Meier and Wendell Bell, "Anomie and Differential Access to the Achievement of Life Goals," *American Sociological Review*, 24 (April, 1959), pp. 189–202.

119. Ephraim H. Mizruchi, "Aspiration and Poverty: A Neglected Aspect of Merton's Anomie," *Sociological Quarterly*, 8 (Autumn, 1967), pp. 439–446; Marven S. Olsen, "Alienation and Political Opinion," *Public Opinion Quarterly*, 29 (Summer, 1965), pp. 200–212; A. Lewis Rhodes, "Anomia, Aspiration, and Status," *Social Forces*, 42 (1964), pp. 434–440; and Richard L. Simpson, "A Note on Status, Mobility, and Anomie," *British Journal of Sociology*, 11 (December, 1960), pp. 370–372.

120. Lewis M. Killian and Charles M. Grigg, "Urbanism, Race, and Anomia," *American Journal of Sociology*, 67 (May, 1962), pp. 661–665; and Rhodes, *supra*, footnote 119.

121. G. Reimamis and S. H. Darol, "Correlates and Prediction of Anomie in a V. A. Domiciliary," *Journal of Social Psychology*, 55 (December, 1961), pp. 237–244.

122. Killian and Grigg, *supra*, footnote 120, Olsen, *supra*, footnote 119.

123. Rhodes, *supra*, footnote 119.

124. T. C. Keedy and M. J. Vincent, "Anomie and Religious Orthodoxy," *Sociology and Social Research*, 43 (September–October, 1958), pp. 34–37; Olsen, *supra*, footnote 119; Alan H. Roberts and Milton Rokeach, "Anomie, Authoritarianism and Prejudice: A Replication," *American Journal of Sociology*, 4 (January, 1956); Srole, *supra*, footnote 93.

125. Keedy and Vincent, *supra*, footnote 124.

126. *Supra*, footnote 121.

127. Melvin M. Tumin and Ray C. Collins, Jr., "Status, Mobility and Anomie: A Study of Readiness for Desegregation," *British Journal of Sociology*, 10 (September, 1954), pp. 253–267.

128. Edward L. McDill, "Anomie, Authoritarianism, Prejudice, and SES: An Attempt at Clarification," *Social Forces,* 39 (March, 1961), pp. 234–245.

129. Dwight G. Dean and Jon A. Reeves, "Anomie: A Comparison of a Catholic and a Protestant Sample," *Sociometry,* 25 (June, 1962), pp. 209–212; W. Y. Wassef, "Influences of Religion, Socio-economic Status, and Education of Anomie," *Sociological Quarterly,* 8 (Spring, 1967), pp. 233–238.

130. L. Bramson, *The Political Context of Sociology* (Princeton, N.J.: Princeton University Press, 1961), p. 1.

131. Nathanial Glazer, "The Alienation of Modern Man," *Commentary,* 3 (April, 1947), p. 378.

132. Melvin Seeman, "The Logic and Limits of Mass Society Theory," unpublished paper delivered at University of California at Los Angeles, 1963.

133. William Kornhauser, *The Politics of Mass Society* (New York: The Free Press, 1959).

134. Gustave Le Bon, *The Crowd* (London: Ernest Bonn Ltd., 1947).

135. José Ortega y Gasset, *The Revolt of the Masses* (New York: W. W. Norton, 1932).

136. Karl Mannheim, *Ideology and Utopia* (London: Routledge and Kegan Paul, 1940).

137. *Supra,* footnote 133, p. 27.

138. Emil Lederer, *State of the Masses* (New York: W. W. Norton, 1940).

139. Hannah Arendt, *The Origins of Totalitarianism* (New York: Harcourt, Brace, 1951).

140. *Supra,* footnote 134, p. 33

141. Daniel Bell, "America as a Mass Society: *A Critique,"* in Daniel Bell, *The End of Ideology* (New York: The Free Press, 1961), pp. 21–22.

142. *Supra,* footnote 134, pp. 33–34.

143. *Ibid.,* p. 39.

144. *Ibid.,* p. 40.

145. *Ibid.,* p. 40–41.

146. *Ibid.,* p. 43.

147. *Ibid.,* p. 236.

148. *Ibid.,* p. 47.

149. These include Raymond A. Bauer and Alice H. Bauer, "America, Mass Society and Mass Media," *Journal of Social Issues,* 16 (1960), pp. 3–66; *supra,* footnote 141; Walter M. Gerson, "Alienation in Mass Society: Some Causes and Responses," *Sociology and Social Research,* 49 (January, 1965), pp. 143–152; S. Leventman, "Race and Mental Illness in Mass Society," *Social Problems,* 16 (1968), pp. 73–78; Joseph D. Lohman and Dietrich C. Reitzes, "Note on Race Relations in Mass Society," *American Journal of Sociology,* 58 (November, 1952), pp. 240–246; and Maurice Pinard, "Mass Society and Political Movements: A New Formulation," *American Journal of Sociology,* 73 (May, 1968), pp. 682–690. Mass society is discussed as a theory in the sense used by Kornhauser in Joseph R. Gusfield, "Mass Society and Extremist Politics," *American Sociological Review,* 27 (February, 1962), pp. 19–30; and Philip Selznick, "Institutional Vulnerability and Mass Society," *American Journal of Sociology,* 56 (January, 1951), pp. 320–331.

150. *Supra,* footnote 132.

151. Edward Shils, "The Theory of Mass Society," in Philip Olson (ed.), *America as a Mass Society* (New York: The Free Press, 1963), p. 315.

152. See, for example, John F. Cuber, William F. Kenkel, and Robert A. Harper, *Problems of American Society* (New York: Holt, Rinehart and Winston, 1964), and Bernard Rosenberg, Israel Gerver, and F. William Howton, *Mass Society in Crisis,* (New York: Macmillan, 1964).

153. Gwinn Nettler, "Antisocial Sentiment and Criminality," *American Sociological Review,* 24 (April, 1959) p. 202.

154. Melvin Seeman, "On the Meaning of Alienation," *American Sociological Review,* 24 (December, 1959), pp. 783–791.

155. *Supra,* footnote 132.

156. *Supra,* footnote 154.

157. Charles J. Browning, Malcolm F. Farmer, H. David Kirk, and G. Duncan Mitchell, "On the Meaning of Alienation," Letter to the Editor, *American Sociological Review,* 26 (October, 1961), pp. 780–781. Merton's typology of adaptation can be similarly used in this context.

A predisposing stage of conformity or ritualism might be followed by a stage of cultural disaffection involving retreatism, which is followed by an adaptation stage of innovation or rebellion.

158. Joseph C. Mouledous and Elizabeth C. Mouledous, "Criticisms of the Concept of Alienation," Commentary and Debates Section, *American Journal of Sociology*, 70 (July, 1964), pp. 78–82.

159. *Ibid.*, pp. 79–80.

160. Daniel Bell, "The Rediscovery of Alienation: Some Notes Along the Quest for the Historical Marx," *Journal of Philosophy*, 56 (November, 1959), pp. 933–952.

161. Erich Fromm, *Marx's Concept of Man* (New York: Frederick Ungar, 1961), Chapter 5.

162. Karl Marx, "Alienated Labor," *Ibid.*, pp. 93–109.

163. Russell Middleton, "Alienation, Race, and Education," *American Sociological Review*, 28 (December, 1963), pp. 973–983.

164. Erich Fromm, *The Sane Society* (New York: Rinehart and Company, 1955), p. 141.

165. Kenneth Keniston, "Alienation and the Decline of Utopia," *The American Scholar*, 29 (Spring, 1960), pp. 163–168.

166. H. Stroup, "A Historical Explanation of Alienation," *Social Casework*, 42 (March, 1961), pp. 107–111.

167. M. Greene, "Alienation within a Problematic of Substance and Subject, "*Social Research*, 33 (Autumn, 1966), pp. 355–374.

168. *Supra*, footnote 155.

169. Dwight G. Dean, "Alienation: Its Meaning and Measurement," *American Sociological Review*, 26 (October, 1961), pp. 754–755.

170. Russell Middleton, "Alienation, Race and Education," *American Sociological Review*, 28 (December, 1963), pp. 973–983.

171. Arthur Neal and Saloman Rettig, "Dimensions of Alienation among Manual and Non-manual Workers," *American Sociological Review*, 28 (August, 1963), pp. 599–608.

172. Robert Blauner, *Alienation and Freedom* (Chicago: University of Chicago Press, 1964).

173. Arthur Neal and Saloman Rettig, "On the Multidimensionality of Alienation," *American Sociological Review*, 32 (February, 1967), pp. 54–64.

174. John C. Whitehorn, "Alienation and Leadership," *Psychiatry*, 24 (May, 1961), pp. 3–7, and Jan Hajda, "Alienation and Integration of Student Intellectuals," *American Sociological Review*, 26 (October, 1961), pp. 758–777.

175. Kenneth Keniston, *The Uncommitted: Alienated Youth in American Society* (New York: Harcourt, Brace and World, 1965).

176. Leonard I. Pearlin, "Alienation from Work: A Study of Nursing Personnel," *American Sociological Review*, 27 (June, 1962), pp. 312–314.

177. Hajda, *supra*, footnote 174.

178. *Ibid.*, Arnold Rose, "Alienation and Participation: A Comparison of Group Leaders and the Mass," *American Sociological Review*, 27 (December, 1962), pp. 834–838, and Melvin Seeman, "Alienation, Membership, and Political Knowledge, a Comparative Study, *Public Opinion Quarterly*, 30 (Fall, 1966), pp. 353–367.

179. *Supra*, footnote 171.

180. L. A. Zurcher, A. Meadow, and S. L. Zurcher, "Value Orientation, Role Conflict and Alienation from Work: A Cross-Cultural Study," *American Sociological Review* 30 (August, 1965), pp. 539–548.

181. M. Aiken and J. Hage, "Organizational Alienation: A Comparative Analysis," *American Sociological Review*, 31 (August, 1966), pp. 497–507.

182. G. A. Miller, "Professionals in Bureaucracy: Alienation among Industrial Scientists and Engineers," *American Sociological Review*, 32 (October, 1967), pp. 755–768.

183. Whitehorn, *supra*, footnote 174.

184. Robert Sommer and Robert Hall, "Alienation and Mental Illness," *American Sociological Review*, 23 (August, 1958), pp. 418–420.

185. H. E. Ransford, "Isolation, Powerlessness, and Violence: A Study of Attitude and Participation in the Watts Riot," *American Journal of Sociology*, 73 (March, 1968), pp. 581–591, and M. Zeitlin, "Alienation and Revolution," *Social Forces*, 45 (December, 1966), pp. 224–236.

186. Michael A. Faia, "Alienation, Structural Strain, and Political Deviancy: A Test of Merton's Hypothesis," *Social Problems,* 14 (Spring, 1967), pp. 389–413.

187. Gwinn Nettler, "Antisocial Sentiment and Criminalty," *American Sociological Review,* 24 (April, 1959), pp. 202–208.

188. J. L. Simmons, "Liberalism, Alienation, and Personal Disturbance," *Sociology and Social Research,* 49 (July, 1965), pp. 456–464.

189. Edward L. McDill and J. C. Ridley, "Status, Anomia, and Political Participation," *American Journal of Sociology,* 68 (Spring, 1962), pp. 205–213.

190. Frederick Templeton, "Alienation and Political Participation: Some Research Findings," *Public Opinion Quarterly,* 30 (Summer, 1966), pp. 244–261.

191. Robert Winslow, *An Organizational Theory of Delinquency and Alienation* (Ann Arbor, Mich.: University Microfilms, 1966).

192. *Supra,* footnote 172.

193. Daniel Bell, "The Theory of Mass Society: A Critique," *Commentary,* 22 (July, 1956), pp. 75–83.

194. See, for example, Morris Axelrod, "Urban Structure and Social Participation," *American Sociological Review,* 21 (February, 1956), pp. 13–18; and Wendell Bell and M. D. Boar, "Urban Neighborhoods and Informal Social Relations," *American Journal of Sociology,* 62 (January, 1957), pp. 391–398.

195. *Supra,* footnote 194.

196. Émile Durkheim, *The Division of Labor,* translated by George Simpson (New York: The Free Press, 1933).

197. H. L. Wilensky, "Mass Society and Mass Culture: Interdependence or Independence?" *American Sociological Review,* 29 (April, 1964), pp. 173–197.

Chapter 4

1. George C. Homans, *The Human Group* (New York: Harcourt, Brace and World, 1950) p. 451, as quoted in Mabel A. Elliott and Francis E. Merrill, *Social Disorganization* (New York: Harper and Row, 1961) p. 51.

2. John Horton, "The Dehumanization of Anomie and Alienation: A Problem in the Ideology of Sociology," *British Journal of Sociology,* 40 (December, 1964), pp. 283–300.

3. Marshall Clinard, *The Sociology of Deviant Behavior* (New York: Holt, Rinehart and Winston, 1962), p. 22.

4. George A. Lundberg, Clarence C. Schrag, and Otto N. Larsen, *Sociology* (New York: Harper and Bros., 1958), p. 349.

5. Erich Fromm, *The Sane Society* (New York: Rinehart and Company, 1955) pp. 68 and 72.

6. Paul Goodman, *Growing up Absurd* (New York: Rinehart and Company, 1955) p. 199.

7. Milton Barron, *The Juvenile in Delinquent Society* (New York: Alfred A. Knopf, 1954).

8. Kenneth Keniston, "Alienation and the Decline of Utopia," *The American Scholar,* 29 (Spring, 1960) pp. 161–200.

9. Émile Durkheim, *The Rules of Sociological Method* (New York: The Free Press, 1938), p. 71.

10. *Ibid.,* p. 70.

11. *Ibid.,* p. 71.

12. These hypotheses about conflict are traced mainly to three classic works: Lewis Coser, *The Functions of Social Conflict,* (New York: The Free Press, 1956); Georg Simmel, *Conflict: The Web of Group Affiliations,* Translated by Kurt H. Wolff, (Glencoe, Ill.: The Free Press, 1955); and Georges Sorel, *Reflections on Violence,* (New York: Collier Books, 1961).

There has been much recent interest in the topic of conflict: For example, see Lewis A. Coser, *The Functions of Social Conflict* (New York: The Free Press, 1956) and Ralf Dahrendorf, *Class and Class Conflict in Industrial Society* (Stanford: Stanford University Press, 1959). The position that deviancy may contribute to positive social change is also taken by Kai T. Erikson, *Wayward Puritans* (New York: Wiley, 1966) and Robert A. Dentler and Kai T. Erikson, "The Functions of Deviance in Groups," *Social Problems,* 7 (1959), pp. 98–107.

13. *Webster's Third New International Dictionary,* p. 1488, definition 2.

14. Throughout the foregoing analysis we may observe three criteria of a good classification system:

1. *Articulation:* The classification should proceed in steps from the general to the specific, so that the material can be examined either in terms of detailed categories or of broad groupings, whichever are more appropriate for a given purpose.

2. *Logical correctness:* In an articulated set of categories those on each step must be exhaustive and mutually exclusive.

3. *Adaptation to the structure of the situation:* The classification should be based on a comprehensive outline of the situation as a whole—an outline containing the main elements and processes in the situation which it is important to distinguish for purposes of understanding, predicting, or policy making.

Paul F. Lazarsfeld and Allen H. Barton, "Some General Principles of Questionnaire Classification," in Paul F. Lazarsfeld and Morris Rosenberg, *The Language of Social Research,* (Glencoe, Ill.: The Free Press, 1955), p. 84.

15. International Association of Chiefs of Police, Committee on Uniform Records, *Uniform Crime Reporting,* (New York: J. J. Little and Ives, 1929), pp. 180–182; See also *Uniform Crime Reports,* 1958, Special Issue, pp. 15–17; 20–25.

16. Theodore N. Ferdinand, *Typologies of Delinquency* (New York: Random House, 1966).

17. Franz Alexander and Hugo Staub, *The Criminal, the Judge, and the Public* (New York: Free Press, 1956), pp. 83–124.

18. David Abrahamsen, *Psychology of Crime* (New York: Columbia University Press, 1960), pp. 123–127.

19. R. Nevitt Sanford, "A Psychoanalytic Study of Three Criminal Types," *Journal of Criminal Psychopathology,* 5 (July, 1943), pp. 57–68.

20. S. Kirson Weinberg, *Society and Personality Disorders* (Englewood Cliffs, N.J.: Prentice-Hall, 1952), pp. 264–69.

21. *Supra,* footnote 16, Chapter 5.

22. Marshall B. Clinard, *Sociology of Deviant Behavior* (New York: Holt, Rinehart and Winston, 1963), p. 211.

23. *Supra,* footnote 16, pp. 119–141. Although Ferdinand's typology refers specifically to juvenile delinquency, it has at least some relevance to adult crime.

24. Duane Strinden, *Parole Prediction Using Criminological Theory and Manifold Classification Techniques* (unpublished master's thesis, University of Washington, 1959).

25. Ruth Shonlie Cavan, *Criminology* (New York: Thomas Y. Crowell, 1962), Chapter 3.

26. Marshall B. Clinard, *Sociology of Deviant Behavior* (New York: Holt, Rinehart and Winston, 1963), p. 425.

27. H. Warren Dunham, "The Social Personality of the Catatonic Schizophrenic," *American Journal of Sociology,* 49 (May, 1944), pp. 508–518; R. E. L. Faris, "Cultural Isolation and the Schizophrenic Personality," *American Journal of Sociology,* 40 (September, 1934), pp. 155–169; R. R. Grinker and J. Spiegal, *Men Under Stress* (Philadelphia: Blakiston, 1945); A. B. Hollingshead, R. Ellis and E. Kirby, "Social Mobility and Mental Illness", *American Sociological Review,* 19 (October, 1954), pp. 578–584; Stanley H. King and Andrew F. Henry, "Aggression and Cardiovascular Reactions Related to Parental Control over Behavior," *Journal of Abnormal Social Psychology,* 50 (1955), pp. 206–210; David Mechanic, "Stress, Illness Behavior, and the Sick Role," *American Sociological Review,* 26 (February, 1961), p. 51; S. Kirson Weinberg, "A Sociological Analysis of a Schizophrenic Type," *American Sociological Review,* 15 (October, 1950), pp. 600–610.

28. R. E. L. Faris, "Reflections of Social Disorganization in the Behavior of a Schizophrenic Patient," *American Journal of Sociology,* 50 (September, 1944), pp. 134–141.

29. Arnold Green describes this neurotic pattern of conformity in "The Middle-Class Male Child and Neurosis," *American Sociological Review,* 11 (February, 1946), pp. 31–41.

30. George E. Simpson and J. Milton Yinger, *Racial and Cultural Minorities* (New York: Harper and Bros., 1953), pp. 105–107.

31. T. W. Adorno, *et al., The Authoritarian Personality* (New York: Harper and Row, 1950); Gordon Allport, *The Nature of Prejudice* (New York: Addison–Wesley, 1954); Bruno Bettelheim and Morris Janowitz, "Ethnic Tolerance: A Function of Personal and Social Control," *American Journal of Sociology*, 55 (1940), pp. 137–145; J. Greenblum and L. I. Pearlin, "Vertical Mobility and Prejudice: A Social Psychological Analysis," in Reinhard Bendix and Seymour Martin Lipset, *Class, Status and Power* (New York: The Free Press, 1953), pp. 480–491; Gunnar Myrdal, *An American Dilemma* (New York: Harper and Row, 1944); Robin M. Williams, Jr., *American Society* (New York: Alfred A. Knopf, 1960), Chapter 11.

32. Émile Durkheim, *Suicide* (New York: The Free Press, 1951), pp. 241–276.

33. Andrew F. Henry and James F. Short, Jr., *Suicide and Homicide* (New York: The Free Press, 1954).

34. Kingsley Davis, "Final Note On a Case of Extreme Isolation," *American Journal of Sociology*, 52 (March, 1947), pp. 432–437; E. Gartly Jaco, "Social Isolation Hypothesis and Schizophrenia," *American Sociological Review*, 19 (October, 1954), pp. 567–577; Melvin L. Kohn and John A. Clausen, "Social Isolation and Schizophrenia," *American Sociological Review*, 20 (June, 1955), pp. 265–273.

35. *Supra*, footnote 31 and Leo Srole, "Social Integration and Certain Corollaries," *American Sociological Review*, 21 (December, 1956), pp. 709–716.

36. *Supra*, footnote 32.

37. Derek L. Phillips, "Rejection: A Possible Consequence of Seeking Help for Mental Disorder," *American Sociological Review*, 29 (December, 1963), pp. 963–972; and "Rejection of the Mentally Ill: The Influence of Behavior and Sex," *American Sociological Review*, 29 (October, 1964), pp. 679–687.

38. *Ibid.*

39. *Supra*, footnote 37.

40. John Cummings and Elaine Cummings, *Closed Ranks: An Experiment in Mental Health Education* (Cambridge: Harvard University Press, 1957); Shirley Star, "The Place of Psychiatry in Popular Thinking," *American Association for Public Opinion Research*, (May, 1957).

41. Eric Hoffer, *The True Believer* (New York: Harper and Bros., 1951).

42. See Adorno, *supra*, note 31, p. 228 for a full description of the authoritarian personality syndrome.

43. The following research findings resulted from a two-year study of seriousness conducted jointly with Delos H. Kelly. An expanded version of these findings is given in Kelly's M.A. thesis, entitled "An Analytical Approach to the Assessment of the Seriousness of Delinquent Behavior," San Diego State College.

44. A number of studies of seriousness of delinquency took place prior to Sellin and Wolfgang's classic work; however, none of these approaches the methodological sophistication of Sellin and Wolfgang's work. These are cited in Thorsten Sellin and Marvin E. Wolfgang, *The Measurement of Delinquency* (New York: John Wiley and Sons, 1964), pp. 62–70.

45. *Ibid.*, pp. 131–144.

46. *Ibid.*, p. 300.

47. *Ibid.*, p. 303.

48. *Ibid.*, p. 249.

49. *Ibid.*, p. 297.

50. See, for example, Solomon Kobrin, "The Conflict of Values in Delinquency Areas," *American Sociological Review*, 16 (1951), pp. 653–661; and Walter B. Miller, "Lower Class Culture as a Generating Milieu of Gang Delinquency," *Journal of Social Issues*, 14 (1958), pp. 5–19.

51. *Supra*, footnote 44, p. 268.

52. G. N. Rose, "Concerning the Measurement of Delinquency," *British Journal of Criminology*, 6 (October, 1966), p. 442.

53. Dogan G. Akman, Robert Figlio, and Andre Normandeau, "Concerning the Measurement of Delinquency—A Rejoinder and Beyond," *British Journal of Criminology*, 7 (October, 1967), p. 442.

54. Rose, *op. cit.*, p. 414.

55. Federal Bureau of Investigation, *Uniform Crime Reporting Handbook*, (Washington, D.C.: Federal Bureau of Investigation, July, 1966), pp. 10–65.

56. *Supra,* footnote 44, pp. 381–386.

57. Dogan G. Akman and Andre Normandeau, "The Measurement of Crime and Delinquency in Canada: A Replication Study, *British Journal of Criminology,* 7 (April, 1967), pp. 129–149.

Chapter 5

1. Several of these theories have proposed a link between crime and social class; however, they have not attempted to look at the trends in class composition of society in relation to increasing (or decreasing) rates of crime and delinquency.

2. Cesare Beccaria, *An Essay on Crime and Punishments* (New York: Stephen Gould, 1809).

3. Robert G. Caldwell, *Criminology,* 2d ed. (New York: The Ronald Press, 1965), p. 168.

4. *Ibid.,* pp. 163–164.

5. Ruth S. Cavan, *Criminology* (New York: Thomas Y. Crowell, 1962), p. 692.

6. Ernest A. Hooton, *Crime and the Man* (Cambridge: Harvard University Press, 1939).

7. These are summarized in W. Norwood East, "Physical Factors in Criminal Behavior," *Journal of Clinical Psychopathology,* 8 (July, 1946), pp. 7–36.

8. William Healy and Augusta F. Bronner, *New Light on Delinquency and Its Treatment* (New York: Yale University Press, 1936); Franz Alexander and William Healy, *Roots of Crime: Psychoanalytic Studies* (New York: Alfred A. Knopf, 1935).

9. Walter C. Reckless, *The Crime Problem* (New York: Appleton-Century-Crofts, 1967), p. 20.

10. Caldwell, *op. cit.,* p. 172.

11. Cavan, *op. cit.,* p. 687.

12. *Ibid.*

13. Edwin Sutherland, *Principles of Criminology* (Chicago: J. B. Lippincott, 1960), Chapter 4.

14. As stated by Richard Cloward and Lloyd E. Ohlin, *Delinquency and Opportunity* (Glencoe, Ill.: The Free Press, 1961), pp. 145–148.

15. Daniel Glasier, "Criminality Theories and Behavioral Images," *American Journal of Sociology,* 61 (March, 1956), pp. 433–444.

16. Solomon Kobrin, "The Conflict of Values in Delinquency Areas," *American Sociological Review,* 16 (October, 1951), pp. 653–659.

17. Walter B. Miller, "Lower Class Culture as a Generating Milieu of Gang Delinquency," *The Journal of Social Issues,* 14 (April, 1958), pp. 5–19.

18. William C. Kvaraceus, Walter S. Miller, *et al., Delinquent Behavior: Culture and the Individual* (Washington, D.C.: Juvenile Delinquency Project, NEA, 1201 Sixteenth St. NW, 1959).

19. Albert K. Cohen, *Delinquent Boys: The Culture of the Gang* (New York: The Free Press, 1955).

20. Albert K. Cohen and James F. Short, Jr., "Research in Delinquent Subcultures," *The Journal of Social Issues,* 14 (April, 1958), pp. 20–31.

21. George B. Vold, *Theoretical Criminology* (New York, Oxford, 1958).

22. *Supra,* footnote 14.

23. Herbert Bloch and Arthur Niederhoffer, *The Gang: A Study in Adolescent Behavior* (New York: Philosophical Library, 1958).

24. President's Commission on Law Enforcement and Administration of Justice, (PCLAJ), *Report of the President's Commission on Crime in the District of Columbia* (Washington, D.C.: U.S. Government Printing Office, 1966), p. 42. Martin E. Wolfgang, *Patterns in Criminal Homicide* (Philadelphia: University of Pennsylvania Press, 1958), p. 207.

25. UCR, 1960, p. 11. D.C. Crime Commission Report, p. 67.

26. D.C. Crime Commission Report, p. 53. Menachem Amir, "Patterns of Forcible Rape" (Ph.D. Dissertation, University of Pennsylvania, 1965) p. 496.

27. *Supra,* footnote 24.

28. *Supra,* footnote 25.

29. *Supra,* footnote 26.

30. UCR, 1965, Table 14, p. 105.

31. D.C. Crime Commission Report, pp. 54–64. The 25 per cent figure for forcible rape refers to percentage of attackers with a weapon. The exact injury statistics are not known.

32. UCR, 1965, p. 51.

33. *Supra,* footnote 24.

34. UCR, 1965, p. 94. Ninety-nine per cent of all negligent manslaughter is due to automobile accident (UCR, 1958, Special Issue, p. 25).

35. Martin E. Wolfgang, *UCR: A Critical Appraisal,* University of Pennsylvania Law Review, III: 704–738 (April, 1963).

36. UCR, 1965, p. 51.

37. PCLAJ, *Task Force Report: Assessment of Crime* (Washington, D.C.: U.S. Government Printing Office, 1967), Chapter 3, notes 30–40, 73–92.

38. UCR, 1965, p. 67.

39. UCR, 1965, p. 107.

40. Phillip H. Ennis, *Criminal Victimization in the United States: A Report of a National Survey* (Field Surveys II, PCLAJ, Washington, D.C.: U.S. Government Printing Office, 1967) — hereafter referred to as the NORC survey.

41. *President's Commission on Law Enforcement and Administration of Justice, Task Force Report: Corrections* (Washington, D.C.: United States Government Printing Office, 1967), p. 215.

42. President's Commission, *The Challenge of Crime in a Free Society* (Washington, D.C.: U.S. Government Printing Office, 1967), p. 55.

43. Source: The President's Commission on Law Enforcement and Administration of Justice, *Criminal Victimization in the U.S.: A Report of a National Survey: Field Surveys II,* (Washington D.C.: U.S. Government Printing Office, 1967), Chapter 11.

44. Representative studies include M. G. Caldwell, "The Economic Status of the Families of Delinquent Boys in Wisconsin," *American Journal of Sociology,* 37 (September, 1931), pp. 231–239; William Lloyd Warner and Paul Lunt, *The Social Life of a Modern Community* (New Haven: Yale University Press, 1941), pp. 373–377; William C. Kvaraceus, *Juvenile Delinquency in the Schools* (Yonkers-on-Hudson, New York: World Book Company, 1945); and Kvaraceus, "Juvenile Delinquency and Social Class," *Journal of Educational Sociology,* 18 (September, 1946), pp. 51–54; August B. Hollingshead, "Selected Characteristics of Classes in A Middle Western Community," *American Sociological Review,* 12 (August, 1947), pp. 385–395.

45. These include Ronald L. Akers, "Socio-Economic Status and Delinquent Behavior: A Retest," *Journal of Research on Crime and Delinquency,* 1 (January, 1964), pp. 38–46; John P. Clark and Eugene P. Wenninger, "Socio-Economic Class and Area as Correlates of Illegal Behavior among Juveniles," *American Sociological Review,* 27 (December, 1962) pp. 826–834; Robert A. Dentler and Lawrence J. Monroe, "Social Correlates of Early Adolescent Theft," *American Sociological Review,* 26 (October, 1961), pp. 733–743; F. Ivan Nye, James F. Short, Jr., and Virgil J. Olson, "Socio-Economic Status and Delinquent Behavior," *American Journal of Sociology,* 63 (January, 1958), pp. 381–389; Austin L. Porterfield, "Delinquency and Its Outcome in Court and College," *American Journal of Sociology,* 49 (November, 1943), pp. 199–208; Herman Schwendinger, *The Instrumental Theory of Delinquency: A Tentative Formulation* (Ann Arbor, Mich.: University Microfilms, Inc., 1963); Arthur L. Stinchcombe, *Rebellion in High School* (Chicago: Quadrangle Books, 1964); Harwin L. Voss, "Socio-Economic Status and Reported Delinquent Behavior," *Social Problems,* 13 (Winter, 1966), pp. 314–324; James S. Wallerstein and Clement J. Wyle, "Our Law-Abiding Law-Breakers," *Probation,* 7 (April, 1947), pp. 355–376; Robert W. Winslow, *An Organizational Theory of Delinquency and Alienation* (Ann Arbor, Mich.: University Microfilms, Inc., 1966). One exception is Reiss and Rhodes's study. However, since they use juvenile court classifications along with self-report criteria, their data are not strictly comparable to these previous studies. See Albert J. Reiss, Jr., and Albert L. Rhodes, "The Distribution of Juvenile Delinquency in the Social Class Structure," *American Sociological Review,* 26 (October, 1961), pp. 720–732.

46. *Ibid.*

47. Donald R. Taft, "Nationality and Crime," *American Sociological Review,* 1 (October, 1936), p. 732.

48. John P. Clark and Eugene P. Wenninger, "Social Class and Area as Correlated of Illegal Behavior among Juveniles," *American Sociological Review,* 27 (December, 1962), pp. 826–834.

49. Commission on Law Observance and Enforcement, *Report on Criminal Statistics* (Washington, D.C.: U.S. Government Printing Office, 1931).

50. Daniel Bell, "The Myth of Crime Waves: The Actual Decline of Crime in the United States," in *The End of Ideology* (New York: The Free Press, 1962), p. 153.

51. *Ibid.*

52. Edwin H. Powell, "Crime as a Function of Anomie," *Journal of Criminal Law, Criminology and Police Science,* 56 (June, 1966), pp. 161–171

53. *Supra,* footnote 50, p. 158.

54. Ruth S. Cavan and Jordan T. Cavan, *Delinquency and Crime: Cross-Cultural Perspectives* (Philadelphia: J. B. Lippincott, 1968).

55. *Ibid.,* p. 221.

56. Paul Goodman, *Growing Up Absurd* (New York: Random House, 1960), p. 13.

57. R. E. L. Faris, "Contemporary and Prospective Social Disorganization," *Sociology and Social Research,* 32 (January–February 1948) pp. 679–684.

58. Robert M. Marsh, *Comparative Sociology* (New York: Harcourt, Brace and World, 1967), pp. 329–336, Appendices 1–2, pp. 337-374.

59. Ivo K. Feierabend and Rosalind L. Feierabend, "Aggressive Behavior within Polities, 1948–1962: A Cross-National Study," *Journal of Conflict Resolution,* 10 (September, 1966), pp. 249–271.

60. Betty A. Nesvold, "Scalogram Analysis of Political Violence: A Cross-National Study," a paper read at the 1967 annual meeting of the American Political Science Association, Pick-Congress Hotel, Chicago, September 5–9, 1967.

61. *Demographic Yearbook,* 1965 (New York: United Nations, 1966), Table 44, pp. 762–775. These are rates per 100,000 population. While these cross-cultural statistics have been questioned as to reliability and validity, they are the only statistics available for a large number of nations. Furthermore, recent studies indicate these rates are more reliable than is generally assumed. Jack P. Gibbs, "Suicide," in Robert K. Merton and Robert A. Nisbet, *Contemporary Social Problems* (New York: Harcourt, Brace and World, 1966), p. 287.

62. James C. Coleman, *Abnormal Psychology in Modern Life* (Chicago: Scott, Foresman), pp. 236–237.

63. Shirley A. Star, "The Screening of Psychoneurotics in the Army: Technical Development of Tests," Chapter 13 in Samuel A. Stouffer, *et al., Measurement and Prediction: Studies in Social Psychology in World War II,* Vol. IV (Princeton, New Jersey: Princeton University Press, 1950).

64. Norman Jollife, "Alcohol and Nutrition: The Diseases of Chronic Alcoholism," in *Alcohol, Science and Society* (New Haven: Yale University Press, 1945), p. 76–77.

65. Ralf Dahrendorf, *Class and Class Conflict in Industrial Society* (Stanford, Calif.: Stanford University Press, 1959), p. 238.

Chapter 6

1. Max Weber, *The Theory of Social and Economic Organization,* translated by A. M. Henderson and Talcott Parons, edited by Talcott Parsons (New York: Oxford University Press, 1947), pp. 329–340.

2. Robert K. Merton, "Bureaucratic Structure and Personality," Robert K. Merton, *et al., Bureaucracy* (New York: The Free Press, 1952), pp. 361–371; H. H. Gerth, C. W. Mills (ed. and trans.), *From Max Weber: Essays on Sociology* (New York: Oxford University Press, 1945), pp. 196–244.

3. Alvin W. Gouldner, *Patterns of Industrial Bureaucracy* (New York: Antioch Press, 1954), pp. 15–24; Chapter 10.

4. Fritz Marx, "Bureaucracy," *Introduction to Politics,* edited by R. V. Peal and J. S. Roucek (New York: Thomas Y. Crowell, 1941), Chapter 19.

5. Talcott Parsons, "Suggestions for a Sociological Approach to the Theory of Organizations," *Structure and Process in Modern Societies* (Glencoe, Ill.: The Free Press, 1960).

6. Peter M. Blau, W. Richard Scott, *Formal Organizations: A Comparative Approach* (San Francisco: Chandler, 1962), pp. 42–45.

7. Franz Neuman, *The Democratic and Authoritarian State* (Glencoe, Ill.: The Free Press, 1957).

8. Amitai Etzioni, *A Comparative Analysis of Complex Organizations* (New York: The Free Press, 1961). The following chapter will draw extensively from this source.

9. *Supra,* footnote 1, p. 152.

10. Chester I. Barnard, "The Theory of Authority," *The Functions of the Executive* (Cambridge, Mass.: Harvard University Press, 1938), pp. 161–184.

11. *Supra,* footnote 1, pp. 324–392.

12. Etzioni defines power as the actor's ability to induce or influence another actor to carry out his directives or other norms he supports.

13. Richard Cloward and Lloyd E. Ohlin, *Delinquency and Opportunity* (Glencoe, Ill.: The Free Press, 1960).

14. Edwin H. Sutherland, *White Collar Crime* (Dryden Press, 1949).

15. Address to the American Sociological Society, 1939.

16. "50 Ways Employees Steal From Their Store," *Life* (December 15, 1967), pp. 70–71.

17. These findings, first reported in *Reader's Digest,* are presented in Riis and Pattie, *The Repairman Will Get You If You Don't Watch Out* (Doubleday, Doran, 1942), pp. 53–184.

18. Austin L. Porterfield, "Delinquency and Its Outcome in Court and College," *American Journal of Sociology,* 49 (November, 1943), pp. 199–208.

19. These self-report studies are discussed more fully in Chapter 5.

20. Robert H. Bolke, "Social Mobility, Stratification Inconsistency, and Middle Class Delinquency," *Social Problems,* 8 (Spring, 1961), pp. 351–363.

21. The details of sampling and methods are given in Robert Winslow, *An Organizational Theory of Delinquency and Alienation* (Ann Arbor, Mich.: University Microfilms, 1966), Chapter 2.

22. Thus there are three independent variables—SES heterogeneity, area status, and racial segregation—and two measures of the delinquency dependent variable—self-report and official. The basis for measurement of the independent variables was the social area data compiled by Vincent Correll, *Effect of School District Size Upon Public Interest in Schools* (Ann Arbor: University Microfilms, 1963). Correll's work, in turn, is based upon the earlier work of R. Shevky and W. Bell, *Social Area Analysis* (Stanford: Stanford University Press, 1955). Assuming the census tracts were of relatively equal population size, summary measures were computed based on the census tracts for a given school attendance area. SES heterogeneity thus was measured by the standard deviation of Shevky-Bell school area status scores. Area status and racial segregation were mean status and segregation scores for a given school area. Self-report delinquency was measured by a nine-item scale drawn from a larger questionnaire by item analysis techniques. The self-report items were various acts of delinquency including larceny, auto theft, narcotics abuse, gang fighting, carrying a concealed weapon, purchasing stolen goods, forgery, and going to school intoxicated. Official statistics were 602 petition rates for Los Angeles County for 1962. These rates were census tract figures recomputed for school areas. Arthur Rowe, *Profiles of Delinquency* (Los Angeles: Department of Community Services, 1963).

23. It should be noted that while alienation is here viewed as institutional in locus, the types of deviant behavior are deviancies with regard to ends of the individual in the larger society. The implications of this are two-fold: First, behavior must be evaluated in terms of individual life goals as well as socially sanctioned means and ends in the larger society. Second, it is possible that the typical adaptations of individuals within a coercive (or utilitarian) setting may be considered "deviant." To illustrate, an individual has need for heterosexual relations, for foods of various types and other health needs. These needs may be denied while in prison. This results in alienative feeling directed toward the prison staff, prison life, even other in-

mates. If an individual engages in homosexual relations and eats prison food, he may come to scale down his needs in order to conform to prison rules (ritualism). He may, on the other hand, refuse to eat and to engage in homosexual relations, rejecting both the prison way of life and the secondary rewards it offers. In a sense, coercive settings are "negative" opportunity structures which prevent an individual from attaining societally induced goals, while utilitarian settings may be "illegitimate opportunity structures" and normative settings "legitimate opportunity structures."

24. J. C. Abegglen, *The Japanese Factory: Aspects of Social Organization* (Glencoe, Ill.: The Free Press, 1958).

25. Monica Baldwin, *I Leap Over the Wall* (New York: Signet, 1957).

26. Phillip Selznick, *The Organizational Weapon* (New York: McGraw-Hill, 1952).

27. A. H. Leighton, *The Governing of Men* (Princeton, N.J.: Princeton University Press, 1945).

28. W. L. White, *The Captives of Korea* (New York: Scribners, 1957).

29. Erving Goffman, *Asylums* (New York: Doubleday, 1961).

30. I. Balknap, *Human Problems of a State Mental Hospital* (New York: McGraw-Hill, 1956).

31. R. H. Hardt and S. J. Feinhandler, "Social Class and Mental Hospitalization Prognosis," *American Sociological Review,* 24 (December, 1959), pp. 815–821.

32. August B. Hollingshead and Frederick C. Redlich, *Social Class and Mental Illness* (New York: John Wiley and Sons, 1958).

33. H. Warren Dunham and S. Kirson Weinberg, *The Culture of the State Mental Hospital* (Detroit: Wayne State University Press, 1960).

34. E. Kogon, *The Theory and Practice of Hell* (New York: Farrar, Straus, 1950).

35. J. McElroy, *This Was Andersonville* (New York: McDowell, 1957).

36. Edgar Schein, "Reaction Patterns to Severe, Chronic Stress in American Army Prisoners of War of the Chinese," *Journal of Social Issues,* 13 (1957), pp. 21–30.

Chapter 7

1. See pp. 169–170 for a detailed discussion of Sutherland's theory of differential association.

2. E. H. Sutherland, *The Professional Thief* (Chicago: University of Chicago Press, 1937).

3. D. W. Maurer, *The Big Con* (New York: Pocket Books, Inc., 1949).

4. D. W. Maurer, *Whiz Mob* (New Haven: College and University Press, 1955).

5. J. B. Marton, *My Life in Crime* (New York: Harper, 1952).

6. J. Hall, *Theft, Law, and Society,* 2d ed. (Indianapolis: Bobbs-Merrill, 1952).

7. The F.B.I's statistics are not tabulated in such a way as to separate professional from other crimes.

8. Edwin H. Sutherland and Donald R. Cressey, *Principles of Criminology,* 6th ed. (New York: J. B. Lippincott, 1955), p. 232.

9. Marshall B. Clinard, *Sociology of Deviant Behavior* (New York: Holt, Rinehart and Winston, 1963), p. 284.

10. Ruth S. Cavan, *Criminology* (New York: Thomas Y. Crowell, 1962), pp. 96–97.

11. *Supra,* footnote 2, p. 207.

12. *Supra,* footnote 9, p. 286.

13. Robert W. Winslow, *Crime in a Free Society: Selections from the President's Commission on Law Enforcement and Administration of Justice* (Belmont, Calif.: Dickenson Publishing Co., 1968), p. 164.

14. *Supra,* footnote 9, p. 273.

15. *Ibid.*

16. *Supra,* footnote 13, p. 203.

17. Harry C. Bredemeier and Jackson Toby, *Social Problems in America* (New York: John Wiley and Sons, 1961).

18. Maurice Leznoff and William A. Westley, "The Homosexual Community," *Social Problems,* 3 (April, 1956), pp. 257–263.

19. Albert J. Reiss, Jr., "The Social Integration of Queers and Peers," *Social Problems,* 2 (Fall, 1961), pp. 102–120.

20. James H. Bryan, "Apprenticeships in Prostitution," *Social Problems,* 12 (Winter, 1965), p. 287.

21. James H. Bryan "Occupational Ideologies and Individual Attitudes of Call Girls," *Social Problems,* 13 (Spring, 1966), p. 444.

22. *Ibid.*

23. Harold Greenwald, *The Call Girl* (New York: Ballantine Books, 1958), p. 140.

24. Edwin Lemert, *Social Pathology* (New York: McGraw-Hill, 1951), p. 240.

25. *Supra,* footnote 23, p. 142.

26. *Supra,* footnote 24, p. 243.

27. David Riesman, *The Lonely Crowd* (New Haven: Yale University Press, 1961), pp. 261–264.

28. Sherri Cavan, *Liquor License* (Chicago: Aldine Publishing Co., 1966).

29. James F. Rooney, "Group Processes Among Skid Row Winos," *Quarterly Journal of Studies on Alcohol,* 22 (June, 1961), pp. 444–60.

30. *Supra,* footnote 28, p. 51.

31. *Supra,* footnote 28, p. 84.

32. *Supra,* footnote 28, p. 171.

33. Alfred R. Lindesmith and John H. Gagnon, "Anomie and Drug Addiction," in Marshall B. Clinard (ed.), *Anomie and Deviant Behavior: A Discussion and Critique* (New York: The Free Press, 1964), pp. 158–188.

34. Robert K. Merton, *Social Theory and Social Structure* (New York: The Free Press, 1967), pp. 142–144.

35. *Supra,* footnote 33, pp. 176, 179, and 183.

36. Talcott Parsons, *The Social System* (New York: The Free Press, 1951), pp. 256–259.

37. Charles Winick, "The Use of Drugs by Jazz Musicians," *Social Problems,* 7 (Winter, 1959–1960), pp. 240–253.

38. Harold Finestone, "Cats, Kicks, and Color," *Social Problems,* 5 (Summer, 1957), pp. 3–13.

39. A "hustle" is any non-violent means of "making some bread" that does not require work. A "kick" is any act tabooed by "squares" that heightens and intensifies the present moment of experience and differentiates it as much as possible from the humdrum routine of everyday life. *Ibid.,* p. 5.

40. *Supra,* footnote 37, p. 249.

41. Frederic M. Thrasher, *The Gang* (Chicago: University of Chicago Press, 1927).

42. Albert Cohen, *Delinquent Boys* (Glencoe, Ill.: The Free Press, 1955).

43. John I. Kitsuse and David C. Dietrick, "Delinquent Boys: A Critique," *American Sociological Review,* 24 (April, 1959), pp. 208–15.

44. See *supra,* footnote 46, Chapter 5, for a list of studies challenging the lower-class conception of gang delinquency.

45. Albert K. Cohen and James F. Short, Jr., "Research in Delinquent Subcultures," *Journal of Social Issues,* 14 (March, 1958), pp. 20–37.

46. In fact, Short had difficulty finding groups representing any of the hypothesized subcultural types, as is evident in the following quote:
"Very early in our study we were impressed by the lack of purity of the hypothesized types. Negro conflict gangs abounded, but they seemed also to do a great deal of stealing, and we could not locate a real criminal gang. There appeared to be cliques or other subunits within the larger gang which engaged in special activities, e.g., systematic theft or strong-arming. . . . We finally located what appeared to be a genuine retreatist group, after a full year of investigation. . . . It is clear that the subcultural emphases specified in the literature are not as exclusive as their descriptions in the literature suggest."
James F. Short, Jr., "Gang Delinquency and Anomie," in Marshall B. Clinard, *Anomie and Deviant Behavior* (New York: The Free Press, 1964), p. 104.

47. R. A. Cloward and L. E. Ohlin, *Delinquent and Opportunity* (Glencoe, Ill.: The Free Press, 1960).

48. Lewis Yablonsky, "The Delinquent Gang as a Near-Group," *Social Problems,* 7 (Fall, 1959), pp. 108–117.

49. David Matza, *Delinquency and Drift* (New York: John Wiley and Sons, 1964).

50. Kenneth Keniston, "Alienation and the Decline of Utopia," *The American Scholar,* 29 (Spring, 1960), pp. 161–200.

51. James S. Coleman, *The Adolescent Society* (New York: The Free Press, 1961).

52. Herman Schwendinger, *An Instrumental Theory of Delinquency: A Tentative Formulation* (Ann Arbor, Mich.: University Microfilms, 1963).

53. We shall use Durkheim's terms because there is explicit reference to the family in Durkheim, which reference we shall draw upon. These four, it should be remembered, are included under our constructive types atomistic, plural, oligarchic, and multipartite, respectively.

54. Elman R. Service, *Profiles in Ethnology,* (New York: Harper and Row, 1953), pp. xx–xxi.

55. Emile Durkheim, *The Division of Labor in Society* (New York: The Free Press, 1933), pp. 58–59.

56. Max Gluckman, *A Custom and Conflict in Africa:* (Oxford: Basil Blackwell, 1960).

57. Evelyn M. Duvall, *Family Development* (Chicago: J. B. Lippincott, 1957).

58. *Ibid.,* pp. 53–54.

59. *Ibid.,* pp. 48–49.

60. *Supra,* footnote 59.

61. *Supra,* footnote 60.

62. Ruth S. Cavan, *The American Family* (New York: Thomas Y. Crowell, 1963), p. 426.

63. Sheldon and Eleanor Glueck, *Unraveling Juvenile Delinquency* (Cambridge: Harvard University Press, 1950).

64. Fritz Redl and David Wineman, *Children Who Hate* (Glencoe, Ill.: The Free Press, 1951).

65. Talcott Parsons, "Age and Sex in the Social Structure of the United States," *American Sociological Review,* 7 (1942), pp. 604–617.

66. Bronislaw Malinowski, *Sex and Repression in Savage Society* (New York: Harcourt, Brace, 1927).

67. Erich Fromm, "Individual and Social Origins of Neurosis," *American Sociological Review,* 9 (1944), p. 380.

68. Erich Fromm, *The Sane Society* (New York: Rinehart, 1955).

69. Arnold Green, "The Middle Class Male Child and Neurosis" *American Sociological Review,* 11 (February, 1946), pp. 31–41.

Chapter 8

1. George H. Mead, *Mind, Self, and Society* (Chicago: University of Chicago Press, 1934), pp. 173–186.

2. In the midtown Manhattan study, two psychiatrists were asked to diagnose various types of mental illness on the basis of symptomatology alone, with no knowledge of the patient's social-class background. The two psychiatrists could not do so reliably and so a more ambiguous, less detailed classification system was developed using six categories: well, mild symptom formation, moderate symptom formation, marked symptom formation, severe symptom formation, and incapacitated. Thomas Langner, *et al., Mental Health in the Metropolis* (New York: McGraw-Hill, 1962). Similarly, in the New Haven study, it was discovered that different psychiatric categories would be assigned the same patient when examined by different psychiatrists. August Hollingshead and Frederick Redlich, *Social Class and Mental Illness* (New York: John Wiley, 1959).

3. Robin Williams, Jr., *American Society* (New York: Alfred A. Knopf, 1960), Chapter 11.

4. R. E. L. Faris, "Cultural Isolation and the Schizophrenic Personality," *American Journal of Sociology,* 40 (September, 1934), pp. 155–169.

5. H. Warren Dunham, "The Social Personality of the Catatonic Schizophrenic" *American Journal of Sociology,* 49 (May, 1944), pp. 508–518.

6. S. Kirson Weinberg, "A Sociological Analysis of a Schizophrenic Type" *American Sociological Review,* 15 (October, 1950), pp. 600–610.

7. S. Kirson Weinberg, *Society and Personality Disorders,* (New York: Prentice-Hall, 1952).

8. A. B. Hollingshead, R. Ellis, and E. Kirby, "Social Mobility and Mental Illness," *American Sociological Review,* 19 (October, 1954), pp. 578–584.

9. Melvin Kohn and John Clausen, "Social Isolation and Schizophrenia," *American Sociological Review,* 20 (June, 1955), pp. 215–273.

10. James Coleman, *Abnormal Psychology in Modern Life,* 2d. ed. (Chicago: Scott, Foresman, 1956), p. 262.

11. *Ibid,* pp. 299 and 314.

12. *Supra,* footnotes 10 and 11.

13. *Supra,* footnote 10, pp. 310 and 316.

14. *Supra,* footnote 10, p. 220.

15. *Supra,* footnote 2.

16. R. E. L. Faris and H. Warren Dunham, *Mental Disorders in Urban Areas* (Chicago: University of Chicago Press, 1934).

17. *Supra,* footnote 2.

18. *Supra,* footnote 2, p. 199.

19. Benjamin Malzberg, *Statistical Data for the Study of Mental Disease among Negroes in New York State* (Albany, New York: Research Foundation for Mental Hygiene, Inc., 1954).

20. Hollingshead and Redlich, *supra,* footnote 2.

21. Abram Kardner and Lionel Oversey, *The Mark of Oppression* (New York: W. W. Norton, 1951).

22. Ruth S. Cavan, *Suicide* (Chicago: University of Chicago Press, 1928), p. 3.

23. Émile Durkheim, *Suicide* (New York: The Free Press, 1951), p. 44.

24. George Allen and Edward Ellis, *The Traitor Within* (Garden City, New York: Doubleday, 1961).

25. Karl Menninger, *Man Against Himself* (New York: Harcourt, Brace, 1938), p. 61.

26. Émile Durkheim, *Suicide* (New York: The Free Press, 1951).

27. *Ibid.,* p. 299.

28. Herbert A. Bloch, *Disorganization, Personal and Social* (New York: Alfred A. Knopf), p. 556.

29. *Ibid.,* p. 556.

30. *Ibid.*

31. Cavan, *op. cit.,* p. 106

32. Allen and Ellis, *op. cit.,* pp. 20–30.

33. Nathan Ackerman and Marie Jahoda, *Anti-Semitism and Emotional Disorder* (New York: Harper and Row, 1950), pp. 3–4.

34. Gordon Allport and B. M. Kramer, "Some Roots of Prejudice," *Journal of Psychology,* (July, 1946), pp. 21–22.

35. George E. Simpson and J. Milton Yinger, *Racial and Cultural Minorities,* 3d ed. (New York: Harper and Row, 1965), p. 10.

36. Robin Williams, Jr., *The Reduction of Intergroup Tensions* (Social Science Research Council, 1947), pp. 37–38.

37. Oliver C. Cox, *Caste, Class and Race* (New York: Doubleday, 1948), p. 393.

38. T. W. Adorno, Else Frenkel-Brunswik, D. J. Levinson, and R. N. Sanford, *The Authoritarian Personality* (New York: Harper and Row, 1950).

39. *Supra,* footnote 35, pp. 66–73.

40. Bruno Bettelheim and Morris Janowitz, *Dynamics of Prejudice* (New York: Harper and Bros., 1950), p. 59.

41. Seymour Lipset, "Democracy and Working Class Authoritarianism," *American Sociological Review,* 24 (August, 1959), p. 489.

42. Alfred R. Lindesmith, *The Addict and the Law* (New York: Vintage Books, 1967).

43. Alfred R. Lindesmith and John H. Gagnon, "Anomie and Drug Addiction," in Marshall B. Clinard, *Anomie and Deviant Behavior* (New York: The Free Press, 1964), p. 162.

44. *Ibid.,* p. 163.

45. Alfred R. Lindesmith, "A Sociological Theory of Drug Addiction," *American Journal of Sociology,* 43 (January, 1938), p. 559.

46. Harold Finestone, "Cats, Kicks, and Color," *Social Problems,* 5 (July, 1957), pp. 3–13.

47. *Supra,* footnote 43, p. 167.

48. *Ibid.,* p. 182.

49. *1965 FBI Uniform Crime Reports,* p. 117 (Table 25).

50. R. Fox and P. Lyon, *Alcoholism: Its Scope Cause and Treatment* (New York: Random House, 1955), p. 8.

51. E. M. Jellinek, "Phases of Alcohol Addiction," *Quarterly Journal Studies on Alcohol,* 13 (1952), pp. 673–684.

52. Charles R. Snyder, "Inebriety, Alcoholism, and Anomie," in *supra,* footnote 43, pp. 204–205.

53. Margaret Cork, *Social Workers Can Help Alcoholics,* (National Council on Alcoholism, Inc., November 1954), p. 45.

Chapter 9

1. Plato, *Five Great Dialogues* (Roslyn, N.Y.: Walter J. Black, 1942).

2. Sir Thomas More, *Utopia* (Rosyln, N.Y.: Walter J. Black, 1947).

3. Aldous Huxley, *Brave New World* (New York: Harper and Bros., 1932).

4. George Orwell, *Nineteen Eighty-Four* (New York: Harcourt, Brace, 1949).

5. B. F. Skinner, *Walden Two* (New York: Macmillan, 1948).

6. Alvin Gouldner, Introduction to Émile Durkheim's *Socialism* (New York: Collier Books, 1962), pp. 18–19.

7. Medford Spiro, *Children of the Kibbutz* (New York: Schocken Books, 1965), p. 1. See also Melford Spiro, *Kibbutz: Venture in Utopia* (New York: Schocken Books, 1963).

8. Spiro, *Children of the Kibbutz,* p. 5.

9. *Ibid.,* p. 8.

10. Robert Blauner, *Alienation and Freedom* (Chicago: University of Chicago Press, 1964).

11. Leo Huberman, "History and Economic Beginnings of the Current Conflict Situation," in Geo. W. Hartman, *Industrial Conflict* (New York: The Gordon Co., 1939).

12. Seymour M. Lipset, Martin Trow, and James S. Coleman, *Union Democracy* (Glencoe, Ill.: The Free Press, 1956).

13. Otto L. Shaw, *Youth in Crisis: A Radical Approach to Delinquency* (New York: Hart Publishing Co., 1960).

14. *Ibid.,* p. 26.

15. H. Ashley Weeks, *Youthful Offenders at Highfields* (Ann Arbor: University of Michigan Press, 1958).

16. Lamar T. Empey and Jerome Rabow, "The Provo Experiment in Delinquency Rehabilitation," *American Sociological Review,* 26 (October, 1961), pp. 679–695.

17. Donald R. Cressey, "Changing Criminals: The Application of the Theory of Differential Association," *The American Journal of Sociology,* 61 (September, 1955), pp. 116–120.

18. Maxwell Jones, *The Therapeutic Community,* (New York: Basic Books, 1953).

19. Herbert J. Gans, *The Urban Villagers* (New York: The Free Press, 1962).

20. Anonymous, *Alcoholics Anonymous* (New York: Works Publishing Co., 1950).

21. Ronald Lippitt and Ralph K. White, "An Experimental Study of Leadership and Group Life," in Eleanor Macaby, *et al., Readings in Social Psychology* (New York: Holt, Rinehart and Winston, 1958), pp. 496–511.

22. *Ibid.,* p. 505.

23. Evelyn M. Duvall, *Family Development* (Chicago: J. B. Lippincott, 1957).

24. *Ibid.,* p. 47.

25. *Loc. cit.*

26. *Ibid.,* p. 53.

27. Richard Christie, in Richard Christie and Marie Jahoda (eds.), *Studies in the Scope and Method of "The Authoritarian Personality"* (Glencoe, Ill.: The Free Press, 1954), p. 159.

28. T. W. Adorno, *et al., The Authoritarian Personality* (New York: Harper and Row, 1950), p. 1.

INDEX

INDEX